Social Entrepreneurship in the Age of Atrocities

Social Entrepreneurship in the Age of Atrocities

Changing Our World

Edited by

Zachary D. Kaufman

Social Entrepreneur, attorney practicing at an international law firm, and Adjunct Professor, George Washington University, USA

Edward Elgar
Cheltenham, UK • Northampton, MA, USA

Published by
Edward Elgar Publishing Limited
The Lypiatts
15 Lansdown Road
Cheltenham
Glos GL50 2JA
UK

Edward Elgar Publishing, Inc.
William Pratt House
9 Dewey Court
Northampton
Massachusetts 01060
USA

A catalogue record for this book
is available from the British Library

Library of Congress Control Number: 2012935316

ISBN 978 1 78100 213 1 (cased)
     978 1 78100 221 6 (paperback)

Typeset by Cambrian Typesetters, Camberley, Surrey
Printed and bound by MPG Books Group, UK

Praise for *Social Entrepreneurship in the Age of Atrocities:*

'*How can anyone make a difference in a world marked by genocide, civil war, refugee crises, disease epidemics? With conscience, hope, and sweat equity, Dr. Zachary Kaufman and the other contributors to this book have offered aid, created organizations serving victims of human rights violations, and learned from set-backs and failures. Their insight into challenges of sustainable fund-raising, organizational design and management, and skepticism about young Western volunteers can inspire and instruct others who hope to address suffering and injustice through initiative, analysis, and commitment.*'
  – **Martha Minow**, Dean of the Faculty of Law and Jeremiah Smith, Jr. Professor of Law, Harvard Law School; Author, *Between Vengeance and Forgiveness: Facing History After Genocide and Mass Violence*

'*This book makes an all too rare and important point: One of the distinguishing characteristics of social entrepreneurs is the way their actions and their example pave the way for peace. Kaufman gives us multiple examples here to demonstrate that the kind of empathetic leadership exhibited by these social entrepreneurs builds an alternative to conflict and contributes to the stability and security of societies.*'
  – **Dr. Diana Wells**, President, Ashoka

'*Under the able editorship of Dr. Zachary Kaufman, an upstander in his own right, this pathbreaking book demystifies social entrepreneurship, namely, citizen-inspired initiatives that may have as much potential to overcome the challenges burdening victims of atrocities and other assaults on humankind as social media has demonstrated in revolutionizing how people communicate in the 21st Century.*'
  – **The Honorable David J. Scheffer**, Mayer Brown/Robert A. Helman Professor of Law and Director, Center for International Human Rights, Northwestern University School of Law; former U.S. Ambassador at Large for War Crimes Issues; Author, *All the Missing Souls: A Personal History of the War Crimes Tribunals*

'The accounts of social entrepreneurs contained in this volume could well inspire a future shortlist for the Nobel Peace Prize. Zachary Kaufman has coupled impressive narratives with compelling analysis in a collection that informs observers but that will also stimulate more young people to take up the challenges of responding to atrocities.'

— **Dr. William A. Schabas**, Professor of International Law, Middlesex University (London); Author, *Genocide in International Law: The Crime of Crimes*; Commissioner, Sierra Leone Truth and Reconciliation Commission

'This splendid book is more than a primer on social entrepreneurship for human rights in the developing world. It is also a compendium of searing testimony about the immense practical challenges that idealistic changemakers can over-come by dint of their unflagging energy, incandescent visions of humanity and justice, and on-the-ground skills and resourcefulness. Zachary Kaufman has performed a great public service in orchestrating this admirable volume about how hope for the future can be vindicated even under the most unpromising conditions.'

— **Peter H. Schuck**, Simeon E. Baldwin Professor Emeritus of Law, Yale Law School

'At last, a compelling narrative of recent achievements to address pressing global issues through social entrepreneurship! This book is a tribute to Dr. Zachary Kaufman's ethical convictions and the generation of innovators that he represents. As Chairman of UNITAID, the first laboratory of innovative financ-ing, I've seen how a small levy on airline tickets can save thousands of lives every year through market solutions. It warms me to see how young thinkers continue to innovate and act to provide global public goods. Pay attention to them!'

— **The Honorable Dr. Philippe Douste-Blazy**, United Nations Under Secretary-General in charge of Innovative Financing for Development; Chairman, UNITAID (international facility for the purchase of drugs against HIV/AIDS, Malaria, and Tuberculosis); former French Minister of Foreign Affairs

'At a time when so many reflexively look to government action as a remedy for today's ills, this valuable book demonstrates the power of social entrepreneurs to take on some of the world's great challenges. Social entrepreneurship is grounded in real-world experience. The projects the book profiles demonstrate the impact of individuals as agents of change – taking ideas and turning them into action that can help transform entire societies.'

— **Dr. Arthur C. Brooks**, President, The American Enterprise Institute; Author, *Social Entrepreneurship: A Modern Approach to Social Value Creation*

'For anyone who doubted one person could change the world or just wondered how to get started, Dr. Kaufman's book is equal parts inspiration and how-to guide. He has lived and studied social entrepreneurship, and provides a serious contribution to the emerging field of social entrepreneurship, particularly as it relates to genocide and other atrocities.'

– **The Honorable Tom Perriello**, former U.S. Congressman; former Special Advisor to the Prosecutor, Special Court for Sierra Leone; Co-Founder, DarfurGenocide.org; current President & CEO, Center for American Progress Action

'Social Entrepreneurship in the Age of Atrocities *is a welcome contribution to the study of one of the most promising social movements in recent time, the mobilization of engaged citizens, or Upstanders, in the face of mass atrocities around the world. Zachary Kaufman incisively investigates how social entrepreneurs are taking on tough issues including conflict prevention and transitional justice, and presents practical lessons learned from the perspective of activists on the ground.'*

– **John Prendergast**, Co-Founder, Enough Project, Center for American Progress; former Director for African Affairs, U.S. National Security Council; Co-Author, *Unlikely Brothers: Our Story of Adventure, Loss, and Redemption*; Co-Author, *Not on Our Watch: The Mission to End Genocide in Darfur and Beyond*

'Social Entrepreneurship in the Age of Atrocities *interweaves two critical movements: social entrepreneurship and human rights. Kaufman is one of the first to explore these intersections in a powerfully informative way. He and his fellow social entrepreneurs provide concrete examples of, and offer practical advice about, the power of ordinary people to confront one of the most intractable problems: mass atrocities. Kaufman demonstrates how we can all be "upstanders" in the face of such conflicts.'*

– **Mark Hanis**, Co-Founder & Board member of United to End Genocide (formerly Save Darfur/Genocide Intervention Network); Ashoka Fellow; Echoing Green Fellow

'Dr. Kaufman's book is a huge addition to the field, and his focus on atrocities is spot on. Looking at social entrepreneurship through the lens offered in this book will provide the field with new insights and inspiration. Bravo!'

– **Peter Brinckerhoff**, Author, *Smart Stewardship for Nonprofits: Making the Right Decision in Good Times and Bad* and *Social Entrepreneurship: The Art of Mission-Based Venture Development*

'Social Entrepreneurship in the Age of Atrocities: Changing Our World *deftly outlines how young global peace entrepreneurs are successfully fostering smart and agile solutions to some of the world's most intractable problems. Gone are the tired images of doves and peace signs, rightfully replaced with laptops and smart phones. This is a must read for all young leaders who strive to have real impact in their careers, as well as the old guard if they care not to be left behind by the winds of change.'*

– **Cameron M. Chisholm**, Founder and President, International Peace & Security Institute

'*In an age of austerity, with governments and international organizations limited in their capacity to address atrocities, Dr. Zachary Kaufman's book is a timely reminder of the power of social entrepreneurs to effect critical change. But this is no romantic account of the ability of inspired individuals to make a difference after mass conflict. As an insiders' view of entrepreneurship, this book gives a warts-and-all account of the personal, political, social, and economic challenges that must be overcome and the energy, risk-taking, and good fortune required to achieve even modest results. Highlighting the crucial work of social entrepreneurs, this collection also provides a necessary critique of the failures of governments and international bodies such as the UN to respond coherently to the challenges of post-conflict societies.'*

– **Dr. Phil Clark**, Lecturer in Comparative and International Politics, School of Oriental and African Studies, University of London; Co-Founder, Oxford Transitional Justice Research, University of Oxford; Author, *The Gacaca Courts, Post-Genocide Justice and Reconciliation in Rwanda: Justice Without Lawyers*; Co-Editor, *After Genocide: Transitional Justice, Post-Conflict Reconstruction, and Reconciliation in Rwanda and Beyond*

'Social Entrepreneurship in the Age of Atrocities *is a bold work of definition and analyses. It presents both concepts and histories – focused on individuals and groups – in response to mass violence and atrocities. This significant study, edited by Zachary Kaufman, is a work of clarification and inspiration.'*

– **Dr. Judith S. Goldstein**, Founder & Executive Director, Humanity in Action

'This book is nothing less than an antidote against despondency. In and of itself an innovation, Dr. Zachary Kaufman's collection of personal narratives by change agents reveals a pattern of how people are bringing light to areas where there seems to be nothing but darkness. The remarkably simple recipe of these social entrepreneurs is to take a good dose of caring, add an innovative solution, and finally knead the project through the phases of iterative testing and growth until impact is achieved. Finally we have in this book an addition to the ever-growing library of literature on human rights and atrocities that is not a call to arms or a cry of accusatory indignation, but a cheerful invitation to roll up one's sleeves.'

    – Dr. Fernande Raine, Social Innovation Leader, Innosight; former Senior Team Member, Ashoka; former management consultant, McKinsey & Company; former Executive Director, Carr Center for Human Rights Policy, John F. Kennedy School of Government, Harvard University

'Dr. Zachary Kaufman provides powerful lessons for anyone committed to preventing atrocities, ending conflicts, building peace, and fostering systematic and sustainable positive social change. The compelling and honest firsthand accounts by leading social entrepreneurs working in diverse sectoral areas help ground the field by providing unique insight into the many opportunities, successes, and challenges encountered through the difficult task of change making. This powerful text will inspire many young people and others to take action and work hard in pursuing innovative ways to address some of the most complex, seemingly intractable problems facing the world today. This book should be required reading for anyone seeking to positively impact the world, one step at a time.'

    – Dr. Craig Zelizer, Associate Director, Conflict Resolution Program, Georgetown University; Founder, Peace and Collaborative Development Network

'Zachary Kaufman's new book expands the term social entrepreneur to include human rights advocates – in this instance, young people from the Global North, who have chosen to speak out, stand up, and intervene in the complex contexts of war, atrocity, and civil conflict. Kaufman's provocative book includes case studies that will help challenge prevailing definitions of this emerging field as it explores how, where, and why social entrepreneurs are engaging with the intersection of geo-politics, international law, and social change.'

    – Kavita N. Ramdas, Executive Director, Program on Social Entrepreneurship, Stanford University; former President & CEO, Global Fund for Women

Contents

Abbreviations

AA	Asylum Access
ACLA	American Comparative Literature Association
AEI	American Enterprise Institute
AFKPL	American Friends of the Kigali Public Library
AGOA	African Growth and Opportunity Act
AID	Americans for Informed Democracy
AIDS	Acquired Immune Deficiency Syndrome
AMERA	Africa and Middle East Refugee Assistance
AUC	American University in Cairo
Project BIG	Project Books for International Goodwill
BSF	*Bibliothèques sans Frontières*
CEO	Chief Executive Officer
CFO	Chief Financial Officer
CHAI	Clinton Health Access Initiative
CoA	Children of Abraham
COO	Chief Operating Officer
DDP	Domestic Discovery Program (Children of Abraham)
DRC	Democratic Republic of the Congo
DUMBO	Down Under Manhattan Bridge Overpass (New York)
EOHR	Egyptian Organization for Human Rights
FINIDP	Friends in Need Integrated Development Project (Uganda)
GDP	Global Discovery Program (Children of Abraham)
GoR	Government of Rwanda
GR	Generation Rwanda
HCA	Helsinki Citizens' Assembly (Turkey)
HIV	human immunodeficiency virus
HRC	Human Rights Commission (Sierra Leone)
IA	Indego Africa
ICC	International Criminal Court
ICG	International Crisis Group
ICTE	International Center for Tolerance Education
ICTJ	International Center for Transitional Justice
ICTR	United Nations International Criminal Tribunal for Rwanda
ICTY	United Nations International Criminal Tribunal for the Former Yugoslavia

IIMP	Istanbul Interparish Migrants' Program
IRLAP	Istanbul Refugee Legal Aid Program
KPL	Kigali Public Library
KPLC	Kigali Public Library Committee
LWB	Libraries Without Borders
MSKPL	Marshall Scholars for the Kigali Public Library
MTN	Mobile Telephone Networks
NGO	non-governmental organization
NVSL	National Vision for Sierra Leone
NYU	New York University
OAA	Orphans Against AIDS
ORAM	Organization for Refuge, Asylum & Migration
OSCE	Organization for Security and Cooperation in Europe
OSI	Open Society Institute
OVCs	orphans and vulnerable children
PIPA	Program on International Policy Attitudes
PRIDE	Post-conflict Reintegration Initiative for Development and Empowerment (Sierra Leone)
Project BIG	Project Books for International Goodwill
RASP	Refugee Advocacy and Support Program
RCK	Refugee Consortium of Kenya
RCKV	Rotary Club of Kigali-Virunga (Rwanda)
RLAP	Refugee Legal Aid Project
RLP	Refugee Law Project (Makerere University)
RSC	Refugee Studies Centre (University of Oxford)
RSD	refugee status determination
RSLAF	Republic of Sierra Leone Armed Forces
RTLM	*Radio Télévision Libre des Mille Collines*
SL TRC	Sierra Leone Truth and Reconciliation Commission
SRLAN	Southern Refugee Legal Aid Network
STAND	Students Taking Action Now: Darfur
SURF	Survivors Fund
UCT	University of Cape Town
U.K. or UK	United Kingdom
U.N. or UN	United Nations
UNAIDS	Joint United Nations Programme on HIV/AIDS
UNDP	United Nations Development Programme
UNESCO	United Nations Educational, Scientific, and Cultural Organization
UNHCR	United Nations High Commissioner for Refugees
UNHRC	United Nations Human Rights Commission
U.S. or US	United States

USAID	United States Agency for International Development
VISTA	Volunteers in Service to the United States
YHRDLJ	*Yale Human Rights & Development Law Journal*
YLPR	*Yale Law & Policy Review*
YLSE	Yale Law Social Entrepreneurs

Contributors' biographies

Dr. Zachary D. Kaufman (editor of this volume) is an attorney, political scientist, professor, author, speaker, and social entrepreneur. He is the founder, president, and chairman of the Board of Directors of the AFKPL and an Honorary Member of the RCKV. Dr. Kaufman was also the co-founder and co-president of MSKPL, which worked with the AFKPL and the RCKV. He will serve on the KPL's Board of Trustees once the library is inaugurated.

Dr. Kaufman is currently an Associate at an international law firm, where, among other matters, he serves as *pro bono* counsel to Ashoka. Dr. Kaufman is also currently an adjunct professor at George Washington University's Elliott School of International Affairs. A frequent writer and commentator on legal and political issues, his first book, *After Genocide: Transitional Justice, Post-Conflict Reconstruction, and Reconciliation in Rwanda and Beyond*, which he co-edited with Dr. Phil Clark and co-authored, was co-published in 2009 by Columbia University Press and C. Hurst & Co. In 2011, Dr. Kaufman was named one of the 'Top 99 Under 33 Foreign Policy Leaders' by *Diplomatic Courier* magazine and Young Professionals in Foreign Policy.

Much of Dr. Kaufman's work has been in the public sector. Dr. Kaufman has served as a law clerk to The Honorable Juan R. Torruella on the U.S. Court of Appeals for the First Circuit, at the U.S. Departments of State and Justice, and at the ICTY and the ICTR. He also was the first American to serve at the ICC, where he was policy clerk to the first Chief Prosecutor. In addition to his work with the KPL, Dr. Kaufman currently serves on the boards or leadership committees of nine other organizations: the U.S. Holocaust Memorial Museum, the Humanity in Action Foundation (of which he is also a Senior Fellow), IA, the Yale Alumni Fund, the Yale Club of D.C., the Yale Law School Association of D.C., the Joseph Slifka Center for Jewish Life at Yale, the *Yale Law & Policy Review* (YLPR), and Yale Law Social Entrepreneurs (YLSE). Dr. Kaufman also serves as a consultant to other non-profit organizations and social enterprises.

In addition, Dr. Kaufman has worked in the private sector on legal and political issues. He has worked as a Summer Associate at O'Melveny & Myers LLP and on Google's Global Public Policy and Government Affairs team.

A former Fellow at Stanford University (in the Freeman Spogli Institute for International Studies' Center on Democracy, Development, and the Rule of

Law), Dr. Kaufman received his Doctor of Philosophy (D.Phil/PhD) and Master of Philosophy (M.Phil) degrees, both in International Relations, from the University of Oxford, where he was a Marshall Scholar. Dr. Kaufman received his Juris Doctor (J.D.) and Bachelor of Arts (B.A.) in Political Science degrees from Yale University. At Yale Law School, he was the Editor-in-Chief of the YLPR, Managing Editor of the *Yale Human Rights & Development Law Journal* (YHRDLJ), Articles Editor of the *Yale Journal of International Law*, co-founder and co-president (both with Scott Grinsell) of YLSE, member of the Non-Profit Organizations Clinic, and an Olin Fellow of the Center for Law, Economics, and Public Policy. Dr. Kaufman now serves on the Advisory Boards of both the YLPR and YLSE. At Yale University, Dr. Kaufman was the student body president, a residential counselor, co-captain of the Yale Wrestling Team, and an All-American and Runner-up National Champion in the National Collegiate Wrestling Association.

Adrienne Bernhard (editorial assistant of this volume) is a freelance editor and, most recently, assistant to the Deputy Editor at *The New Yorker Magazine*. She is currently pursuing a second Master's degree, in Education, at Columbia University. Ms. Bernhard has worked as a freelance writer and editor for numerous periodicals and publishing houses, including Random House, *The New York Times*, Farrar Straus & Giroux, Encounter Books, *The New Criterion*, *The Jewish Review of Books*, and *Abroad Magazine*.

Ms. Bernhard earned her first Master's degree, in American Literature, from Yale University in 2008. She presented twice at the American Comparative Literature Association (ACLA) and led a seminar at the 2009 ACLA Conference entitled 'Global Orientalism: a Paradigm Shift of the East-West Axis.' During 2007–08, she served as an editor of Volume XI of the YHRDLJ, in which she published commentary on corporate social responsibility.

Ms. Bernhard graduated with departmental honors from Northwestern University in 2006 with a dual degree in English and French and was awarded Northwestern University's Study Abroad Research Award for her senior thesis. Ms. Bernhard spent her junior year of college abroad at St. Hilda's College, University of Oxford. She currently lives in New York City.

Ari Alexander was a co-founder and co-Executive Director of CoA. He currently serves as the Director of Independent Software Vendor and Channel Sales Enablement at Salesforce.com, an enterprise cloud computing company that was named the world's most innovative company by *Forbes Magazine*. From December 2009 to September 2011, Mr. Alexander served as Senior Advisor to the Administrator and the Director of the Center for Faith-Based and Community Initiatives at USAID. In recognition of his contributions to

USAID and the Obama Administration, Mr. Alexander was invited to the Oval Office for a one-on-one meeting with President Obama. Previously, Mr. Alexander served as a Senior Fellow with the President's Advisory Council on Faith-based and Neighborhood Partnerships. He has presented and lectured about international development and interfaith cooperation all over the world, including in Cambodia, Egypt, Ethiopia, Georgia, Indonesia, Morocco, Peru, Qatar, Senegal, South Africa, South Korea, Tunisia, and Turkey.

Mr. Alexander completed two Masters' degrees in the United Kingdom as a Marshall Scholar: a Master of Arts (M.A.) in Comparative Ethnic Conflict from the Queen's University of Belfast and an M.Phil. in Modern Middle Eastern Studies from the University of Oxford. His research led him to live in Beirut, Damascus, and Jerusalem. He graduated Phi Beta Kappa from the University of Pennsylvania with a B.A. in History. He has also served as an English teacher in the Yarmouk refugee camp in Syria, as a counselor and facilitator at Seeds of Peace International Camp and Face to Face / Faith to Faith, as well as an educator for Jewish teenagers participating in United Synagogue Youth and at the Lauder Camp in Hungary.

Emily E. Arnold-Fernández, the founder and Executive Director of AA, is a social entrepreneur and human rights pioneer. A lawyer who has advocated nationally and internationally for the human rights of women, children, and other vulnerable individuals, Ms. Arnold-Fernández first became involved in refugee rights in 2002, when she represented refugees in UN proceedings in Cairo, Egypt. Her first client was a young Liberian who had fled to Egypt to avoid being abducted and forced to fight as a child soldier. Denied refugee status, he was at constant risk of arrest, detention, and deportation by Egyptian authorities unless he could get the decision reversed. Ms. Arnold-Fernández's legal advocacy won her client protection and safety in Egypt until his eventual resettlement in the U.S. Cairo was one of very few places where refugees had access to legal assistance. Ms. Arnold-Fernández founded AA to change this.

For her innovative approach to the global refugee crisis, Ms. Arnold-Fernández was honored by the Dalai Lama as one of 50 'Unsung Heroes of Compassion' from around the world (2009). She has also been recognized as Pomona College's Inspirational Young Alumna (2006), awarded the prestigious Echoing Green Fellowship (2007), and recognized as the New Leaders Council's 40 Under 40 (2010). Her ground-breaking work with AA has earned her international speaking invitations and widespread media attention, including the Rotary International Peace Symposium (2008, 2009), the UN High Commissioner for Refugees' Annual Consultations (2008, 2009), a cover feature in the *Christian Science Monitor* (September 2009), and the *San Francisco Examiner*'s Credo column (July 2011). She holds a B.A. *cum laude* from Pomona College and a J.D. from Georgetown University Law Center, and taught Social Entrepreneurship as an adjunct professor at the University of San Francisco in Fall 2010.

Amy Chua is the John M. Duff, Jr. Professor of Law at Yale Law School. Professor Chua is the author of *World on Fire: How Exporting Free Market Democracy Breeds Ethnic Hatred and Global Instability* (Doubleday, 2002), *Day of Empire: How Hyperpowers Rise to Global Dominance – And Why They Fall* (Doubleday, 2007), and *Battle Hymn of the Tiger Mother* (Penguin Press, 2011).

Professor Chua is an expert on international business transactions, law and development, ethnic conflict, and globalization and the law. She has an A.B. and a J.D. from Harvard University. In 2011, *Time* named Professor Chua one of the top 100 most influential people in the world, *The Atlantic* named her one of their annual 'Brave Thinkers,' and *Newsweek* and the *Daily Beast* named her one of the '150 Women Who Shake the World.'

Mauro De Lorenzo was a founding board member of AA and continues to serve as an advisor to the organization. He is Senior Research Scholar and Deputy Director of the Urbanization Project at the Stern School of Business, New York University. From 2009 to 2012, he was Vice President for Freedom and Free Enterprise at the John Templeton Foundation. From 2006 to 2009, he was a Resident Fellow in foreign and defense policy at the American Enterprise Institute (AEI), where he led a project to re-imagine the place of foreign aid and development policy in U.S. foreign policy toward developing countries. He remains a Visiting Fellow at AEI.

Mr. De Lorenzo received a B.A. in Cognitive Science and an M.A. in Linguistics from the University of Delaware. He then earned a Master of Science (M.Sc.) degree in Social Anthropology at the University of Oxford, where he was a Rhodes Scholar and a research associate at both the American University in Cairo and the Makerere Institute of Social Research in Kampala, Uganda, focusing on refugee policy and the dynamics of the wars in Congo, Rwanda, and Burundi. In 2002, he was associate producer and head of research for 'The Price of Aid,' a BBC/ARTE documentary about U.S. food aid to Africa and the institutional misdiagnosis of famines. In 1996–97 he was assistant to the coordinator of refugee elections for Bosnia-Herzegovina at the Organization for Security and Cooperation in Europe (OSCE). From 2007 to 2010, he served as the official 'plus one' and policy advisor to former U.S. Senate Majority Leader Bill Frist for his service on the Board of Directors of the Millennium Challenge Corporation, an innovative multi-billion dollar U.S. foreign aid agency.

Dr. Cheryl L. Dorsey is the President of Echoing Green. She is the co-author of *Be Bold: Create a Career with Impact* (Echoing Green, 2006).

An accomplished social entrepreneur with expertise in health care, labor issues, and public policy, Dr. Dorsey is the first Echoing Green Fellow to lead this global non-profit organization, which has awarded more than $30 million in start-up capital to over 500 social entrepreneurs worldwide since 1987. In 1992, Dr. Dorsey's Echoing Green Fellowship enabled her to launch the Family Van, a community-based mobile health unit that provides basic health care and outreach services to at-risk residents of inner-city Boston neighborhoods.

Dr. Dorsey has served in two presidential administrations as a White House Fellow and Special Assistant to the U.S. Secretary of Labor (1997–98), Special Assistant to the Director of the Women's Bureau of the U.S. Labor Department (1998–99), Transition Team Member of the Innovation and Civil Society subgroup of the Technology, Innovation, and Government Reform Policy Working Group (2008–09), and Vice Chair for the President's Commission on White House Fellowships (2009–present).

Currently, Dr. Dorsey serves on several boards, including the Harvard Board of Overseers, the SEED Foundation, and Northeast Bank. She has received numerous public service awards and recognition for her work, including the Leonard J. Siff Prize for best History of Science Senior Thesis (1985), Robert Kennedy Distinguished Public Service Award (1992), First Recipient, Jane Rainie Opel '50, Young Alumna Award, Radcliffe College Alumnae Association (1995), Henry Crown Fellow, Aspen Institute (2006), and Prime Movers Fellow, Hunt Alternatives Fund (2007). In 2009, Dorsey was named one of 'America's Best Leaders' by *U.S. News & World Report* and the Center for Public Leadership at Harvard University's John F. Kennedy School of Government. In 2010 and 2011, she was named as one of *The Nonprofit Times'* 'Power and Influence Top 50.' Like Professor Chua, in 2011, *Newsweek* and the *Daily Beast* named Dr. Dorsey one of the '150 Women Who Shake the World.'

Dr. Dorsey holds a B.A. in History and Science *magna cum laude* with highest honors from Harvard-Radcliffe Colleges, a Doctor of Medicine (M.D.) from the Harvard Medical School, and a Master of Public Policy (M.P.P.) from Harvard University's John F. Kennedy School of Government. She completed her pediatric residency at Children's National Medical Center in Washington, D.C.

Bill Drayton is the Founder, Chair, and CEO of Ashoka: Innovators for the Public, the global association of the world's leading social entrepreneurs. Ashoka: Innovators for the Public supports individual social entrepreneurs – financially and professionally; brings communities of social entrepreneurs together to help leverage their impact, scale their ideas, and capture and disseminate their best practices; and helps build the infrastructure and financial systems needed to support the growth of the citizen sector and facilitate the spread of social innovation globally. Since 1981, Ashoka: Innovators for the Public has elected over 3,000 leading social entrepreneurs from more than 70 countries. Mr. Drayton also pursues his social entrepreneurship work through Ashoka's Youth Venture and Get America Working!.

Mr. Drayton worked for 10 years as a management consultant for McKinsey & Co. and for four years as Assistant Administrator of the U.S. Environmental Protection Agency. He has taught at Stanford Law School and Harvard University's John F. Kennedy School of Government.

Mr. Drayton is a graduate of Harvard University, Yale Law School, and the University of Oxford, where he was a Rhodes Scholar. He has received many awards for his achievements. Mr. Drayton was elected one of the early MacArthur Fellows for his work, including the founding of Ashoka. Yale University's School of Management gave him its annual Award for Entrepreneurial Excellence. The American Society of Public Administration and the National Academy of Public Administration jointly awarded him their National Public Service Award, and Common Cause gave him its Public Service Achievement Award. He has also been named a Preiskel-Silverman Fellow for Yale Law School and is a member of the American Academy of Arts and Sciences. In 2005, he was selected one of 'America's Best Leaders' by *U.S. News & World Report* and Harvard University's Center for Public Leadership. In the same month he was the recipient of the Yale Law School's highest alumni honor, The Yale Law School Award of Merit, for having made a substantial contribution to Public Service.

David 'Dai' Ellis co-founded GR. He currently serves as CEO of the Boston-based Excel Academy charter school network, where he is responsible for leading Excel's expansion. Excel is building a leading network of high-performing charter schools in Boston and eventually beyond.

Before joining Excel, Mr. Ellis spearheaded the Clinton Foundation's work on improving the marketplace for HIV/AIDS and malaria drugs, diagnostics, and other essential health products. While at the Clinton Health Access Initiative (CHAI) he built an expert in-house technical team of former pharmaceutical industry chemists and sourcing specialists; this team helped CHAI develop proprietary new chemistry and support its partner manufacturers in lowering the price of HIV/AIDS treatment by more than 50 percent.

Prior to his work at CHAI, Mr. Ellis worked at McKinsey & Co. serving clients in the pharmaceutical and biotechnology industries. He later joined the Center for Global Health and Economic Development at Columbia University under Dr. Jeffrey Sachs. His work at Columbia took him to Rwanda, where he worked as the advisor to the Director of the National AIDS Commission and helped to launch a national HIV/AIDS prevention and treatment program. Mr.

Ellis received his J.D. from Yale Law School and his A.B. in Biochemistry from Harvard University.

Conor B. French is the President and Chief Operating Officer of IA and a committed business partner to more than 400 women entrepreneurs in Rwanda. Quarterbacking IA's functional and operational strategies, Mr. French is dedicated to meticulously building out every stage of its entrepreneurial model for economic justice from innovation to impact.

Prior to joining IA, Mr. French practiced law at the global law firm of Latham & Watkins LLP. He represented public and private companies, investment banks, private equity firms, and investors in a wide range of leveraged finance and other business transactions. As *pro bono* counsel to Ashoka, Mr. French structured joint ventures, strategic partnerships, and other collaborations that provided critical support for Ashoka's global network of leading social entrepreneurs.

Mr. French currently chairs the audit committee on the Board of Directors of Red Hen Press and serves on the Board of Directors of New York University (NYU) School of Law's Alumni Association. A recipient of Bet Tzedek's Access to Justice Award and an honorary member of 85 Broads' *Guys Who Rock*, Mr. French is a Truman National Security Fellow and member of the New York State Bar Association's Committee on Attorney Professionalism. He is the editor-in-chief of the blog *Social Enterprising* and frequently speaks on issues related to social innovation and impact, economic development, micro-enterprise in Africa, business and philanthropy, and non-profit leadership.

Mr. French received a B.A. in History and English from Georgetown University and a J.D. from NYU School of Law, where he was an editor of the *Journal of International Law & Politics* and taught at the High School Law Institute. He is qualified to practice before the California, District of Columbia, Massachusetts, and New York bars.

Seth Green is the founder and a current Board Member of AID, and served as AID's chief executive from 2002 to 2007. During his time leading AID, Mr. Green built a network that includes more than 23,000 members; created partnerships with leading think tanks, NGOs, businesses, and foundations; and raised over US$1 million for the organization's programming. Mr. Green has also worked at the Brookings Institution, the *American Prospect*, Taxpayers for Common Sense, Lazard Freres, McKinsey & Co., the Job Opportunity Investment Network, and Youth Organizations Umbrella.

Mr. Green is an expert on youth social change movements. A Marshall Scholar, he graduated *summa cum laude* from Princeton University and earned Masters' degrees in Development Studies from the London School of

Economics and in Women's Studies from the University of Oxford. He also completed a J.D. degree at Yale Law School, where he was named an Olin Fellow by the Center for Studies in Law, Economics, and Public Policy. Mr. Green has served on the Board of Directors of AID, 20/20 Vision, Citizens for Global Solutions, and Thinking Beyond Borders.

Scott Grinsell is a Partner in and Project Director for Uganda of OAA, where, in addition to co-founding OAA's program in Uganda, he has focused his work on issues of governance and the formation of the organization's Board of Directors. Mr. Grinsell graduated *summa cum laude* and Phi Beta Kappa from Williams College, where he received the Erastus C. Benedict Prize. He then studied as a Marshall Scholar at Magdalen College, University of Oxford, where he received an M.Phil., with Distinction, in Modern History.

Mr. Grinsell received a J.D. from Yale Law School in 2009, where he was a Coker Teaching Fellow, Comments Editor of the *Yale Law Journal*, Executive Editor of the YLPR, co-founder and co-president (both with Dr. Zachary Kaufman) of YLSE (the Advisory Board of which he now serves on), and a research assistant to Professor Heather Gerken on constitutional law. Mr. Grinsell's academic work has been published in the *Yale Journal of International Law* and the *Michigan Journal of Race & Law*. After law school, he served as a law clerk to Judge Rosemary S. Pooler on the U.S. Court of Appeals for the Second Circuit. Mr. Grinsell is currently an Associate at the law firm of Wachtell, Lipton, Rosen & Katz in New York.

Dr. Barbara Harrell-Bond is a global leader in refugee studies and refugee rights advocacy. She was the founding director of the Refugee Studies Centre at the University of Oxford (1982–1996), the world's first institution dedicated to the study of refugees. She went on to establish the Refugee Law Project at Makerere University in Kampala, Uganda (1997) and a refugee legal aid program in Cairo, Egypt (2000) that is now AMERA-Egypt. Dr. Harrell-Bond currently sits on the Board of Directors of AMERA-UK, AMERA-Egypt's parent organization. She also previously chaired the Board of Directors of AA (2005–2009), and remains a Founding Patron of the organization. Currently, Dr. Harrell-Bond directs the Refugee Program of the Fahamu Trust, an international NGO working on social justice issues and the founding Secretariat of the SRLAN, a network of refugee rights advocacy organizations throughout the Global South.

Dr. Harrell-Bond's pivotal contributions to refugee studies and the global refugee rights movement have been widely recognized. Among other accolades, she received the Distinguished Service Award from the American Anthropological Association in 1996, and in 2005 was made an Order of the British Empire 'for services to refugee studies' in the Queen's Birthday

Honors List. She is an Honorary Fellow at Lady Margaret Hall, University of Oxford, and an Emeritus Associate at the University of Oxford's Refugee Studies Centre.

Dr. Harrell-Bond studied social anthropology; she received a Diploma, an M.Litt. based on fieldwork in an urban housing estate, and a D.Phil. from the University of Oxford based on fieldwork in Sierra Leone.

Jamie Hodari is the Executive Director of GR. Mr. Hodari came to GR from Birch Run Capital, a hedge fund in New York City, where he analyzed businesses and served as legal counsel. Prior to joining Birch Run, he was an Associate in the New York office of the law firm Sullivan & Cromwell LLP, where he worked primarily in Asian and Latin American project finance.

Mr. Hodari also served as a manager in Ohio on President Obama's 2008 presidential campaign. Before graduate school, he worked at the *Times of India* as a political and economic reporter. Mr. Hodari received his J.D. from Yale Law School, his M.P.P. from Harvard University's John F. Kennedy School of Government, and his B.A. from Columbia University.

Andrew Klaber is the founder and president of OAA. A *summa cum laude* Ethics, Politics & Economics and International Studies graduate of Yale College, Mr Klaber earned dual M.Sc. degrees in Financial Economics and Economic History as a Marshall Scholar at the University of Oxford. Mr. Klaber also holds a J.D./M.B.A. from Harvard Law School and Harvard Business School, where he graduated with Distinction. He received the President's Environmental Youth Award at the White House and was invited to speak at the World Economic Forum in Davos. He has been named a *USA Today* Academic All-American, a Goldman Sachs Global Leader, a Truman Scholar, and a Udall Scholar. Mr. Klaber rowed on the Yale lightweight crew (2002 national champions), biked across the United States (New Haven to San Francisco) to raise money and awareness for Habitat for Humanity, and has run in the Berlin, Boston, London, New York, Paris, and Valencia marathons. He serves on the boards of several organizations, including the Yale Alumni Fund, the Harvard Law School Board of Overseers, the Echoing Green Social Investment Council, the Association of Marshall Scholars, and the Russell Trust Association.

Mr. Klaber aims to promote symbiotic relationships between the private, public, and non-profit sectors that increase social and economic empowerment. He currently lives in New York City and works as an investment professional at Paulson & Company, a multi-strategy investment firm.

Rachel Levitan is an independent consultant based in Washington, D.C., where she works with non-profit organizations and international agencies engaged in human rights advocacy, rule of law, and refugee protection issues. She conducts training and program evaluation, coordinates thematic working groups, and designs campaigns and field-based research. Until early 2012, Ms. Levitan worked as the Director of Advocacy for the Organization for Refuge, Asylum & Migration (ORAM), where, through legal representation and policy advocacy, she worked to increase international protection for individuals who flee persecution based on sexual orientation and gender identity. Before joining ORAM, Ms. Levitan co-founded the Refugee Advocacy and Support Program of Helsinki Citizens' Assembly (HCA), Turkey's first and only legal clinic for refugees. As HCA's Legal Director, Ms. Levitan managed legal services for thousands of refugees, primarily from Iran, Afghanistan, and Somalia. Ms. Levitan also set advocacy strategy, conducted legal training, and carried out fundraising for the program.

Prior to her work in Turkey, Ms. Levitan litigated race- and gender-based employment discrimination cases in federal court in New York. She also advocated for immigrant workplace rights, having coordinated a project to improve the working conditions of immigrant household workers. Ms. Levitan's publications include 'Unsafe Haven: Security Challenges Facing LGBT Asylum Seekers and Refugees in Turkey,' in *Praxis: The Fletcher Journal of Human Security*; 'Refugee Protection in Turkey,' in *Forced Migration Review*; and 'Unwelcome Guests: The Detention of Refugees in Turkey's "Foreigners' Guesthouses,"' in *Refuge: Canada's Periodical on Refugees*. Ms. Levitan received a B.A. from McGill University and a Bachelor of Laws (LL.B.) from the University of British Columbia.

Leah Maloney served as a Senior Political Analyst at AID during the summer of 2006. She graduated *magna cum laude* and was elected Phi Beta Kappa at Boston College, earning highest honors in the Political Science Department's honors program, with a dual major in Islamic Civilizations and Societies. While at Boston College, Ms. Maloney was editor-in-chief of the Political Science Department's journal *Uncommon Sense*. Ms. Maloney served as a Peace Corps volunteer in Jordan teaching English and working on women's development projects. She is currently attending George Washington University Law School, where she is focusing on public interest law and plans to earn her J.D. in 2013.

Matthew T. Mitro is the Founder and Chairman of the Board of Directors of IA. Mr. Mitro's founding vision for IA is to use the power of social enterprise to transform the lives of economically-vulnerable but highly-skilled artisans in Africa. Mr. Mitro has a longstanding interest in African development, stemming from his six years living in Nigeria and his personal experience working with African women.

Mr. Mitro's professional training includes three years spent as a practicing attorney at Akin Gump LLP in Washington, D.C., where he coordinated the legal aspects of financing large-scale infrastructure projects in developing countries such as Bolivia, Morocco, and the Democratic Republic of Congo. Prior to joining Akin, Mr. Mitro was a federal law clerk in the Eastern District of Virginia and spent time in the U.S. Departments of State and Justice working on international legal issues.

Mr. Mitro graduated *magna cum laude* from American University's Washington College of Law in 2003 and holds a bachelor's degree in economics and history from Washington University in St. Louis. He has conducted published legal research on the topic of combating exploitative child labor through the global trading system and is conversational in French and German. Mr. Mitro is a Fellow of the Wittenberg Center for Global Ethics and the StartingBloc Institute for Social Innovation, where he focuses on social entrepreneurship in Africa. Mr. Mitro has traveled to more than 60 countries, living extensively in seven countries on four continents.

In August 2011, Mr. Mitro joined Google as a University Program Specialist for the Middle East & Africa. Mr. Mitro is responsible for building out Google's strategic hiring programs and acting as Google's ambassador at target academic institutions across the region. Mr. Mitro was recently recognized by Devex as one of '40 under 40 International Development Leaders in London.'

Gul Rukh Rahman is currently consulting with the Edmond de Rothschild Foundation in New York. From 2005 to 2009, Ms. Rahman served as the co-Executive Director of CoA. In February 2008 she relocated to Paris, where she worked with a division of France's Ministry of Defense to create an educational and experiential center that would address intercultural, interfaith, and intra-community dialogue between young French men and women. The experiential center aimed to address issues of social cohesion through economic empowerment and education.

Ms. Rahman earned her Master's degree at Tufts University's Fletcher School of Law and Diplomacy. Prior to joining CoA, Ms. Rahman worked as a software engineer in the Bay Area of Northern California. She has also worked as a freelance journalist for many South Asian and Arab media outlets, writing about human rights, Afghan refugees, and other social, cultural, and economic issues. In the past, she volunteered her time consulting with several non-governmental organizations that advocated for Afghan refugees in Pakistan.

Sophie Raseman is former full-time director of the NVSL and was one of its founding members as it transitioned into an independent organization. In addition to working at the NVSL, Ms. Raseman has served in a range of public interest positions, including in the non-profit and public sectors. Ms. Raseman currently holds a position at the U.S. Department of Treasury, in the Office of Financial Institutions, where she specializes in financial services policies affecting consumers. Ms. Raseman has also worked as a management consultant at McKinsey & Co. in New York City, where she served large financial services companies. Ms. Raseman was born and raised in New York City. She has a J.D. from Yale Law School and graduated *magna cum laude* and Phi Beta Kappa from Yale University.

Dr. Oliver Rothschild founded and continues to chair the board of GR. He currently works as a consultant with McKinsey & Co. advising clients working in international development and global health as well as a range of health-care clients in the private sector.

Dr. Rothschild came to McKinsey & Co. from rural Rwanda, where he served as Special Advisor to the Director at Partners In Health-Rwanda under Dr. Paul Farmer, helping to manage a network of hospitals providing care to more than 10 percent of Rwanda's population and advising the Ministry of Health on HIV/AIDS policy. Prior to joining Partners In Health, Dr. Rothschild worked with the Center for Global Health and Economic Development at Columbia University under Dr. Jeffrey Sachs and at the Clinton Foundation, where he supported the launch of Rwanda's first national pediatric HIV program. Outside Rwanda, he has worked in health and economics at the United Nations in Paris and in medical research studying infectious disease at Rockefeller University in New York.

Dr. Rothschild received a B.A. in Economics and Computer Science from the University of Chicago, and holds an M.D. from Yale Medical School.

Benjamin D. Stone is the CEO of IA. With an unwavering enthusiasm, Mr. Stone leads IA's market-driven approach to empowering women in Africa. He received a B.A. in English Literature from Washington University in St. Louis in 2000, a J.D. from NYU School of Law in 2004, and in 2010 completed the Stanford Graduate School of Business Executive Program in Social Entrepreneurship.

Mr. Stone frequently speaks about global leadership, management, international affairs, social enterprise, and the law at a wide range of professional, academic, and industry venues, including Harvard Business School, the U.S. Chamber of Commerce, NYU Stern School of Business, Columbia Law School, Boston University's School of International Relations, NYU School of Law, and the Presidential Summit on Entrepreneurship. On June 5, 2011, Mr. Stone delivered his high school *alma mater*'s Commencement Address, encouraging students to 'stand bold' and 'get nerdy.'

In 2011, Mr. Stone was named one of *Diplomatic Courier* magazine's 'Top 99 Under 33 Foreign Policy Leaders' and received The Global Leaders' Future Global Leader Award. Mr. Stone is also an honorary member of 85 Broads' *Guys Who Rock*, a five-time Empire State Counsel honoree, and a member of the Young Strategic Forum and the Bar of the State of New York. Mr. Stone also won the 2009 Fair Trade Federation Photography Award and has exhibited his photos and mini-documentaries at galleries across the U.S.

Prior to joining IA, Mr. Stone practiced law in New York City for four years as a complex commercial litigation and white collar defense attorney at Orrick, Herrington & Sutcliffe LLP, where he managed multi-million-dollar representations of big four accounting firms, technology manufacturers, energy companies, and individuals in business disputes and government investigations.

Anthea Zervos is a founding member and was the longest-serving director of the NVSL. Ms. Zervos has worked on a number of rule of law and justice initiatives in post-conflict West Africa since 2003. These include the NVSL project with the Sierra Leone Truth and Reconciliation Commission, the Outreach Section of the Liberia Truth and Reconciliation Commission, and the Labor Law Reform initiative with the Liberia Ministry of Labor. From October 2009 through December 2011, Ms. Zervos worked with the American Bar Association Rule of Law Initiative in Liberia in the position of Program Manager for the initiative's program focusing on reducing prolonged pre-trial detention in Monrovia Central Prison. Ms. Zervos is originally from Athens, Greece. She completed her Bachelor of Science (B.S.) degree in Theater at Skidmore College in 2002, and her M.Sc. degree in Violence, Conflict, and Development at the University of London's School of Oriental and African Studies in 2007.

Acknowledgements

First, I want to thank all of the contributors to this book: Ari Alexander, Emily Arnold-Fernández, Professor Amy Chua, Mauro De Lorenzo, Dr. Cheryl Dorsey, Bill Drayton, Dai Ellis, Conor French, Seth Green, Scott Grinsell, Dr. Barbara Harrell-Bond, Jamie Hodari, Andrew Klaber, Rachel Levitan, Leah Maloney, Matt Mitro, Gul Rukh Rahman, Sophie Raseman, Dr. Oliver Rothschild, Ben Stone, and Anthea Zervos. Conceiving of, assembling, co-authoring, and editing this book has provided me with a special opportunity to work with each of these amazing individuals. Through this joint effort, my enormous admiration for them and their work has grown even greater, and it has been a tremendous honor to work together. Thank you to Shannon Howard, Fernande Raine, and Sally Stephenson of Ashoka for facilitating Mr. Drayton's Foreword and to Armand Biroonak, Shalena Broadnax, and Jesse Gerstin of Echoing Green for facilitating Dr. Dorsey's Afterword.

More gratitude than I could ever express is also due to Adrienne Bernhard, my talented Editorial Assistant and lovely cousin. She thoroughly edited multiple drafts of the manuscript and improved it significantly, in substance, structure, and style. Thank you, as well, to Christina Beasley, James Montana, and Alex Treuber for precise, plentiful, and punctual research assistance.

In addition to all of those mentioned above, several other people have also served as particularly influential sounding boards as I have developed my ideas on social entrepreneurship and pursued this book project. Roshan Paul, Ilaina Rabbat, Paul Rodolfo Rodríguez, David Sullivan, Philip Ugelow, and David Wishnick have continuously offered critical insight on social entrepreneurship. Fahim Ahmed, Fawzi Jumean, Ilya Podolyako, and Yong Suh have always provided excellent input on management, business, and strategy. Dr. David Backer, Dr. Samuel Charap, Christopher L. Griffin, Jr., Scott Grinsell, Richard James 'Jim' Mitre, Dr. Vipin Narang, and Katherine Southwick have consistently offered wonderful feedback on law, politics, and international relations. Dr. Phil Clark and Mauro De Lorenzo have been valuable and cherished colleagues through years of studying, discussing, working on, and traveling through Africa, particularly Rwanda. Several other friends and colleagues have been especially helpful, including Ligia Abreu Medina, Carolyn Crandall, Dr. Brendon Graeber, Arvind Grover, Elizabeth Katz, Tisana 'O' Kunjara Na Ayudhya, Dianne Liu, Brendan & Lacey Lupetin,

Sarah Martin, Jackson Muneza Mvunganyi, Tanusri Prasanna, Eve Semins, Dr. Michelle Semins, Vance Serchuk, Dr. Tamara 'Tammy' Vanderwal, Lauren Vestewig, Dr. Sunil Wadhwa, and Dr. Jared Williamson.

Since I was a child, librarians have been my teachers and friends, and libraries have been my sanctuaries and playgrounds. Librarians at Yale University generously contributed their research skills, expert advice, and encouragement. Thank you to the following individuals from Yale Law School's Lillian Goldman Law Library: Femi Cadmus, former Associate Librarian for Administration (current Director, Cornell Law Library); Margaret Chisholm, Reference Librarian; Ryan Harrington, Reference Librarian for Foreign & International Law; S. Blair Kauffman, Law Librarian & Professor of Law; Evelyn Ma, Reference Librarian; Teresa Miguel, former Associate Librarian for Foreign & International Law (current Associate Librarian for Administration); John B. Nann, Associate Librarian for Reference & Instructional Services; and Camilla M. Tubbs, Head of Research Instruction. And thank you to the following individuals from Yale University Library: Ann Okerson, former Associate University Librarian for Collections & International Programs, and Dorothy Woodson, Curator, African Collection.

Thank you to Peter Schuck, the Simeon E. Baldwin Professor Emeritus of Law at the Yale Law School, and Dr. Judith Goldstein, Executive Director of Humanity in Action, for their mentorship. Their generosity of guidance and kindness knows no bounds, and they have been inspiring and encouraging forces in this book and everything else in my life for more than a decade.

My loving family is wonderfully supportive, and I am deeply grateful. Thank you to my father, Dr. Howard H. Kaufman; my mother, Romaine H.M. Kaufman; my brother, Ezekiel 'Zeke' A. Kaufman; my sister-in-law, Chan Joo 'C.J.' Park; my niece, Stella Anne Kaufman; my nephew, Julian Alexander Kaufman; my grandfather, Rabbi Dr. Shalom Coleman; my uncle, Martin 'Marty' Coleman; my aunt, Heidi Zajd; and my cousin, Alexandra 'Lexie' Amy Coleman. Thank you, as well, to my late grandmother, Stella Lande Kaufman, a generous philanthropist and news junky, who taught me early on about public service and politics, and the promise and pitfalls of their inter-sections.

I am indebted to several institutions for their support as this book grew from an idea to a reality. I thank the University of Oxford, Stanford University, and Yale Law School, where I spent several years developing these ideas and which were flexible in allowing me to pursue this project while I was primarily focused on my graduate and law school work. Thank you to the College of William & Mary, Columbia University's School of International & Public Affairs, Dartmouth College, Dartmouth's Tuck School of Business, George Washington University's Elliott School of International Affairs, Georgetown University, New York University School of Law, Stanford University, the

University of Connecticut Law School, the University of Oxford, Yale University, and Yale Law School; Rotary clubs and conventions in Rwanda, Spain, and the U.K.; the International Youth Assembly of the YMCA-YWCA in Umeä, Sweden; the Institute for International Mediation and Conflict Resolution in The Hague, The Netherlands; and Unite For Sight's annual Global Health & Innovation Conferences (particularly the fourth one, on April 15, 2007, at Stanford University Medical School; the fifth one, on April 12, 2008, at Yale University; and the sixth one, on April 18, 2009, also at Yale University) for inviting me to give lectures that grew into this book. Thank you to Yale Law School for providing funding to support my work on the manuscript, and to its former Associate Dean, Mark Templeton, for facilitating that grant. I also thank Google Inc. and The Honorable Juan R. Torruella of the United States Court of Appeals for the First Circuit, for granting me time while I worked in their offices to continue laboring on this book.

Thank you to my former colleagues from the United States Department of Justice – particularly Carl Alexander, Faye Ehrenstamm, William 'Bill' Lantz, James 'Jim' Silverwood, and Pierre St. Hilaire – who sent me on my very first trip to Rwanda, where I initially became inspired to study and work in the field of social entrepreneurship. It was during that first visit to Rwanda that I became involved in the effort to build the Kigali Public Library (see Chapter 4), and it is my past and present colleagues in that endeavour – including Karin Alexander, Lauren Baer, Caroline Batambuze, Beth Bensman, Page Brannon, Urmi de Baghel, Michelle Drucker, Jill Fenton, Neil Fenton, Rose Gahire, Benjamin Heineike, Amanda Hektor, Neil Helfand, Jonathan Home, Sarah Ingabire, Diana Kakoma, Sarah Kakoma, Sam Kebongo, William 'Bill' Kosar, Vivek Krishnamurthy, Janet Labuda, Gwenn Laviolette, Beth Haines Levitt, Dr. Martin Levitt, Abbie Liel, Binu Malajil, Paul Masterjerb, Dr. Jolly Mazimhaka, Jennifer McCard, Edson Mpyisi, Gerald Mpyisi, Ambassador Zephyr Mutanguha, Grace Nkubana, Andrew Park, Beth Payne, Michael Rakower, Raj Rajendran, Dr. Geoffrey Rugege, Sheba Rugege-Hakiza, Duhirwe Rushemeza, Liliane Rusheeza, Joan Rwanyonga, Jelena Šljivić Mishina, Janepher Turatsinze, Dudu Thabede, Violette Uwamutara, Priya Vallabhbhai, Viresh Vallabhbhai, Claudia Veritas, Gitau Wamukui, and Nils Zirimwabagabo – to whom I am most grateful for inspiring me to reflect upon and share the lessons we have learned.

Last but certainly not least, I am indebted to Edward Elgar Publishing's Executive Editor, Alan Sturmer; Assistant Editor, Alexandra Mandzak; Desk Editor, David Fairclough; Copyeditor, Rebecca Wise; and their anonymous expert reviewers for their encouragement, insights, and feedback in refining this book. Any errors are, of course, my own.

Zachary D. Kaufman

Dedications and donations

This book is primarily dedicated to Artemis Christodulou. Artemis, my class-mate at Yale University, was in a serious car accident on May 23, 2004, in Sierra Leone while she was scouting for a new location to display contributions to the National Vision for Sierra Leone, one of the projects profiled in this book (see Chapter 2). The accident caused severe injuries, and she remains impaired. Artemis sacrificed much in the service of others, and she epitomizes the essence of a young social entrepreneur. I will donate half of the book's royalties to the Christodulou family for Artemis's medical costs. The Christodulou family welcomes this dedication and contribution, and further welcomes support from anyone else who would be willing to donate. Please make checks payable to 'Artemis Christodulou' and mail them to:

Artemis Christodulou
96 Agricultural Avenue
Rehoboth, Massachusetts 02769
United States

For more information about Artemis, please visit her family's website at: http://www.christodulou.com/. Please also visit The Artemis Project (http://ylsmediaserv.law.yale.edu/webwork/trc2005/artemis.htm), an online database hosted by Yale University and named after Artemis that archives truth commission documents.

This book is also dedicated to the social enterprises profiled herein. I will donate an equal division of the other half of the book's royalties to the ventures that continue to operate. As such, this book itself is a form of social entrepreneurship.

Finally, this book is dedicated to victims of atrocities, whom we will always remember, and to survivors of atrocities, who inspire us with their courage and hope.

Zachary D. Kaufman

Foreword

Bill Drayton

The past two and a half decades have witnessed a rapid and profound change in human history. Health, the environment, human rights, development, education, emergency relief, housing, energy, and other social issues have become as entrepreneurial and competitive as business. Several consequences have flowed directly from this phenomenon. There are now major new career and part-time opportunities for men and women of all ages and backgrounds to become involved in the citizen sector on a paid or volunteer basis.[1] In fact, the citizen sector is by far the fastest growing economic sector. It generates jobs at three times the rate of the rest of the economy. From 1990 to 2000 alone, the number of registered international citizen groups increased 450 percent,[2] and there has been an explosion of such groups since. Social entrepreneurs – individuals with innovative, system-changing solutions to society's most pressing social problems – have become both more competitive and more collaborative with one another and with business, increasing productivity and quality. Indeed, the productivity of citizen groups is rising so quickly that the productivity gap with business is decreasing by half every 10 to 12 years in countries and regions where the citizen sector is large and active.

Social entrepreneurs change society by seizing opportunities, improving systems, inventing new approaches, and creating solutions. It is about finding what is not working and persuading entire societies to take new leaps. There is nothing more powerful than the combination of a big idea with a good entrepreneur. We are in the middle of the biggest structural change since the Agricultural Revolution, and social entrepreneurs are right at the heart of it.

Recognizing that most people are not yet aware of these significant changes, this book offers concrete illustrations of social entrepreneurs in action. It demystifies who they are and how they succeed. *Social Entrepreneurship in the Age of Atrocities: Changing Our World* helps reveal that magic moment when entrepreneurs have not only conceived an idea that sparked the next step in the field, but also learned how to cause major structural social change in order to do so.

Ashoka is the global association of the world's leading social entrepreneurs. When we started, the concept of 'social entrepreneurs' was so new that we had to invent the very phrase. Since 1981, we have implemented a five-step selection process (focusing on pattern-change ideas, creativity, entrepreneurial quality, social impact, and ethical fiber) to find and launch over 3,000 leading social entrepreneurs as Ashoka Fellows. We help them fly by providing them with living stipends, professional support, and welcome into a global network of peers in more than 70 countries.[3] Over half have changed national policy within five years of their launch. Three-quarters have changed the patterns of their field nationally.

Ashoka's core belief is 'Everyone a Changemaker™.' Beyond simply building an entrepreneurial, competitive citizen sector, our mission is to create a world where everyone has the freedom, confidence, and ability to turn challenges into solutions. The world now needs nothing short of a democratic revolution: a transformative, contagious movement that not only impacts the citizen sector, but all other spheres, including government, business, academia, and journalism.

Young people – the focus of this book – are critical. Because of their age, motivation, and, for some, a counterintuitively high level of competence and responsibility, young people can be powerful, long-term changemakers – people with the confidence and skills to take initiative and create change. For any society to succeed in a world increasingly defined by accelerating change, it must now ensure that all of its young people do develop this confidence and the skills that must underpin it: empathy, teamwork, leadership, and changemaking. To be a changemaker in life, one must first be and practice being a changemaker in one's youth. Society urgently needs to help, but the chief responsibility rests with every young person. He or she must be able to give him/herself permission – permission to see a problem knowing that he or she will be able to solve it, permission to change how the world works.

If young people do not give themselves such permission and then act, it is all too easy to slip into a life of powerlessness. That was sad before; soon it will be a tragedy. By the time today's young people reach their thirties, there will be very little demand for anyone who cannot contribute to change.

Without a high level of empathetic skills, for example, one will hurt people and groups and be thrown out of the game. How can one be a team member without both teamwork and leadership skills serving changemaking? How can one develop complex, learned skills required to be a changemaker without a lot of practice?

Young people standing up, organizing a team, and solving the problems around them is now essential. For them and for their futures. To solve the problems. And to ensure, in the only way possible, that we will soon be living in a society of changemakers. This is critical to opening the way to our 'Everyone a Changemaker™' future. That world will be fundamentally different and far safer, happier, more equal, and more successful. There is no way that the problems can outrun the solutions.

To this end, Ashoka and many partners are building Ashoka's Youth Venture, a global movement of young changemakers.[4] We hope it will spark changes analogous to those triggered earlier by the women's movement and the civil rights movement. All young people need to be changemakers now so that they can be changemakers later in life.

Inspired by and utilizing a liberal education that has made them knowledgeable and committed to shaping themselves and the world around them, the contributors to this book, many of whom are current or recent students, embody the ideal of the modern young social entrepreneur. Through their studies and travels, these proactive, critical thinkers saw problems around them, began to experience and appreciate needs and opportunities in the flesh, and felt compelled to act.

Social entrepreneurs are not content just to give a fish or to teach how to fish. They will not rest until they have revolutionized the fishing industry. The chapters ahead illustrate the needs of particular 'industries' and communities and then describe how these activities and groups are being revolutionized: whether through the promotion of creative outlets for those surviving recent horrors in Sierra Leone; the offering of legal assistance to asylum seekers; the creation of Rwanda's first public library; the partnership with Rwandan women's collectives to sell their goods abroad and to return profits and skills training; the provision of scholarships and services for socially vulnerable youth in Rwanda; the easing of the educational and healthcare needs of children orphaned by HIV/AIDS worldwide; the facilitation of young Americans in confronting global challenges; and efforts to ease the dysfunctional and destructive interrelations between Muslim and Jewish youth. Indeed, atrocity responses, the subject matter of this book, have been especially impacted by the citizen sector. For example, the primary reason we now have the International Criminal Court (ICC), the world's first permanent tribunal for war crimes, and other crimes against humanity, is that 2,000 citizen groups got together and blasted it out of the attic where the nation states had kept it locked up for over 50 years.[5]

This book demonstrates some key lessons about the modern era generally, and social entrepreneurship specifically. First, many of the world's problems must be addressed at the global level. Today's needs, exemplified in this book by atrocities, are often so complicated and challenging that they demand international collaboration on solutions. Second, entrepreneurship is often most successful when it is driven by values-based faith. From motivating the individual to engage in the entrepreneurial activity in the first place, to persuading others around her to support the initiative and trust the entrepreneur, deeply rooted and life-defining values inspire and compel. Third, social entrepreneurs must and do catalyze new local changemakers into being. To be truly self-sustaining and expansive, a movement must become more than its originator and have local ownership and commitment. Finally, social entrepreneurship can be the rule, not the exception. The individuals profiled in this book are not astrophysicists. They are good people, and they gave themselves permission to change the world where it needed change. They then went to work and succeeded by solving problems as they came into sight. You could do this. I hope these stories of caring and creativity will serve as a beacon and encourage many, many others to care and to take initiative.

Though increasingly popular and clearly most necessary, social entrepreneurship is still in the early stages of focused scholarship. This book helps fill a gap in the study and practice of the field by providing in-depth profiles written by young social entrepreneurs themselves. Congratulations and thanks to Dr. Zachary Kaufman for assembling, editing, and contributing to this valuable collection – and also for his own work changing the world.

Everyone can indeed be a changemaker, like those whose work is featured in this book. Please consider it. The world needs you, the changemaker. And there is no more rewarding life.

NOTES

1. Ashoka and a growing number of other organizations ask that everyone stop defining us as 'non-profit' or 'non-governmental' organizations. We instead suggest the use of 'citizen sector' and 'citizen organization.' Citizens – people who care and take action to serve others and cause needed change – are the essence of the sector. We believe that when one or several people get together to cause positive social change, they instantly become citizens in the fullest sense of the word. As I have argued elsewhere, these linguistic differences matter. *See* Bill Drayton, *Words Matter: Time to Switch*, ALLIANCE, Sept. 2007, at 22.
2. Bill Drayton, *Where the Real Power Lies*, ALLIANCE, Mar. 2005, at 29–30.
3. For the official website of Ashoka, see http://www.ashoka.org/.
4. For the official website of Ashoka's Youth Venture, see http://www.ashoka.org/youthventure/.
5. For the official website of the ICC, see http://www.icc-cpi.int/.

Preface

Amy Chua

After the fall of the Berlin Wall, a consensus emerged, not only in the United States, but also to a considerable extent around the world. Markets and democracy, working hand in hand, would transform the world into a community of modernized, productive, peace-loving nations. In the process, ethnic hatred, religious zealotry, and other 'backward' aspects of underdevelopment would be swept away.[1] Unfortunately, something very different has happened. Since 1989, we have seen the proliferation of ethnic conflict, intensifying fundamentalism and anti-Americanism, wars and war crimes, two genocides of magnitudes unprecedented since the Nazi Holocaust, and a rising tide of worldwide terrorism.[2]

Sometimes, states respond to these problems with massive force. Other times, they are unwilling or unable to respond at all. Either way, these new and often horrific challenges are too important and too complex for states alone to address. Even when states do get involved, they usually leave instability and festering wounds in their wake. Social entrepreneurship, an emerging theme in global political, economic, development, and cultural issues, helps fill this crucial gap.

Some have argued that the twenty-first century needs an 'American Empire' to deal with rogue states and spreading violence.[3] Others believe that American unilateralism and militarism have fueled global turbulence.[4] Whatever one's politics, this book has refreshingly demonstrated that civil society – including young people with big ideas and a lot of heart – has great potential to address atrocities, often in ways states, international institutions, or large foundations can't or won't.

'Social entrepreneurship' is difficult to define. In his Introduction to this book, Dr. Zachary Kaufman, both a thinker on and practitioner of social entrepreneurship, has offered a helpful theoretical definition, while the subsequent case study chapters illustrate the concept in practice. Whether by building libraries for post-genocide societies, supporting orphans in developing countries, or empowering young Americans to address global issues, social entrepreneurship is an exciting and diverse field of research and work that is changing the way we think about the relationship between small-group initiatives and large-scale problems that were once under the exclusive purview of government. My own experience in the field is partially based on my service on the Advisory Board of Americans for Informed Democracy, which Seth Green and Leah Maloney profile in this book.[5] It has become clear to me – and to many others – that social entrepreneurship, properly structured and harnessed, can help attack critical and persistent problems in new and successful ways while engaging stakeholders that may have otherwise been excluded from the process.

Contrary to the view of many proponents of globalization, the spread of markets and democracy has had the unintended consequence of aggravating ethnic conflict and violence in many parts of the developing world.[6] But globalization offers solutions as well as problems. Social entrepreneurship, often engaging providers, recipients, and foreign and local partners across national boundaries using modern communication, transportation, and technology, is a form of globalization capable of mitigating and counteracting some of these unintended consequences.

Specifically, social entrepreneurship can help bring necessary material, medical, educational, technological, or other assistance to desperate communities. By aiding these communities in their development, social entrepreneurship can ease the economic hardships and disparities that can heighten ethnic conflict. In particular, resentment and violence directed against what I have called 'market-dominant minorities'[7] might be avoided or reduced if members of those wealthy minority communities initiate or participate in social entrepreneurship, visibly benefiting and demonstrating their concern for the larger, poorer portions of the population. Social entrepreneurship goes beyond philanthropy, aligning incentives and capitalizing on generosity and common interests. Moreover, when engaged in by Westerners, such as the bright, young, motivated individuals featured in this book, social entrepreneurship can be a way of allaying anti-Westernism, including global anti-Americanism.

In a recent book, I wrote about the rise and fall of history's 'hyperpowers': the strikingly few societies in history that amassed such economic and military might that they basically dominated the world.[8] I argued that the secret to world dominance has been, surprisingly, *tolerance* – defined not in the modern, human rights sense, but simply as the willingness to let people of different ethnicities, religions, and backgrounds live, work, and prosper in society. To be globally (not just regionally or locally) dominant, a society must be at the forefront of the world's technological, military, and economic frontiers. And at any given moment, the most valuable human capital the world has to offer – whether in terms of intelligence, skills, networks, creativity, or drive – is never found within any one ethnic or religious group. To be world dominant, a society must be able to pull in and motivate the *world's* 'best and brightest.'

In my view, a similar notion of tolerance underlies the social entrepreneurship described in this book – and gives it tremendous creative, global, on-the-ground potential. Essentially, international social entrepreneurship draws on and derives its energy from diverse people working together across vast distances, involving local communities, government, foundations, and corporations. In that sense, social entrepreneurship is globalization as tolerance in the best sense.

This book offers a wise and wide-ranging reflection on the past and present of social entrepreneurship, providing a guide for its future. Given the repeated failure of states to address some of the world's most urgent problems, it would be worthwhile for us all to take to heart the inspiring successes described in this book.

NOTES

1. *See, e.g.,* THOMAS L. FRIEDMAN, THE LEXUS AND THE OLIVE TREE: UNDERSTANDING GLOBALIZATION (2000); FRANCIS FUKUYAMA, THE END OF HISTORY AND THE LAST MAN (1992).
2. *See generally* AMY CHUA, WORLD ON FIRE: HOW EXPORTING FREE MARKET DEMOCRACY BREEDS ETHNIC HATRED AND GLOBAL INSTABILITY (2004) [hereinafter CHUA, WORLD ON FIRE].
3. *See, e.g.,* NIALL FERGUSON, COLOSSUS: THE PRICE OF AMERICA'S EMPIRE 301–02 (2004).
4. *See, e.g.,* NOAM CHOMSKY, HEGEMONY OR SURVIVAL: AMERICA'S QUEST FOR GLOBAL DOMINANCE (2003); PATRICE L. R. HIGONNET, ATTENDANT CRUELTIES: NATIONAL AND NATIONALISM IN AMERICAN HISTORY (2007).
5. *See* Chapter 8.
6. CHUA, WORLD ON FIRE, *supra* note 2, at 9.
7. *Id.* at 6.
8. See AMY CHUA, DAY OF EMPIRE: HOW HYPERPOWERS RISE TO GLOBAL DOMINANCE – AND WHY THEY FALL (2007).

1. Social entrepreneurship in the age of atrocities: Introduction

Zachary D. Kaufman

INTRODUCTION

One of the tensions generated by globalization is that advanced technologies and our ever-shrinking world empower not only state actors but also individuals to act increasingly in either constructive or destructive ways. Although 'social entrepreneurship'[1] is not a new type of human endeavor, its impact is greater than at any previous point in history. Contemporary 'social entrepreneurs'[2] are, in fact, anti-terrorists.[3]

This book focuses on social entrepreneurship concerning 'atrocity'[4] issues. This introductory chapter provides an overview of social entrepreneurship itself. The chapter then considers potential perils and pitfalls of social entrepreneurship and, finally, presents an overview of the book, explaining its purposes and describing the profiled social enterprises.

SOCIAL ENTREPRENEURSHIP: A BRIEF OVERVIEW

This part first considers existing definitions of 'social entrepreneurship' before suggesting a refined, expanded version. Next, it explores the history of and institutions involved in social entrepreneurship and then moves on to a description of the various qualities social entrepreneurs themselves possess. The part ends by discussing social entrepreneurship as a particular type of venture.

Definition

What, exactly, is social entrepreneurship? Tony Sheldon, Executive Director of the Program on Social Enterprise at Yale University's School of Management, has said, in echoing U.S. Supreme Court Justice Potter Stewart, that '[s]ocial entrepreneurship is a little like pornography. It's hard to define, but you know it when you see it.'[5]

Bill Drayton, the author of this book's Foreword, is often credited with coining the term 'social entrepreneurship' roughly 20 years ago.[6] Drayton is a former management consultant at McKinsey & Company and Assistant Administrator at the U.S. Environmental Protection Agency. In 1980, he founded Ashoka, an organization focused on identifying and supporting leading social entrepreneurs.[7] Citing examples such as women's rights leader Susan B. Anthony, environmentalist David Brower, education philosopher Mary Montessori, conservationist John Muir, nursing pioneer Florence Nightingale, landscape architect Frederick Law Olmsted, sex educator and birth control activist Margaret Sanger, and Drayton himself, Ashoka provides the following description of social entrepreneurship:

> [T]he most powerful force for change in the world is a new idea in the hands of a leading social entrepreneur. The job of a social entrepreneur is to recognize when a part of society is stuck and to provide new ways to get it unstuck. He or she finds what is not working and solves the problem by changing the system, spreading the solution and persuading entire societies to take new leaps. Social entrepreneurs are not content just to give a fish or teach how to fish. They will not rest until they have revolutionized the fishing industry.[8]

J. Gregory Dees, Professor of the Practice of Social Entrepreneurship and Nonprofit Management at Duke University's Fuqua School of Business, has provided a more specific description. Social entrepreneurship, Professor Dees says,

> combines the passion of a social mission with an image of business-like discipline, innovation, and determination commonly associated with, for instance, the high-tech pioneers of Silicon Valley. ... Social entrepreneurs play the role of change agents in the social sector, by:
>
> • Adopting a mission to create and sustain social value (not just private value),
> • Recognizing and relentlessly pursuing new opportunities to serve that mission,
> • Engaging in a process of continuous innovation, adaptation, and learning,
> • Acting boldly without being limited by resources currently in hand, and
> • Exhibiting heightened accountability to the constituencies served and for the outcomes created.[9]

Social entrepreneurship is usually viewed as innovation that uses business skills to pursue socially-beneficial goals instead of – or in addition to – the traditional entrepreneurial goal of financial profit. For example, Pamela Hartigan, Director of the University of Oxford's Skoll Center for Social Entrepreneurship and former Founding Managing Director of the Schwab Foundation for Social Entrepreneurship, describes a social entrepreneur as 'what you get when you combine Richard Branson and Mother Theresa – a hybrid between business and social value creation.'[10]

But that definition is too narrow. As the field of social entrepreneurship has become more popular and widespread, its definition has similarly broadened. Based on developments in the theory and practice of social entrepreneurship, I define the term to mean an innovative venture – whether for-profit, not-for-profit, or some combination – which seeks to further a social goal.[11] Such endeavors may or may not focus on using typical business skills – although all certainly do use at least some, such as accounting, networking, fundraising, public relations, asset acquisition and management, competition with other ventures for material and human resources, staff recruitment and supervision, effective use of technology, and organizational formation, incorporation, and administration.[12] This expanded definition of social entrepreneurship overlaps with volunteerism, activism, philanthropy, and charity,[13] but it is the *entrepreneurial* nature – that pioneering spirit – of this particular social work that sets it apart. As such, different kinds of entrepreneurs – like policy entrepreneurs, business entrepreneurs, or norm entrepreneurs[14] – can be social entrepreneurs. Admittedly, those who embrace the more traditional, and limiting, definition may not consider some of the ventures profiled in this book to qualify as social entrepreneurship.

History and Institutions

Social entrepreneurship is in essence the privatization and secularization of activities that used to be considered the sole responsibility and province of government and religion. Social entrepreneurship often serves to ameliorate market failures. Not only do social entrepreneurs seek to fill gaps in existing political, social, economic, and legal systems, but these entrepreneurs also endeavor to rectify many of the very problems these systems often inadvertently create, such as inequality and, as Professor Chua observes in her Preface to this book, conflict.[15]

The practice of social entrepreneurship has a rich history, even if the term itself is relatively new. When, exactly, social entrepreneurship became a distinct field in corporate and academic lexicons is difficult to determine because many who would qualify as social entrepreneurs do not refer to or even think of themselves as such, often out of lack of familiarity with the term. Not only is it a vague and only recently-popular concept, but 'social entrepreneur' as a label is also sometimes seen as self-congratulatory or self-promotional.

Early missionaries might be considered among the first social entrepreneurs. The Manhattan Institute's Social Entrepreneurship Initiative, which presents annual awards to outstanding social entrepreneurs in the United States, traces the roots of modern social entrepreneurship to the Gilded Age as well as the Victorian and Edwardian eras – all between 1850 and 1910 – in the United States and the United Kingdom. The Manhattan Institute sees today's resurgence in social entrepreneurship as a renewal of the spirit that flourished in the late 19th and early 20th centuries, a spirit that saw the foundations of today's independent, non-profit sector built by individuals who saw it as their responsibility to act to ameliorate society's problems on their own without significant government oversight or involvement.[16]

The Manhattan Institute identifies 12 individuals as embodying this spirit: Robert Baden-Powell, founder of Boy Scouts and Girl Guides/Scouts; Thomas John Barnado, founder of Barnado's homes for poor children; Clara Barton, founder of the American Red Cross; William Booth, founder of the Salvation Army; Peter Cooper, founder of the Cooper Union for the Advancement of Science and Art; William Wilson Corcoran, founder of the Corcoran Gallery of Art; Edward Flanagan, founder of Boys Town; Edgar J. Helms, founder of Goodwill Industries; Octavia Hill, founder of the National Trust; Enoch Pratt, founder of Enoch Pratt Free Library; Mary Harriman Rumsey, founder of the Junior League; and Henry Shaw, founder of the Missouri Botanical Garden.[17] The breadth of social enterprises these individuals launched – from children's leadership groups to artistic, educational, environmental, healthcare, and welfare organizations – provided early insight into the grand scope that contemporary social entrepreneurship would later embrace.

Modern social entrepreneurship could be considered to have started with Dr. Muhammad Yunus's innovation of microfinance, which he developed in Bangladesh in the mid-1970s when he founded the Grameen Bank.[18] Dr. Yunus's and the Grameen Bank's social entrepreneurship were celebrated by their joint award of the 2006 Nobel Peace Prize.[19] This modern era of social enterprise also began with some high-profile initiatives. Musician and activist Bob Geldof helped raise – and popularize – support for famine relief in Ethiopia with his July 13, 1985 'Live Aid' concert. Twenty years later, 'Live Aid' inspired the 'Live 8' concerts, similarly focused on political, social, and economic problems in Africa and in which Geldof was also involved.

Today, numerous organizations (including foundations, academic institutions, and networks), publications (including books, articles, journals, and blogs), fellowships, conferences, and competitions are dedicated to the field of social entrepreneurship.[20] Wealthy and/or famous individuals (often political or entertainment celebrities), such as Michael Bloomberg,[21] Sergey Brin and Larry Page,[22] Warren Buffett,[23] Jimmy Carter,[24] Joey Cheek,[25] Bill Clinton,[26] Bill and Melinda Gates,[27] Paul Hewson (a.k.a. Bono),[28] Catherine Reynolds,[29] George Soros,[30] and Oprah Winfrey[31] have established foundations that support, or have otherwise contributed significantly to, social entrepreneurship. Students, often through organizations they lead at professional schools,[32] and other ordinary citizens have also increasingly engaged in and impacted social enterprise.[33] The broadening composition of social entrepreneurs signifies a democratization of the field. Not only have the participants in social entrepreneurship changed over time,[34] but so has the practice itself. Instead of utilizing a hierarchical and centralized structure as in the past, today's social entrepreneurship is more decentralized and collaborative.[35]

Social entrepreneurship is in the public eye now more than ever before. Journalists – such as *New York Times* columnist Nicholas Kristof, a part-time social entrepreneur himself[36] – increasingly cover and even collaborate with social entrepreneurs.[37] Websites and blogs – including one of each relating to this book[38] – are also now dedicated to social entrepreneurship.

Qualities of Social Entrepreneurs

No particular background, experience, or education defines or ensures a successful social entrepreneur. However, certain personal qualities are essentially required if the venture is to be effective.

A social entrepreneur is a leader. Often because of her infectious enthusiasm and compelling vision, she possesses the ability to persuade others to adopt her approach to tackling a problem. She also is skilled at communicating with and managing the various staff members who flow into and out of the organization.

A social entrepreneur is a team player. She cooperates and collaborates with others within and outside her organization to achieve the results she seeks. Indeed, through such joint efforts, whole groups, beyond mere individuals, can be entrepreneurial.

A social entrepreneur is driven by purpose. She embraces Mohandas 'Mahatma' Gandhi's charge to '[b]e the change you wish to see.'[39] A social entrepreneur realizes that in an increasingly globalized world, positive and negative effects of worldwide interconnectedness impact us all – through politics, economics, culture, religion, health, technology, and in every other conceivable way. We are the generation of HIV/AIDS, the Rwandan genocide, Srebrenica, Darfur, 9/11, the 'Global War on Terror,' the proliferation of weapons of mass destruction, raging conflict in the Middle East, Abu Ghraib, Guantánamo, the South Asia Tsunami, Hurricanes Katrina and Rita, catastrophic earthquakes in Haiti and Japan, massive inequality, and global financial crises, pandemics, and climate change. Social entrepreneurs try to ameliorate or even prevent these and other tragic events from occurring in the first place and do not rely on governmental beneficence to do so. As then-United Nations (UN) Secretary-General Kofi Annan said about the 1994 Rwandan genocide and the atrocities perpetrated during the 1990s in the former Yugoslavia:

> Why did not one intervene? The question should not be addressed only to the United Nations, or even to its Member States. *Each of us as an individual has to*

take his or her share of responsibility. No one can claim ignorance of what happened. All of us should recall how we responded, and ask: What did I do? Could I have done more? Did I let my prejudice, my indifference, or my fear overwhelm my reasoning? Above all, how would I react next time?[40]

Social entrepreneurs believe that their work not only *can* be done but that it *must* be done. Social entrepreneurs cannot help trying to help – they are inherently, or consciously choose to become, active change agents rather than passive observers. They see problems and respond. They are not bystanders, but 'upstanders'[41] against significant social problems. Some view social entrepreneurs as naïve, idealistic, or fanciful, but in fact many social entrepreneurs are – and must be – realists and pragmatists.

A social entrepreneur is deeply committed to her particular cause. The passion she feels and conveys for her project will directly relate to her ability to recruit staff, fundraise, and raise public awareness. This passion often leads a social entrepreneur to be less concerned with personal income and more with the venture's outcome.

A social entrepreneur is proactive. She is equal parts thinker and doer. More than someone who cares in the abstract, she actually works on critical issues in the flesh.

A social entrepreneur is creative. She possesses the ability to innovate, adapt, and implement new methods of addressing old or emerging problems. This creativity is a necessary correlate to the social entrepreneur's commitment; without it, most ventures would founder.

A social entrepreneur is risk-accepting (or even risk-seeking). If an individual is averse to visiting foreign and potentially dangerous regions, spending time with strangers who may be involved in suspicious activities, or investing her own or others' money in a project that may never become self-sustaining (let alone profitable), then that person is probably unsuited for the often thrilling and fruitful stakes and challenges of social entrepreneurship. While a social entrepreneur may be daring, she should also recognize and manage exposure to unnecessary risk-taking, such as illness, injury, or the violation of local laws.[42]

A social entrepreneur makes time to invest in her project. Since social entrepreneurs often have other responsibilities or jobs, good time-management skills and allocating sufficient time to expend on their project will ensure that the project is well run, especially when confronting devilish details that become more time-consuming than originally predicted.

A social entrepreneur is patient. Given the obstacles she will encounter – the difficulties associated with fundraising, raising public awareness, teaching, negotiating, and all other components of a social enterprise – she must be willing to endure challenges and setbacks over long periods of time. As part of this process, a social entrepreneur must take note of lessons learned throughout her work and then analyze and apply them along the way.

All of these characteristics combine to produce a particular kind of person: a collaborative leader who is not discouraged by traditional obstacles, who possesses and can articulate a transformative vision of the world, and who passionately and proactively yet patiently address its problems (or, as social entrepreneurs often refer to them, 'opportunities'). These traits have led some commentators to refer to social entrepreneurs as 'unreasonable people,' 'radicals,' or even 'crazy.'[43] But such has been said of luminaries throughout history. As George Bernard Shaw reminds us, 'All progress depends on the unreasonable man.'[44]

Social Entrepreneurship as a Particular Type of Venture

Several factors make social entrepreneurship involving human atrocities, the focus of this book, a special and particularly difficult type of venture. These factors can be divided into two categories – resources and distance – which are further discussed throughout the case studies and in the concluding chapter.

Social entrepreneurs almost always face severe limitations on available resources with which to execute their ventures. Staff members, often volunteers, tend to be few in number and do not necessarily possess relevant experience. Usually the venture operates on a shoestring budget, with the likelihood or amount of additional funding unknown. Social entrepreneurs will often work in suboptimal spaces, perhaps part of another's office or someone's home. Communication and transportation – the latter a commonly expensive service in the contexts discussed – may also be extremely constrained by insufficient capital and unreliable due to underdeveloped technological access.

Distance among project sites, staffers, and supporters is a second category of factors that renders social entrepreneurship concerning atrocities an especially challenging endeavor. Staff and donors may work in different locations, possibly in different countries or continents, which makes interactions within and among staff and donors difficult. Furthermore, because at least some of an initiative's staff may not work at the project site, there may be great distances between staff and the project base. These distances complicate communication and transportation, making it hard to ensure quality control or meaningful and productive relationships among all involved. Separation between a social enterprise's project site and home base may also require staff to venture into regions that are dangerous, even deadly.

SOCIAL ENTREPRENEURSHIP: POTENTIAL PERILS AND PITFALLS

The practice of social entrepreneurship is not free from controversy. Indeed, some have referred to social entrepreneurship as 'a wolf in sheep's clothing.'[45] Two controversial aspects of social entrepreneurship are its potential unintended consequences and general criticisms of the endeavor and participants themselves.

Unintended Consequences

Social entrepreneurship includes the possibility of causing more harm than good, even if inadvertently. As the old proverb goes, '[t]he road to hell is paved with good intentions.'[46] A social enterprise may generate unintended negative consequences, perhaps exacerbating a problem or, because of the delicate interconnectedness of needy situations, a related issue.

A social entrepreneur must anticipate as much as possible the likelihood of mistakes or other complications occurring and then decide whether to take the risk. Even if a negative consequence results, the project may be worthwhile. The good may outweigh the bad, or the bad may only be temporary and completely overshadowed by the good that is being – or will be – done.

Just as there may be unintended negative consequences, so too may there be unintended positive consequences, the flip side of interconnection and issue linkage.

Criticisms

Criticism of social entrepreneurship can be divided into charges aimed at social entrepreneurs themselves and charges aimed at their projects. Some suspect that, while altruism may compel many to become involved in social enterprises, at least a few individuals engage in this field out of mixed motives. Some social entrepreneurs may be driven by ego, including a desire to leave a self-promoting personal legacy or a competitive spirit to accomplish something no one else has.[47] Social entrepreneurs may thus be criticized for being self-serving – individuals who seek to pad their résumés (to improve their public image or, as is popularly thought of Andrew Carnegie, to balance out their misdeeds[48]); to achieve fame; or to make money. And it's true: some may be motivated by these factors. As with many other human endeavors, sometimes it is the case that social entrepreneurs are driven by a combination of selfless and selfish interests. Social entrepreneurs might also be condemned for being naïve, unwelcome, unaccountable, inexperienced, unqualified, occasionally dishonest, officious intermeddlers, all of which may also be valid.[49]

Social enterprises themselves are sometimes pilloried on several different grounds. They may focus too narrowly on the issues or facts that fit their agenda. For example, an organization that seeks to promote the UN could be criticized for ignoring problems within that institution. UN peacekeeping missions allegedly have fomented conflict in the Democratic Republic of the Congo (DRC) because peacekeepers have committed horrible crimes, including rape, pedophilia, and prostitution,[50] and similar charges have been leveled against many other UN peacekeeping missions (e.g., Burundi, Haiti, Ivory Coast, Kosovo, Liberia, Sierra Leone).[51] By refusing to take a more critical view of UN activities, a particularly pro-UN organization could be accused of whitewashing the fact that one of the most significant and destructive forces the international institution has to battle against is itself.

Another criticism of social enterprises is that they may misrepresent their methodology, objectives, or activities. The self-characterization of social enterprises can be disingenuous and simply wrong, perhaps intentionally so. An extreme, albeit imperfect example (because not all of these organizations would qualify as social enterprises) is that, through executing the 'Global War on Terror,' we have learned that some seemingly innocent and helpful charities are, in fact, fronts for terrorist organizations.[52] As a result of such misreporting, donors and staff may be completely unaware of the general purposes and specific projects they support and may not have contributed had they known the truth from the outset.

Others may criticize the methodology of a social enterprise, even if they agree with its goals. Paul Theroux, a writer and former Peace Corps volunteer in Malawi, decries the general 'more money' approach to Africa's problems that he says celebrities, such as Bono, and others advocate. Theroux suggests instead that Africa needs better, less corrupt governance and leadership as well as more Africans staying in or returning to their home countries to help.[53] William Easterly, a professor of economics at New York University, argues that foreign aid can cause more harm than good.[54] Even some aid proponents, such as Kristof, concede the point, acknowledging that foreign aid can promote dependency and yield similarly unwanted – and unintended – effects, such as when importing food promotes longer-term famine by discouraging locals from producing their own sustenance in the future.[55]

What should we make of these criticisms of social entrepreneurship? As a first step, we must acknowledge their potential legitimacy. Therefore, as with any emerging field of work and scholarship, we should identify, study, and propose solutions to problems in the theory and practice of social entrepreneurship. Certainly, as with other public and private sector ventures, social enterprises would benefit from increased accountability and transparency. Social entrepreneurs should make more – and more accurate – information about their plans, work, and staff available to the public, particularly to potential and existing donors, members of the communities in which they operate, and other stakeholders. Social enterprise managers should take more seriously their responsibility to thoroughly vet all staff (including volunteers) before hiring them. These same administrators must also be willing to fire staff when appropriate or necessary. A field that relies so significantly on volunteers must still demand accountability and professionalism of those volunteers, especially because the stakes involved in social entrepreneurship (i.e., the benefits and drawbacks to the problems and people targeted for assistance) are so great.

These and other critical challenges distinguish social entrepreneurship from other types of ventures. However, despite its potential perils, pitfalls, and obstacles, social entrepreneurship is still a promising endeavor. As anthropologist Margaret Mead once said, '[n]ever doubt that a small group of thoughtful, committed citizens can change the world: Indeed, it is the only thing that ever has.'[56] Such ventures are most crucial where traditional aid (including for atrocity victims) – provided through governmental or religious institutions – is unavailable, insufficient, or ineffective.

OVERVIEW OF THE BOOK

Purposes

Despite the recent growth of and focus on corporate philanthropy, corporate social responsibility, private sector investment in developing countries, public-private partnerships for social causes, non-governmental organizations (NGOs), and social entrepreneurship itself, comprehensive discussion on the topic of social entrepreneurship is still lacking. Many people are intrigued by social entrepreneurship: they are interested in who undertakes these activities as well as why, how, when, and where. Some also want to draw lessons from the experiences – successes *and* failures – of social entrepreneurs in order to pursue their own initiatives.

The authors of this book have thus identified a clear need for further examination of social entrepreneurship and have set out to fulfill five goals. First, we hope to contribute to the field of social entrepreneurship through our personal insight. Although it has been practiced in one form or another for centuries, social entrepreneurship is a relatively new, increasingly self-aware field. As a result, the existing literature on the topic is fairly modest.[57] Because context is crucial – principles and practices of social entrepreneurship that work well in one place may not elsewhere – it is difficult to generalize from varied experiences, requiring additional case study analysis. Therefore, as Dr. Cheryl Dorsey emphasizes in her Afterword, this book, as one of the early volumes addressing social entrepreneurship, contributes to the emerging field by helping to inform, instruct, and build the community of social entrepreneurs.

Second, we seek to help clarify the concept of social entrepreneurship. This chapter defined the concept and introduced its history and the theory behind it. The case studies that follow illustrate the concept of social entrepreneurship in practice. The concluding chapter, in which I offer detailed comparisons among the preceding case studies, then draws lessons to be learned from the profiled initiatives. The similarities among the case studies that I highlight and analyze in that chapter concern youth leadership, motivation, luck, failure, institution-building, management, friends and family, technology, intersections with academia, and potential personal risks, costs, and benefits. The differences I identify and consider concentrate on design and operations, scalability and obsolescence, staff, the role of local leadership, and social entrepreneur 'multipliers.' Reflecting on the unique initiative that is social entrepreneurship through the case studies elucidates the contours, aims, and functions of the field.

Third, we undertake to raise public awareness about social entrepreneurship. The book profiles several social enterprises in order to spread knowledge about the projects themselves and about the field of social entrepreneurship more generally. We hope not only that the profiles are inherently interesting and informative, but also that they provide insight and serve as models for budding social enterprises. That said, the views expressed by the contributors to this book are not necessarily shared by any of the other contributors, including myself.

Fourth, we explore leadership in innovative activist organizations. As such, the book directly and indirectly examines qualities of a social enterprise's visionary and trailblazer. We also hope to give the reader practical advice on how to initiate and manage an international public service project and to draw from our experiences with our own endeavors to confront specific issues.

Fifth and finally, by focusing on initiatives in or relating to regions that have suffered atrocities, we endeavor to discuss the challenges, obstacles, and opportunities for social entrepreneurship in a particular – and particularly critical – context. These issues concern conflict prevention, 'transitional justice,'[58] and post-conflict reconstruction, reconciliation, healing, and memorialization. Such matters may take generations to ameliorate and affect not only individuals in the immediate vicinity of atrocities but also those in neighboring regions and in a victimized community's diaspora around the world.

In order to convey the specific subject-matter focus within social entrepreneurship and how pressing it is today, the title of this volume partially mimics the subtitle of Samantha Power's Pulitzer Prize-winning book, '*A Problem from Hell': America and the Age of Genocide.*[59] As Bill Drayton notes in his

Foreword, social entrepreneurship has been crucial for inhibiting and repairing the devastation wrought by atrocities; for example, social entrepreneurs contributed to the establishment of the International Criminal Court (ICC), the world's first permanent international war crimes tribunal.[60] Individuals and organizations working on issues related to atrocities have increasingly gained recognition and praise as social entrepreneurs. For example, the Skoll Foundation presented its 2009 Skoll Award for Social Entrepreneurship to the International Center for Transitional Justice (ICTJ) to recognize and support ICTJ's 'pioneering integrated, comprehensive, and localized approaches to transitional justice with tools, expertise and comparative knowledge necessary to help countries heal.'[61]

While this book primarily focuses on social entrepreneurship in the context of atrocities, it necessarily also involves social entrepreneurship concerning other issue areas. The profiled case studies relate to, for example, education, literacy, economic and legal empowerment, and healthcare.

Profiles

This book profiles social enterprises led by young Westerners who focus on atrocity issues, whether ongoing or post-conflict.[62] I have deliberately selected these criteria to provide coherence to the group of profiled enterprises and also to narrow an otherwise enormous number and type of social enterprises. This focus in no way suggests that other social ventures – whether led by older people or by individuals actually from the regions addressed, or initiatives focusing on other issues – are any less important. Rather, they simply fall outside the scope of this particular book.[63] Indeed, much of the most creative and crucial social entrepreneurship originates from individuals in the developing world.[64]

As the editor of this book, I consciously chose the profiled organizations because their similarities and differences highlight various, and sometimes competing, approaches to social entrepreneurship.[65] And like some other books that feature social entrepreneurs, I decided to limit the number of case studies to fewer than 10 in order to ensure sufficient space for detailing each initiative.[66]

I asked the founders and leaders of the profiled social enterprises themselves to discuss their projects,[67] rather than to write about them myself.[68] This format enables individuals who know most about a venture and the needs it addresses to discuss them, as well as organizational members' motives, goals, challenges, successes, and failures. This book thus provides the opportunity for the contributors to report on their work and to reflect more deeply on and share lessons learned from their experiences. Such an approach necessarily entails certain drawbacks; for example, while the contributors are best informed about their work, they may not be the most objective. By reflecting on the case studies as a whole, the concluding chapter aims to provide a more detached perspective.

The eight social enterprises profiled differ with respect to their history, purpose, design, size, and status. The two organizations that no longer operate open and close this anthology. The first case study, in Chapter 2, examines the National Vision for Sierra Leone (NVSL), an outgrowth of the Sierra Leone Truth and Reconciliation Commission (SL TRC), which used dialogue and artistic expression to help promote reconciliation, healing, and remembrance following atrocities committed in West Africa. The case studies start with this chapter for two reasons. First, this chapter contains a helpful rubric for approaching social entrepreneurship, particularly concerning the use of limited resources, which the reader should keep in mind when learning about the other profiled ventures. Second, echoing this introductory chapter, the NVSL case study also considers the definition of social entrepreneurship itself, similarly offering a broad meaning of the term.

Whereas the NVSL helped alleviate problems that refugees, among others, have faced by providing them with an outlet for expressing their emotions and aspirations, in Chapter 3, Asylum Access (AA) and related organizations showcase a different approach to refugee assistance. AA and its sister groups provide on-the-ground legal counsel and representation for refugees in Africa, Asia, and Latin America, and they advocate for refugee rights worldwide.

Chapters 4 through 6 concern social enterprises that focus on Rwanda, the population and infrastructure of which was decimated by genocide in 1994. Chapter 4 highlights the Kigali Public Library (KPL), which is the first national public library in Rwanda. This chapter begins the trio of Rwanda-related case studies because it includes background on events surrounding the genocide that the other cases then reference. Indego Africa (IA), profiled in Chapter 5, partners with cooperatives of women artisans in Rwanda on a fair trade basis to sell their hand-made accessories and home décor products and invests profits from sales and fundraising into skills training programs for cooperative members. In some of these cooperatives, women work alongside the wives of imprisoned *génocidaires* who had killed their families during the genocide. Chapter 6 focuses on Generation Rwanda (GR), which contributes financial and other support to help orphans and other vulnerable children in Rwanda earn university degrees and hopefully become community leaders. Not only are IA and GR grouped together because they operate in Rwanda, but also because of their organizational partnership.

Orphans Against AIDS (OAA), the subject of Chapter 7, immediately follows the case study on GR for comparative purposes, because both social enterprises concern the same type of beneficiaries: disadvantaged children who are particularly susceptible to certain physical, psychological, and economic harms. OAA provides academic scholarships, basic supplies, and healthcare to African and Asian children orphaned and otherwise made vulnerable by HIV/AIDS, in some cases exposed intentionally during atrocities.

The final two cases studies, in Chapters 8 and 9, concern social enterprises that have fostered dialogue toward achieving greater understanding of certain communities and current events. Americans for Informed Democracy (AID) uses various forums (e.g., seminars, summits, meetings, media, and videoconferences) to inform and engage Americans on U.S. foreign policy and international relations issues. Children of Abraham (CoA) sought to promote positive relations between Muslim and Jewish youth through online and in-person activities. This final case study is intentionally included in the anthology as an example of an ultimately unsuccessful social enterprise. Just as valuable lessons for social entrepreneurship can be gleaned from the more effective ventures, CoA's missteps provide equally helpful guidance to nascent social entrepreneurs.

Social Entrepreneurship in the Age of Atrocities: Changing Our World is aimed at illustrating crucial conflict-related problems and crafting effective solutions. The contributors and I hope that the pages ahead inspire and inform you in your own study or practice of social entrepreneurship.

NOTES

1. 'Social entrepreneurship' is also sometimes referred to as 'social enterprise,' 'social innovation,' or 'social venture.' Kristof has termed one type of such entrepreneurship 'Do-It-Yourself Foreign Aid.' Nicholas D. Kristof, *The D.I.Y. Foreign-Aid Revolution*, N.Y. TIMES MAG., Oct. 24, 2010, at 48 [hereinafter Kristof, *The D.I.Y. Foreign-Aid Revolution*]. Kristof says that this concept 'starts with the proposition that it's not only presidents and United Nations officials who chip away at global challenges. Passionate individuals with great ideas can do the same, especially in the age of the Internet and social media.' *Id.*
2. 'Social entrepreneurs' are sometimes referred to as 'social innovators,' 'change agents,' 'changemakers,' or 'philanthrocapitalists.' *See, e.g.*, MATTHEW BISHOP & MICHAEL GREEN, PHILANTHROCAPITALISM: HOW THE RICH CAN SAVE THE WORLD (2008).
3. Of course, who qualifies as a terrorist – or social entrepreneur – may be a matter of perspective. As the old adage goes, 'One man's terrorist is another man's freedom fighter.' GERALD SEYMOUR, HARRY'S GAME: A THRILLER 62 (Overlook Press 2007) (1975). Similarly, one man's social entrepreneur may be another man's mischief-maker.
4. According to the first U.S. Ambassador-at-Large for War Crimes Issues and now international law scholar David J. Scheffer, there are five criteria that define an 'atrocity.' They are:

    > [i] high impact crimes [ii] that are of an orchestrated character, [iii] that shock the conscience of humankind, [iv] that result in a significant number of victims, and [v] that one would expect the international media and the international community to focus on as meriting an international response holding the lead perpetrators accountable before a competent court of law.

    David J. Scheffer, *The Future of Atrocity Law*, 25 SUFFOLK TRANSNAT'L L. REV. 389, 400 (2002). For more legalistic and detailed criteria, see *id.* at 399.

Typically, in both International Relations and International Law, 'atrocities' has referred to genocide, war crimes, and crimes against humanity. *See, e.g.*, ENCYCLOPEDIA OF GENOCIDE AND CRIMES AGAINST HUMANITY (Dinah L. Shelton ed., 2005); WILLIAM A. SCHABAS, GENOCIDE IN INTERNATIONAL LAW (2nd ed. 2009); WILLIAM A. SCHABAS, WAR CRIMES AND HUMAN RIGHTS: ESSAYS ON THE DEATH PENALTY, JUSTICE, AND ACCOUNTABILITY (2008); Elena A. Baylis, *Parallel Courts in Post-Conflict Kosovo*, 32 YALE J. INT'L L. 1, 3 (2007); Adrienne Bernhard, *Response: Sara L. Seck, Home State Responsibility and Local Communities: The Case of Global Mining*, 11 YALE H.R. & DEV. L.J. 207, 212 (2008).

Along with the crime of aggression, these offenses are within the subject-matter jurisdiction of the ICC. Rome Statute of the International Criminal Court art. 5, July 17, 1998, 2187 U.N.T.S. 90.

Increasingly, as conceptions of heinous crimes have broadened, terrorism and ethnic cleansing are now also considered types of atrocities. *See, e.g.*, U.S. DEP'T OF STATE, FACT SHEET: AL QAEDA AND TALIBAN ATROCITIES (2001), *available at* http://usinfo.org/wf-archive/2001/011123/epf503.htm; 2005 World Summit Outcome, G.A. Res. 60/1, ¶ 138-39, U.N. Doc. A/RES/60/1 (Oct. 24, 2005).

5. D.D. Guttenplan, *Business Schools with a Social Conscience*, N.Y. TIMES (Global Edition), Jan. 24, 2011, at 7. Justice Stewart's original quotation is: 'I shall not today attempt further to define the kinds of material I understand to be embraced within that shorthand description ["hard-core pornography"]; and perhaps I could never succeed in intelligibly doing so. But I know it when I see it … .' Jacobellis v. Ohio, 378 U.S. 184, 197 (1964) (Stewart, J., concurring).

6. *See, e.g.*, Caroline Hsu, *Entrepreneur for Social Change*, U.S. NEWS & WORLD REP. (Oct. 31, 2005), *available at* http://www.usnews.com/usnews/news/articles/051031/31drayton. htm.

7. For the official website of Ashoka, see http://www.ashoka.org. For a discussion of some of the Fellows Ashoka selects, see ASHOKA, LEADING SOCIAL ENTREPRENEURS: ELECTIONS IN 2002 AND 2003 (2004); ASHOKA, LEADING SOCIAL ENTREPRENEURS: ELECTIONS IN 2004 AND 2005 (2006); ASHOKA, LEADING SOCIAL ENTREPRENEURS: ELECTIONS IN 2006 AND 2007 (2008) [hereinafter ASHOKA, LEADING SOCIAL ENTREPRENEURS 2006–07]. For independent publications about Ashoka, see, e.g., DAVID BORNSTEIN, HOW TO CHANGE THE WORLD: SOCIAL ENTREPRENEURS AND THE POWER OF NEW IDEAS 11–19, 47–67, 264–79 (2004) [hereinafter BORNSTEIN, HOW TO CHANGE THE WORLD]; Todd Cohen, *Social Entrepreneurs: Web of Connections Fuels Growth*, NON-PROFIT TIMES, Apr. 15, 2002, at 21. For publications by Ashoka staff about the organization, see, e.g., Susan Davis, *Social Entrepreneurship: Towards an Entrepreneurial Culture for Social and Economic Development* (July 31, 2002), http://www.ashoka.org/resource/4541; William Drayton, *Knowing History, Serving It: Ashoka's Theory of Change* (Sept. 2003), http://www.ashoka.org/node/986; William Drayton, *Everyone A Changemaker: Social Entrepreneurship's Ultimate Goal*, INNOVATIONS, Winter 2006, at 1; William Drayton, *The Entrepreneur's Revolution and You* (Aug. 2, 2000), http://www.ashoka.org/entrepreneurrevolution.

8. Ashoka, *What is a Social Entrepreneur?*, http://www.ashoka.org/social_entrepreneur (last visited Nov. 17, 2011).

9. J. Gregory Dees, *The Meaning of 'Social Entrepreneurship,'* 1, 4 (May 30, 2001), http://www.caseatduke.org/documents/dees_sedef.pdf.

10. Pamela Hartigan, *Everybody's Business: Social Entrepreneurs aren't just in it for the Bottom Line – Or Out of a Desire to 'Do Good,'* FOR A CHANGE, Apr.–May 2005, at 18, 18.

11. For other similarly broad definitions of social entrepreneurship, see, e.g., JANE WEI-SILLERN, JAMES E. AUSTIN, HERMAN LEONARD & HOWARD STEVENSON, ENTREPRENEURSHIP IN THE SOCIAL SECTOR 4 (2007) (Social entrepreneurship is 'an innovative, social value-creating activity that can occur within or across the nonprofit, business, or government sector.'); RYSZARD PRASZKIER & ANDRZEJ NOWAK, SOCIAL ENTREPRENEURSHIP: THEORY AND PRACTICE 13 (2011) ('The definition of social entrepreneurship implies that its practitioners come up with new ideas for solving pressing social problems and replacing old, ineffectual ones; they are creative and purposeful, determined to spread their ideas beyond their immediate circle; moreover, they are highly ethical.'); William Drayton, Foreword (Social entrepreneurs are

'individuals with innovative, system-changing solutions to society's most pressing social problems.'); Nicholas D. Kristof, Op-Ed., *The Age of Ambition*, N.Y. TIMES, Jan. 27, 2008, § WK, at 18 [hereinafter Kristof, *The Age of Ambition*] (Social entrepreneurs are 'those who see a problem in society and roll up their sleeves to address it in new ways.').

12. For an overview of the business development, planning, and skills integral to successful social entrepreneurship, see PETER C. BRINCKERHOFF, SOCIAL ENTREPRENEURSHIP: THE ART OF MISSION-BASED VENTURE DEVELOPMENT (2000); ARTHUR C. BROOKS, SOCIAL ENTREPRENEURSHIP: A MODERN APPROACH TO SOCIAL VALUE CREATION (2008).

13. For a discussion of the connections between social entrepreneurship and non-profit or charitable activities, see Arthur C. Brooks, *Philanthropy and the Non-Profit Sector*, *in* UNDERSTANDING AMERICA: THE ANATOMY OF AN EXCEPTIONAL NATION 539 (Peter H. Schuck & James Q. Wilson eds., 2008).

14. For a definition and discussion of 'norm entrepreneurs,' see, e.g., Martha Finnemore & Kathryn Sikkink, *International Norm Dynamics and Political Change*, 52 INT'L ORG. 887 (1998). For a discussion of these and other types of entrepreneurs, see David E. Pozen, *We Are All Entrepreneurs Now*, 43 WAKE FOREST L. REV. 283 (2008).

15. Kavita N. Ramdas, Great Soul Gandhi: Activist or Entrepreneur, http://www.huffington post.com/kavita-n-ramdas/social-entrepreneurship_b_991518.html (Oct. 4, 2011, 16:55 EST).

16. Henry Olson, *Introduction* to MARTIN MORSE WOOSTER, BY THEIR BOOTSTRAPS: THE LIVES OF TWELVE GILDED AGE SOCIAL ENTREPRENEURS i, i (2002).

17. *See generally* WOOSTER, *supra* note 16.

18. *See, e.g.*, DAVID BORNSTEIN, THE PRICE OF A DREAM: THE STORY OF THE GRAMEEN BANK AND THE IDEA THAT IS HELPING THE POOR TO CHANGE THEIR LIVES (2005) [hereinafter BORNSTEIN, THE PRICE OF A DREAM]; MUHAMMAD YUNUS, BANKER TO THE POOR: MICRO-LENDING AND THE BATTLE AGAINST WORLD POVERTY (1999).

19. Celia A. Dugger, *Peace Prize to Pioneer of Loans for Those Too Poor to Borrow*, N.Y. TIMES, Oct. 14, 2006, at A1.

20. For a selection of institutions and resources focusing on social entrepreneurship, see the Appendix.

21. In July 2006, Bloomberg took initial steps to establish a self-financed foundation he will manage after finishing his term as mayor of New York City. *See, e.g.*, Diane Cardwell, *Bloomberg to Put His Charity in Building on Upper East Side*, N.Y. TIMES, July 2, 2006, at A25.

22. Brin and Page are the founders and leaders of the Google Foundation (http://www.google.org/).

23. In June 2006, Buffett pledged about US$31 billion to the Gates Foundation and several more billion dollars to foundations that he and his late wife, Susan Thompson Buffett, established and that are run by their three children, Susie, Howard, and Peter. *See* Jeff Bailey, *Buffett Children Emerge as a Force in Charity*, N.Y. TIMES, July 2, 2006, at A1; Timothy L. O'Brien & Stephanie Saul, *Buffett to Give Bulk of Fortune to Gates Charity*, N.Y. TIMES, June 26, 2006, at A1; Eugene Robinson, Op-Ed., *Disbursal of Fortune: Buffett Bets on the Gateses' Philanthropic Acumen*, WASH. POST, June 27, 2006, at A21; Editorial, *Warren Buffett's Fortune: The World's Biggest Philanthropic Foundation Just Got a Whole Lot Bigger*, WASH. POST, June 27, 2006, at A20.

24. Carter founded and leads the Carter Center (http://www.cartercenter.org/).

25. Cheek donated the US$40,000 from his 2006 Winter Olympic medal bonuses to Right to Play and has campaigned to raise awareness about the atrocities in Darfur. *See* Lynn Zinser, *Another Chapter for Cheek's Notebook*, N.Y. TIMES, May 18, 2006, at D6.

26. Clinton founded and leads the William J. Clinton Foundation (http://www.clinton foundation.org/). *See also* BILL CLINTON, GIVING: HOW EACH OF US CAN CHANGE THE WORLD (2007).

27. The Gateses founded and lead the Bill and Melinda Gates Foundation (http://www.gates foundation.org/).

28. Bono co-founded ONE (http://www.one.org/) and Product (RED) (http://www.joinred.com/red/).

29. Reynolds founded and leads the Catherine B. Reynolds Foundation (http://www.cbrf.org/).
30. Soros founded and leads the Open Society Institute and the Soros Foundations network (http://www.soros.org/).
31. Winfrey is a self-described television pioneer, producer, magazine founder, educator, and philanthropist. For Oprah's official website, see http://www.oprah.com/.
32. For example, the author and Scott Grinsell co-founded Yale Law Social Entrepreneurs, a student organization at Yale Law School.
33. Kiva.org provides a method for ordinary individuals to engage in social entrepreneurship. *See, e.g.*, John S. Johnson, *Kiva.org and the Wealth of Networks: Revolutionary Philanthropy with $31 billion or 25 bucks*, HUFFINGTON POST, July 2, 2006, http://www. huffingtonpost.com/john-s-johnson/kivaorg-and-the-wealth-o_b_24003.html. For the official website of Kiva.org, see http://www.kiva.org/.
34. For a survey of social entrepreneurs of various backgrounds, see CLINTON, *supra* note 26.
35. *See, e.g.*, Daniel Gross, *Giving it Away, Then and Now*, N.Y. TIMES, July 2, 2006, at C4.
36. *See* NICHOLAS D. KRISTOF & SHERYL WUDUNN, HALF THE SKY: TURNING OPPRESSION INTO OPPORTUNITY FOR WOMEN WORLDWIDE xxii (2009) (stating the objective of recruiting readers 'to join an incipient movement to emancipate women and fight global poverty by unlocking women's power as economic catalysts').
37. Kristof has profiled the work of at least one of the social entrepreneurs who contributed to this book, Andrew Klaber. *See* Kristof, *The Age of Ambition*, *supra* note 11. Kristof has also provided space on his *New York Times* blog to at least one other social entrepreneur whose work contributed to this book, Michael Brotchner (GR's former Executive Director). *See* Posting of Michael Brotchner & Josh Ruxin to On the Ground by Nicholas D. Kristof, http://kristof.blogs.nytimes.com/2009/04/11/rwanda-15-years-on/ (Apr. 11, 2009, 22:18 EST). In addition, Kristof has written about other social entrepreneurs, such as John Wood, the founder and chair of the Board of Directors of Room to Read, which focuses on literacy and gender equality in education. *See, e.g.*, Nicholas D. Kristof, Op-Ed., *His Libraries, 12,000 So Far, Change Lives*, N.Y. TIMES, Nov. 6, 2011, § SR, at 11 [hereinafter Kristof, *His Libraries, 12,000 So Far, Change Lives*]. For the official website of Room to Read, see http://www.roomtoread.org/.
38. For the official website of this book, *Social Entrepreneurship in the Age of Atrocities: Changing Our World*, see http://www.socialentrepreneurship-book.com/. This website includes book reviews, a list of social entrepreneurship resources and institutions that is updated periodically, relevant news, and information about associated events (such as lectures by contributors). This book's companion blog is available at the same url and includes entries by contributors to the book about profiled social enterprises.
39. Carmella B'Hahn, *Be the Change You Wish to See: An Interview with Arun Gandhi*, RECLAIMING CHILDREN & YOUTH, Spring 2011, at 6, 7.
40. Kofi Annan, Sec'y-Gen, United Nations, Ditchley Foundation Lecture XXXV at the Ditchley Foundation: Intervention (June 26, 1998), http://www.ditchley.co.uk/page/ 173/lecture-xxxv.htm (emphasis added).
41. In various works, Samantha Power has popularized the term and concept of 'upstanders.' *See, e.g.*, Samantha Power, *Why Can't We?*, NATION, May 23, 2006, *available at* http://www.thenation.com/article/why-cant-we [hereinafter Power, *Why Can't We?*].
42. For a guide to legal issues social entrepreneurs confront, see Bruce Hopkins, *Appendix A: Social Entrepreneurs' Brief Guide to the Law*, *in* ENTERPRISING NONPROFITS: A TOOLKIT FOR SOCIAL ENTREPRENEURS 299 (J. Gregory Dees, Peter Economy & Jed Emerson eds., 2001); BRUCE HOPKINS, STARTING AND MANAGING A NONPROFIT ORGANIZATION: A LEGAL GUIDE (2001).
43. *See generally* JOHN ELKINGTON & PAMELA HARTIGAN, THE POWER OF UNREASONABLE PEOPLE: HOW SOCIAL ENTREPRENEURS CREATE MARKETS THAT CHANGE THE WORLD (2008).
44. The Unreasonable Institute, an incubator and network for social entrepreneurs, derives its name from George Bernard Shaw's epigram. *See* Hannah Seligson, *Unreasonable, Maybe, but it's on a Social Mission*, N.Y. TIMES, Oct. 23, 2011, § BU at 1.
45. Alex Nicholls & Rowena Young, *Preface* to SOCIAL ENTREPRENEURSHIP: NEW MODELS OF SUSTAINABLE SOCIAL CHANGE vii, vii (Alex Nicholls ed., 2006).

18   *Social entrepreneurship in the age of atrocities*

46. BOSWELL'S LIFE OF JOHNSON 412 (George Birbeck Hill ed., 1887).
47. *See, e.g.*, BROOKS, *supra* note 12, at 104–08 (2008).
48. *See, e.g.*, David Nasaw, Op-Ed., *Billionaires to the Rescue*, N.Y. TIMES, July 4, 2006, at A15.
49. For example, in April 2011, author Jon Krakauer and investigative journalists from CBS News' *60 Minutes* questioned claims Greg Mortenson has made about the genesis and financial, managerial, and logistical operations of his educationally-oriented social enterprises in Afghanistan and Pakistan. *See* JON KRAKAUER, THREE CUPS OF DECEIT: HOW GREG MORTENSON, HUMANITARIAN HERO, LOST HIS WAY (2011); *Questions Over Greg Mortenson's Stories*, CBS NEWS' 60 MINUTES, Apr. 15, 2011, http://www.cbsnews.com/stories/2011/04/15/60minutes/main20054397.shtml.
50. For media reports and commentary about the scandal, see, e.g., Laura S. Applestein, Ltr. to the Ed., *Call a Rapist a Rapist*, WASH. POST, Aug. 26, 2006, at A20; Jonathan Clayton & James Bone, *Sex Scandal in Congo Threatens to Engulf UN's Peacekeepers*, TIMES ONLINE, Dec. 23, 2004, http://www.timesonline.co.uk/article/0,,3-1413501,00.html; Warren Hoge, *Report Finds U.N. Isn't Moving to End Sex Abuse by Peacekeepers*, N.Y. TIMES, Oct. 19, 2005, at A5; Joseph Loconte, *The U.N. Sex Scandal*, WEEKLY STANDARD, Jan. 3, 2005, *available at* http://www.weeklystandard.com/Content/Public/Articles/000/000/005/081zxelz.asp; *U.N. Investigating New Sex Allegations in Congo*, WASH. POST, Aug. 18, 2006, at A18. For two of the UN's own reports on this scandal, see NICOLA DAHRENDORF, SEXUAL EXPLOITATION AND ABUSE: LESSONS LEARNED STUDY: ADDRESSING SEXUAL EXPLOITATION AND ABUSE IN MONUC (2006), *available at* http://www.peacekeepingbestpractices.unlb.org/pbps/Pages/PUBLIC/ViewDocument.aspx?docid=752; U.N. Office of Internal Oversight, *Investigation by the Office of Internal Oversight Services into Allegations of Sexual Exploitation and Abuse in the United Nations Organization Mission in the Democratic Republic of Congo*, U.N. Doc. A/59/661 (Jan. 5, 2005) (prepared by Dileep Nair, Under-Sec'y-Gen. for Internal Oversight).
51. *See, e.g.*, Colum Lynch, *U.N. Faces More Accusations of Sexual Misconduct*, WASH. POST, Mar. 13, 2005, at A22.
52. *See, e.g.*, U.S. DEP'T OF THE TREASURY, PROTECTING CHARITABLE GIVING (2010), *available at* http://www.treasury.gov/resource-center/terrorist-illicit-finance/Documents/Treasury%20Charity%20FAQs%206-4-2010%20FINAL.pdf.
53. Paul Theroux, Op-Ed., *The Rock Star's Burden*, N.Y. TIMES, Dec. 15, 2005, at A35.
54. WILLIAM EASTERLY, THE WHITE MAN'S BURDEN: WHY THE WEST'S EFFORTS TO AID THE REST HAVE DONE SO MUCH ILL AND SO LITTLE GOOD (2006). For a critical review, see Amartya Sen, *The Man Without a Plan*, FOREIGN AFF., Mar.–Apr. 2006, at 171 (reviewing EASTERLY, *supra*). For other, more recent critical views of aid, see DAMBISA MOYO, DEAD AID: WHY AID IS NOT WORKING AND HOW THERE IS A BETTER WAY FOR AFRICA (2009) (arguing that the concept of foreign aid is flawed because aid can be diverted for other purposes and creates perverse incentives and unintended consequences); Jagdish Bhagwati, *Banned Aid: Why International Assistance Does Not Alleviate Poverty*, FOREIGN AFF., Jan.–Feb. 2010, at 120 (reviewing MOYO, *supra*).
55. Nicholas D. Kristof, Op-Ed., *Foreign Aid Has Flaws. So What?*, N.Y. TIMES, June 13, 2006, at A23.
56. Rushworth M. Kidder, *Every Tourist a Diplomat*, CHRISTIAN SCI. MONITOR, June 1, 1989, at 14 (quoting Mead).
57. For some existing literature in the emerging field of social entrepreneurship, see the Appendix.
58. 'Transitional justice' refers to both the process and objectives of societies employing judicial and/or non-judicial mechanisms to address past or even ongoing atrocities and other serious human rights violations. *See generally* AFTER GENOCIDE: TRANSITIONAL JUSTICE, POST-CONFLICT RECONSTRUCTION, AND RECONCILIATION IN RWANDA AND BEYOND (Phil Clark & Zachary D. Kaufman eds., 2009); Zachary D. Kaufman, *The Future of Transitional Justice*, 1 ST. ANTONY'S INT'L REV. 58 (2005); Zachary D. Kaufman, From Nuremberg to The Hague: United States Policy on Transitional Justice (Oct. 7, 2011) (unpublished D.Phil. dissertation, University of Oxford) (on file with author).
59. SAMANTHA POWER, 'A PROBLEM FROM HELL': AMERICA AND THE AGE OF GENOCIDE (2002) [hereinafter POWER, 'A PROBLEM FROM HELL'].

60. For the official website of the ICC, see http://www.icc-cpi.int/.
61. Skoll Foundation, Skoll Foundation Adds Seven Organizations to its Portfolio of Leading Social Entrepreneurs (Mar. 12, 2009), http://www.skollfoundation.org/skoll-foundation-adds-seven-organizations-to-its-portfolio-of-leading-social-entrepreneurs/. For the official website of ICTJ, see http://www.ictj.org/.
62. By 'young' I mean that these individuals were current or recent students when they launched their social enterprises. By 'Westerners' I mean individuals from developed countries, also known as the 'Global North.' For a discussion of the 'Global South,' see Chapter 3.
63. Other volumes on social entrepreneurship have been similarly focused. For an example of a book that also concentrates on young people, see SHEILA KINKADE & CHRISTINA MACY, OUR TIME IS NOW: YOUNG PEOPLE CHANGE THE WORLD (2005). For an example of a book that highlights individuals living in the U.K. or the U.S. between 1850 and 1910, see WOOSTER, *supra* note 16.
64. *See, e.g.*, ASHOKA, LEADING SOCIAL ENTREPRENEURS 2006–07, *supra* note 7.
65. Some other books have focused on a single social entrepreneur or venture. *See, e.g.*, BORNSTEIN, THE PRICE OF A DREAM, *supra* note 18; ALEX COUNTS, SMALL LOANS, BIG DREAMS: HOW NOBEL PRIZE WINNER MUHAMMAD YUNUS AND MICROFINANCE ARE CHANGING THE WORLD (2008); TRACY KIDDER, MOUNTAINS BEYOND MOUNTAINS: THE QUEST OF DR. PAUL FARMER, A MAN WHO WOULD CURE THE WORLD (2004); SAM ROBERTS, A KIND OF GENIUS: HERB STURZ AND SOCIETY'S TOUGHEST PROBLEMS (2009); PAUL TOUGH, WHATEVER IT TAKES: GEOFFREY CANADA'S QUEST TO CHANGE HARLEM AND AMERICA (2008).
66. *See, e.g.*, BORNSTEIN, HOW TO CHANGE THE WORLD, *supra* note 7, at x.
67. For other books that also feature social entrepreneurs writing about their own work, see DARRELL HAMMOND, KABOOM!: HOW ONE MAN BUILT A MOVEMENT TO SAVE PLAY (2011); WENDY KOPP, ONE DAY ALL CHILDREN. ...: THE UNLIKELY TRIUMPH OF TEACH FOR AMERICA AND WHAT I LEARNED ALONG THE WAY (2003); GREG MORTENSON, STONES INTO SCHOOLS: PROMOTING PEACE WITH BOOKS, NOT BOMBS, IN AFGHANISTAN AND PAKISTAN (2009); GREG MORTENSON & DAVID OLIVER RELIN, THREE CUPS OF TEA: ONE MAN'S MISSION TO FIGHT TERRORISM AND BUILD NATIONS — ONE SCHOOL AT A TIME (2006); JACQUELINE NOVOGRATZ, THE BLUE SWEATER: BRIDGING THE GAP BETWEEN RICH AND POOR IN AN INTERCONNECTED WORLD (2009); JOHN WOOD, LEAVING MICROSOFT TO CHANGE THE WORLD: AN ENTREPRENEUR'S ODYSSEY TO EDUCATE THE WORLD'S CHILDREN (2006); YUNUS, *supra* note 18.
68. For two of the most prominent examples of books that provide in-depth profiles of a limited number of social entrepreneurs, see BORNSTEIN, HOW TO CHANGE THE WORLD, *supra* note 7; LESLIE R. CRUTCHFIELD & HEATHER MCLEOD GRANT, FORCES FOR GOOD: THE SIX PRACTICES OF HIGH-IMPACT NONPROFITS (2008). For examples of another type of edited, multi-contributor volume on social entrepreneurship, see ENTERPRISING NONPROFITS, *supra* note 42; STRATEGIC TOOLS FOR SOCIAL ENTREPRENEURS: ENHANCING THE PERFORMANCE OF YOUR ENTERPRISING NONPROFIT (J. Gregory Dees, Peter Economy & Jed Emerson eds., 2002); SOCIAL ENTREPRENEURSHIP: NEW MODELS OF SUSTAINABLE SOCIAL CHANGE, *supra* note 45.

2. 'I pray never to see again what I saw': The National Vision for Sierra Leone

Sophie Raseman and Anthea Zervos

'I Saw'
by Mohamed Sekoya[1]

I saw the atrocities in Sierra Leone
Yes I saw
I saw the people running for their lives from cities to towns, towns to villages, villages to the bush
Yes I saw
I saw rebels, Sierra Leone Army and Kamajors shooting in the streets, killing, attacking and looting
Yes I saw
I saw children crying for food
Yes I saw
I saw abomination between man and woman, man and man, woman and woman, adults and children
Yes I saw
I saw a victim helping a victim
Yes I saw
I saw the United Nations peacekeeping forces and I was happy
Yes I saw
I saw the rebels coming home for peace
Yes I saw
I pray never to see again what I saw in my beloved Sierra Leone

PREFACE: ARTEMIS CHRISTODULOU

On May 23, 2004, Artemis Christodulou, a founding member of the National Vision for Sierra Leone (NVSL), was in a near-fatal car accident outside the remote town of Lunsar, Sierra Leone. Years later, she is still recovering from the serious head injuries she suffered in the crash and is cared for by her family at their home in Massachusetts. It is impossible to overstate the deep sorrow and devastation experienced after the accident by all who know this courageous young woman. Artemis was, and still is, a beacon of light and inspiration for many people around the world. At the time of the accident, she was a PhD candidate in Comparative Literature at Yale University as well as a consultant to the International Center for Transitional Justice (ICTJ), where she specialized in memorials and human rights. Her work took her to Peru, East Timor, Sierra Leone, and the United States. Artemis's role in building the NVSL was invaluable, and the energy and drive she committed to her work in Sierra Leone played an integral part in the NVSL's success. Her legacy continues in Sierra Leone, where those who knew her will never forget how much she contributed to the NVSL – both as a pioneering social entrepreneur and as a caring and generous human being.

INTRODUCTION

Sierra Leone, a small West African nation that is one of the least-developed countries in the world, experienced civil war from 1991 to 2002. This conflict devastated the nation, leaving thousands dead or displaced from their communities.[2]

The Sierra Leone Truth and Reconciliation Commission (SL TRC) launched the NVSL as part of its mission to address the devastation caused by the civil war.[3] At the end of the SL TRC's mandate in December 2003, a group of volunteers, including Sierra Leoneans and ex-patriots, mostly Westerners in their twenties, spearheaded the project's transition into an independent social enterprise of the same name. The NVSL's approach used artistic and cultural communication activities – including drama, art, poetry, and music – to engage Sierra Leoneans in an ongoing dialogue about the future of the nation, the legacy of the SL TRC, human rights, and reconciliation.

The NVSL's original approach makes it a compelling case study in social entrepreneurship. Many of the challenges the NVSL faced, and the strategies it adopted to overcome those challenges, help illuminate issues that can arise in social enterprises. A unique aspect of the NVSL, which we discuss in the following part, was its status as an independent project initially sponsored by a restorative justice institution, the SL TRC. In the next part we discuss strategic planning, organizational concerns, empowerment, and operational issues relevant to other social enterprises in post-conflict and developing contexts. We conclude the chapter with a reflection on the concept of social entrepreneurship, arguing for an inclusive definition of the term that recognizes the achievements of all types of individuals who undertake innovative actions to change the world for the better.

BRIEF HISTORY OF THE NVSL

Sierra Leone's Conflict and the SL TRC

Before describing the work of the NVSL it is necessary to address the background of Sierra Leone's conflict and the establishment of the SL TRC. The civil war in Sierra Leone, which featured severe violations of human rights and international humanitarian law, began in March 1991 when the Revolutionary United Front entered the country from Liberia to overthrow the government of President Joseph Saidu Momoh. According to the SL TRC, which set out to create an impartial record of the conflict, each of the warring factions that emerged throughout the civil war victimized civilians and plundered from the nation.[4] The SL TRC documented numerous atrocities, including killings, amputations, forced cannibalism, abductions, assault, torture, and rape and other sexual abuse (including sexual slavery).[5] The SL TRC also found that children were targeted with some of the most brutal human rights violations, including forced recruitment into combat, abduction, and sexual abuse.[6] After almost a decade of warfare, a peace agreement was signed at Lomé, the capital of Togo, in July 1999.[7] Fighting continued after the signing of the Lomé Peace Agreement, however. Following further international military intervention by the UN, the Sierra Leone civil war was officially declared over in January 2002.[8]

At the end of the conflict, Sierra Leone faced the daunting task of rebuilding its shattered infrastructure and addressing the traumatic legacy of more than a decade of violence and instability. One initiative supporting Sierra Leone's transition to peace and unity was the SL TRC. The SL TRC was part of a wave of 'transitional justice' institutions known as 'truth commissions' that have been established in countries emerging from conflict or state repression.[9] Such commissions have focused on restorative justice goals, such as truth-telling and reconciliation, as opposed to retributive justice objectives, such as the prosecution of perpetrators of crimes.[10]

The SL TRC's mandate had several major components. The Lomé Peace Agreement stated that the SL TRC would 'address impunity, break the cycle of violence, provide a forum for both the victims and perpetrators of human rights violations to tell their story, and get a clear picture of the past in order to facilitate genuine healing and reconciliation.'[11] The 'clear picture of the past' took the form of a final report on the SL TRC's activities, which provided a detailed account of the causes and nature of the conflict. In addition, this report contained a section of recommendations that aimed at 'providing an impartial historical record, preventing the repetition of violations or abuses suffered, addressing impunity, responding to the needs of victims[,] and promoting healing and reconciliation.'[12]

The Origins of the NVSL in the SL TRC and its Transition to an Independent Initiative

The SL TRC initiated the NVSL to engage Sierra Leoneans in a dialogue on the future of the nation.[13] The SL TRC stated that the purpose of the NVSL was to encourage the public to envision the future society that the SL TRC recommendations were designed to help the nation achieve.[14] The SL TRC did not limit the form that submissions could take and, instead, called on the public to consider providing creative contributions such as slogans, poems, songs, paintings, and photographs.[15] This open-ended call to the public encouraged a broad range of people to participate and made it more likely that the contributions would be accessible to a diverse audience, including those with little or no formal education.

The NVSL was promoted across the country. International and local partners distributed pamphlets and flyers with information about the NVSL's 'Call for Contributions' for a 'National Vision' for Sierra Leone throughout educational institutions and communities in every province. The SL TRC hosted radio shows, conducted interviews, and placed articles and advertisements in newspapers. SL TRC staff visited the central prison in Freetown, Sierra Leone's capital, to inform inmates about the NVSL and to provide supplies, such as paint, wood, and paper, to enable these individuals to produce and submit their 'Visions.' SL TRC staff also held workshops at the SL TRC's offices and provided materials to a variety of individuals – including students, unemployed youth, and former combatants – to facilitate participation.

Initially, the SL TRC conceived of the NVSL as a short-term campaign, an open 'Call for Contributions' to the public that would last for two months. The success of the campaign, however, suggested that the SL TRC should continue to pursue the initiative. Numerous organizations, institutions, schools, colleges, and individuals throughout Freetown and the provinces responded enthusiastically to the NVSL's 'Call for Contributions.' A diverse group of Sierra Leoneans submitted contributions to the NVSL: men and women of all ages, including students, artists, former combatants, civil society activists, and prisoners. Submissions came in a variety of forms, including written contributions (e.g., essays, poems), visual media (e.g., paintings, carvings, sculptures), and dramatic works recorded on film. The submissions conveyed the contributors' aspirations for the future of the nation as well as descriptions of challenges the nation still faced. The submissions also set forth ideals of peace and unity for Sierra Leone that would enable the country to reconcile and rebuild.

The NVSL was launched as an exhibit in December 2003 at the National Stadium in Freetown (where approximately 20 percent of the total Sierra Leonean population lives[16]) before a large and enthusiastic crowd. Following the launch, the NVSL exhibit was hosted for six months at the National

Museum, also in Freetown, where the contributions continued to generate participation, publicity, and interest. Hundreds of people attended the launch and the museum exhibition, including students, members of the military, and government leaders. After the deadline for the initial 'Call for Contributions' had passed, the public continued to submit contributions, and contributors frequently visited the SL TRC offices to ask how they could further aid the NVSL effort.

In light of the burst of energy the NVSL campaign sparked, demand grew both from participants and the public that the NVSL should continue. The NVSL momentum drew the attention of, and garnered support from, people outside Sierra Leone, including from South Africa, where both Archbishop Desmond Tutu and the former vice-Chairman of the South Africa TRC, Alex Boraine, provided strong endorsements of the NVSL's mission. The SL TRC recommended in its final report that NVSL activities should continue in the light of the importance – and reception – of the initiative.[17] The SL TRC set forth recommendations for the future of the project, including that it should 'become a permanent open, interactive civic space for all stakeholders in Sierra Leone to engage in dialogue through artistic and scholarly expression on political, moral[,] and social issues of the past, present[,] and future.'[18] The SL TRC also recommended that future NVSL activities adhere to the principles that animated the SL TRC itself, including to 'serve the preservation of peace, [to] strive for unity and promote healing and reconciliation[,]' and to '[r]emain independent and non-partisan.'[19]

The SL TRC could not serve as a long-term parent institution, as its formal operations would end in December 2003. The SL TRC thus proposed in its recommendation for the future of the NVSL:

> that the [NVSL] fall under the wing of the [SL] TRC's successor body, the proposed National Human Rights Commission (HRC); or, alternatively, that the [NVSL] work in close collaboration with the HRC. Pending the formation of the HRC, the [SL TRC] recommends that civil society and government commit to keep the [NVSL] alive and establish a provisional vehicle or structure under which its activities can continue.[20]

The HRC was established by an Act of Parliament in 2004,[21] but it did not immediately become operational. In the period following the launch of the exhibit, the need to preserve and to build on the momentum and enthusiasm generated by the NVSL prompted the individuals involved with the project (the NVSL 'team') – mostly young Sierra Leonean and foreign volunteers – to respond to the public demand and the SL TRC recommendations. In early 2004, the team established the NVSL as an independent social enterprise based in Freetown, aided by the advice and guidance of an advisory coalition made up of 15 prominent Sierra Leoneans who were inspired by the enthusiasm of the initial public response.

A serious accident involving NVSL team members marked the early stages of the NVSL's transition into an independent initiative. On May 23, 2004, less than six months after the launch of the NVSL, two team members, who were serving as the day-to-day project coordinators of the NVSL at the time, sustained critical injuries in a car accident near Lunsar, a small town in the provinces far from Freetown. One of the volunteers in the accident, Anthea Zervos, a co-author of this chapter, recovered from her injuries and was eventually able to return to Sierra Leone to rejoin the NVSL team. The other volunteer in the accident, Artemis Christodulou, to whom this book is dedicated, sustained more serious injuries, as discussed in this chapter's preface. The accident caused personal devastation and threw into jeopardy the survival of the NVSL as an independent initiative after the end of the SL TRC's mandate. As with many social enterprises, the passion of its volunteer leaders fueled the NVSL. When those leaders became incapacitated, the initiative was jeopardized at a critical time in its development. But supporters of the NVSL and team members succeeded in keeping the project alive, coming together with renewed drive and dedication to ensure that the project to which Artemis and many others had dedicated inspiring effort would not be lost.

It may not seem to be an obvious choice to include the NVSL, which was initiated by an international institution (the SL TRC), in a book on social entrepreneurship. But in many ways the NVSL exemplified social entrepreneurship, even while it was part of the SL TRC, and not simply because the project's design was innovative in the context of a truth commission. A number of the familiar traits of social enterprises – many of which are identified by Dr. Zachary Kaufman in the first and final chapters of this book – prevailed in this 'pocket of entrepreneurship' within a larger, official institution. The novelty of the NVSL's mission and the freedom to experiment that the team enjoyed allowed the group to innovate. The project's minimal resources demanded discipline and creativity from team members. In addition, the NVSL from the beginning exemplified the volunteerism integral to many social enterprises. At its inception, the project was fueled by the sacrifices of a small group of SL TRC staff and others who, in addition to their full-time jobs researching and writing the SL TRC's final report, volunteered their time to the NVSL in raising public awareness and soliciting submissions. This spirit of volunteerism continued throughout the life of the NVSL. As with many social enterprises, the NVSL's management structure was non-hierarchical. All participating individuals became part of 'the team,' with a say in organizational decision-making. Furthermore, the team faced a number of challenges, including communication complexities posed by distance, since team members hailed from six countries: Canada, Greece, Sierra Leone, South Africa, the United Kingdom, and the United States.

Another common feature of social entrepreneurship that emerged early in the NVSL was the youthful makeup of the team. Youth brings both benefits and costs for social entrepreneurs, as Dr. Kaufman's concluding chapter to this book describes, and the NVSL was no exception. The youth of many of the team members brought a great appetite for experimentation and a passion for change, but it also posed certain challenges. For example, a serious issue was the high turnover rate among young volunteers. Many team members were not able to provide more than a one- or two-year time commitment because of other priorities, such as graduate school or jobs in other countries. Yet the NVSL team continued its mission despite these obstacles.

The NVSL's Life after the SL TRC

After establishing the project as an independent venture, the NVSL team continued to pursue the ideals of the SL TRC. From the outset, the NVSL team used the expanding exhibit of 'Visions' as a forum for educational activities, with beneficiaries that included schoolchildren and university students, civil society, youth groups, public officials, women's groups, ex-combatants, artists and artisans, the international community, UN troops stationed in Sierra Leone, and the Republic of Sierra Leone Armed Forces (RSLAF). Beginning with the six-month exhibition at the Sierra Leonean National Museum in Freetown in December 2003, the team conducted guided tours, showcasing submissions and sharing background information supplied by the creators of the 'Visions'. Following guided tours of the NVSL exhibit, the team facilitated discussions on themes raised in the submissions, such as justice, unity, equality, reconciliation, transparency, human rights, education, good governance, peace-building, and the history of the conflict in Sierra Leone. Participants explored the works on display and talked about their own aspirations for their lives and for Sierra Leone. The NVSL also hosted radio programs at local stations in Freetown and in the provinces. These programs featured team members and program participants, as well as members of government, students, and journalists.

From the time of the launch of the NVSL in December 2003, the exhibit was on display, accompanied by complementary activities, in diverse locations in Sierra Leone, including a number of venues in Freetown. These venues included the National Stadium (where the NVSL launch was held), the National Museum, the British Council, the National Library, the Bintumani Hotel, the RSLAF Horton Academy, the headquarters of the UN Mission in Sierra Leone, and schools in the provinces. When the exhibit was not on display, submissions could be viewed at the NVSL office in downtown Freetown, in space donated by a civil society organization dedicated to the reintegration of ex-combatants. Distinguished visitors to the NVSL exhibit included leaders and ambassadors from Europe, high-level UN officials, members of Parliament and the then-President of Sierra Leone, Alhaji Ahmad Tejan Kabbah, who pledged his support for the NVSL during a nationally televised event at the opening of the exhibit at the National Museum in December 2003.

With the release of the SL TRC final report and the video companion to the report, 'Witness to Truth,'[22] the NVSL incorporated public education about the work of the SL TRC into its activities, workshops, and exhibit venues. In May 2005, the NVSL team produced a Handbook to the SL TRC final report, a short, accessible summary of the findings and recommendations of that report.[23] The team produced and distributed the Handbook in conjunction with civil society organizations in Freetown and Sierra Leonean Diaspora groups. Using 'Witness to Truth' and the Handbook, the NVSL raised awareness of the SL TRC's findings and recommendations. In collaboration with the organization WITNESS,[24] and several Sierra Leonean Diaspora groups, the NVSL team organized a conference, 'Where Are We Now? Taking Stock of TRC Follow-Up Activities,' at the British Council in Freetown in May 2005. Special guest speakers included members of the Sierra Leone government, civil society activists, and UN Goodwill Ambassador Angelina Jolie. The aim of the conference was in part to raise public awareness about the recommendations of the SL TRC in order to generate grassroots support for their implementation.

CLOSING THE NVSL OFFICES

Throughout the NVSL's activities from 2003 to 2007, first as an SL TRC program and later as an independent initiative, the NVSL was fueled by the engagement of diverse communities in Sierra Leone. The public support for the NVSL pointed to a strong desire for a shared space where individuals and communities could engage in a dialogue on recovery, reconciliation, and unity. The NVSL began as part of a transitional body, the SL TRC, whose mission was time-bound: the SL TRC sought to examine and document the conflict in Sierra Leone and make recommendations for reforms. Similarly, the NVSL's independent mission was time-bound, focused on a particular momentum and need expressed by Sierra Leoneans as their country began emerging from conflict. In early 2007, after more than three years of activities in Sierra Leone, the NVSL team came to the conclusion that their role in the NVSL operations should come to a close. Following the SL TRC's recommendations for the future of the NVSL, the HRC has become the custodian of the original 'Visions' submitted during the NVSL's 2003 'Call for Contributions.' In early 2011, the HRC began touring the exhibit in schools, using the collection of 'Visions' as a platform to engage students in discussions about the history of the civil war, the mandate and legacy of the SL TRC, the purpose and goals of the HRC, and the responsibility of younger generations towards building a country that embodies the hopes and ideals set forth in the exhibit.[25] The HRC has expressed its commitment to preserve the NVSL for future generations, with the submissions continuing to serve as memorials to the country's troubled past.

LESSONS FROM THE NVSL EXPERIENCE

The NVSL achieved some of its goals; it also faced challenges and endured significant setbacks along the way. Both the achievements and the challenges the initiative experienced can provide insight for those interested in understanding social entrepreneurship and for those embarking on their own social enterprises. We examine several of those lessons in the following section, touching on consensus-based decision making, empowering local entrepreneurs, project planning with limited resources, and ensuring safety.

Maximizing the Effectiveness of Consensus-based Decision-making

One of the greatest challenges the NVSL team faced in coordinating activities and identifying goals resulted from the non-hierarchical organizational structure. As the NVSL transitioned from a body within the SL TRC to an autonomous organization, the egalitarian and consensus-based team structure that had emerged during its time under the SL TRC became the management structure of the new entity. Despite the efficiency benefits the NVSL team could have obtained by imposing a more hierarchical structure, the team retained a consensus-driven approach to questions of substance. As Dr. Kaufman discusses in his concluding chapter, social entrepreneurs, who are often motivated by a commitment to egalitarianism and who are often bound together with their colleagues through pre-existing personal relationships, are often attracted to this more horizontal management structure. But this organizational structure can give rise to significant decision-making difficulties. On several occasions NVSL team members diverged substantially in their views on particular projects or partnerships that the organization considered pursuing.

Given the NVSL's commitment to governing by consensus, it became important to explicitly define decision-making procedures. For a team of social entrepreneurs making a similar commitment to consensus, it will be important to clearly define the decision-making roles of the various parties involved, such as the day-to-day supervisors and the larger team (be it an advisory board or decision-making body, such as a governing board). The team should also explicitly describe the rules governing the consensus process (for example, a rule that individuals must submit all significant proposals to the team within X days of the decision date and submit all responses within Y days after that). While these policies may appear to overly formalize basic processes, they provide a defense against the potential pitfalls of consensus.

Many organizations will opt to avoid using consensus as a primary means of decision-making due to the difficulties discussed above. Such groups may choose to adopt alternative management structures such as the top-down approach or decision by majority vote. As Dr. Kaufman's Conclusion discusses, these alternatives have strengths and weaknesses. For example, a majority vote decision-making approach offers some of the benefits of a consensus approach in that it preserves a flat management structure and a sense of equal participation for all participants. But the majority-vote approach may alienate the 'losers,' particularly if the same individuals frequently find themselves on the minority side. Top-down decision making, on the other hand, enhances efficiency, but may cause those low in the hierarchy to disengage. Social entrepreneurs must weigh the costs and benefits of each approach in the specific context of their own ventures to determine the optimal approach.

Empowering Local Social Entrepreneurs

While this book focuses on the entrepreneurial activities of young Westerners, it is also important to address the value of empowering local partners within social enterprises. Dr. Kaufman's concluding chapter touches on some of the benefits of involving local communities in social enterprises spearheaded by young Westerners, including drawing on local knowledge and garnering support. Among other important benefits of engaging local partners is nurturing indigenous social entrepreneurship. From the beginning, the NVSL team was committed to fostering participation and leadership among Sierra Leonean volunteers and paid staff. One of the positive outcomes of the NVSL was its impact on these individuals. Some of these Sierra Leoneans were combatants in the civil war who had come to the NVSL through a local partner organization, the Post-conflict Reintegration Initiative for Development and Empowerment (PRIDE), a Sierra Leonean NGO that worked with ex-combatants, who faced substantial challenges reintegrating into their communities after the end of the conflict.

Project Planning with Limited Resources

The NVSL never operated on more than a modest budget and survived in large part thanks to volunteer efforts. Many social entrepreneurs face a similar challenge: how to have a significant impact by making modest resources go a long way. We believe that all organizations, even small, informal ones, should engage in careful strategic planning to ensure that their goals are both worthwhile and manageable. Below we propose a step-by-step approach that other social entrepreneurs can use to engage in strategic planning. Our approach focuses on maximizing a budding venture's impact in the face of resource and capability limitations. The steps include (1) asset and capabilities assessment, (2) project brainstorming, (3) project assessment, (4) building assets and capabilities, (5) executing the strategies, and (6) ongoing strategic review.

Before laying out the project design steps in the following section, it is important to discuss the practicalities of how to implement them in a real-world organization.[26] A good venue for the planning process is an in-person workshop with all the relevant stakeholders. The group should set aside a period of time, such as a half-day or day, commensurate with the size of the group and the complexities of the issues addressed. Before the day of the workshop, designated facilitators (members of the team or outsiders) should gather information that can serve as a starting point for the discussion and circulate the planned discussion points so that individuals can prepare their contributions. The day of the workshop, the facilitators should create an ongoing record of the conversation by flipchart or other visual means. Facilitators should actively manage the group discussion to ensure that the group completes all the necessary steps. The group does not have to answer every question raised to count its session as a success. In fact, the team will very likely bring up some issues it can only resolve through additional work (e.g., through sub-committees or follow-up sessions of the whole team). Finally, the facilitators should synthesize the decisions made during the planning session and share them with the team, both as a final check that everyone has the same understanding of what was agreed upon and as a basis for beginning implementation.

Steps for project planning with limited resources

Step 1: Asset and capabilities assessment   Step 1 involves taking careful stock of the team's assets. A framework of the major categories of assets can be a useful way to inventory what an organization possesses, which may be more (or less) than team members may initially assume:

1. Financial assets: Financial assets are the most obvious category of assets. These are the organization's funds from individual and institutional donors. In some cases, as in the NVSL experience, social entrepreneurs may even donate money themselves to their projects, in addition to their time and skills.

2. Human resources and expertise: Human resources are often the greatest assets available to social entrepreneurs. Whether it is the willingness of one individual to burn the midnight oil without compensation or the contribution of a larger team, manpower is the vital ingredient in a recipe for a social enterprise.

    The exercise of taking an inventory of available talent and manpower raises critical issues for a social enterprise. As Dr. Kaufman's Conclusion discusses, staff and volunteer attrition pose significant challenges to social entrepreneurs. Organizations should take into account in their planning processes that it can be difficult for individuals who are committed to a cause and personally committed to their co-workers to broach the topic of the limits on the time they can contribute. Social entrepreneurs should confront these issues directly, however, in order to avoid risks like having to close down a project midstream due to the unexpected departure of a key team member. The NVSL, as a primarily volunteer-driven organization, faced the challenge of attrition of volunteers on a number of occasions. In the instances when the limitations on time commitments from team members had not been made explicit, the organization was not able to plan properly. With the proper level of transparency and skillful management, however, an organization can survive and even thrive in the context of the inevitable attrition of a volunteer workforce.

    One important aspect of human resources to consider is the specific expertise of individuals involved with a project. Often those who are interested in addressing a problem in a new or creative way have previous experience in the field. The knowledge and skill sets they have developed through their work should be among the primary determinants of project design, given the role expertise plays in determining where the organization's comparative advantage lies. Examples of this category of asset include knowledge of local languages, customs, industries, and people, as well as functional skills like workshop facilitation, grant writing, and technical knowledge.

3. Reputation: Reputation can be of significant value to social entrepreneurs. Some projects can capitalize on the reputation and public awareness of parent institutions, as the NVSL could by virtue of its roots in the SL TRC. Other social enterprises, however, must build their reputations over time. In the early stages, important sources of reputational assets include the cachet of team members' institutional associations and the names of prestigious institutions or prominent individuals that have supported the venture financially or symbolically. For example, the eloquent endorsement of Desmond Tutu in the first year of the project enhanced the NVSL's stature in the eyes of funders and programming partners.

4. Relationships: The relationships between social entrepreneurs and outside individuals and institutions represent an important resource for social enterprises. The following are several key types of relationships:

    a. Relationships with potential individual supporters: The first type of relationship is with individuals who can contribute to the venture, such as by donating funds. It is also important to consider carefully other potential ways that individuals connected to the team can help further the venture's mission. For example, individuals may help make valuable introductions or provide in-kind support, such as resources or advice.
    b. Relationships with potential institutional supporters: A second type of relationship is with institutions that can support social entrepreneurial work. In its simplest form, this support can be financial backing. Relationships with individuals inside grant-making institutions constitute a substantial asset for a venture. Less obvious but often just as valuable are relationships with institutions and groups that can offer in-kind support. Established organizations can offer a budding organization many crucial resources at limited cost to themselves, such as the use of office facilities. The NVSL benefited from the generosity of numerous partners in Sierra Leone, generosity made even more meaningful because many of those who contributed had extremely limited resources themselves. The diverse benefits the NVSL received from its partners, primarily Sierra Leonean NGOs, included office space in downtown Freetown, storage space for the exhibition when it was not on display, transportation for staff and program participants, and venues for workshops and conferences.

        A social enterprise can partner with institutions to further both organizations' missions. For example, the NVSL and the RSLAF partnered to provide senior army officers training on the SL TRC, to share the NVSL exhibition, and to solicit 'Visions' from the officers. The venture succeeded because it met pre-existing goals of both organizations: for the NVSL, to educate the public about the work of the SL TRC, and for the RSLAF, to raise the Sierra Leonean officers' awareness of human rights issues. Partner institutions with complementary missions like the RSLAF played a strong role in much of the NVSL's activities. Throughout its life, the NVSL partnered with diverse groups, from international human rights NGOs, to United States- or United Kingdom-based Sierra Leonean Diaspora organizations.

5. Other assets: Not all assets will fit into the categories described above; the list provided is merely a starting point. Social entrepreneurs should create

their own categories, and include a catchall category, in order to ensure that they are capturing all of the important resources upon which their venture can draw.

Step 2: Project brainstorming   Once the team has thoroughly catalogued the assets at its disposal, the team should brainstorm a large list of potential strategies the organization can pursue. In the brainstorming session, it is particularly important for the facilitators to be aware that some quieter team members may need to be given extra encouragement to participate. Facilitators should remain neutral in order to foster openness. At this stage, it is not necessary to strike any proposals from the list, even if the facilitators or other team members are strongly opposed. Since the ideas will be evaluated and filtered later, it is recommended that the facilitators err on the side of inclusiveness in this step.

Step 3: Project assessment   After a brainstorming process, the team of social entrepreneurs should vet the potential projects rigorously. We propose the 'strategy assessment chart,' shown in Figure 2.1, as a prioritization tool. The chart has two axes: one that measures the degree to which a strategy furthers the organization's mission ('degree of impact') and another that measures how difficult the strategy is to execute ('feasibility'). The feasibility score should be informed by knowledge gained through the asset assessment exercise. Once the team has placed the proposed strategies along the two axes it becomes easier to make comparisons and to select which strategies to pursue. The strategy assessment chart is divided into four quadrants that suggest how to proceed with each idea. Each quadrant is explained in the Notes below Figure 2.1.

Step 4: Building assets and capabilities   Now that specific strategies have been identified, the team must identify what gaps exist between current assets and capabilities (which were inventoried in Step 2) and those necessary to execute the current plan. The team must develop and implement a plan to close these gaps through activities such as fundraising, volunteer recruitment, and staff hiring. Since the team already rated the feasibility of the selected strategies as high, the required capability build-out should be manageable, although not necessarily easy.

Step 5: Executing the strategies   Execution is of course critical. Success here will depend partly on how well the team carried out the previous planning steps. While there are many key factors that affect the success of the execution (for example, management structure), they fall outside the scope of the current discussion.

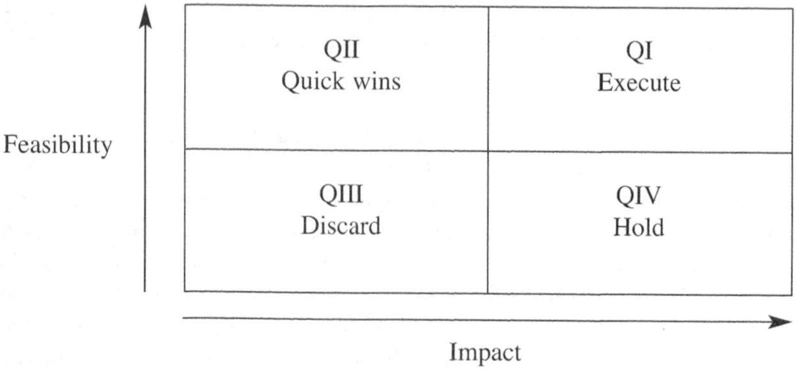

Figure 2.1   Strategy assessment chart

Notes:

Quadrant I: Execute
Strategies found in Quadrant I, those that are both high impact and high feasibility, are the 'winner' ideas that the organization should strongly consider pursuing.

Quadrant II: Quick Wins
Quadrant II strategies, which are relatively low in impact but are easy to execute, are quick wins that can play an important role, particularly when a venture is getting off the ground and needs to establish credibility with donors and the constituent community. These types of quick wins can also bolster team morale. One should be aware of the limits of organizational capacity concerning Quadrant II strategies. It is important not to risk threatening higher impact strategies by allocating too much staff and volunteer time on a long list of quick win projects.

Quadrant III: Discard
In Quadrant III fall the strategies that are low in impact and hard to execute. These strategies should be discarded.

Quadrant IV: Hold
Quadrant IV is the most complicated. While desirable from an impact standpoint, these strategies are not realistically achievable given the current constraints of the organization. The team should shelve these ideas. Although the ideas are not feasible now, they may become more realistic as the team's capacity evolves. Dealing with the ideas that fall in Quadrant IV can be difficult because passionate social entrepreneurs may find it hard to wait to launch projects that are likely to have large impact.

The NVSL encountered some of its most daunting challenges in addressing what to do with strategies that would fall within Quadrant IV. On one occasion, the team drew up plans to carry out a traveling exhibition to a remote region of Sierra Leone for which the team did not have a good chance of receiving sufficient funding in the short term. When the project ultimately did not take place, not only did the team fail to meet the project's objectives, but it also missed out on pursuing more realistic opportunities. Furthermore, morale – one of the primary intangible assets of a volunteer-based organization – deteriorated. Taking time to go through the exercises of idea generation and vetting would have saved the team from losing time and experiencing disappointment.

Step 6: Ongoing strategic review The steps outlined above are not intended to be a one-time process. It is vital to the success of a venture that the team revisit and refine the strategic planning process as time goes on and circumstances change. Lessons learned from previous strategic exercises and from executing strategies will inform subsequent rounds of planning.

Staying Safe

Social entrepreneurs should rigorously vet their projects for safety. The NVSL team was particularly sensitized to safety issues due to the tragic car accident that involved two of its members, but all social entrepreneurs operating in high-risk areas and activities should make safety a priority. Young social entrepreneurs should take into account the increased risks posed by having youthful team members, especially college-age or younger, who are likely to have minimal prior experience in high-risk settings such as post-conflict regions, and may appear to be easy targets to outsiders.

Social entrepreneurs can reduce their risks in a number of ways. First, in designing projects, they should take into account the costs of minimum safety procedures (e.g., equipping vehicles with a radio). Second, they should determine where projects fall along the spectrum of safety (taking into account the realistic safety procedures available) and reject any projects that fall below the minimum that the group or any affected individual will accept. The team should accept that many great ideas will fall below this minimum safety standard. At several points the NVSL team had to pass over attractive opportunities due to safety concerns. For example, the team declined to take on an otherwise qualified additional member due to concerns for the safety of the individual, who was a college student with limited experience in countries like Sierra Leone. The team also focused its operations within Freetown, the nation's capital, where safety precautions were relatively inexpensive, rather than pursuing potential opportunities to work in rural Sierra Leone, despite a great need in such areas. While safety limitations may be disappointing, teams must remain vigilant and avoid activities that are too dangerous.

TOWARDS AN INCLUSIVE DEFINITION OF SOCIAL ENTREPRENEURSHIP

The boundaries of what is considered social entrepreneurship are still evolving. We believe that it is important to define social entrepreneurship in a way that is inclusive. Inclusiveness is particularly important in the developing world and conflict and post-conflict situations, where it is critical to foster local leadership. In light of these issues, and in light of the NVSL's experience, we propose two principles to inform the definition of social entrepreneurship to enhance its accessibility to all those who are committed to making positive change.

First, we believe social entrepreneurship can be informal. Social enterprise often takes place outside the boundaries of formally established institutions, such as officially recognized NGOs. While establishing a formal NGO can be useful, seeking official organizational status is not possible, appropriate, or worthwhile for every social enterprise.

The ability to formalize one's socially entrepreneurial activities can be constrained by time, resources, capabilities, or even social status. Sierra Leonean members of the NVSL team repeatedly came up against this last constraint. At one point during the process to seek formal status for the NVSL, a Sierra Leonean member of the team (an individual whose appearance and speech mark him as not being a member of the local elite) found it difficult to navigate the process to register the NVSL as a national NGO. The authors, two international team members, encountered less trouble when they attempted the same task.

Second, the definition of social entrepreneurship should celebrate the contributions of all members, no matter their place in the organizational hierarchy. Social entrepreneurship's ethos should be egalitarian and community-oriented. Egalitarianism should extend to the daily practices of a social enterprise. A culture that recognizes the contributions of all participants strengthens the relationships among team members and encourages all individuals to take an active role in shaping the common social enterprise.

It is our hope that the principles laid out above will accomplish two purposes: First, we want to encourage readers, no matter their social or economic circumstances, to feel that they can become social entrepreneurs. Second, we want to promote a non-hierarchical, community-oriented spirit within the field of social entrepreneurship. The danger of our attempt to expand the definition of social entrepreneurship is that it becomes so inclusive that it loses its value as a distinct category. What is the difference between social entrepreneurship and any work one might do for the social good? We would argue that social entrepreneurship is distinguished by innovation and experimentation. These core traits are what make social entrepreneurship a powerful force for change.

NOTES

1. Poem submitted to the NVSL in 2003. The poem is also reproduced in the final report of the SL TRC. *See* SIERRA LEONE TRUTH & RECONCILIATION COMM'N, 3B WITNESS TO TRUTH: REPORT OF THE SIERRA LEONE TRUTH & RECONCILIATION COMMISSION 509 (2004), *available at* http://www.sierra-leone.org/TRCDocuments.html [hereinafter SL TRC, 3B FINAL REPORT].

2. For rich accounts of the Sierra Leonean conflict, its causes, and its consequences, see, e.g., CHRIS COULTER, BUSH WIVES AND GIRL SOLDIERS: WOMEN'S LIVES THROUGH WAR AND PEACE IN SIERRA LEONE (2009); LANSANA GBERIE, A DIRTY WAR IN WEST AFRICA: THE RUF AND THE DESTRUCTION OF SIERRA LEONE (2005); INT'L CRISIS GROUP, LIBERIA AND SIERRA LEONE: REBUILDING FAILED STATES (2004); DAVID KEEN, CONFLICT AND COLLUSION IN SIERRA LEONE (2005); PAUL RICHARDS, FIGHTING FOR THE RAINFOREST: WAR, YOUTH AND RESOURCES IN SIERRA LEONE (1996); Ibrahaim Abdullah, *Bush Path to Destruction: The Origin and Character of the Revolutionary United Front/Sierra Leone*, 36 J. MOD. AFR. STUD. 203 (1998).

3. For additional information on the SL TRC, see, e.g., PRISCILLA HAYNER, THE SIERRA LEONE TRUTH AND RECONCILIATION COMMISSION: REVIEWING THE FIRST YEAR (CASE STUDY SERIES) (2004); BJORN PETTERSON, POST-CONFLICT RECONCILIATION IN SIERRA LEONE: LESSONS LEARNED 7-31 (2005); AMADU SESAY, DISCUSSION PAPER 36: DOES ONE SIZE FIT ALL? THE SIERRA LEONE TRUTH AND RECONCILIATION COMMISSION REVISITED (2007); Beth Dougherty, *Searching for Answers: Sierra Leone's Truth & Reconciliation Commission*, 8 AFR. STUD. Q. 39 (2004); Lyn Graybill & Kimberly Lanegran, *Truth, Justice, and Reconciliation in Africa: Issues and Cases*, 8 AFR. STUD. Q. 1 (2004); William Schabas, *The Relationship Between Truth Commissions and International Courts: The Case of Sierra Leone*, 25 HUM. RTS. Q. 1035 (2003).

4. SIERRA LEONE TRUTH & RECONCILIATION COMM'N, 1 WITNESS TO TRUTH: REPORT OF THE SIERRA LEONE TRUTH & RECONCILIATION COMMISSION 12 (2004), *available at* http://www.sierra-leone.org/TRCDocuments.html.

5. *Id.* at 11; SIERRA LEONE TRUTH & RECONCILIATION COMM'N, 3A WITNESS TO TRUTH: REPORT OF THE SIERRA LEONE TRUTH & RECONCILIATION COMMISSION 465-564 (2004), *available at* http://www.sierra-leone.org/TRCDocuments.html (describing the nature of the conflict).

6. SL TRC, 3B FINAL REPORT, *supra* note 1, at 233–339 (describing the role of children in the conflict).

7. U.S. DEP'T OF STATE BUREAU OF AFR. AFFAIRS, BACKGROUND NOTE: SIERRA LEONE (2011), http://www.state.gov/r/pa/ei/bgn/5475.htm.

8. *Id.*

9. 'Transitional justice' is a term of art used by practitioners in post-conflict settings that includes activities such as truth commissions. ICTJ defines the term as follows:

    > Transitional justice refers to the set of judicial and non-judicial measures that have been implemented by different countries in order to redress the legacies of massive human rights abuses … . Transitional justice is not a 'special' kind of justice, but an approach to achieving justice in times of transition from conflict and / or state repression. By trying to achieve accountability and redressing victims, transitional justice provides recognition of the rights of victims, promotes civic trust and strengthens the democratic rule of law.

    Int'l Ctr. for Transitional Justice, What is Transitional Justice?, http://www.ictj.org/en/tj/ (last visited Nov. 17, 2011). ICTJ lists the following as some of the basic approaches to transitional justice: criminal prosecutions, truth commissions, reparations programs, institutional reforms, and memorialization. *Id.*

10. For an overview of truth commissions, see PRISCILLA B. HAYNER, UNSPEAKABLE TRUTHS: TRANSITIONAL JUSTICE AND THE CHALLENGE OF TRUTH COMMISSIONS (2nd ed. 2010).

11. Peace Agreement Between the Government of Sierra Leone and the Revolutionary United Front of Sierra Leone, art. 26(1) (1999), *available at* http://www.sierra-leone.org/lomeaccord.html.

12. SIERRA LEONE TRUTH & RECONCILIATION COMM'N, 2 WITNESS TO TRUTH: REPORT OF THE SIERRA LEONE TRUTH & RECONCILIATION COMMISSION 117 (2004), *available at* http://www.sierra-leone.org/TRCDocuments.html.

13. For a detailed description of the NVSL's activities under the TRC, see SL TRC, 3B FINAL REPORT, *supra* note 1, at 449–520 (also containing images and excerpts from the 'Visions' submitted to the NVSL).

14.   *Id*. at 499.
15.   *Id*. at 502 (reproducing the NVSL's 'Call for Contributions').
16.   Central Intelligence Agency, The World Factbook: Sierra Leone, https://www.cia.gov/library/publications/the-world-factbook/geos/sl.html (last visited Nov. 17, 2011).
17.   SL TRC, 3B FINAL REPORT, *supra* note 1, at 514–18.
18.   *Id*. at 514.
19.   *Id*. at 516.
20.   *Id*. at 515.
21.   The Human Rights Commission of Sierra Leone Act (Aug. 20, 2004), *available at* http://www.sierra-leone.org/Laws/2004-9p.pdf.
22.   'Witness to Truth' was produced at the invitation of the SL TRC by WITNESS, a U.S.-based NGO that uses video to raise public awareness about human rights abuses. *See* WITNESS TO TRUTH (WITNESS 2005), *available at* http://www.witness.org/index.php?option=com_rightsalert&Itemid=178&task=view&alert_id=16.
23.   NAT'L VISION FOR SIERRA LEONE, HANDBOOK TO THE TRC FINAL REPORT (2005).
24.   WITNESS uses video advocacy to promote human rights. For the official website of WITNESS, see http://www.witness.org/.
25.   Ibrahim Tarawallie, *Sierra Leone: HRC Takes TRC Vision to Schools*, ALL AFR. NEWS, Mar. 21, 2011, *available at* http://allafrica.com/stories/201103220823.html.
26.   The approach we propose here is ideal, but social entrepreneurs should obviously modify it to fit specific organizational circumstances (e.g., a 'one-woman team,' a team that cannot meet in person).

3. Starting a movement for refugee rights in the Global South: Asylum Access and beyond

Emily E. Arnold-Fernández, Mauro De Lorenzo, Barbara Harrell-Bond, and Rachel Levitan[1]

INTRODUCTION

Refugees across the Global South are frequently deprived of fundamental rights,[2] often for a decade or more.[3] Since the late 1990s, advocates across the Global South and around the world, including young people, outraged by this phenomenon and feeling that traditional refugee humanitarian organizations were ignoring the rampant violation of refugees' rights, have begun to pursue an alternative mode of refugee assistance: a movement to make human rights a reality for refugees in the Global South.

The movement's first and still primary tool is legal aid. Refugees need legal assistance as soon as they arrive in a host country. Their lives may depend on the outcome of a refugee status determination (RSD) proceeding. Failure to gain such status exposes a refugee to the risk of forcible repatriation and subsequent persecution. Recognition of refugee status is also a prerequisite for other basic rights guaranteed to refugees by international law, such as the right to seek employment, to move freely, and to obtain education and healthcare on the same terms as citizens.

Typically, governments determine refugee status. Where they are unwilling or unable to do so, the Office of the United Nations High Commissioner for Refugees (UNHCR) makes the determination. In 2010, UNHCR conducted status determination for nearly 100,000 individuals in more than 50 countries,[4] making its RSD system the world's largest after that of South Africa.[5] Although UNHCR's focused mandate to protect refugees distinguishes it from states, RSD serves the same gate-keeping function regardless of who conducts it. Consequently, refugees need legal aid in proceedings before UNHCR as urgently as they do before host governments.

This is the story of the earliest days of the worldwide movement for refugee rights in the Global South. In East Africa, socio-legal research on refugee rights identified an urgent need for permanent legal aid for refugees.[6] Researchers and lawyers established the first formal programs in Uganda and Kenya in 1998, and in Egypt in 2000.[7]

Funding for refugee rights advocacy abroad, especially refugee legal aid, is rare and fickle. The programs discussed in this chapter have all faced the threat of closure because of changes in donor funding priorities. To address this risk, activists from the Netherlands, the U.K., and the U.S., who had volunteered in the programs in Uganda and Egypt, started advocacy and fundraising organizations. The ability of Western volunteers to secure resources and invest 'sweat equity'[8] was a critical initial component of the refugee rights movement.

Within a few years of their creation, the Uganda, Kenya, and Egypt programs were cooperating with similar efforts in Ecuador, Hong Kong, Israel, Lebanon, South Africa, Senegal, Tanzania, Thailand, Turkey, and Zambia. As a result, host governments and UNHCR increasingly recognize that demands for legal aid should not be seen as a threat to the power of decision-makers, but as a cornerstone of an effective refugee protection regime. Still, none of the programs could have survived without scores of dedicated volunteers, mostly young and from Western countries, who worked to scale up the first embryonic legal aid providers into mature human rights organizations.

THE CONTEXT

Most refugees will never be resettled (offered a permanent home) in the West, and many will never be able to go home. In 2010, 22 countries offering resettlement – mainly Australia, Canada, and the U.S. – admitted 98,800 refugees from a global total estimated at 15.8 million refugees.[9] The remainder will spend their years of exile in another country of the Global South. There, as a matter of policy, many refugees are confined to camps or otherwise 'frequently and systematically denied [their] rights under international law, sometimes for decades, in a practice known as "warehousing".'[10]

Many of the refugees who seek resettlement abroad must undergo an individual RSD interview. Most refugees prepare their cases themselves and are interviewed, without representation, by a host government official or a UNHCR protection officer. Rejected refugees are often given no reason for the rejection, nor are they told of appeal procedures, if appeal procedures even exist.[11] Serious procedural deficiencies are commonplace in both UNHCR and host government RSD.[12] Some procedural improvements have occurred in correlation with advocacy by the organizations described here and others that comprise the refugee rights movement.[13]

KENYA AND UGANDA: HOW THE MOVEMENT BEGAN

In 1993, Hannah Garry, an American, then an undergraduate student,[14] travelled to a refugee camp in Ethiopia to participate in a UNHCR program for students. The human rights violations she observed appalled her. One refugee was shot fleeing unlawful detention, and combatants from Sudan raided the camp to round up children to fight as soldiers. Because of her experience, Garry enrolled at the Refugee Studies Centre (RSC) at the University of Oxford the following year.

There, Garry met Dr. Barbara Harrell-Bond, the RSC's founder and director, and Guglielmo Verdirame, a young Italian lawyer conducting research on the weakness of enforcement mechanisms in human rights law. Garry, Dr. Harrell-Bond, and Verdirame designed a research program carried out in Kenya and Uganda between 1997 and 2000 to investigate the extent to which refugees can actually access their rights.[15] Their work culminated in *Rights in Exile: Janus-Faced Humanitarianism*, a book about the flaws in refugee protection.[16] The first refugee legal aid programs outside South Africa – Refugee Law Project (RLP) at Makerere University in Kampala, Uganda;[17] the Refugee Consortium of Kenya (RCK);[18] and Africa and Middle East Refugee Assistance (AMERA) in the U.K.[19] and Egypt[20] – were born from this research.

Virtually every refugee who approached the *Rights in Exile* team required legal assistance. The team helped hundreds of people prepare testimony and represented them in RSD interviews. The team also trained the Ugandan police in refugee rights and wrote about refugee rights in local newspapers. Dr. Harrell-Bond worked with Pamela Reynell, a young Ugandan-British barrister, to establish a law clinic at Makerere University and to offer refugee-related coursework for law students there. With funding from the Amberstone Trust in the U.K., the RLP, discussed further below, was created in 1999.

EGYPT: STARTING REFUGEE LEGAL AID IN CAIRO

In 2000, the American University in Cairo (AUC) invited Dr. Harrell-Bond to establish a graduate program in refugee studies. Refugees learned of her arrival and began lining up outside her office to request help with their applications to UNHCR, the asylum decision-maker in Egypt.

Verdirame arranged for a British law student, Mark Pallis, to travel to Cairo at his own expense to help Dr. Harrell-Bond cope with the demand. In 2001, 14 self-funded volunteers, mainly from the U.K. and the U.S., joined Pallis. That year, the Danish embassy and the Amberstone Trust pledged US$100,000 for two years and the Refugee Legal Aid Project (RLAP) began, initially under the Egyptian Organization for Human Rights (EOHR). RLAP trained and employed Egyptian lawyers and paralegals and accepted self-funded foreign interns, who reported that the work changed their lives. Asylum Access (AA) founder Emily Arnold-Fernández was one such volunteer in 2002.

The two-year grant ran out in November 2003, and the U.K.-based AMERA-UK was founded as a charity.[21] The main purpose of AMERA-UK was to put funding for refugee legal aid in the Global South on a firmer footing.[22] In 2004, RLAP was renamed AMERA-Egypt. AMERA-Egypt was established in Egypt as a foreign 'branch office' of AMERA-UK. AMERA-Egypt's goal was to be the model refugee legal aid provider in the Global South, not only helping refugees in Egypt, but also serving as a training hub for practitioners from around the world.

AMERA-Egypt receives 10 to 12 young foreign interns, lawyers, paralegals, and psychosocial workers three times a year.[23] The volunteers first complete two weeks of intensive training from AMERA staff before beginning to work on refugee cases. Interns have hailed from 34 different countries, but most have come from Australia, Canada, Denmark, the Netherlands, New Zealand, Norway, Sweden, the U.K., and the U.S.

AMERA's experience with interns was bumpy at the start. Some had difficulty adjusting to cultural differences, such as the requirement that women dress modestly. AMERA found it was necessary to introduce regulations into its office manual against fraternizing between AMERA staff and refugee clients. Still, the interns brought new ideas and new skills and allowed AMERA to serve more refugees. Interacting with foreign interns greatly enhanced the Egyptian staff's command of English. By 2011, more Egyptians than foreign interns worked at AMERA-Egypt, and most team leaders were Egyptian.

REACHING OUT: RSDWATCH

Michael Kagan travelled to Egypt as a law student in the summer of 1998 for a seven-month internship with an Egyptian human rights group. While there, an Algerian graduate student asked for help with his application to UNHCR. Kagan agreed to help because, at the time, there was no legal aid for refugees in Egypt. Kagan was shocked when the Algerian was rejected by UNHCR: a staff member announced his decision with a small slip of paper on which the letters 'REJ' were scribbled. Kagan prepared the Algerian's appeal, and the refugee's status was eventually recognized. In the process, and in large part because of his disillusionment with UNHCR, Kagan decided to specialize in refugee law. Equally important, he resolved to return to Egypt to develop legal aid for refugees. While Kagan completed law school at the University of Michigan, his Algerian client began his own form of activism. Fluent in four languages, the Algerian began recording testimonies from fellow asylum-seekers, sending them by email to Kagan, who returned questions and prepared legal memoranda to UNHCR. The Algerian put Kagan in touch with a Southern Sudanese refugee and researcher at the AUC, Leben Nelson Moro, who did the same for Sudanese refugees. Working remotely by email with the Algerian and Moro, Kagan prepared 19 applications to UNHCR, all success-ful. Kagan's Algerian client put him in touch with Dr. Harrell-Bond. In 2000, at Dr. Harrell-Bond's request, Kagan wrote a concept paper for a refugee legal aid program targeting UNHCR's RSD and resettlement procedures. Dr. Harrell-Bond wrote him back a one-line email: 'Talk about vision!' She began circulating it in Cairo.

Kagan returned to Egypt in the summer of 2001. For the next year and a half he split time between Dr. Harrell-Bond's RLAP and a program called Musa'adeen (meaning 'helpers' and based at All Saints Cathedral in the Zamalek neighborhood of Cairo), which trained refugees to assist other refugees to prepare applications to UNHCR.[24] After 2002, Kagan increasingly devoted his time to pressuring UNHCR to reform its RSD procedures. There had been barely any mention of the subject in academic literature until Michael Alexander, an Australian lawyer working in Southeast Asia, published an article in the *International Journal of Refugee Law* in 1999. Kagan updated this piece with a study of UNHCR procedures in Cairo in 2002,[25] and followed it with papers illustrating the effectiveness of refugee legal aid.[26]

This academic effort complemented AMERA's campaign that began in Cairo in 2001 to convince UNHCR to provide more detailed reasons for rejec-tion of refugees. The general call for reform – especially reasons for rejection, access to evidence, and independent appeals – was, beginning in 2004, carried to UNHCR's headquarters in Geneva annually by staff from AMERA, Frontiers Ruwad Association,[27] RCK, and RLP. This call for reform was endorsed by joint NGO statements at the annual UNHCR Executive Committee meetings. In early 2005, Kagan launched RSDWatch.org,[28] which has become a focal point for the campaign for RSD reform at UNHCR. Later that year, Kagan helped co-found AA, and RSDWatch.org became a formal project of the fledgling organization.

THE MOVEMENT SPREADS TO TURKEY

In 1991, a group of about 10 churches in Istanbul founded a small charity, the Istanbul Interparish Migrants' Program (IIMP), to assist migrants who had joined their churches. Building on the momentum in Uganda and Egypt, in 2003, five activists from Europe and North America – including three who also volunteered with AMERA-Egypt – began providing legal assistance to

IIMP clients applying for refugee status with the UNHCR in Turkey. When the number of refugees in need of legal aid outgrew the tiny IIMP office, the volunteers paid for a one-room apartment in bustling central Istanbul. They called their group the Istanbul Refugee Legal Aid Program (IRLAP), a nod to RLAP in Egypt. While at first most clients were Somali, when the word spread, IRLAP soon began advising clients from the Democratic Republic of Congo (DRC), Ethiopia, Iran, and Sudan, among other countries.

IRLAP volunteers soon realized they would need funding to make the initiative sustainable. Since only Turkish NGOs could legally apply for funding, the program was 'adopted' by a registered Turkish NGO, the Helsinki Citizens' Assembly-Turkey (HCA), which decided to integrate refugee legal services into its overall human rights agenda.

HCA's first funding came in 2004 from George Soros's Open Society Institute (OSI) Assistance Foundation-Turkey, which provided approximately US$90,000 to pay six staff and all running costs. The team spent hours drafting their first policies and procedures in a tea shop before receiving funding for their first real office. The original IRLAP volunteers were now employed as HCA legal advisors. The program attracted smaller donations of between US$5,000 and US$15,000 from the Dutch Consulate, the Canadian Embassy, and the Heinrich Böll Foundation, and it began to attract larger numbers of volunteers from Turkey and abroad.

The relationship between HCA and UNHCR Turkey was strained at first, in part because UNHCR staff had never interacted with refugee legal advocates. Over time, however, that relationship improved. HCA's first victory was to be permitted to represent clients during RSD interviews, something that UNHCR still does not allow in all of its countries of operation. By December 2005, UNHCR agreed to allow HCA's legal advisors to review UNHCR internal assessment forms documenting the reasons for rejection, a practice that took place in only one other UNHCR country office.[29]

Despite these gains, HCA staff were factionalized by the end of the first year. Some believed that decisions should be made by consensus, while others felt that a growing organization required more formal management structures. Two British co-founders left in February 2006 and were replaced by Turkish legal advisors.

Around the same time, OSI decided not to renew funding because its strategic priorities had shifted away from 'direct legal services' toward 'policy advocacy.' The temporary gap in funding proved catalytic, however. After intensive internal debate, the HCA team submitted a new proposal to OSI that included quarterly press campaigns, a public newsletter written by refugees, a pilot project to involve Turkish university students in refugee advocacy, and an ambitious training program for refugees and members of NGOs and local agencies in other cities throughout Turkey.

For the next five months, while waiting for OSI to evaluate the reworked funding application, the HCA program – now renamed the Refugee Advocacy and Support Program (RASP) to reflect its expanded mission – had no financial reserves. As a result, the staff went unpaid, reduced their legal services, and found part-time work to survive.

By July 2006, OSI decided to renew funding, and the European Union provided additional financial support for HCA to carry out a 'satellite city'[30] training program. The UN Voluntary Fund for Victims of Torture funded RASP's legal and psychological services for torture survivors. In October 2006, the European Commission made a two-year grant of more than €700,000 to cover most of the funding needs of the RASP constellation of projects. Two years later, HCA partnered with Stichting 3R, the Dutch NGO, which secured a further €700,000 from the Dutch Ministry of Foreign Affairs.

A human rights activist and founder of Amnesty International Turkey became the RASP program coordinator, and Turkish activists continued to replace the foreign founders and interns. As of August 2011, most RASP staff and interns are Turkish, though foreign legal advisors and fellows continue to represent refugees in UNHCR's RSD procedure. Thus a volunteer program for refugees initiated by Western activists has become part of the Turkish human rights establishment and the leading voice on refugee rights in Turkey. Moreover, the program found ways to diversify its funding sources and expand its mission without losing the focus on refugee legal aid services that inspired the founders to create the organization in the first place.

As of August 2011, RASP has served more than 2,500 clients from close to 50 countries. The program engages in extensive government and international advocacy, especially on *refoulement* (expulsion of rightful refugees) and the situation in Turkey's foreigners' detention facilities; carries out legal representation not only at the UNHCR but at the European Court of Human Rights and in domestic administrative courts; leads a group of human rights organizations advocating for refugee rights domestically; trains lawyers and NGO staffers across the country on refugee protection; publishes *Refugee Voices*, a newsletter written by refugees; distributes legal education materials in six languages; and evaluates UNHCR's compliance with its own RSD standards. RASP is Turkey's leading civil society voice on refugee rights.

ASYLUM ACCESS: THE MOVEMENT GOES MULTINATIONAL

In summer 2002, fresh from her first year of law school at Georgetown University, Arnold-Fernández travelled to Egypt, with the financial assistance of only a small university-supported stipend, to work as a legal advisor at

RLAP in Cairo. The RLAP program was still very informal; she was shown around the office by a volunteer who had arrived two weeks before, attended a two-hour training lecture on the 1951 Refugee Convention, and then was assigned her first client: a young Liberian who fled to Egypt to avoid being abducted and forced to fight as a child soldier. He had been denied refugee status and was at constant risk of arrest and deportation by Egyptian authorities, so he sought RLAP's help. Arnold-Fernández was shocked that she, a first-year law student, was the boy's best hope to get the decision reversed. Arnold-Fernández had never before represented a client in a legal proceeding – much less one that meant life or death for a teenage boy. After she worked extremely hard for that client, Egypt granted him refugee status and Arnold-Fernández found a calling.

Convinced that more and better-qualified U.S. lawyers would be eager to help if they understood the enormous dearth of legal assistance for refugees in the Global South, Arnold-Fernández began a dialogue with Dr. Harrell-Bond and, later, other young activists. These meetings culminated in the founding of AA.

Although young, AA's 'startup team' of activists collectively brought a wealth of on-the-ground experience in developing and providing legal aid to refugees in the Global South. Amalia Greenberg started as a legal advisor at AMERA (formerly RLAP) and then worked in Turkey during the early days of what is now RASP. Marina Sharpe and Suzanne Bach were legal advisors at AMERA, and Sharpe then worked at RLP in Uganda. Mauro De Lorenzo had worked with Dr. Harrell-Bond in the early phases of both the Uganda and Egypt programs and had spent several years conducting fieldwork on the war in eastern DRC. Kagan went to Egypt as a law student and initiated a refugee legal aid project that predated RLAP, then served in a leadership role at RLAP and again later when RLAP became AMERA. In between, he also worked with other refugee legal aid centers, including Frontiers Ruwad Association in Lebanon and a legal aid clinic at the University of Tel Aviv.

In initial conversations, conducted intermittently from 2002 to 2005 mostly by email, AA team members saw their goal as raising funds to support AMERA-Egypt. As the AA team began to formalize its ideas with incorporation documents and a business plan, however, the team's ambitions expanded. AA's impact could be far greater, the team agreed, if the organization looked beyond supporting existing refugee legal aid to catalyzing the movement itself. With an expanded mission came the need for something more than a volunteer team, and in mid-2005 Arnold-Fernández agreed to serve as the first executive director, with the rest of the team serving on the board of directors.[31] Her task was to build an entirely new human rights organization from the ground up, including raising funds for the executive director's salary.

To catalyze the expansion of refugee legal aid in the Global South, the AA team's first idea – in retrospect naïve – was to raise funds to give grants to organizations wishing to develop new refugee legal aid programs. None of the board members could provide or secure significant startup capital for this activity, however. Board-level conversations focused more on anticipated power dynamics in AA's relationships with prospective grantees than on an analysis of funding prospects. Like many activists with great passion but little fundraising experience, AA board members believed funding would follow magically from the moral strength of the cause. Any experienced fundraiser, in a for- or non-profit field, would have immediately identified the team's financing approach as flawed. As events later proved, the team was also mistaken about another key piece of the model: the interest of organizations in developing new refugee legal aid.

AA issued a call for Letters of Interest[32] as a way to gauge the field of potential grantees. Around the same time, Arnold-Fernández took the lead in three fundraising efforts: She held an 'office-warming party' in her apartment, which served as AA's first office; she asked a handful of friends earning moderate salaries as junior staff in legal or information technology businesses to make contributions, telling them, 'you may not feel rich, but you're one of the richest people *I* know'; and she sent a holiday appeal letter to everyone she had known since seventh grade, blessing her parents' habit of keeping mementos of her school years as she scoured junior and high school directories, chorus rosters, cross-country team lists, and college lookbooks to create a list of 600 addresses. In total, she raised around US$5,000. The largest gift was US$800. A few other members of the startup team sent out a handful of letters as well; Kagan's heartfelt appeal to his family netted the next-largest total, around US$500.

Meanwhile, 12 Letters of Interest arrived, including one from AMERA, one from the Jesuit Refugee & Migrant Services office in Ecuador, which Greenberg had helped found, and two from universities in Cape Town, South Africa. All of these organizations already provided legal assistance to refugees, but used their letters to propose a specific project to expand existing refugee legal aid. The rest of the letters proposed projects that were mostly or entirely unrelated to refugee legal aid.

In early 2006, AA found itself with no significant funds and no significant grantee prospects, with the exception of organizations already providing refugee legal aid. The initial strategy was thus apparently unworkable, but the mission, the founders believed, remained critically important. Over the course of that year, the organization struggled to redefine its approach to find an effective way to meet this challenge.

SCALING REFUGEE RIGHTS

Two key experiences during this period helped AA to shift course. One was Arnold-Fernández's first application to Echoing Green,[33] a seed funder for social change with a rigorous application process focused on the development of a coherent organizational business plan.

Echoing Green is one of a growing handful of funders that invest philanthropic capital in individual social entrepreneurs who apply lessons from business and other sectors to create bold, innovative solutions to social problems. Echoing Green's application requires social entrepreneurs to create a business plan, including a competitive analysis of the market[34] and a plan to scale impact.[35] In the 2006 competition, Arnold-Fernández advanced to the semi-final round, but was not selected for the fellowship. Still, the effort invested in developing AA's strategy for competitive advantage and scaling paid off handsomely.

The second key experience that prompted AA's shift was its decision to fund a project proposed by the University of Cape Town (UCT) refugee law clinic, a six-month intensive training for refugee leaders interested in becoming community legal advisors for other refugees. One lesson that emerged from Arnold-Fernández's 2006 Echoing Green application and AA's decision to fund the UCT project proposal was the importance of building on existing models of refugee legal aid with a proven track record of success, rather than on the general idea of refugee legal aid. The promise of funding had not proven to be sufficient incentive to induce human rights organizations to develop new refugee legal aid programs. Moreover, the Letters of Interest demonstrated that few organizations even understood what refugee legal aid was. To catalyze the spread of legal aid, AA would have to educate potential service providers on refugee legal aid based on proven models. This approach was not only likely to be effective, but it also fit more closely with AA's main asset: expertise in the development of refugee legal aid in the Global South.

Accordingly, AA began making plans to open refugee legal aid offices in countries where refugees currently lacked access to legal assistance, using the model developed at AMERA-Egypt, RLP in Uganda, and elsewhere: unpaid foreign volunteers supervised by paid local staff. This approach would allow the organization to test this model in new contexts and to demonstrate that the lessons learned within the movement were transferable throughout the Global South.

Questions about scaling impact were particularly vexing for AA. Having recently and painfully learned that success does not automatically follow from a good idea, the AA team asked itself: How can legal aid – by nature an intensive, individualized form of assistance – reach a sufficient number of refugees to make a difference? Part of the answer came from Arnold-Fernández's experience in U.S. legal non-profit organizations, which often use policy advocacy and strategic litigation to advance a human rights agenda.

Another part of the answer came from the UCT law clinic's Letter of Interest. The UCT law clinic proposed that AA provide funding to train a group of refugee community leaders to offer legal assistance within their communities, with a focus on practical resolution of rights violations. The problem facing refugees in the Western Cape region of South Africa was xenophobic violence combined with lack of government protection. The violence started with rocks thrown through refugee-owned shop windows; it soon escalated, culminating in the murders of several refugees from Somalia. The refugee community wanted to demand the equal protection of the law to which they were entitled in South Africa, but didn't know how to do so.

With funding from AA and others, the UCT law clinic trained 50 refugee leaders over six months, educating them on South Africa's judicial and executive branch enforcement mechanisms and bringing in government officials as guest lecturers. Halfway through the project, 87 percent of the participants had already shared what they learned with other members of their communities who consulted them for advice. At the end of the project, at least three graduates were hired by other non-governmental or community-based organizations to advise other refugees on a full-time, paid basis.

For AA, the UCT project proved to be a model of refugee-based assistance that could provide an important alternative to reliance on foreign volunteers. Foreign volunteers are by nature transitory, and even though they are not paid, training and managing them is not without administrative cost. Drawing advocates from within the refugee community itself, however, will ensure that the pool of resources always matches the need. AA decided to fund this project as much for the potential impact as for the opportunity to experiment with a promising new business model.

As the South Africa project was finalized in January 2007, Arnold-Fernández reapplied for the Echoing Green fellowship. This time, she was able to articulate a scalable business plan that focused on securing not only asylum but also other refugee rights, including access to employment. This made her proposal far more viable: her approach was innovative, she addressed root causes (refugee dependence on international aid has at its roots the denial of the rights to employment and free movement), and she had added policy advocacy, strategic litigation, and community legal empowerment to the less-scalable legal aid model. These ideas formed the core principles that eventually led AA to success.

FAITH + PERSEVERANCE = SUCCESS

Throughout 2007, AA headquarters' operations in San Francisco were run by Arnold-Fernández and a collection of up to 10 interns, law students, and young professionals who held other jobs while working for AA part-time. AA staff provided their own laptops and worked on TV trays in Arnold-Fernández's living room, her kitchen, and her nine-by-seven-foot 'office.'

Arnold-Fernández had mixed feelings about the demands AA placed on her personal life in the organization's early stages. She was working to enforce the human rights of people who had often suffered tremendously; complaining about the lack of pay or the pervasive presence of interns in her home seemed unjustified when she heard what AA's clients had experienced. At the same time, the realities of running a small non-profit organization were stressful: neither she nor her husband could take a sick day, because interns would arrive at 9 o'clock each workday morning. Until September 2007, when the Echoing Green funding arrived, Arnold-Fernández was still working part-time as a civil rights litigator, so she would instruct the interns before heading off to her other job, then review their work in the evening. When AA invited refugee speakers, they stayed in Arnold-Fernández's living room on a pull-out couch bed.

When AA launched refugee rights operations in Ecuador and Thailand in October 2007, its initial directors were also forced to be entrepreneurial, creative, and endure less than ideal working conditions. When the Ecuador director, Michelle Arévalo-Carpenter, was hired, she was told that AA was in discussions with a potential funder for her salary, but had no guaranteed funding for her or the office. One of her first responsibilities was to secure donated office space.

The team in Thailand, led by Sanjula Weerasinghe and Vivienne Chew, faced the added challenge of running an unregistered organization. AA was advised that the Thai government would not allow an organization openly promoting refugee rights to operate as a legally-registered entity. For the first two years of its existence, AA Thailand maintained a low profile, only providing legal aid and community legal education while seeking a way to obtain registration so that it could press for broader, more sustainable change.

AA's perseverance paid off. By June 2011, AA was headquartered in a downtown office in San Francisco with six paid staff and not a single TV tray. The AA offices in Ecuador, Thailand, and a new one in Tanzania had five, four, and three paid staff respectively, around 25 foreign and local volunteer legal advocates, and dozens of refugee community legal advisors. All offices could utilize the full range of AA's tools: legal aid, community legal empowerment, strategic litigation, and policy advocacy.

Few plans survive first contact with reality, of course, and the measured approach Arnold-Fernández articulated to Echoing Green is no exception. Planning responsibly, AA had determined that it would only begin policy advocacy after a full year of operation in a country. Then, just six months after the Ecuador office opened, Arévalo-Carpenter had a chance to appear before the Ecuadorian National Constituent Assembly, charged with rewriting the Ecuadorian Constitution. The opportunity was too precious to pass up. Heading a delegation of representatives from seven refugee-led community groups around the country, Arévalo-Carpenter testified before the Assembly.

Shortly thereafter, the Assembly added a constitutional provision stating that the state must guarantee refugees full enjoyment of their rights. The final Constitution included other refugee human rights protections, including a prohibition on employment discrimination that meant Ecuador's estimated 250,000 refugees could now, for the first time, work and feed their families on an equal basis with Ecuadorian nationals.

At AA Thailand, a lack of registration and a dearth of Thai staff meant progress was slower than in Ecuador. Securing Thai staff was challenging, both because of funding limitations and because the office required someone fluent in legalistic English to direct the legal aid services, which centered on UNHCR RSD. Nonetheless, even without registration and with a foreign director, the office was still serving hundreds of refugees annually by the end of 2008 with legal aid and community legal education.

Finally, in March 2010, AA Thailand was officially registered as a project of the Human Rights and Development Foundation, a Thai umbrella organization, much as the legal aid program in Turkey had done some years before. Later that year, AA hired its first Thai country director and began to move forward with ambitious policy advocacy plans. By June 2011, AA Thailand had co-led advocacy efforts by the Asia Pacific Refugee Rights Network that secured the release of nearly 100 refugees from Bangkok's Immigration Detention Center in the first mass release of refugees in Thailand's history.

Globally, as of June 2011, AA was providing legal information, advice, and representation to over 3,500 refugees per year in its offices in Africa, Asia, and Latin America. Using policy advocacy, strategic litigation, and community legal empowerment for broader impact, the organization estimated that from its inception until June 2011 it had directly impacted the lives of over 700,000 refugees.

ACHIEVING GLOBAL IMPACT

AA's successes to date have proven that the refugee legal aid model is exportable beyond Africa and the Middle East, where the movement began. They have also shown that coupling legal aid with strategies designed for broader change – community legal empowerment, strategic litigation, and policy advocacy – can multiply success.

Moving forward, AA plans to launch three new offices in 2013–14, and is developing a Refugee Rights Toolkit, an 'office in a box' that allows other activists to replicate AA's model. Building the global refugee rights movement remains the fundamental purpose of AA. The organization's early growing pains taught it to learn and to adapt in order to accomplish that purpose.

THE MOVEMENT COMES TOGETHER

In January 2007, 13 NGOs, two African NGO networks (representing NGOs in 16 African countries), and three law clinics assisting refugees convened in Nairobi for the five-day Southern Refugee Legal Advocates Conference.[36] The purpose of the conference was to establish a code of ethics for refugee legal aid practitioners and to create a network for the Global South to advocate collectively on behalf of refugees. Conference participants produced two documents that have already begun to shape the future of refugee legal advocacy: the Model Rules of Ethics for Legal Advisors in Refugee Cases (known as the Nairobi Code) and the Charter for the Southern Refugee Legal Aid Network (SRLAN),[37] a network of refugee legal aid providers across the Global South.[38]

SRLAN links its member organizations through a web interface that serves as a one-stop-shop source for refugee legal aid organizations and advisors in the Global South. A moderated listserv allows legal aid providers to exchange information and to solicit help on cases, such as urgent anonymous requests for input on cases they represent.

A monthly Fahamu Legal Aid eNewsletter began in March 2010. This electronic newsletter aims to provide, in the first instance, a monthly forum for wider reflection on the provision of refugee legal aid. It includes an overview of highlights of important issues related to refugees; major events relevant to legal aid providers' concerns; recent developments in the interpretation of refugee law; cases which can be used as precedent from other jurisdictions; reports and helpful resources for refugee legal aid NGOs; and stories of struggles and of success in the work of refugee legal aid. The newsletter also follows up on issues raised in the SRLAN listserv. SRLAN legal advisors represent refugees in RSD adjudication; defend refugees in local courts against criminal charges, arbitrary detention, charges of illegal entry, and *refoulement*; assist refugees in registering births, marriages, and divorces; and design strategic litigation to promote refugee rights under the 1951 Refugee Convention and human rights law.

Since 2004, refugee legal aid NGOs have attended UNHCR's annual consultations with NGOs. SRLAN holds its annual meetings in conjunction with these consultations. The gradual improvements in UNHCR's RSD policies over the past decade would not have occurred without the activism of the global refugee legal aid movement.

CONCLUSION

Before the late 1990s, there was virtually no legal aid for refugees in the Global South.[39] Refugees' human rights were violated so routinely that even envisioning an alternative seemed unthinkable. A small but determined group of activists, however, did envision an alternative – and their determination brought into being a network of refugee legal aid organizations and birthed a vibrant movement for refugee rights.

The refugee rights movement initially was driven by young people from the West – those with the time and money to volunteer – in partnership with activists in refugee-affected countries of the Global South, some of whom were themselves current or former refugees. As increased funding has made possible the participation of more and more highly-qualified local leaders, the refugee rights campaign has now become an entrenched, indigenous movement within countries across Africa, Asia, and Latin America.

The RLP, a semi-autonomous clinic attached to Makerere University, originally run out of a foreign researcher's apartment, is now a permanent fixture of the Ugandan human rights landscape. It is the most important voice on refugee policy in the country. AMERA-Egypt, begun by foreign volunteers, now has a permanent Egyptian staff that oversees the work of the 30 new interns that visit every year. It is one of the largest human rights organizations created in Egypt in recent years. In Turkey, HCA-RASP has transitioned from a volunteer legal aid program run by Westerners to an established Turkish-run human rights advocacy organization, incorporating legal assistance into broader advocacy strategy. AA absorbed the early lessons of all of these organizations, and then built on their examples to create a model that includes a comprehensive portfolio of advocacy tools and can be replicated by local activists in any refugee-hosting country.

Because this chapter is written by, and addresses the experiences of, Western activists who played a leadership role in the earliest days of the refugee rights movement, it does not capture the voices or experiences of refugee rights activists from the Global South who are now increasingly the movement's primary leaders. These individuals face new and different challenges as the movement grows, and the lessons they learn will inform future phases of the movement.

While no longer its primary leaders, however, young people from the West continue to fill a variety of roles in the Global South in furthering the refugee rights movement. These youthful Westerners include volunteers and educators, refugee legal advocates, and leaders of international advocacy and support organizations. At the same time, refugee rights remains predominantly a young people's movement. Perhaps this is because young Western activists have a greater sense of kinship and shared culture with young activists from the Global South than do older professionals in the refugee or human rights fields. Perhaps it is because entry to the movement is still frequently by way of volunteering, which may be easier for students and other young people not yet embarked on a career. Or perhaps it's simply a matter of money: perhaps the movement does not yet pay enough to attract older, more experienced leaders. Finding the human and financial resources for refugee legal aid is not easy, but young people have quickly grasped the possibilities for refugee legal aid and have eagerly embraced the challenge of building a new system of refugee assistance.

Traditional international funders have been slow to embrace this new idea. Since refugee legal aid in the Global South is a completely new proposition, it was unfamiliar to funders, who tend to associate refugee assistance in the Global South with humanitarian aid to meet immediate needs. It is difficult to convince these funders to see the issue through a different lens: how by investing in legal aid to ensure that refugees' rights are respected they will make it possible for refugees to meet their own needs. Only a few innovative donors – like Echoing Green, Comic Relief, the Sigrid Rausing Trust, and the Amberstone Trust – have embraced the idea that legal aid is vital to sustainable solutions for refugees.

In response to funding challenges, the refugee rights movement has innovated ways to raise public awareness and to educate donors – both in countries hosting refugees as well as those that are the largest sources of funding. Educating foundation donors is one method. Another is community events, such as fairs or lectures planned or hosted by refugees themselves, particularly in refugee-hosting countries where the public is rarely invited to learn more about refugees in a positive, relaxed forum. Community outreach in countries with large donor populations, especially the U.S., also helps to raise funds from individuals, who form the backbone of non-profit funding in the U.S. However, the struggle to ensure fiscal viability of refugee legal aid in the Global South is ongoing, and none of the organizations described here has yet perfected a magic formula to set it free from financial worries.

Without the 'sweat equity' of young social entrepreneurs from Western countries, none of the legal aid service organizations discussed in this chapter would have ever gotten into a position to qualify for significant philanthropic investments. Those donors, in turn, pushed the organizations to widen their scope beyond addressing the suffering and injustice before their eyes to innovative forms of policy advocacy and public education that can have truly transformative effects on human rights protection.

Since the peak of the mid-1990s, the number of refugees in the world had been on a downward trend. The exoduses from Darfur and Iraq, and the situations in North Africa and Syria, have reversed that trend.[40] Given the fragility of contemporary geopolitics, it is inevitable that new wars, large and small, will produce additional refugees even as some are able to return home. With barriers to asylum being raised higher in the West,[41] advocacy for refugee rights in the Global South is the best hope for those who remain behind.

NOTES

1. We thank Michael Kagan and Christian Mommers for substantive input and feedback.
2. In this chapter, 'Global South' refers to Africa, Asia, and Latin America.
3. While precise global statistics on the extent of the problem are unavailable, UNHCR estimates that as of 2003, the average time in exile was 17 years. *See, e.g.*, UNHCR, *10 Stories the World Should Hear More About*, http://www.un.org/events/tenstories/06/story.asp?storyID=2600 (last visited Nov. 17, 2011). The U.S. State Department's Bureau of Population, Refugees, and Migration states that two-thirds of refugees live in 'protracted refugee situations,' defined by UNHCR as a situation in which, inter alia, 'their basic rights … remain unfulfilled after years in exile.' U.S. Dep't of State, Bureau of Population, Refugees, and Migration, *Protracted Refugee Situations*, http://www.state.gov/documents/organization/157622.pdf (last visited Nov. 17, 2011).
4. UNHCR, 60 YEARS AND STILL COUNTING: UNHCR GLOBAL TRENDS 2010, 2 (2011), *available at* http://www.unhcr.org/4dfa11499.html [hereinafter UNHCR 2010 GLOBAL TRENDS].
5. For many years, UNHCR's RSD system was the world's largest. Starting in 2008, however, the number of asylum applications in South Africa exceeded refugee status claims submitted to UNHCR. *Id.* at 25.
6. *See* BARBARA HARRELL-BOND & GUGLIELMO VERDIRAME, RIGHTS IN EXILE: JANUS-FACED HUMANITARIANISM (2005); Natalie Briant & Andrew Kennedy, *An Investigation of Perceived Needs and Priorities held by African Refugees in an Urban Setting in a First Country of Asylum*, 17 J. REFUGEE STUD. 437 (2004).
7. The programs are the RLP and the RCK. The program in Egypt was originally based at the AUC.
8. 'Sweat equity' can be defined as equity created in a venture through the diligence of the venture's staff.
9. UNHCR 2010 GLOBAL TRENDS, *supra* note 4, at 2, 19. This number includes persons displaced outside their countries of refuge but whom UNHCR has not yet determined to be refugees. It does not include internally displaced persons.
10. *See* U.S. Comm. for Refugees & Immigrants, Campaign to End Warehousing, http://www.refugees.org/our-work/refugee-rights/warehousing-campaign/ (last visited Nov. 17, 2011).
11. For key texts on RSD, see, e.g., Michael Kagan, *Assessment of Refugee Status Determination Procedures at UNHCR's Cairo Office, 2001–2* (FMRS Program, American University in Cairo, Working Paper No. 1, 2002) [hereinafter Kagan, *Assessment of RSD Procedures*]; Barbara E. Harrell-Bond & Michael Kagan, *Protecting the Rights of Refugees in Africa: Beginning with the UN Gatekeeper*, PAMBAZUKA NEWS, Nov. 11, 2004, http://www.pambazuka.org/en/category/features/25612; *see also* Mauro De Lorenzo, *Dignity, Safety, and Health for Refugees*, WASHINGTONPOST.COM, May 2, 2007, http://www.washingtonpost.com/wp-dyn/content/article/2007/05/01/AR2007050101056.html.
12. For more specific information on issues of fairness, accountability, and transparency in RSD proceedings, see RSD Watch, http://www.rsdwatch.org (last visited Nov. 17, 2011).
13. *See, e.g., id.*
14. Garry subsequently became director of the International Human Rights Clinic at the University of Southern California School of Law. Hannah Garry, http://lawweb.usc.edu/who/faculty/directory/contactInfo.cfm?detailID=69366 (last visited Nov. 17, 2011).
15. The research was funded by the European Union, the Ford Foundation, the Norwegian Ministry of Foreign Affairs, the Nuffield Foundation, and the Rotary Foundation. A generous personal grant to Dr. Harrell-Bond from the Ford Foundation extended the research in Uganda to 2000.
16. HARRELL-BOND & VERDIRAME, *supra* note 6.
17. For the official website of RLP, see http://www.refugeelawproject.org/.
18. For the official website of RCK, see http://www.rckkenya.org/.
19. For the official website of AMERA-UK, see http://www.amera-uk.org/.

20. For the official website of AMERA-Egypt, see http://www.amera-egypt.org/.
21. AMERA-UK has obtained most of its funding from Comic Relief, but other financial sources include former interns, the Sigrid Rausing Trust, the Ford Foundation, the Oak Foundation, the UN Voluntary Fund for Victims of Torture, the War Trauma Foundation (Netherlands), and the Bromley Trust. The founding members of AMERA-UK were Dr. Harrell-Bond, Caroline Moorehead, Pallis, Lyndall Passerini, and Verdirame. Pallis, Moorehead, and Passerini spent months in Cairo recording the testimonies of young Liberians. Out of this experience, Moorehead wrote a book. *See* CAROLINE MOOREHEAD, HUMAN CARGO: A JOURNEY AMONG REFUGEES (2005).
22. The following year, in 2004, a similar organization, Stichting 3R, was formed in the Netherlands, inspired by the work of AMERA-UK and led by Cees ten Thije and Christian Mommers (the latter a former RLP and AMERA intern). For the official website of Stichting 3R, see http://www.stichting3r.nl/.
23. Most individuals are self-funded and stay for a minimum of six months. However, one group – students of law schools with which AMERA has contracts – stay for three months during their summer recess.
24. *See* Michael Kagan, *Frontier Justice: Refugee Legal Aid and UNHCR Refugee Status Determination in Egypt*, 19 J. REFUGEE STUD. 45, 50–51 (2006).
25. *See* Kagan, *Assessment of RSD Procedures*, *supra* note 11.
26. *See* RSDWatch.org, Other Readings, http://rsdwatch.wordpress.com/more-resources/other-reading/ (last visited Nov. 17, 2011) (including Kagan's publications).
27. Frontiers Ruwad Association is a refugee legal aid organization based in Beirut, Lebanon. For the official website of Frontiers Ruwad Association, see http://www.frontiersruwad.org/.
28. For the official website of RSDWatch.org, see http://www.rsdwatch.org/.
29. Only Frontiers Ruwad Association had access to internal UNHCR reasons for rejection at the time. This practice in Lebanon has since ended. As of August 2011, HCA was the only NGO with access to internal UNHCR rejection reasons and was in discussions to review interview transcripts as well. At the same time, UNHCR Turkey was in the process of rolling out personalized letters to rejected applicants explaining the reasons for rejection.
30. 'Satellite cities' are small towns in Turkey's interior where asylum seekers are required to reside while waiting for their claims to be evaluated by the UNHCR. Asylum seekers and refugees need police permission to leave a satellite city for any reason.
31. Arnold-Fernández began serving as AA's executive director in September 2005, during which she worked part-time as a civil rights litigator to support herself. Arnold-Fernández did not begin receiving a salary for her AA work until September 2007.
32. Letters of Interest, or Letters of Inquiry, typically provide a brief description of a project or organization and are a common tool used by grant-makers to identify prospective grantees.
33. For the official website of Echoing Green, see http://www.echoinggreen.org/. Echoing Green's president, Dr. Cheryl L. Dorsey, is the author of this book's Afterword.
34. In the social entrepreneurship field, the 'market' is often defined broadly as other players, including not only competitors for resources but also complementary organizations and potential partners. Echoing Green's 2007 application form required an analysis of other organizations using a similar model or working with a similar population.
35. 'Scaling' impact refers to increasing an organization's impact in a logarithmic rather than linear way, such that if X resources yield Y impact, then 2X resources might yield something like 4Y impact, and 10X resources might yield 100Y impact.
36. The conference, the first of its kind, was funded by the U.S. Institute for Peace and organized by AMERA and AA. It was hosted locally by the Hebrew Immigrant Aid Society, Refugee Trust of Kenya, and RCK.
37. For the official website of SRLAN, see http://www.srlan.org/.
38. As of August 2011, SRLAN was led by a Steering Committee of nine member organizations, including Asylum Access, AMERA, and HCA-RASP in Turkey, and coordinated by a Secretariat, Fahamu Refugee Programme. *See* SRLAN, About Us, http://srlan.org/content/about-us (last visited Nov. 17, 2011). For the official website of the Fahamu Refugee Programme, see http://www.srlan.org/.
39. An exception was the work of a British barrister, Pamela Baxter in Hong Kong, who died of

cancer in 2002. She resigned from the Hong Kong Legal Aid Department in 1990 after contravening policy by granting legal aid to an entire boatload of Vietnamese refugees. She set up law offices in her home, gathered a group of young activist lawyers, and began defending refugee clients. She explained at the time that she was 'simply irritated at the injustice.'

40. *See, e.g.*, Shiv Malik, *UNHCR Report Says Refugee Numbers at 15-Year High*, GUARDIAN, June 20, 2011, *available at* http://www.guardian.co.uk/world/2011/jun/20/unhcr-report-refugee-numbers-15-year-high.

41. *See, e.g.*, CONTROLLING FRONTIERS: FREE MOVEMENT INTO AND WITHIN EUROPE (Didier Bigo & Elspeth Guild eds., 2005).

4. Social entrepreneurship in a post-genocide society: Building Rwanda's first public library, the Kigali Public Library

Zachary D. Kaufman

The Kigali Public Library (KPL) is Rwanda's first-ever national library that is open to all in a country that less than a generation ago experienced one of the worst atrocities in history. The Rotary Club of Kigali-Virunga (RCKV) in Rwanda initiated the campaign to construct and outfit the KPL, which has been supported by the American Friends of the Kigali Public Library (AFKPL) in the United States and other individuals and organizations around the world. After several years of fundraising and logistical coordination, the KPL opened on April 16, 2012.[1] The KPL will soon incorporate even more resources, will require ongoing maintenance, and may even expand.

This chapter begins by providing background information about the 1994 Rwandan genocide and by identifying one of many related problems – namely media access – that demands a response. The chapter then focuses on how that problem became the inspiration for building the KPL. Next, the chapter explores the KPL's staffing, organizational design, fundraising, communication, and management and sustainability challenges. The chapter then considers some potential unintended consequences of the KPL. In conclusion the chapter reflects on the past, present, and future of the KPL.

BACKGROUND: THE RWANDAN GENOCIDE

Rwanda, about the size of Maryland and located in the Great Lakes region of Africa, is the most densely populated country on the continent.[2] In July 2011, Rwanda had an estimated population of 11.4 million people.[3] For decades, its landlocked citizens had suffered from isolation, violence, and extremism, which culminated in the April to July 1994 genocide in which approximately 1 million Tutsi and moderate Hutu (a total of over 10 percent of the population, and over 80 percent of the Tutsi) were killed.[4] One historian of the genocide, Philip Gourevitch, notes, 'the dead of Rwanda accumulated at nearly three times the rate of Jewish dead during the Holocaust. It was the most efficient mass killing since the atomic bombings of Hiroshima and Nagasaki.'[5]

IDENTIFYING A PROBLEM: MEDIA IN RWANDA

The Rwandan literacy rate is relatively low compared to the rest of the world[6] and written materials are sparsely available.[7] Indeed, all of sub-Saharan Africa is facing literacy challenges, as the number of illiterates in the region is expected to rise in the coming years.[8]

Immediately before and during the genocide, Hutu hardliners monopolized and manipulated print and broadcast media in Rwanda. The newspaper *Kangura* and other periodicals, as well as *Radio Télévision Libre des Mille Collines* (RTLM, or 'Hate Radio') and Radio Rwanda were 'voice[s] of extremism' that dehumanized and demonized Tutsi.[9] Not only did these widely popular media outlets spew virulent anti-Tutsi propaganda that incited the genocide, but they also directly helped execute those atrocities by distributing specific information about the identity and whereabouts of targeted individuals and instructions and images encouraging the use of mass violence against Tutsi.[10] Hutu extremists subtly directed other propaganda tools at youth. For example, at least one pre-genocide elementary school math course included the following arithmetic problem: 'If three Hutu are in a room with two Tutsi and the Hutu kill the Tutsi, how many people are left?'[11]

Rwandans were bombarded with such propaganda, while having little formal education and scarce access to outside information with which they could have judged the messages' veracity. Poorly informed and frightened, many Rwandans thus believed – and acted on – official statements that Tutsi were conspiring to kill Hutu, and so concluded that Tutsi should be preemptively slaughtered.[12] This deadly misinformation – combined with other factors, such as extreme poverty, over-population, a history of unaddressed violent ethnic conflict, and pressure on Hutu from friends, relatives, neighbors, and authority figures to lash out at Tutsi and their sympathizers – formed a recipe for the catastrophe that manifested in 1994.

On December 3, 2003, the United Nations International Criminal Tribunal for Rwanda (ICTR),[13] in a joint trial popularly known as the 'Media Case,' convicted the following individuals of genocide, conspiracy to commit genocide, direct and public incitement to commit genocide, and crimes against humanity: Jean-Bosco Barayagwiza and Ferdinand Nahimana, co-founders and senior officials of RTLM, and Hassan Ngeze, the founder and editor-in-chief of *Kangura*. The ICTR sentenced both Nahimana and Ngeze to life imprisonment; because of a violation of his rights during the course of his trial, the ICTR sentenced Barayagwiza to a lesser term of 35 years' imprisonment.[14] While some of these convictions were overturned and the sentences were reduced on appeal,[15] this trial nonetheless acknowledged the role the media can play in promoting and perpetrating atrocities and established important precedents in international law that criminalize genocidal hate speech.[16] It was the first judgment to address these issues since the post-World War II International Military Tribunal at Nuremberg (popularly known as the Nuremberg Tribunal) convicted Julius Streicher, the founder, publisher, and editor of *Der Stürmer*, an anti-Semitic weekly Nazi propaganda newspaper, of crimes against humanity and sentenced him to death by hanging.[17]

ADDRESSING MEDIA DISTORTION AND ILLITERACY: BUILDING RWANDA'S FIRST PUBLIC LIBRARY

Before the KPL, there was no public library in the entire country of Rwanda. It was shocking that, in the twenty-first century, any country in the world would not have at least one such fundamental civic institution. The absence of open access to accurate information, which a public library provides, has been particularly tragic in Rwanda, as this absence directly and indirectly contributed to the genocide in 1994. A 2009 study found 'evidence that the ability to access independent information can mitigate the propaganda effects' on participation in violent conflict and that 'the propaganda [in Rwanda in 1994] caused more violence because there was a lack of alternative information sources that could contest the content broadcasted by ... RTLM'[18] and printed by *Kangura*.

Many of us – Rwandans and others concerned about Rwanda – felt compelled to confront the issue head-on, and so decided to collaborate in designing, building, stocking (with books, audio-visual media, and computers), staffing, and maintaining a public library in Rwanda's capital city of Kigali. The library is now open to the public. In the future, we may partner with a bookmobile – a truck that would carry a portion of the KPL's books to rural communities, lend the books, and return to collect them – which would make the library's resources even more accessible to the majority of Rwandans, who live and work outside of Kigali.

The rationale for building Rwanda's first public library was clear.[19] The inscription over the door of the Library at Thebes in Ancient Greece simply read: 'Balm of the Soul.'[20] Even then, over 2,000 years ago, humanity understood the important relationship between literacy and the health of a society. The KPL campaign recognizes the significance of providing access to knowledge, especially for a nation recovering from genocide.

The construction of the KPL sends a strong message to the Rwandan people and to the world that Rwanda is opening a new chapter in its history – one committed to peace, progress, equality, and the belief that education will strengthen and improve the country's social, economic, and political fabric. By enriching minds and encouraging critical thought, a public library can combat the stultifying burdens of ignorance and conformity; its existence signifies the extent to which a democratic society values knowledge, truth, and justice. A public library helps safeguard freedom and spurs the development of a healthy democracy by providing access to information with which citizens can more effectively govern themselves. We recognize that a key aspect to ending violence and preventing further genocide is to make uncensored information and ideas accessible to all Rwandans, regardless of income, ethnicity, religion, or other factors. As Andrew Carnegie, the founder of the modern public library, said, 'there is not such a cradle of pure democracy upon the earth as in the Free Public Library, this republic of letters, where neither rank, office[,] nor wealth receives the slightest consideration; where all men are equal.'[21] Carnegie recognized – and helped popularize – the crucial ties between public libraries, self-determination, and egalitarianism, just as we hope to do in Rwanda. Gerald Mpyisi, a Rwandan who served as the second chairperson of the KPL Committee of the RCKV, articulated this hope early in the project's history when he stated:

> One cannot overemphasize the role of a public library in the development of a country. Most of us are convinced that ignorance and lack of information played a major role in the genocide that took place in this country in 1994. By deciding to construct and equip a public library with tools of knowledge, we hope to enhance the spirit of reconciliation and forgiveness in our children, which is essential for the development of our country, Rwanda.[22]

Now that users, with the support of trained professional librarians, have access to the KPL's materials, these patrons also will have the opportunity to gain knowledge that could help them secure employment or start a business. In this way, the library will not only promote independent thinking and informed decision-making, but will also help fulfill the dream of equality and development in Rwanda.

In addition, a public library in Rwanda will help to build a common national identity. This institution will house special collections on such topics as Rwandan history and literature, which will serve to preserve the past and showcase shared experiences. We will ensure that the histories and heritage represented in the library's collection are selected and maintained by a qualified editorial board.

Finally, Rwanda's first public library will strive to play an important role in childhood education. A library can transport children from the realm of the

everyday to that of the extraordinary. Its resources will spark their imagina-
tions, inspire their creativity, and expose them to a world filled with ideas and
wonder. From story hours for preschoolers to career- and education-planning
for secondary students, the library and its dedicated librarians will make a
difference by encouraging the intellectual development of each individual who
enters the building. The library's staff and resources will also encourage children to take an active interest in their civic responsibilities by sharing the
history of the Rwandan country and its people, thus promoting conscientious
action and providing a more secure future for all Rwandans. The KPL will
give the gift of knowledge to thousands of Rwandan children, providing them
with tools to lead their country down the path to liberty, democracy, and a
bright future. Similarly, John Wood, who founded and serves as the chair of
the Board of Directors of Room to Read, states that his social enterprise builds
libraries around the world to relegate 'the notion that any child can be told
"you were born in the wrong place at the wrong time and so you will not get
educated" ... to the scrapheap of human history.'[23]

For these reasons, the RCKV, chartered in October 2000, committed itself
to building a public library in Kigali. This effort was soon joined by the
AFKPL, which I founded in 2001, and Marshall Scholars for the Kigali Public
Library (MSKPL), which my class of Marshall Scholars founded in 2002. By
2005, the MSKPL had fulfilled its fundraising, publicity, and construction
objectives. Together, the RCKV and the AFKPL comprise the Kigali Public
Library Committee (KPLC), which has directed the campaign to fundraise and
collect books for, to increase public awareness about, and to build, equip, and
staff the KPL.

RECRUITING HELP: RWANDANS AND NON-RWANDANS, SKILLED AND UNSKILLED ALIKE

Recruiting staff as well as securing informal and *ad hoc* assistance to build
Rwanda's first public library has not been difficult, primarily because most
Rwandans and foreigners view the project as indisputably positive and necessary. Moreover, the KPL project resonates with many different stakeholders
eager to participate. Some are concerned about media and education issues in
Rwanda: Rwandans themselves, current and former Government of Rwanda
(GoR) officials, current and former American and other donor government
officials in Rwanda, and teachers, librarians, authors, journalists, corporations,
and NGOs working in Rwanda or on Rwandan issues. Other participants are
close to individuals already working on the KPL, such as friends, relatives,
and significant others. A third group of volunteers comprises those not
connected to the KPL or involved in related issues but who still want to

provide assistance. This group includes those who are outraged by the Rwandan genocide and those who are similarly outraged by the idea of any country not having a public library or access to the many resources libraries provide.

Volunteers on the KPL project report that their experience has been positive, in terms of what they have learned and contributed as well as the relationships that they have developed. For example, AFKPL Vice President and Board Member Michael Rakower states:

> Working on matters relating to the Rwandan genocide reminds people of how precious life is. Engaging in a shared endeavor to build Rwanda's first public library provides volunteers with an opportunity to forge common ground and thereby develop a worldwide voice against intolerance and oppression. I have found my work with the AFKPL to be fulfilling, as I know that my efforts will assist in improving the lives of many deserving people, and enjoyable, as I have worked cooperatively with others who share a similar vision. Humanitarian undertakings like the construction of the Kigali Public Library do not happen overnight or by accident, and it pleases me to know that I have contributed to something that will have a lasting effect on a group of people seeking positive change.[24]

We have found, however, that not all volunteers have participated effectively in the initiative. Some volunteers, particularly the younger among them, are enthusiastic but do not contribute meaningfully to the cause because they are either unwilling or unable to provide skills that are useful to our efforts. As a result, we have sometimes expended valuable time on briefing and training volunteers who end up not contributing much or at all. Where volunteers have not fulfilled their duties, we have asked them to depart from the organization, so that they do not deplete time, energy, or other resources that could be expended on a more useful volunteer or other endeavor. In this way, we have often treated volunteers like paid employees who are expected to live up to certain responsibilities while part of the organization and who are asked to leave if they do not.

Consequently, we have been mindful to enlist individuals who possess particular skills necessary to build Rwanda's first public library. Among others, we have recruited: (1) librarians and others with a background in library sciences to advise us on how to build, stock, and manage the first public library in a country; (2) attorneys to draft and negotiate contracts involving goods and services, such as construction supplies and transportation equipment; (3) individuals with a background in financial development to work on our fundraising campaign; (4) accountants to help manage our budget and process necessary paperwork to various governments and other institutions about our funding and spending; (5) architects to design and oversee construction of the library; (6) engineers and construction workers to build the library; and (7) publicists to assist our public awareness campaign. We have

been grateful for how many individuals who work full-time in highly professionalized and demanding industries have volunteered their technical services.
We have tasked volunteers to particular activities or projects, so both they and
their manager within the organization are clear and in continuous communication about expectations.

While staff recruitment has been relatively easy, retaining KPLC staff
beyond the initial core group has proven more challenging. The great distance
among an entirely volunteer, part-time staff within the KPLC in multiple countries has sometimes translated to communication, travel, and other logistical or
organizational difficulties, including fostering a sense of community. The
duration of this project has also led to a significant degree of KPLC staff
turnover. These developments were inevitable and, as discussed below, the
KPL community has sought to overcome them in multiple ways.

ORGANIZATIONAL FORMATION AND STRUCTURE: LEAN AND MEAN

Those of us who serve in the RCKV and AFKPL have found that establishing
ourselves as legal, official organizations with flexible institutional structures
has been critical to undertaking a long-term, dynamic, multidimensional,
international social enterprise like the KPL.

The RCKV is organized along the lines of many Rotary Clubs throughout
the world. Such clubs are a collection of professionals who meet weekly to
volunteer in their communities and embrace the motto 'Service Above Self.'[25]
The leadership of the RCKV rotates annually among its members. A dedicated
KPL committee of the RCKV – led in its early years by the visionary, generous, and effective Raj Rajendran – manages this project and has its own officers who do not necessarily rotate as often. The RCKV has an office for its
KPL committee on the site of the KPL itself.

The AFKPL opted to follow a traditional organizational structure compris-
ing a Board of Directors, officers, and committees. The individuals who have
served in those positions, and the size of the organization, have changed over
time, although the overall purpose of each position and the group as a whole
has remained constant. Such change is expected, given that the project began
in 2001 and some people have since moved, changed jobs, or reprioritized
their commitments.

Membership on the AFKPL Board of Directors significantly overlaps with
the group's officers. The Board is led by a chairperson, who also serves as the
AFKPL's president, and some of the Board members also serve in various,
sometimes multiple, officer positions, whether as vice-president, treasurer,
secretary, public relations specialist, grants specialist, library specialist, or

legal advisor. The AFKPL's leadership has created and dissolved the organization's committees as necessary. These committees have focused on, among other duties, fundraising, grant applications, designing and managing special events, construction of the library itself, legal issues, and relations with our past and present partner organizations, MSKPL and RCKV. The AFKPL does not have any dedicated office space; AFKPL directors and officers maintain official records in their homes and conduct meetings in their homes, workplaces, or at restaurants.

As a not-for-profit venture based in the United States, the AFKPL was formally established as a 501(c)(3) organization, the U.S. tax code designation of all officially recognized public charities in the United States. This label helped establish the AFKPL's credibility at the outset, when some doubted that Rwanda was stable enough to warrant investment in a public library and others suspected the organization of being some sort of scam.

DESIGNING THE PROJECT: FIRST THINGS FIRST

Designing the KPL involved consideration not only of the physical structure of the building itself, but also of its current and future capacity to provide resources.

The Physical Structure

The RCKV hosted a competition for the design of the library building in which five local architectural firms participated. The winning design (by Balkan S.A.R.L.[26]) is a modern structure that will allow physical expansion of the library as more funds become available. Its architectural style reflects the elegance of Rwandan art and culture and promises to stand as a landmark for years to come.

Book Collection, Storage, and Transportation

The KPLC confronted questions about the appropriate timing, sourcing, and sequencing of events in obtaining, sorting, transporting, and storing books for the library. For the first several years of the campaign, the KPL was unprepared to accept many books, as we were in the midst of our major fundraising and design campaigns. If we had accepted more books, we would have had to store them off-site, either in Rwanda or elsewhere, which would have been costly and would have diverted funds from the design and construction of the library itself – our priority at the time. Books can also deteriorate, mildew, or mold if they are not stored in climate-controlled facilities, which are expensive to operate. We therefore asked most book donors to hold their pledged books until construction neared completion.

Early in our fundraising and publicity campaign, many who heard about the KPL offered to donate books in addition to – but often instead of – contributing financially. This should not have come as a surprise, given that libraries need such materials, but these offers typically included no information about the quality, quantity, or content of the books, or the cost to ship the books either to a centralized location in their home country or directly to Rwanda. In other words, a substantial number of people were willing to give us varying numbers of boxes of an unspecified quantity and type of books they had been storing in, say, their attics, but would or could not provide an inventory describing the books or their condition. Instead, these individuals merely offered to arrange a time for the boxes to be picked up. We were grateful for these offers, but not necessarily any closer to stocking the KPL's limited shelves with the books we most desired and needed, which were a combination of Rwandan and African history and literature; children's books; great works of fiction; nonfiction in the humanities, social sciences, and sciences; and reference books, including encyclopedias, dictionaries, and almanacs.

Besides the storage and selection of books, another dimension of the book collection challenge concerned transportation. It is expensive and slow to ship books to Rwanda because of the country's limited accessibility and unusual geography. To travel from the United States, for example, a container filled with books must be sent by ship, which sails from New York, across the Atlantic Ocean, around South Africa's Cape of Good Hope, and through the Indian Ocean to reach the eastern coast of Africa. Because Rwanda is landlocked, the container must then be off-loaded at a nearby port, one of the closest of which is in Mombasa, Kenya. Since no rail line yet exists connecting nearby ports to Kigali, the container must then be transported via truck. Because we initially prioritized constructing the library, hiring staff, and purchasing requisite equipment (i.e., security system, computers) that would not be provided in-kind, the KPL had little funds remaining to collect and transport books. We researched grant applications to ship books to Rwanda, but had we even secured such funding, the administrative burden of managing hundreds of pick-ups from homes would have been prohibitively expensive.

The KPLC thus concluded that *ad hoc* book donation was inefficient, in that it would result in the expensive and logistically-challenging task of gathering from numerous locations around the world what could turn out to be duplicate, inappropriate, or shabby books. Our decision to reject such piecemeal book donations may have offended some potential donors who viewed our pragmatic decision as ungrateful. We determined, however, that we could solve this coordination problem by pursuing some sort of centralized system for book collection, storage, and transportation to Rwanda. We were aware that there were organizations specifically designed to provide these services. So, in 2009, AFKPL initiated a KPLC partnership with Project Books for International Goodwill (BIG)[27] and Libraries Without Borders (LWB)[28] to obtain the books we need for the KPL's initial operations. Many of the individuals who had stored books for the KPL's use then offered to ship the boxes to a centralized location that LWB established. Those books were then included in the shipment LWB made to the KPL. Project BIG has also delivered the books it pledged.

Private libraries and schools in Rwanda have also benefited from our experience in efficiently collecting and transporting books to the country. After soliciting our advice, the Wellspring Academy Library[29] in Kigali also obtained from Project BIG a pledge in 2010 for a significant number of books.[30] On April 20, 2012, just four days after the KPL opened, the KPL facilitated the donation of thousands of books from the U.S.-based Children International to 25 schools in Rwanda's Gasabo district.[31]

Language

Because the KPL is a public institution, the KPLC necessarily remains mindful of relevant political developments in Rwanda's history. Many Rwandans harbor deep resentment towards Belgians because of Rwanda's tragic past under Belgian colonial rule. It was under the Belgian government that mandatory ethnic identity cards were issued to Rwandans. These cards were later used, in combination with lists identifying the ethnicity of each community's residents, to single out targets of the genocide.[32] In addition, Rwandans have for years blamed France for its role in training and otherwise supporting genocidal forces leading up to and during 1994.[33] On November 29, 2009, Rwanda joined the Commonwealth, only the second country (after Mozambique) that had not been a British colony to do so.[34]

Rwanda's move from the Francophone to the Anglophone sphere generated important consequences for the KPL. For example, English is now more likely to be taught in Rwanda and used more frequently in commerce and everyday discourse than ever before.[35] The KPLC has thus confronted sensitive questions about just what portion of the KPL's limited holdings should be in English in comparison to French and Kinyarwanda, the native language. Resolving these questions will require ongoing consultation with educators and professional librarians to determine what will be most useful for Rwandans as the KPL operates over time.

FUNDRAISING

Fundraising Campaign

By 2012, approximately 11 years after its inception, the KPLC finished collecting the pledges and donations needed to complete our multi-million dollar fundraising campaign to construct the KPL.

In the process, the past and present main component groups of the KPL community – the RCKV, the AFKPL, and the MSKPL – have inspired the creation of several spin-off organizations, which have multiplied the main groups' impact. For example, individuals have founded AFKPL chapters in Southern Michigan; Chicago, Illinois; and the greater Tulsa, Oklahoma area. With guidance and assistance from the AFKPL, these chapters have hosted their own successful fundraising and public awareness campaigns.

The most popular fundraising events within Rwanda have been used-book sales hosted by the RCKV. At these events, donated books that were unsuitable for or unnecessary duplicates of the library's permanent collection have been sold. The Rwandan community has been thrilled to be able to buy affordable books, and these sales helped fill the book void in Rwanda while the library was under construction.

In addition to used-book sales, two other components of the KPL community's fundraising campaign are particularly noteworthy. First, the KPL community has effectively solicited contributions from individuals, foundations, corporations, governments, and inter-governmental organizations.[36] Second, the KPLC has hosted successful fundraising events, which have been educational[37] or entertaining[38] (or both) in nature and focus.[39] Some of these events have been intentionally limited to close contacts of the KPLC's active participants.[40] Attendees at KPL fundraisers have stated that they enjoyed the events and, for those events that were informational, learned much about Rwanda, its fascinating and tragic history, and its promising post-conflict reconstruction. The KPLC has also initiated various informational events without a fundraising component that have been designed to raise public awareness about the KPL.[41]

While the KPL's fundraising campaign was successful, it took longer than initially expected. There are several reasons for the campaign's prolonged timeframe (including its periods of low fundraising activity).

The first phase of fundraising was difficult. Despite worldwide press coverage about the 1994 genocide and impressive developments in Rwanda since, the country remains in many foreigners' minds a distant land, physically as well as emotionally. Thus, many foreigners were disinclined to rally around causes there. Even for those familiar with the country and its history, some did not believe that it would be stable enough to sustain such a major aid initiative less than 10 years after a genocide that decimated its population and infrastructure. There were even some who insinuated that Rwandans might use the library's books or other resources as weapons against each other. Others doubted the utility of building a library for a population with a relatively low literacy rate. Still others questioned whether there were not more important issues in Rwanda – such as healthcare, justice, reconciliation, rehabilitation, and economic development – on which available resources, including funding and volunteers' time, should be spent. We improved public awareness about the stability of Rwanda as well as the utility of building a public library (even amidst a host of other pressing concerns), and eventually raised enough money for the KPL campaign to gain credibility, popularity, and momentum.

Over time, other issues emerged that affected the fundraising rate, sometimes negatively so. In addition to the aforementioned concerns about Rwanda itself, competing interests in the areas of education and literacy in other countries attracted funds that might have otherwise gone towards the KPL. Furthermore, significant developments in other countries regarding issues unrelated to education and literacy also drew funds that may have been contributed to the KPL. For example, the terrorist attacks on the United States on September 11, 2001, and the subsequent U.S.-led invasion and occupation of Afghanistan and Iraq compelled many to support charities raising money for the provision of humanitarian goods and services to the Islamic world. The South Asia earthquake/tsunami of December 26, 2004; hurricanes Katrina (late August 2005) and Rita (mid-September 2005); and the earthquakes in Haiti (January 12, 2010), Chile (February 27, 2010), and Japan (March 11, 2011) elicited significant donations to charities working on disaster relief. Over the years, the KPL campaign has also witnessed some fatigue among donors who have wanted to see the organization progress more quickly than it has.

Donor Benefits

The KPL campaign employs a tiered system of recognition and benefits based on the contribution amount. The top eight 'Premier Donors' – the first eight donors to give US$45,000 or more – receive, among other recognitions, a seat on the Board of Trustees and the privilege of having one of the main reading rooms named after them. The other four donor levels and their corresponding amounts are: VIP Donors (US$10,000–$44,499), Founding Members (US$1,000–$9,999), Contributing Members (US$450–$999), and Friends (US$100–$449), with each level receiving various corresponding benefits. Contributors to the lowest level of sponsorship receive a T-shirt with the inscription: 'I Helped Build the Kigali Public Library, Rwanda.'[42]

Several of the most generous donors to the KPL will be able to use the library as a vehicle to further their own valuable causes. For example, the Dian

Fossey Gorilla Fund International,[43] a VIP Donor, will have the opportunity to employ the library's resources to promote conservation awareness about the silverback gorilla, which inhabit the mountain range in western Rwanda (a range that extends into Uganda and the DRC). PEN (poets, playwrights, essayists, editors, and novelists),[44] another generous donor, whose pledge to the KPL was facilitated by Philip Gourevitch, renowned writer and Rwandan genocide historian, will be able to capitalize on the KPL's outreach and initiatives to encourage and promote the production of indigenous literature in Rwanda.

Fundraising Phases

The KPL campaign has implemented different phases of fundraising, with varying solicitation strategies and aims.

Phase I: Obvious aims
In the first phase of fundraising, the KPL focused on potential donors with the most obvious interest in the project. We did so through both direct solicitations and through events directly related to the KPL, such as used-book sales.

All sorts of people contributed. We can already tell that children are especially excited about the KPL. Recently, a young Rwandan boy who visited our Kigali office dug into his pocket, pulled out a Rwandan franc, placed it on the desk, and declared: 'This is to help build *my* library.' Other individual donors are prominent members of Rwandan society, including GoR officials, such as President Paul Kagame and First Lady Jeannette Kagame (both of whom have attended KPL fundraising events as guests of honor) and the mayor of Kigali; Rwandan business executives; and expatriates living or working in Rwanda, including diplomats from Belgium, Germany, the United Kingdom, and the United States. For example, the very first fundraising event to benefit the KPL was hosted on November 30, 2000, by then-U.S. Ambassador to Rwanda George Staples, who was a member of the RCKV. That event, held at the U.S. Ambassador's residence and which President Kagame attended as the guest of honor, raised US$250,000 in pledges and actual contributions, which was used to pay for the early work of the KPL's architect and building contractor. As another example, on July 7, 2001, the GoR embassy in Washington, DC (then led by Ambassador Dr. Richard Sezibera) hosted one of the AFKPL's first fundraisers. Others who contributed during this first phase of fundraising were supportive of the KPL or its staff, including volunteers working for the RCKV, AFKPL, and MSKPL, and associates (e.g., friends, family, colleagues) of those volunteers.

Several foundations also contributed in this first phrase of fundraising, including the Dian Fossey Gorilla Fund International, Rwanda Children's

Fund, Human Help Network,[45] the Rotary Foundation,[46] the Rotary Clubs of Kigali-Virunga, Rwanda, and Littleton, Colorado, U.S., and the Ruettgers Family Charitable Foundation. The Magdalen College Trust of Magdalen College, University of Oxford,[47] has been the most frequent institutional donor to the KPL, having already contributed on six separate occasions.

Private sector institutions that contributed during this first phase include both Rwandan businesses and foreign corporations operating in Rwanda. Rwandan businesses include Tri-Star Investments, SORWATHE (a tea plantation), UTEXRWA (a textile plant), various banks (National Bank of Rwanda, Bank of Kigali, Rwandan Development Bank, and Bank of Commerce, Development, and Industry), various utilities (Electrogaz, Mobile Telephone Networks (MTN),[48] and MTN Rwanda Cell), and other local businesses and organizations (Alliance Express, Hotel Chez Lando, and the Kigali Institute of Science, Technology, and Management). Expatriate and multi-national businesses that donated early on include KK Security, DHL International, and Shell Rwanda. Total,[49] another multi-national corporate donor to the KPL, launched an innovative campaign to fundraise for the KPL. Total pledged to the KPL a portion of the cost of each liter of gasoline it sells in Rwanda. To promote its campaign, Total released bumper stickers, which have also been posted on windows and doors and can be seen all over the country, that read: 'I *Total*ly Support the Kigali Public Library!' Rwandan telecommunications company MTN launched a similarly inventive initiative tied to its services to raise funds for the KPL. MTN pledged to the KPL a portion of the cost of each text message its customers send. These initiatives of Total and MTN were mutually beneficial, as both companies likely attracted customers because of their support for the KPL, support which these companies' customers can increase by using their products and services.

Governments that were early supporters, many of which are concerned about and actively support Rwanda's post-conflict development, include those of Canada, Switzerland, and Belgium. That Rwanda's former colonial ruler has contributed to this civic institution that promotes self-governance signifies the extent to which relations between the two countries have improved over time. The GoR itself has been the most generous donor to the KPL, not only by contributing the largest single donation to date, but also by providing in-kind donations, such as the two-hectare plot of land near the center of downtown Kigali that serves as the KPL's physical site. This location is within easy walking distance or a short bike, bus, taxi, or car ride for the majority of the Kigali population. That the GoR has been such a generous donor to the KPL should quell fears that the GoR will spend resources on a nefarious project that otherwise would go to this charitable venture.[50]

Like governments, some intergovernmental organizations involved in Rwandan development issues and projects have supported the KPL. For example, the European Union provided the funding to build the physical foundation of the library.

As with customers of Total and MTN, consumers of other goods and services have indirectly supported the KPL. For example, Dr. Phil Clark, my co-editor of *After Genocide: Transitional Justice, Post-Conflict Reconstruction, and Reconciliation in Rwanda and Beyond* (a book published in 2009 about post-genocide Rwanda) and I have donated profits from the book to the KPL.[51] Just as with purchases of Total and MTN products, some individuals have purchased *After Genocide* with the specific intention of supporting the KPL. Similarly, profits of this book will be donated to the KPL (and the other ongoing profiled social enterprises),[52] so perhaps individuals who purchase this book do so at least in part to support these ventures.

Phase II: Non-obvious aims
Having exhausted all sources with obvious interests in the KPL, the KPLC focused on less apparent potential donors in the second phase of our fundraising campaign. We brainstormed and pursued potential sources with less directly-demonstrated interest in Rwandan development issues, including actors, talk show hosts, and authors. Non-obvious foundations from which we have received funding include the World Council of Credit Unions and Partners in Conservation/The Columbus Zoo. Corporations that do not have close connections with Rwanda but yet have donated include the Boeing Company and the Target Corporation.

Fundraising Challenges

While we have been grateful for the many pledges we have received, we have been disappointed that not all potential donors have followed through in actually donating funds or in-kind goods or services. We continue to hope that these potential donors will soon deliver on their promises.

In the course of fundraising, we have been surprised that some individuals and groups have decided *not* to contribute to our cause. For example, some wealthy people and foundations with stated missions to support children, education, and Africa have declined to provide funds or even respond to our solicitations. We plan to continue submitting grant requests to some of these potential donors in the hopes that they will change their minds, as some of our other donors have done.

Not all offers of donations can or should be accepted. For example, in 2003, a major book publisher pledged 12,500 books to the KPL. The publisher offered the books but would neither transport them to Kigali nor store them in their home city or in Kigali. In order to make use of the books the KPL would have had to pay for shipping and storage until the KPL was built and ready to move books on to its shelves. Either endeavor would have been expensive, given the amount of books and the financial and logistical challenges in transporting them to Rwanda. Only later was it revealed that the books were, in fact, several hundred copies each of 11 outdated (some dating back to the 1970s) university-level textbooks in economics, biology, organic chemistry, American literature, and U.S. government. These books were completely unsuitable for the KPL, because they were too advanced or obsolete, and they were donated in quantities unnecessary for a nascent public library, which usually has capacity for, at most, a few copies of any particular book. While the publisher's offer may have been motivated by a sincere desire to help, some suspected more self-serving intentions, such as an objective to dump old and unwanted books on the KPL while obtaining a tax break for the 'charitable contribution.' Had we accepted these thousands of inappropriate books, we or other donors would have spent precious resources on shipping and storage that could have gone towards more useful endeavors.

As with many bricks-and-mortar projects, the KPL budget increased over time. We realized that our broad fundraising campaign had foreseeable limits and that it would be most efficient for a limited number of donors to provide large contributions to help us reach our goal. The GoR, which obviously had a great interest in seeing this project completed, offered to provide most of the remaining funds necessary to complete the KPL. The GoR also provided technical assistance on the KPL construction site, but control over the KPL will remain in the hands of the KPL's Board of Trustees.

COMMUNICATION

The KPL community has produced a significant amount of print and electronic promotional materials, including a website, blog, brochures, press releases, electronic newsletters, flyers, advertisements, and publications (opinion editorials and articles),[53] which we have distributed to our wide and ever-growing network. Newspapers and magazines outside of Rwanda have provided significant press coverage of the KPL campaign.[54] The UN Educational, Scientific, and Cultural Organization (UNESCO) published an appeal for assistance for the KPL.[55] Additionally, the KPL has been featured multiple times in a radio talk show on Voice of America, which has a global audience.[56] The local media in Rwanda has also given significant press coverage to the KPL. Some reports have discussed the general KPL initiative, while others have focused on particular events. For example, *Newsweek* reported on a July 2004 trip several MSKPL members took to Rwanda to deliver a contribution to the RCKV, participate in the physical construction of the KPL, and visit schools around Rwanda to raise interest in education and the KPL itself.[57]

The KPLC has also availed itself of modern technology to host internal discussions and information-sharing, and to fundraise. Skype has provided a free, effective means of organizing real-time conversations among volunteers around the world.[58] These efforts have proven invaluable to the development of a sense of community among KPLC members in the United States, Rwanda, and elsewhere – members who may never actually meet face-to-face. As another example of a social media application, the KPLC has used Facebook to share pictures and news of the KPL under construction and related projects, to fundraise, and to generate even greater interest in the project.[59] While these technological innovations have greatly benefited the effort to build the KPL, we still believe, based on our experience, that there is no substitute for in-person communication: real-life interaction forges stronger, more genuine relationships. For this reason, KPLC members make every effort to meet donors, and each other, in person.

MANAGEMENT AND SUSTAINABILITY

Rwandan Prime Minister Bernard Makuza placed the cornerstone of the KPL on May 11, 2001, and construction began in October 2001. The building has since been erected.[60] After an extensive search for qualified and appropriate candidates, in mid-2011 we hired the KPL's first full-time Executive Director, Janepher Turatsinze, a Rwandan fluent in English, French, and Kinyarwanda who had been Chief Librarian and the Director of Library Services at the Kigali Institute of Education, one of the leading universities in Rwanda.

With the support of a Fulbright grant, Dr. Martin Levitt, Librarian of the American Philosophical Society, travelled to Rwanda in 2011 to work on-site with the KPLC. Dr. Levitt completed much of the preliminary work on developing the KPL's governing documents, structure, operating procedures, and strategic plan.

Once the library is fully staffed, stocked with books and journals, and equipped with computers, the KPLC will hand over the project to its Board of Trustees. The Board will be comprised of members of the RCKV and the AFKPL and representatives of the top eight donors to the library, including the GoR. The Board, working with the Executive Director, will determine the initial by-laws and governing structure of the library.

The KPL will be a living institution, constantly in need of maintenance and support. It will require additional funds, new books, more audio-visual materials, and extra staff and volunteers who can offer their time and contacts with corporations, foundations, associations – as well as with specialists in the fields of library sciences, professional fundraising, development, and law. We may eventually decide to expand the size and scope of the KPL or even build branch public libraries or partner with a bookmobile in Rwanda, with the goal of providing the library's resources to Rwandans throughout the country, especially those who cannot visit Kigali. To maintain and sustain the KPL even after it opens will thus require continued support of its resources and programs, an initiative the Board will direct and oversee.

POTENTIAL UNINTENDED CONSEQUENCES

Unintended consequences of building Rwanda's first public library can be divided into potential drawbacks and potential misuse, although neither consequence is necessarily negative in the long run.

Potential Drawbacks

Economic issues
The establishment of a publicly accessible institution from which patrons can borrow books and at which patrons can access the Internet may diminish or eliminate business at local bookstores and Internet cafés, forcing some of them to close. However, this potential negative effect may never manifest. Patrons of bookstores and Internet cafés may not use the KPL or may choose not to alter their spending habits, preferring the smaller size and perhaps greater convenience of these private businesses. Wealthier Rwandans or others living in Rwanda who can afford to buy books in Rwanda may continue to do so even if they can borrow them, as many people around the world with access to public libraries still often prefer to buy some or all of their own books. Additionally, even with access to Internet-accessible computers at the KPL, many may still choose to pay for that service at Internet cafés – for additional privacy, shorter lines, and the opportunity to use a computer for longer periods of time.

If business at local bookstores or Internet cafés is negatively impacted, the effects may nevertheless be short-term. The establishment of the KPL may even help promote business at local bookstores and Internet cafés and the opening of new businesses in the long run, as the KPL helps build a culture and client base of reading and Internet use, which in turn could increase demand for commercial outlets for those goods and services.

Individuals who work at local businesses that may be adversely affected by the opening of the KPL may be able to transfer into other employment opportunities prompted by the KPL. Since Rwanda has never had a public library and has only a few private libraries, there is a dearth of available, experienced librarians to staff the KPL. Bookstore employees possess a similar skillset to librarians with respect to sorting, cataloguing, processing, and otherwise working with reading materials and providing customer service. The KPL will thus include those individuals in the pool of candidates when seeking to hire our librarians. Those who work in Internet cafés have technical expertise with computers and familiarity with user problems, skills the KPL will seek when staffing our Internet-accessible computer center.

In response to the concern that the advent of the KPL may negatively affect local businesses, there are three possible outcomes. First, there may be no harmful effects whatsoever. Second, whatever the harmful effects, they may only manifest in the short term, as the KPL may actually promote related commercial activities in the long term. Finally, whatever the time horizon on the KPL's harmful effects, the library may mitigate these negative consequences by recruiting and hiring staff from local businesses into the KPL's own operations.

Cultural issues
Rwandans may find offensive or alienating certain operational aspects of building and managing the KPL's lending system and infrastructure. The KPL will likely need to issue identification cards and maintain membership lists used in lending books and distributing other resources to patrons. However, as discussed above, both identification cards and lists have played a notorious role in Rwanda's past. Furthermore, security measures may require patrons either to open their personal effects (e.g., purses) to verify that library resources have not been deliberately or unintentionally placed inside without being properly checked out, or to leave those personal effects at a check-in counter near the entrance to the KPL. These and other operational systems may be unfamiliar to some of the KPL's patrons at first, but, in time, patrons should become more familiar and, hopefully, less uncomfortable.

Potential Misuse

As with any public space or resource, the KPL could potentially be misused, by either government officials or patrons. As is possible in any public library, authorities could seek to use the collections as propaganda or try to ban or censor certain reading materials. Patrons could damage, destroy, or steal books and other media, a real problem for any public library. Users could monopolize computers or network bandwidth. Visitors could use the building itself as a meeting place for potentially nefarious purposes.

Any of these potentially negative applications of the KPL and its holdings is a risk, but one that KPL managers can mitigate through effective governance, education, and security. Given the enormous potential benefits of the KPL, the chance is certainly worth taking. The Board of Trustees, which will have a diverse membership and will oversee the Executive Director's work, will maintain editorial control over the KPL. By posting notices and conducting vigilant surveillance, library administrators can deter or otherwise prevent and address patron abuse.

Furthermore, not all misuses are harmful. For example, since social bonding can occur for positive as well as negative purposes, some groups, such as genocide survivors who would like to discuss their experiences, may occasionally use the KPL's building for informal or official meetings. We have also discussed the possibility of permitting patrons to host weddings and other social functions on the library's rooftop, which features a beautiful view of the capital.

CONCLUSION

The campaign to build Rwanda's first public library has witnessed collaboration between Rwandans (Hutu *and* Tutsi), Americans, Canadians, Europeans, and countless others. This joint project is tangible proof that the Rwandan nation has come together to build a better future, and that many other individuals and groups actively support that effort.

Now operational, the KPL holds the potential to partner with other types of social enterprises, including some of those profiled in this book. Such joint endeavors could be related to the KPL's mission: for instance, the KPL could partner with Indego Africa (IA),[61] Generation Rwanda (GR),[62] or Orphans Against AIDS (OAA)[63] to craft programs and provide educational resources particularly useful to the students and other young people whom these organizations support. Alternatively or in addition, such partnerships may not be directly related to the KPL's primary objectives; for example, the KPL might host the types of ethnic reconciliation activities the National Vision for Sierra Leone (NVSL)[64] and Children of Abraham (CoA)[65] directed or discussions like Americans for Informed Democracy (AID)[66] facilitates.

The KPL campaign has taken more time and involved more challenges than we initially imagined, but our experience, with all of the unexpected and politically, culturally, and logistically complicated steps, is typical for many social enterprises. The KPLC has been forced many times to acknowledge its limits, in terms of both knowledge and resources, which has demanded that its members exercise patience, dedication, and humility. Where these limitations have been most prominent, such as with construction and library science expertise, we have thus sought external assistance.

Only in time will we know the full impact of the KPL on Rwanda's emerging civil society. We are nevertheless confident that the library will not only help educate current and future generations of Rwandans, but also that it will serve as one of many initiatives and institutions that will help bring a once war-torn people together and foster mutual understanding in post-genocide Rwanda.

NOTES

1. *See* Stevenson Mugisha, *Kigali Public Library Opens*, NEW TIMES (Rwanda), Apr. 18, 2012, *available at* http://www.newtimes.co.rw/news/index.php?i=14966&a=52579.
2. For an overview of challenges contemporary Rwanda faces, see AFTER GENOCIDE, *supra* Chapter 1 note 58.
3. CENT. INTELLIGENCE AGENCY, THE WORLD FACTBOOK: RWANDA, https://www.cia.gov/library/publications/the-world-factbook/geos/rw.html (last visited Nov. 17, 2011).
4. For the seminal work on the 1994 Rwandan genocide, see MICHAEL BARNETT, EYEWITNESS TO A GENOCIDE: THE UNITED NATIONS AND RWANDA (2002); ROMÉO DALLAIRE, SHAKE HANDS WITH THE DEVIL: THE FAILURE OF HUMANITY IN RWANDA (2003); ALISON DES FORGES, LEAVE NONE TO TELL THE STORY: GENOCIDE IN RWANDA (1999); ALAIN DESTEXHE, RWANDA AND GENOCIDE IN THE TWENTIETH CENTURY (1995); SCOTT R. FEIL, PREVENTING GENOCIDE: HOW THE EARLY USE OF FORCE MIGHT HAVE SUCCEEDED IN RWANDA (1998); THE PATH OF A GENOCIDE: THE RWANDA CRISIS FROM UGANDA TO ZAIRE (Howard Adelman & Astri Suhrke eds., 1999); PHILIP GOUREVITCH, WE WISH TO INFORM YOU THAT TOMORROW WE WILL BE KILLED WITH OUR FAMILIES: STORIES FROM RWANDA (1998); LINDA MELVERN, A PEOPLE BETRAYED: THE ROLE OF THE WEST IN RWANDA'S GENOCIDE (2000) [hereinafter MELVERN, A PEOPLE BETRAYED]; LINDA MELVERN, CONSPIRACY TO MURDER: THE RWANDAN GENOCIDE (rev. ed. 2006) [hereinafter MELVERN, CONSPIRACY TO MURDER]; POWER, 'A PROBLEM FROM HELL,' *supra* Chapter 1 note 59, at 329–89; GÉRARD PRUNIER, THE RWANDA CRISIS: HISTORY OF A GENOCIDE (2nd ed. 1997).
5. GOUREVITCH, *supra* note 4, at 3.
6. The Human Development Report of the United Nations Development Programme (UNDP) calculated that, in 1980, Rwanda had an adult literacy rate of 38.2 percent, which improved to 57.9 percent by 1990 but then flat-lined around 64.9 percent from 2000 to 2010. *See* UNDP, International Human Development Indicators, Adult Literacy Rate, http://hdrstats.undp.org/en/indicators/6.html (last visited Nov. 17, 2011). UNDP defines 'adult literacy rate' as the '[p]ercentage of people aged 15 years and older who can, with understanding, both read and write a short simple statement on their everyday life.' *Id.* In 2011, UNDP ranked Rwanda as having the 166th lowest adult literacy rate in the world. *See* UNDP, International Human Development Indicators, Adult Literacy Rate, http://hdrstats.undp.org/en/indicators/101406.html (last visited Nov. 17, 2011).
7. This observation is based on the author's first-hand experiences in Rwanda, where he has seen few and small bookstores, private libraries, or personal collections as compared to in other countries he has visited.
8. Simon Ellis, *Knowing Your Readers and Your Community*, *in* LIBRARY STATISTICS FOR THE TWENTY-FIRST CENTURY WORLD 115 (Michael Heaney ed., 2009) ('[T]he global number of illiterates is expected to fall from 692 million in 2005 to 657 million in 2015…. [A]lthough the literacy rate in Sub Saharan Africa is expect [*sic*] to decrease[,] the number of illiterates is expected to *rise* by over 13 million adults between 2005 and 2015. This contrast is explained by rising populations and the "patchy" quality of the education system.') (emphasis in original).
9. DES FORGES, *supra* note 4, at 99.
10. For an overview of the role of RTLM, *Kangura*, and other propaganda in the genocide, see, e.g., *id.* at 65–96, 248–60; LINDA KIRSCHKE, BROADCASTING GENOCIDE: CENSORSHIP, PROPAGANDA & STATE-SPONSORED VIOLENCE IN RWANDA 1990–1994 (1996); Jamie Frederic Metzl, *Rwandan Genocide and the International Law of Radio Jamming*, 91 AM. J. INT'L L. 628 (1997).
11. A schoolteacher cited this arithmetic problem to the author during the author's first trip to Rwanda, in 2001.
12. Some recent literature has sought to quantify the impact of such media during the genocide. *See, e.g.*, David Yanagizawa, Propaganda and Conflict: Theory and Evidence from the Rwandan Genocide (Nov. 21, 2009) (unpublished manuscript, on file with author).
13. On November 8, 1994, the UN Security Council established the ICTR to address the 1994

Rwandan genocide. *See* S.C. Res. 955, U.N. Doc. S/RES/955 (Nov. 8, 1994); Statute of the International Tribunal for Rwanda, Nov. 8, 1994, 33 I.L.M. 1602. For discussion of the ICTR's origin, operation, and controversies, see Zachary D. Kaufman, *The United States Role in the Establishment of the United Nations International Criminal Tribunal for Rwanda*, *in* AFTER GENOCIDE, *supra* note 2, at 229; Zachary D. Kaufman, *The United Nations International Criminal Tribunal for Rwanda*, *in* THE ENCYCLOPEDIA OF TRANSITIONAL JUSTICE (Lavinia Stan & Nadya Nedelsky eds., forthcoming 2012).

14. Prosecutor v. Nahimana, Barayagwiza & Ngeze, Case No. ICTR-99-52-T, Trial Chamber Judgment Summary (Dec. 3, 2003), *available at* http://www.unictr.org/Portals/0/Case/ English/Nahimana/judgement/Summary-Media.pdf [hereinafter ICTR Media Trial Judgment Summary]. *See also* DINA TEMPLE-RASTON, JUSTICE ON THE GRASS: THREE RWANDAN JOURNALISTS, THEIR TRIAL FOR WAR CRIMES, AND A NATION'S QUEST FOR REDEMPTION (2005); Metzl, *supra* note 10.

15. Nahimana, Barayagwiza & Ngeze v. Prosecutor, Case No. ICTR-99-52-A, Appeals Chamber Judgment (Nov. 28, 2007), *available at* http://www.unictr.org/Portals/0/Case/ English/Nahimana/decisions/071128_judgement.pdf.

16. For example, in delivering its judgment against Nahimana, the trial chamber declared: 'Without a firearm, machete or any physical weapon, you caused the deaths of thousands of innocent civilians.' ICTR Media Trial Judgment Summary, *supra* note 14, at 29.

17. NUREMBERG TRIAL PROCEEDINGS: VOLUME 22: TWO HUNDRED AND EIGHTEENTH DAY: TUESDAY, 1 OCTOBER 1946, The Avalon Project at Yale Law School, *available at* http://avalon.law.yale.edu/imt/10-01-46.asp. *See also* RANDALL L. BYTWERK, JULIUS STREICHER: NAZI EDITOR OF THE NOTORIOUS ANTI-SEMITIC NEWSPAPER DER STÜRMER (2001). For general information on the Nuremberg Tribunal, see Zachary D. Kaufman, *The Nuremberg Tribunal v. The Tokyo Tribunal: Designs, Staffs, and Operations*, 43 J. MARSHALL L. REV. 753 (symposium issue on 'International Law in the 21st Century: The Law and Politics of the International Criminal Court') (2010); Kaufman, From Nuremberg to The Hague, *supra* Chapter 1 note 58. In delivering its judgment in the Media Case, the ICTR trial chamber observed:

> This case raises important principles concerning the role of the media, which have not been addressed at the level of international criminal justice since Nuremberg. The power of the media to create and destroy fundamental human values comes with great responsibility. Those who control such media are accountable for its consequences.

ICTR Media Trial Judgment Summary, *supra* note 14, at ¶ 8. The Chamber further noted that

> Julius Streicher was convicted at Nuremberg of persecution for anti-semitic writings that significantly predated the extermination of Jews in the 1940's. In Rwanda, the virulent writers of *Kangura* and the incendiary broadcasts of RTLM functioned in the same way, conditioning the Hutu population and creating a climate of harm, as evidenced in party by the extermination and genocide that followed.

Id. at ¶ 115

18. Yanagizawa, *supra* note 12, at 3–4.

19. The author is indebted to Beth Payne, an American diplomat who served as the first chairperson of the KPL Committee of the RCKV, for formulating an earlier version of the rationale for the KPL. *See also* Elisha R. T. Chiware & Buhle Mbambo-Thata, *Current Trends in the Collection and Use of Statistics in Academic and Public Libraries in Africa*, *in* LIBRARY STATISTICS FOR THE TWENTY-FIRST CENTURY WORLD, *supra* note 8, at 71, 72 ('[L]ibraries provide access to our cultural and scientific heritage; contribute to the development of knowledge economy; support the democratic process; help bridge the digital divide; support lifelong literacy; and represent good value for money.').

20. SICULUS DIORORUS, DIORORUS *ON EGYPT* 65 (Edwin Murphy trans., 1985).

21. *See* Sidney Ditzion, Arsenals of a Democratic Culture 154 (1947).
22. E-mail interview with Gerald Mpyisi, Chair, Kigali Pub. Library Comm., Rotary Club of Kigali-Virunga (2002).
23. Kristof, *His Libraries, 12,000 So Far, Change Lives*, *supra* Chapter 1 note 37 (quoting Wood).
24. Telephone interview with Michal Rakower, Vice President & Member, Bd. of Dirs., Am. Friends of the Kigali Pub. Library (Nov. 15, 2011).
25. For the official website of Rotary International, see http://www.rotary.org/.
26. For the official website of Balkan S.A.R.L., see http://www.balkan.co.rw/.
27. Project BIG was initiated by the Parole Rotary Club of Annapolis, Maryland, but is now an independent non-profit entity. For the official website of Project BIG, see http://www.big-books.org/. Project BIG pledged to provide the KPL with – and subsequently delivered – a total of 20,000–25,000 books.
28. LWB, based in New York City, is the American subsidiary of Paris-based Bibliothèques sans Frontières (BSF). For the official website for LWB, see http://www.librarieswithout borders.org/. For the official website of BSF, see http://www.bibliosansfrontieres.org/. LWB pledged to provide the KPL with – and subsequently delivered – a total of 12,000–15,000 books, including at least 6,000 books in English and 4,000 books in French.
29. For the official website of the Wellspring Academy, see http://www.thewellspring foundation.com/.
30. E-mail from David Polisi, Dev. Officer, Wellspring Found., to author (July 19, 2010, 14:55 EST) (on file with author) ('We've been successful in obtaining a shipment of 20,000 books for the Wellspring Academy Library in Kigali. Many thanks for the information that lead [*sic*] me to Books for International Goodwill; it proved fruitful.').
31. *Kigali Public Library Donates Books to Schools in Gasabo District*, Hope Mag. (Rwanda), Apr. 21, 2012, http://www.hope-mag.com/news.php?option=lnews&ca=1&a=134. For the official website of Children International, see http://www.children.org/.
32. *See* Des Forges, *supra* note 4, at 37, 40, 42, 90; Melvern, Conspiracy to Murder, *supra* note 4, at 5–6; Melvern, A People Betrayed, *supra* note 4, at 10–11.
33. For an overview of French involvement in Rwanda's past, see Andrew Wallis, Silent Accomplice: The Untold Story of France's Role in the Rwandan Genocide (2006).
34. Mike Pflanz, *Rwanda Joins the Commonwealth*, Telegraph (London), Nov. 29, 2009, *available at* http://www.telegraph.co.uk/news/worldnews/africaandindianocean/rwanda/6685316/Rwanda-joins-the-Commonwealth.html.
35. *See* Scott Baldauf, *French-Speaking Rwanda Turns to English*, Christian Sci. Monitor, Sept. 25, 2007, *available at* http://www.csmonitor.com/2007/0925/p01s05-woaf.html.
36. A list of the most generous donors to the KPL is available on the KPL's website. *See* Donor List, Kigali Public Library, http://www.kigalilibrary.org/list.html (last visited Nov. 17, 2011).
37. Examples of educational fundraising events the KPLC has hosted include historical presentations about Rwanda at popular venues, such as the Embassy of the Republic of Rwanda in the United States, for which attendees purchased tickets or were expected to donate; and a screening of the film 'Hotel Rwanda,' which was co-hosted with MGM/United Artists, for which attendees purchased tickets, and which was followed by a panel discussion.
38. Examples of entertaining fundraising events the KPLC has hosted include a talent show at the University of Oxford; a silent auction and art benefit in Chicago, Illinois, USA; African dance parties; auctions of African art; a music and dance recital of Marshall and Rhodes Scholars; and talent shows. Another example of such events has been the sale of 'Peace Baskets' provided by Gahaya Links, a Rwandan handicraft company. For more information about Gahaya Links, see Chapter 5. For the official website of Gahaya Links, see http://www.gahayalinks.com/.
39. Examples of hybrid educational/entertaining fundraising events the KPLC has hosted include multi-media presentations about Rwanda followed by receptions at such venues as the Embassy of the Republic of Rwanda in the United States, the headquarters of the International Monetary Fund in Washington, DC, the University of the District of Columbia; a Rwanda film festival held at the University of Oxford; and book drives at Messiah College

in Grantham, Pennsylvania, and at the University United Methodist Church at the University of Tulsa in Tulsa, Oklahoma.

40. Examples of personal fundraisers include campaigns centered around staff members' birthdays or participation in activities, such as an Ironman competition.

41. Examples of public awareness events the KPLC has hosted or participated in include lectures on social entrepreneurship, using the KPL as a case study, at the College of William & Mary, Columbia University, Dartmouth College, Dartmouth College's Tuck School of Business, George Washington University's Elliott School of International Affairs, Georgetown University, New York University School of Law, Stanford University, the University of Connecticut Law School, the University of Oxford, Yale University; academic conferences commemorating the 10th and 15th anniversaries of the genocide that were held at the University of Oxford; and presentations about Rwanda or the KPL in other popular venues, including the Alliance Française in Washington, D.C., USA; a high school in Portland, Oregon, USA; the Globetrotters Club in New York City, New York, USA; the Institute for International Mediation and Conflict Resolution in The Hague, The Netherlands; the International Rotary Convention in Barcelona, Spain; the International Student House in Washington, D.C., USA; the International Youth Assembly of the YMCA-YWCA in Umeå, Sweden; and the Rotary Clubs of Oxford, United Kingdom; Cambridge, United Kingdom; Palm Beach, Florida, USA; and West Palm Beach, Florida, USA.

42. The list of donor benefits per contribution level is available on the KPL website. *See* Donor Benefits, Kigali Public Library, http://www.kigalilibrary.org/benefits.html (last visited Nov. 17, 2011).

43. For the official website of the Dian Fossey Gorilla Fund International, see http://www.gorillafund.org/.

44. For the official website of PEN, see http://www.pen.org/.

45. For the official website of Human Help Network, see http://www.hhn.org/.

46. For the official website of the Rotary Foundation, see http://www.rotary.org/foundation/.

47. Magdalen College, University of Oxford, was the residential college for the author's post-graduate work at the University of Oxford, and he served on the Executive Committee of the Magdalen College Trust. For the official website of the Magdalen College Trust, see http://www.magd.ox.ac.uk/college/societies/trust.

48. For the official website of MTN, see http://www.mtn.com/.

49. For the official website of Total, see http://www.total.com/.

50. Kristof, *The D.I.Y. Foreign-Aid Revolution*, *supra* Chapter 1 note 1, at 48 ('[C]haritable construction of schools and hospitals may sometimes free up governments in poor countries to use their money to buy weapons instead.').

51. *See* AFTER GENOCIDE, *supra* note 2, at viii.

52. *See* the 'Dedications and Donations' section of this book, *supra*.

53. For publications authored by KPL staff, see, e.g., Lauren Baer, Op-Ed., *Making Good on the Promise of 'Never Again'* JEWISH J. (Jewish newspaper of northern Palm Beach, Florida), Apr. 6, 2004, at 26, 30; Lauren Baer, & Zachary D. Kaufman, *American Students Launch 'Marshall Plan' for Rwanda's First Public Library,* BULL. (publication of the Association of Commonwealth Universities), Aug. 2003, at 26; Lauren Baer & Zachary D. Kaufman, *Launching a 'Marshall Plan' for Rwanda's First Public Library*, MARSHALL UPDATE: NEWS FOR MARSHALL SCHOLARS, Vol. 2, No. 1: 5–7 (Winter 2003–04); ZACHARY D. KAUFMAN, MARSHALL SCHOLARS' PUBLIC SERVICE PROJECTS 8–10 (2010); Zachary D. Kaufman, *Social Entrepreneurship in a Post-Genocide Society: Building Rwanda's First Public Library*, SOC'Y & DIPLOMATIC REV. 52–54 (2006); Zachary D. Kaufman, *World Community Failed Rwanda*, KIGALI PUB. LIBR. NEWSL., Sept. 2001, at 1; Zachary D. Kaufman, *Building Rwanda's First Public Library*, 40 CENT. AFR. MAG. 31–32 (2001); Zachary D. Kaufman, Ltr to the Ed., *Open Books*, WASH. POST, Sept. 2, 2006, at A28; Zachary D. Kaufman, Ltr to the Ed., *Rwanda and Jews*, JERUSALEM POST, Aug. 14, 2007, at 14; Abbie Liel, *We Are Not So Very Different*, THIS I BELIEVE, Feb. 14, 2006, http://thisibelieve.org/essay/10812/; Andrew Park, Op-Ed., *Knowing the Meaning of 'Never Again'* PIONEER PRESS, Sept. 30, 2004, at 13; Michael Rakower, Op-Ed., *An Appeal for Help in Rwanda*, GLOBETROTTERS CLUB E-NEWSL., Aug. 2003, *available at* http://www.globetrotters.co.uk/newsletter/ archive/744.

54. For publications about the KPL, see, e.g., Tab Abbady, *Life and Death Lessons: S. Florida Scholar Hopes a Library Will Help Bring Peace*, FLA. SUN-SENTINEL, Aug. 30, 2004, at 1B; Christina Kent, *Assignment Baghdad*, ROTARIAN (magazine of Rotary International), Oct. 2003, at 38–41; Oscar Kimanuka, Op-Ed., *Kigali Gets a Public Library*, E. AFR., May 16, 2005, at 13; Helen Lewis, *Money-Makers Among Us*, OXFORD STUDENT, Oct. 23, 2003, at 6–7; Jordana Lewis, *Marshalls: A Real Class Act*, NEWSWEEK, July 26, 2004, at 12; Robert Nurden, *A Country's First Public Library Takes Shape*, LONDON PRESS SERVICE, Aug. 26, 2003; Genevieve Suzuki, *Building a Library Is Just the Beginning*, STUDENT LAW. (magazine of the American Bar Association's Law Student Division), Jan. 2008, at 96; Jennifer T. Ries-Taggart, *Tales from the Front: Building a Library in Rwanda*, PUB. LIBR. (magazine of the American Library Association), July–Aug. 2001, at 204.

55. UNESCO, *Building Rwanda's First Public Library*, Oct. 20, 2002, http://portal.unesco.org/ci/en/ev.php-URL_ID=5784&URL_DO=DO_TOPIC&URL_SECTION=201.html.

56. On March 27, 2002, the author first appeared on Voice of America (on a show entitled, 'Talk to Africa') to discuss the KPL. Since then, the author has appeared on various shows on Voice of America – particularly the 'Upfront Africa' show, co-hosted by Jackson Muneza Mvunganyi and Nadia Samie, on the Africa News and Features program – to discuss the KPL.

57. Jordana Lewis, *supra* note 54.

58. Skype provides subscribers with, among other things, free video calling. For the official website of Skype, see http://www.skype.com/.

59. Facebook is a social networking website. For the official website of Facebook, see http://www.facebook.com/. The Causes application on Facebook is 'the world's largest platform for activism and philanthropy. We empower individuals to create grassroots communities called "causes" that take action on behalf of a specific issue or nonprofit organization.' *See* About Causes, Causes, http://www.causes.com/about (last visited Nov. 17, 2011). For the official website of Facebook Causes, see http://apps.facebook.com/causes/.

60. Pictures of the library under construction are available on the KPL website. *See* The Building – Construction Photos, Kigali Public Library, http://www.kigalilibrary.org/building.html (last visited Nov. 17, 2011).

61. For more information about IA, see Chapter 5.

62. For more information about GR, see Chapter 6.

63. For more information about OAA, see Chapter 7.

64. For more information about NVSL, see Chapter 2.

65. For more information about CoA, see Chapter 9.

66. For more information about AID, see Chapter 8.

5. 'Stand bold': Indego Africa's business case for Rwandan women

Conor B. French, Matthew T. Mitro, and Benjamin D. Stone

INTRODUCTION

Long-term partnerships, global markets, and education drive Indego Africa's social enterprise approach to empowering thousands of entrepreneurial businesswomen in Africa. A non-profit organization incorporated in the U.S., Indego Africa (IA) forges long-term business and development partnerships with for-profit cooperatives of female artisans in Rwanda. IA exports, markets, and sells its artisan partners' accessories and home décor products on its e-commerce website and to major U.S. retail chains. IA then pools 100 percent of its profits from sales with donations to fund training programs in business management, entrepreneurship, literacy, and technology for its artisan partners.

Through their partnership with IA, artisan women generate income through product sales to meet their families' critical needs while also acquiring the necessary skills to run their own profitable businesses over the long-term. By focusing on both market access and training equally, IA merges two normally divergent development approaches: the traditional aid model and the purely profit-driven commercial model. Similarly, to achieve sustainability in its approach, IA draws financial support for its programs by bringing together two typically separate development funding sources: philanthropic investment in women's education and the consumer goods market.

IA adheres to the premise that '[a] company can outperform rivals only if it can establish a difference that it can preserve.'[1] For IA, the path toward a durable competitive advantage has meant patiently constructing business infrastructure for scale and sustainability.

Perhaps counterintuitively, IA was built by fashion-challenged lawyers and has grown into a grassroots movement of thousands of supporters, volunteers, interns, academic institutions, corporations, and NGOs. The IA story – both the determination of its leadership and the journey towards prosperity of its partners – illuminates the potential for social enterprise in the most challenging of social contexts.

THE BEGINNING (NOVEMBER 2006 TO AUGUST 2007)

Background

Born in Houston, Texas, in 1978, Matt Mitro was inspired early on by women who overcame systemic poverty through their own entrepreneurship, whether in his own family or in Africa. His father was a finance director at Chevron and, as a result, the Mitros lived in Nigeria during Mitro's formative years, from 1982 to 1985 and again from 1991 to 1993. The spirited resourcefulness and tenacity of African women in the communities around him left a lasting impression on Mitro. These women reminded him of his own grandmother, who rose from a poverty-stricken childhood to found a small business that paid tuition for Mitro's father to attend college.

Mitro quickly patterned himself as an organizer and a leader. After tackling law school, Mitro joined a global law firm in Washington, D.C., Akin Gump Strauss Hauer & Feld LLP, where he found success as a project finance attorney.[2] But a commitment to Africa's women persisted. Between regular visits to Angola – the next stop for his parents – and other trips, Mitro traveled to more than 20 African countries by age 25. What he recurrently found were instances of talented, driven women precluded from earning a livable income by lack of economic opportunity and access to education.

In May 2006, Mitro's parents commissioned a local artisan group in Angola to produce 400 colorful textile wine coasters for his sister's wedding. The guests adored the coasters – the intricate designs and the moving story. 'How could we get more,' they asked. Mitro made a mental note: *a market existed for African handicrafts that carried social meaning.* Mitro and his father agreed, however, that true economic empowerment required more than export market access heavily facilitated by a *mzungu*[3] organization. The business model must provide opportunities for women to blaze a pathway to independence. This sentiment would evolve into the central innovative structural feature of IA: reinvest 100 percent of the profits from product sales into customized training programs for the producer artisan groups.

The Leap

In August 2006, Mitro quit his law firm job to focus full time on IA. With no seed funding from other sources, Mitro estimated that he had saved up enough to forgo pay for about one year. Despite this ticking clock, Mitro patiently built business infrastructure first. Together with his father, Mitro drafted and adopted organizational policies governing everything from accounting, internal controls, and regulatory compliance to donor privacy and conflicts of interest.[4]

Mitro opted for a non-profit, rather than for-profit, corporate form. The unrestricted nature of donations bought the new enterprise valuable time to build infrastructure without the tight repayment schedule of investments. A non-profit corporate form also freed IA to spend a majority of its enterprise revenue on capacity-building training for artisan groups that would have, in a traditional for-profit context, represented its transactional counterparties.

In October 2006, Mitro dispatched an email to his network of friends and family, outlining his vision and asking for support. Soon thereafter a small founding board of directors convened. The board chose the name 'Indego Africa.'[5] But a major question lingered: in what country should the organization first operate?

To Rwanda

Mitro did not follow a non-profit formation narrative where a founder encounters a distant developing community, falls in love with it, and returns determined to find a way to make a difference there. Mitro had never even been to Rwanda. He and his father initially favored Angola because of their personal ties to the region, but they had difficulty identifying appropriate business partners and found Angola's commercial system opaque.[6] Prerequisites for any location included relative safety, a navigable commercial and regulatory framework, and a population of already-skilled artisans. Urged on by new board member Lyse Hunger, a Rwandan friend of the Mitro family, the Mitros arrived in Kigali, Rwanda's capital city, in August 2007.

Landlocked and the most densely populated country in Africa,[7] Rwanda still bore palpably fresh scars from the 1994 genocide.[8] And yet, more recently, Rwanda had risen from ignominy to become a shining continental star, with policies prioritizing anti-corruption,[9] relative ease of doing business,[10] education,[11] and gender equality.[12] Rwanda has shown encouraging signs of national growth,[13] but the majority of Rwandan people remain mired in extreme poverty.[14] Rwanda's unique history also offered the chance to do something more: deploy economic empowerment as a tool of reconciliation and healing.[15]

Through meetings with district, ministerial, and national government officials in Rwanda, the Mitros found near-immediate traction for IA. In 2006, Rwanda was turning to the handicraft sector as an important revenue-generator for the country. A for-profit handicraft business called Gahaya Links[16] (which was owned and operated by two well-connected Rwandan women) was contracted by a U.S.-based for-profit intermediary to purchase 31,000 *plateau* baskets for Macy's.[17] Almost overnight, government-sponsored training programs in basket weaving sprouted up all over the country.[18] Apart from Gahaya Links, however, no other companies had succeeded in exporting handicrafts from Rwanda on a large scale.[19]

First Artisan Partners

Encouraged, Hunger brokered meetings with two artisan groups – Ange and *Cooperative de Vannerie de Nyamata* (Covanya) – which would become IA's first partners. Ange was an association of 35 textile seamstresses near Kigali and Covanya was a cooperative[20] of 35 basket weavers in Nyamata, one of the villages most severely affected by the genocide.[21] Ange, located on a remote hilltop, sporadically sold products to the local market. The government formed Covanya and trained its staff, but the cooperative's customers consisted only of rare tourists or occasional expatriate passersby.

Mitro entered into donation and assistance agreements with Ange and Covanya that governed the relationship between the parties on issues such as communication, management, allocation of funds, and financial affairs. At IA's request, representatives of the relevant Rwandan district governments countersigned each agreement pledging their assistance to the partnership. The Mitros then placed small test orders for products already produced for the local market by each artisan group – sets of textile wine coasters from Ange and *plateau* baskets from Covanya.[22] These test orders provided occasion to evaluate production quality and timeliness while also, if successful, resulting in a small sample collection which the Mitros could use in the U.S. to gauge export market demand.

IA calculated its payments to each artisan group in strict adherence to the Fair Trade Federation's per-product, per-woman 'fair trade wage,' which included an examination of a daily 'living wage.'[23] To absorb commercial risk from socio-economically vulnerable women, IA prepaid 50 percent to its artisan partners and paid the remaining 50 percent upon delivery in Rwanda. This transaction structure increased IA's order financing costs, but preserved its artisan partners' ability to obtain raw materials (when necessary) and to meet urgent daily needs, such as feeding their families, while working on an order.

IA featured the name and signature of each artisan on its product hangtags so that end customers could forge a direct and personal connection with that artisan. The Mitros packaged and shipped the products to their home in Houston, Texas, duty-free under the African Growth and Opportunity Act (AGOA).[24]

Before leaving Rwanda, the Mitros hired a Rwandan to oversee IA's in-country operations. The Mitros considered retaining bank account control as integral to preventing fraud. The resulting cash management structure only permitted their new, remotely-supervised hire to access cash from a smaller account with a strict withdrawal limit. The Mitros periodically replenished this smaller account from a larger account controlled exclusively by them. The Mitros also instituted *pro forma* invoices and bank-to-bank transfers (rather than petty cash) where practicable.

LAUNCHING THE COMPANY (AUGUST 2007 TO SEPTEMBER 2008)

Gathering Steam

On his return to Washington, D.C., Mitro sought *pro bono* legal counsel on issues related to customs, trade regulations, intellectual property rights, corporate registration, and taxes. At the same time, Mitro's close friend from college, Benjamin Stone, was practicing commercial litigation at the global law firm of Orrick, Herrington & Sutcliffe LLP (Orrick).[25] When Mitro solicited Stone's help with IA, Stone leapt at the opportunity to use business-minded principles to drive social change. In August 2007, Orrick engaged IA as its *pro bono* client and Stone set about aggressively recruiting attorneys from various Orrick offices and practice groups to get involved.

In fall 2007, Mitro crisscrossed the U.S. with a neon orange suitcase stuffed full of IA products. Altogether, he visited 200 stores across 13 cities and often would be silenced or shown the door before getting through the first sentence of his pitch. By the conclusion of Mitro's tour, however, IA had secured orders from several receptive museum shops and fair trade boutiques, including the Houston Holocaust Museum and the U.S. Holocaust Memorial Museum in Washington, D.C.[26]

In November 2007, Mitro and Stone hosted a fundraiser for IA in New York City, which drew about 40 friends and family and raised US$2,000. The 2007 holiday season wound down with minimal sales, but significant enthusiasm for the coming year.[27]

Return to Rwanda

Implementing the training programs

In June 2008, Mitro returned to Rwanda for two months, where he hired an expatriate and a Rwandan law school graduate as part-time consultants. Stone joined Mitro in Rwanda in July – Stone's first time in Africa – to see firsthand IA's in-country operations and to help set up its training programs at Ange and Covanya.

Financial and organizational management formed the starting points for IA's training curriculum. Introductory topics include recordkeeping, budgeting, pricing, payments, banking, governance, and government licensing. Once a participating cooperative started to grasp these principles, the curricular emphasis then shifts to entrepreneurship, including market analysis and trends, pricing, profit margins, shipping, contracts, business communication, public relations and marketing, and quality control. IA holds three-hour classes twice weekly at each partner cooperative.

IA created its own proprietary education materials from scratch, consulting source materials from a wide range of development organizations and experts, including UNESCO, UNICEF, government agencies in Rwanda, and Mitro's father. Rooted in a pedagogy of adult participatory learning, IA's training programs tied directly to a partner cooperative's income-generating activities and consistently incorporated feedback from both cooperatives and trainers.

A pivotal partner: Generation Rwanda
Mitro originally thought that IA would hire part-time employees as trainers, but then he met Michael Brotchner, then the executive director of Generation Rwanda (GR). GR is a young NGO that provides merit-based university scholarships for orphans and other socially-vulnerable youth in Rwanda to attend university and also facilitates internship opportunities for those individuals.[28] GR rigorously vetted program participants during its candidate selection process,[29] but often struggled to find quality local internship opportunities for their scholarship recipients. Together, IA and GR developed a program that not only assured IA a steady pipeline of capable local trainers, but also provided high-potential university students with invaluable professional experience.

IA planned and implemented a 'training of the trainers' program, which included weekly discussion groups and monthly in-depth professional development sessions with its trainers on everything from participatory training techniques to curriculum preparation. The collaboration between IA and GR would also serve as a feeder system for standout trainers to eventually earn full-time paid positions with IA.

From Ange to Cocoki: The rise of meritocracy
Meanwhile, in Kicukiro, Rwanda, an informal audit revealed that a local male pastor was conspiring with Ange's current president to embezzle cooperative funds. Mitro resisted fully entangling IA in a partner cooperative's internal decision-making, but he did approach Ange with his discoveries and scheduled an immediate lesson to educate Ange's membership in cooperative law, voting rights, and governance. At the same time, IA advised members of Ange that they themselves needed to seize their business's future. Into this vortex stepped Emelienne Nyiramana, a shy but perceptibly sharp young cooperative member.[30] Nyiramana marshaled member support to dissolve Ange and, shortly thereafter, to form a new cooperative called *Cooperative de Couture de Kicukiro* (Cocoki), comprised primarily Ange members not complicit in the corruption.

In choosing an inaugural cooperative leadership at Cocoki, Nyiramana exhorted members to focus on a candidate's technical qualifications when casting their vote. The membership initially elected Nyiramana to be an advisor and later to be the treasurer. 'People like to trust me; I think it's because

I'm bigger than all of them,' joked the petite Nyiramana.[31] Cocoki operated out of Nyiramana's modest home for its first four months.

THE NEXT LEVEL (SEPTEMBER 2008 TO JULY 2010)

Building a Grassroots Movement

Profoundly moved by his experiences in Rwanda, Stone requested a leave of absence from Orrick to work full-time with IA without pay. Beyond any expectation, Orrick agreed not only to sign off on Stone devoting all of his time to IA, but also to underwrite his new activities by continuing to pay him a portion of his firm salary.[32] This unusual pact between law firm and repurposed attorney felt like just the break IA needed.

At the same time, Mitro significantly upgraded IA's e-commerce platform and supply chain. Now IA had an easy-to-use e-commerce site and an automated warehousing and fulfillment system through Amazon. IA's artisan partners bar-coded the product hangtags, which Amazon then scanned and processed in the U.S.

In December 2008, IA hosted galas in New York City and Washington, D.C., which collectively raised US$23,000, ending 2008 on a promising note.[33]

In early 2009, social enterprise initiatives at both New York University School of Law and Columbia University Law School[34] catapulted Mitro and Stone on to a circuit of speaking engagements.[35] Recognizing that its growing profile would promote sales, IA took to social media and launched a blog called *Social Enterprising*.[36] In February 2009, Stone attended a conference at Harvard Business School on social enterprise where he found a sympathetic ear in faculty member Kathleen McGinn, the Cahners-Rabb Professor of Business Administration.[37] Soon after, McGinn embarked upon a Harvard Business School case study of IA.[38]

Before long IA drew interest from dozens of young professionals across the U.S. IA arranged volunteers in major U.S. cities into regional boards, which took strategic direction from Mitro and Stone, but also relied on their own executive committees and tailored regional strategic plans. Less than a month later and largely without Mitro's or Stone's involvement, the New York and Washington, D.C. regional boards organized events that generated both profits and public interest.[39]

In April 2009, Orrick not only renewed its year-long arrangement with Stone, but the firm also seconded an additional associate to work full-time with IA for a year. With breathing room in the U.S., Mitro and Stone returned to Rwanda to upgrade and expand in-country operations.

Twiyubake and the Literacy Challenge

In June 2009, Mitro and Stone visited Twiyubake Family Cooperative
(Twiyubake), a cooperative of 35 banana leaf weavers, all older women whom
Mitro and Stone first met in July 2008. Originally assembled by the Prison
Fellowship of Rwanda, Twiyubake consisted of genocide widows working
side-by-side with the wives of imprisoned *génocidaires* who had killed their
families. Twiyubake's composition attempted to foster unity and reconciliation
through economic community. Situated in Kayonza, a town 50 kilometers
outside of Kigali, Twiyubake had no access to running water, let alone market
opportunities, and a majority of its members were illiterate.

After purchasing 100 banana leaf platter baskets from Twiyubake a year
earlier, IA returned to integrate Twiyubake into its full suite of partnership
programming. IA tasked one of its top GR trainers, Valens Rutizahana, with
implementing its business management courses there. Rutizahana, an accounting student at Rwanda's School of Finance and Banking, took to his position
with enthusiasm. 'Working at Indego is my contribution to build my country,'
he remarked.[40]

Twiyubake's striking literacy challenges clarified additional priorities for IA's
training programs. In October 2009, IA launched an adult literacy program for
its artisan partners in Rwanda that focused on functional applications of reading
and writing in English and Kinyarwanda.[41] English soon became the women's
favorite subject, mirroring the sweep at that time of the English language across
academic, government, and economic sectors of Rwanda.[42]

Verifiable Impact

IA's bottom line sunk in the non-holiday months of 2009. In September 2009,
Mitro and Stone received a message from Mitro's father, then IA's part-time
Chief Financial Officer (CFO), wryly warning of 'our somewhat diminishing
cash situation.'[43] Mitro gatecrashed New York City's Great Bridal Expo and
circulated through the crowd peddling products. Regional boards and social
media supporters led another grassroots-fueled fourth quarter push. But IA's
product sales had decreased from 2008.[44]

At the same time, IA's first social impact report presented positive outcomes.
Between March 2008 and March 2009, when IA conducted the two social
impact assessments,[45] Cocoki and Covanya members saw dramatic improvements in income, food security, numbers of children attending school, housing
conditions, bank account access, and quality of life.[46] In recognition of its
impact, IA won the Fair Trade Federation's award for 'Most Positive Change in
a Producer Community.'[47] Nevertheless, a sluggish first two quarters in 2010
led to serious concerns about whether IA could sustain itself much longer.

PROMISING PROGRESS (JULY 2010 TO JANUARY 2011)

Abasangiye: A New Type of Cooperative Partnership

To encourage a cooperative's eventual independence, IA generally follows a set of prescriptions in engaging artisan groups. First, IA only partners with women who are already members of a cooperative or who have demonstrated a previous intent to work with one another. Second, IA subsidizes costs (like rent, capital improvements, electricity, and security guards) only when and where necessary. Third, IA only integrates additional partner cooperatives after it has identified a market demand for that cooperative's products. Finally, in the interest of furthering reconciliation through economic development, each of IA's partner cooperatives consists of both Hutu and Tutsi.

In March 2010, however, two NGOs presented IA with an opportunity to test its assumptions about cooperative partnerships and receive a much-needed capital infusion. Survivors Fund (SURF),[48] which helps survivors recover from the genocide, and Foundation Rwanda,[49] which raises funds for children in Rwanda born of rape from the genocide to attend school, offered to pay IA to form and train a sewing cooperative consisting of women participating in their programs.[50]

Hailing from isolated villages in Kayonza District, each of the 25 charter members of the new cooperative, Abasangiye, was Tutsi and mother of a child born of rape. None of the members knew how to sew, could afford to travel to a common production facility, or had met each other. Eugene Nteziyaremye, a GR trainer from the Kigali Institute of Education tapped by IA to launch literacy programs at Abasangiye, however, praised his pupils' studiousness: 'Abasangiye is a very special group of women; they care so much about learning and have very open minds to trying new things. They are my favorite co-op to teach because of their enthusiasm.'[51] IA also hired Jacqueline Muteri and Gloriose Umatesi, seamstresses at Cocoki, to travel to Kayonza to host twice-weekly sewing workshops.[52]

Abasangiye members found a safe environment in which to open up to one another about their experiences during the genocide. An IA staff member, who sat in on one particularly emotional session, recounted some of the women's words:

All of them [Abasangiye members] were taken by the *interahamwe* [mobile killing squads] and forced to become their wives. One woman shared how she wanted to become a nun. Instead she was impregnated by 'the killers' and is now HIV positive. Her son is now 16 and she says that she wants to meet God and ask him 'Why?' Another woman tried to commit suicide by throwing herself down a latrine where she instead lived for days while people urinated and defecated on her. She had seven kids by her captor but five survived. Another woman was only 12 when she was taken. She was so young that when she became pregnant she didn't know what was happening to her body and thought that her captor had poisoned her. Shockingly, these women see their perpetrators on the streets all of the time. 'This is our life,' they say.[53]

Independent Businesswomen

In July 2010, Nyiramana leveraged her training at IA to earn one of 25 spots from a pool of 500 applicants in the Goldman Sachs *10,000 Women* Entrepreneurship Certificate Program at Rwanda's School of Finance and Banking.[54] At Nyiramana's *10,000 Women* graduation six months later, the president of Cocoki, Muteteri, proudly proclaimed: 'Emelienne won this certificate because of her bravery. Despite the challenges in her family and her life, Emelienne thought not of the present, but of the future.'

Nyiramana excelled in her classes in marketing, public relations, human resources, management, bookkeeping, accounting, strategies for accessing capital, and Rwandan law. She also became the first *10,000 Women* participant to blog about her experience. Writing in *Social Enterprising* in September 2010, Nyiramana noted: 'My favorite subject is accounting and bookkeeping ... Cocoki now does a better job at recording our inventory and material.'[55] Nyiramana also invoked the phrase 'stand bold,' which quickly became a rallying cry for Cocoki and IA.[56]

Increased production and export market penetration uncorked considerable financial growth, with annual revenue at Cocoki jumping by 500 percent in 2009 and by another 147 percent in 2010.[57] Nyiramana earned more than RWF 2000 (approximately US$3.38) per day in 2010 at Cocoki, compared to RWF 200 (approximately US$0.36) per day at Ange in 2007.[58] Cocoki even started to develop its own brand recognition in the U.S.[59]

The Tipping Point

By July 2010, Mitro's personal financial sacrifices to found and lead IA had taken a toll, and he knew that an organized succession was critical.[60] Stone was a logical next Chief Executive Officer (CEO), as long as his Orrick deal remained in effect. Effectively running and scaling IA required more than one executive, however.

Around this time, Mitro and Stone met Conor French, a seasoned corporate finance attorney from another global law firm, Latham & Watkins LLP.[61] French's upbringing in a heavily Cape Verdean neighborhood of New Bedford, Massachusetts, spurred him toward formative experiences living abroad in East Africa and Bahia, Brazil's most African-imprinted state. His prior involvement in a range of social enterprise models and applications as *pro bono* counsel to Ashoka primed him for the challenges and opportunities

IA faced.[62] A deep sense of professional and personal fellowship with Mitro and Stone persuaded him to consider and join an African-focused model of economic development with a direct social impact on women, families, and communities. In July 2010, French agreed to succeed Mitro's father as CFO. Like each of IA's leaders before him, French was willing to work full-time on an unpaid basis until IA could absorb additional executive payroll.[63]

Soon after, a 2010 law school graduate, Deirdre McGuigan, joined IA for ten weeks on a legal fellowship sponsored by Brooklyn Law School. With McGuigan flashing project management potential and a keen eye for product design and fashion, IA moved in November 2010 to add her as its first paid U.S. Retail Director.

IA concurrently felt a marketing jolt when, in July 2010, Polo Ralph Lauren placed an order for banana leaf bracelets produced by Twiyubake.[64] Polo Ralph Lauren showcased the bracelets in stores in New York City, the Hamptons, and Vail, Colorado, sparking increased media interest in IA's brand.[65] Then, in late August 2010, a meeting between IA and representatives for fashion designer Nicole Miller set off a fast-tracked design collaboration between the organizations.[66] IA passed prototypes between its partner cooperatives and Nicole Miller and, just a couple of weeks later, Nicole Miller placed a customized order for 133 textile bangle sets made by Cocoki and 100 woven bracelets made by Covanya.

Throughout the fall and winter of 2010, Nicole Miller hosted product launch events for the bracelets in New York City, Los Angeles, and Chicago. StyleCaster.com declared the bracelets 'globally friendly wrist candy' and Elle.com declared them to be 'a tribute to [Rwandan] culture's unique designs' and 'a fun way to brighten up your look.'[67]

At the same time, IA delivered on a logistically complicated knitwear order for the chain retail store Anthropologie.[68] Guided by one of Anthropologie's veteran designers, IA partnered with the Ingenzi Knit Union – 127 knitters drawn from four knitting cooperatives in Rwanda – to produce 850 'Thousand Hills Cowls' for the chain's fall 2010 knitwear collection, a collaboration profiled in *The New York Times Style Magazine* and *VOGUE Knitting*.[69]

This sequence of events not only put IA squarely at the forefront of fair trade and socially conscious fashion, but also precipitated a significant shift in how IA engaged the wholesale market. Instead of only pitching previously-developed product lines, IA evolved to embrace highly-customizable design collaborations with established retailers, brands, and cutting-edge designers. With IA's intimate style of artisan partnership giving buyers more control over the end product, these buyers showed an increased willingness to undertake bigger orders and capitalize on the rise in the global ethical consumer base.[70] By the end of 2010, IA's product sales revenues and fundraising increased from the prior year by 265 percent and 183 percent, respectively.[71]

TEARING UP THE SOCIAL ENTERPRISE WORLD (JANUARY 2011 TO PRESENT)

Management Shifts

A favorable growth outlook reinforced IA's need for leadership in Rwanda, and so the organization recruited an experienced non-profit executive as a full-time country director. Keith Curtis Cobell, Jr., then 40, had just returned to San Francisco after a five-month around-the-world adventure with his wife, and fond memories of their time in Rwanda endured. IA could offer Cobell only a modest salary, but he accepted the challenge and moved to Rwanda with his wife in January 2011.

Cobell assumed oversight of all in-country banking and rented IA office space in Kigali. Cobell then re-engineered IA's in-country internship program, which had ballooned from two to 14 interns in just one year. Improvements included tiered compensation and benefits based on seniority and performance, a more formalized training of the trainers program, and enhanced evaluation, communication, and reporting mechanisms. IA also hired three full-time employees: an accounting and operations assistant (a high-performing GR trainer, Yves Ndashimye), a production director (an expatriate), and an operations manager (a Rwandan who received her Master's degree in the U.S.).

Back in the U.S., IA's once piecemeal coalition of graduate student interns increasingly functioned like a cohesive staff, overlapping and routinely continuing on beyond their intended tenure. IA worked from conference rooms at Orrick's offices in midtown Manhattan. With Stone securing a fourth year of sponsorship from Orrick and accepting the CEO role, Mitro executed his long-planned transition out of IA's day-to-day operations.[72]

A Market-driven Enterprise

By July 2011, IA projected again more than doubling annual product sales.[73] The cornerstone of this expected growth was a US$108,882 purchase order from Anthropologie for 4,490 knitwear pieces. Ingenzi Knit Union would again produce the line, which IA believed would constitute the largest commercial knitwear order ever produced in and exported out of Rwanda to the U.S. IA's partnership with Nicole Miller continued to vault IA and its partner cooperatives further into the public eye.[74] Determined to meet her co-designers, Miller herself traveled to Rwanda in October 2011 to teach advanced sewing and to execute the first direct purchase order between an artisan cooperative in Rwanda – in this case, Cocoki – and a major U.S. label.[75] IA also developed relationships with on-trend fashion lines, like DANNIJO Jewelry, and popular retail outlets, such as Shopbop and Steven Alan.[76]

IA also caught up to the production schedules of larger retailers and brands – which often buy eight to 12 months in advance of products hitting stores – and, as a result, finalized a ground-breaking relationship with J.Crew for the spring / summer 2012 season.[77] For the first time in its history, market demand for IA's products outstripped its current artisan partners' production capacities. IA could now pivot toward a long-standing goal of increasing the number of its partner cooperatives.

Transformation in Rwanda

Back in Rwanda, Abasangiye, led by its president, Eugenie Ufitikirezi – who cared for 15 children, including five of her own and ten who were orphaned when her sisters were killed in the genocide – successfully executed a series of trial orders for IA (including 50 tote bags for Anthropologie). Three members of Abasangiye told IA staff that, before the literacy training started, they 'didn't even know how to hold a pen.'[78] Now learning how to read and write, these women felt 'especially proud to write their names.'[79] Ufitikirezi also noted how before business planning training, 'none of [Absanagiye's members] had ever felt like we could enter a bank with pride.'[80] A geographically dispersed membership, however, limited Abasangiye to a two-day work week. IA became worried that cooperatives like Abasangiye would require extensive subsidies in perpetuity while adding very little production capacity to help IA keep pace with its rapidly growing consumer base. While IA resisted overtures to replicate the Abasangiye model, IA stood by its partnership with Abasangiye and increased its investment in the cooperative's continued progress.

At the same time, IA reached out to dozens of export-ready cooperatives across Rwanda, experimenting with various production capacities, raw materials, cooperative compositions, and locations. Mentored and emboldened by Nyiramana, several women from Cocoki, Covanya, Twiyubake, and Ingenzi Knit Union applied to the Goldman Sachs *10,000 Women* program. After Therese Iribagiza, the vice president of Cocoki, gained admission to the program in July 2011, IA arranged for Nyiramana, Iribagiza, and Ndashimye to visit New York City and Washington, D.C. in October 2011 to connect directly with customers, retailers, brands, designers, business leaders, and supporters.[81]

CHALLENGES

Achieving Independence for Artisan Partners

IA's founders set forth an ambitious vision that, if artisan women in Rwanda could gain commercial experience and participate in targeted training for an extended period of time, they could eventually deal directly with foreign buyers. Achieving this goal, however, while not necessarily impossible, will take decades, not years. IA's partner cooperatives have made significant strides since 2007, when many members could not even read or write, let alone manage complex quality control and production processes. After three years of training, however, IA's artisan partners still have difficulty conceiving designs for foreign markets, fully ensuring their products meet high quality control standards and, with the exception of Nyiramana, communicating effectively in English for business purposes. IA continues to provide strategic introductions, handle export and payment logistics, and support its partner cooperatives financially with rent assistance and raw material purchases.

Reasons for partner cooperatives' protracted dependence on IA are manifold. IA struggles to fully fund training programs for all of its artisan partners, and the programs themselves sometimes lack consistent instruction and clear outcomes. Artisans also have an immediate need for income and, thus, IA prioritizes its sales efforts, which can divert attention from fundraising and curriculum development for training programs with longer-term goals. Even when training is excellent, many artisan women have family and child-rearing obligations that adversely affect attendance and detract from the time and attention they can devote to unpaid classroom learning. Only select artisan partners have fully committed to acquiring all of the skills necessary to run a profitable business independently.

IA also assumes risks related to strict quality and delivery requirements on large orders from demanding buyers and is, accordingly, reticent to delegate certain critical tasks to its partner cooperatives. For example, IA incurred nearly all of the upfront costs on the 2011 order for Anthropologie months in advance of receiving final payment.[82] Failure to deliver the order perfectly could have seriously imperiled IA's financial outlook.[83] With regularly-occurring situations requiring significant investments and reputational risks, IA has chosen not to hand over export paperwork, shipping logistics, or final quality control to its artisan partners, who unfortunately do not yet reliably demonstrate the required skills or experience.

With these challenges in mind, IA constantly looks to re-evaluate and enhance the structure of its programs. Some of IA's artisan partners prefer simpler and less frequent training, whereas others – in particular, cooperative leaders – would like more comprehensive, higher-level training. In many ways, certain instances of ambivalence toward comprehensive training reflect how some artisan women conceive of economic independence as steady employment rather than entrepreneurship or business leadership, a distinction certainly apparent in the U.S. workforce as well.

With projected increases in fundraising for 2011, IA can hopefully better afford to fund expanded and more specifically tailored training programs for its artisan partners. In addition, a new partnership between IA and the Goldman Sachs *10,000 Women* program in Rwanda holds immense promise for enabling many top Rwandan artisan leaders to take the next step in their business education.[84] As time goes on and cooperative members' skills strengthen, IA is committed to transitioning more business functions to its eager artisan partners.

Sustaining Human Capital

The complexity of IA's business model requires more than one or two full-time employees to adequately conduct operations in both the U.S. and Rwanda. With very little financial flexibility in its infancy, IA relied solely upon volunteers and low-paid staff in Rwanda – who cycled in and out of the organization frequently – rather than paying market rates to hire and retain key employees. With little opportunity for in-person team-building, IA leadership also had difficulty infusing the organizational values of flexibility, transparency, and professionalism in the Rwanda team from afar. As a result, performance in Rwanda often suffered. Underpaid expatriates with little management experience did not always effectively mentor Rwandan staff or anticipate business issues that would arise at partner cooperatives. The physical distance between the U.S. and Rwanda teams also fostered miscommunication and sometimes cultivated an atmosphere of disunity. In one instance, two expatriates working for IA coerced their Rwandan counterpart to actively conceal information from the U.S. team about internal Rwanda team conflicts that might not have reflected well on the expatriates. The shift towards a more professional staff paid at market rates, however, has allowed IA to grow into a more unified and cohesive organization.

LESSONS LEARNED

Social Context is Paramount

Despite its emphasis on a business-minded approach, IA could never escape the post-genocide social context in Rwanda and, as a result, must constantly balance individual artisan expectations with internal cooperative dynamics. For example, when cooperative members feel idle or are disappointed in the income they earn from their business, the cohesion between cooperative members from different ethnic and economic backgrounds can easily break. This threat suggests IA should move quickly in procuring product orders. On the other hand, large influxes of income into a cooperative can engender conflicts borne from managerial inexperience – particularly in cash disbursement and record-keeping. This threat suggests that IA should emphasize business skills training. A foreign organization may view such issues as amenable to business-related solutions or program changes, but sometimes such organizations can only navigate these complex Rwandan social dynamics through neutral arbitration.

IA has consequently learned to rely heavily on its Rwandan staff and interns to attune themselves to potentially deeper social issues at play and act as impartial (and local) mediators. At times IA has needed to slow down its ambitious production or training expectations when disputes have erupted within a partner cooperative. For example, during a slow period of product orders, Covanya mishandled a large loan issued by an international NGO that, in IA's opinion, provided inadequate follow-up oversight. Between June and September 2011, festering internecine conflicts at Covanya split the cooperative into two competing factions. Informal discussions revealed that social rather than business dynamics underlay the discord. In close counsel with Bugesera District government officials overseeing Covanya's formal division, IA diligently supported the development of Covanya's membership with orders and training even through this period of uncertainty and unrest. Nevertheless, morale at Covanya and IA's confidence in its partnership with the cooperative each remain deeply shaken.

IA also learned that, to prove itself an unbiased and trusted partner, it needs to demonstrate to its partner cooperatives its honest intentions and its ability to consistently deliver tangible (and highly-desired) benefits. Since its first interaction with artisan women, IA has practiced transparency (like sharing its pricing calculations and internal cost structure) and a candid openness to artisan partner input (like revising training programs to reflect ongoing feedback). Most importantly, IA has succeeded in providing what its artisan partners value most: regular income.

Smart Partnerships are Crucial

IA quickly understood that it needed a cadre of loyal partners to achieve its broad mission and competing objectives. While IA's early leadership understood law and business in Africa very well, in addition to possessing boundless energy, IA as an organization had virtually no experience in product design, sales, supply chains, fundraising, or development programming. Based on mutual benefit and frequently involving no exchange of money, partnerships with organizations and individuals proved essential in filling operational gaps without overburdening IA's constrained budget. The GR partnership provided a ready source of trainers to multiple cooperatives – whom IA could not have otherwise initially afforded – and vocational experience and professional development opportunities for socially-vulnerable university students.

VisionSpring supplied its vision assessment tools and eye-glass sourcing connections to IA in exchange for a market entry point into Rwanda that included social impact reporting and market assessments.[85] In light of IA's human capital challenges, these partnerships widened the breadth of programming and established an organization-wide prerogative of cost-effectiveness, innovation, and openness.

Finding the right retailers, brands, and designers with whom to partner also influenced IA's trajectory towards scale and profitability. At first – and in many instances still – some buyers expressed skepticism that their customers would care about a product's backstory or that African materials repurposed into fashion items could enhance their brand. Some retailers also required pricing schemes that mirrored their traditional relationships with producers in China or other countries known for low production costs. Some further assumed that collaborating with IA would simply represent a one-off charitable endeavor that, while valuable from a public relations perspective, would not ever become a profitable relationship. In an effort to challenge these industry-wide assumptions, IA targeted pricing schemes that would allow each party along the supply chain – the artisans, IA, and the retailer – to turn a profit, while also developing product lines that appealed to customers in both design and aesthetic. Now, with an established brand and several blueprints for successful collaboration, IA only aligns with brands that fully embrace long-term business partnerships and IA's mission.

Differentiate Yourself and be Persistent

The IA team, first led by Mitro and Stone, and later joined by French and many others, learned to unabashedly draw distinctions between IA and similar organizations while doggedly pursuing its own strategy. In its infancy, IA struggled to demonstrate that its business model improved upon the traditional handicraft model of economic development. Government officials in Rwanda registered initial apprehension, expecting IA to treat artisan women the way that other intermediaries had in the past: signing them to exclusivity agreements, paying them too little, and exploiting their images as women in need. Even when it meant initially fewer sales or other difficulties, IA did not alter its founding vision. Through example and an outspoken viewpoint, IA proved that its approach was different and worked.

IA team members often faced similar self-doubt when balancing their time between business and social objectives. IA's model emphasizes both short-term income and long-term development through training. The latter objective required large upfront investments that most handicraft businesses would not incur, such as more frequent trips to Rwanda, advance payments to artisans, and hiring additional non-sales staff. IA forecast future profitability on the commercial side, but only if it could achieve the necessary volume of sales, which would take time. Accordingly, IA constantly invested in non-revenue-generating infrastructure with mostly long-term benefits – like curriculum development and social impact assessment – rather than focusing single-mindedly on immediate sales or fundraising. Relying on its infrastructure, IA has met steadily increasing demand for products and has built its brand while maintaining the integrity of its social business model.

The arc of IA also suggests that intellectual flexibility and brazen aggressiveness are two key attributes of a successful social entrepreneur. Social entrepreneurs and social enterprises must not only aggressively tackle new skill sets on a daily basis, but also commit to staying nimble and making constant adaptations and calibrations – and testing assumptions – at every turn. A social entrepreneur must also relish making the occasional counter-intuitive decision about his or her professional trajectory. Prior careers as high-paid attorneys in global law firms gave Mitro, Stone, and French time to build IA without significant, or any, initial financial support. But a social entrepreneur's personal economic insecurity, while often outwardly perceived as inspirational or a badge of honor, eventually undermines his or her organization's growth.

CONCLUSION

With steady income and access to education, IA's artisan partners are reclaiming control over their futures. Each woman has an opportunity to translate her experiences of financial security and increased productivity into a lasting sense of self-worth and pride, knowing that she can accomplish anything by working together with others and relying on her own strength.

IA is also an investment in Rwanda's future generations. Women apply income earned through market access to enrolling blood-related and, especially because of the genocide, adopted sons, daughters, nephews, and nieces in schools. In addition, dividends from their own educational progress encourage women to prioritize their children's schooling over early entry into the local workforce.

IA's progress to date is the result of thousands of people in Rwanda and the U.S. boldly pushing forward the organization's ambitious vision undaunted by occasional failures or setbacks. Asked why she thought other members of Cocoki looked up to her, Iribagiza mulled the question over before declaring, 'First off, because Therese has no fear.' She then paused dramatically before stating, 'Second, because Therese has no fear!'[86]

NOTES

1. Michael Porter, *What is Strategy?*, HARV. BUS. REV., Nov. 1996, at 61, 62.
2. For the official website of Akin Gump Strauss Hauer & Feld LLP, see http://www.akingump.com/.
3. *Mzungu* is defined as 'white person,' but is colloquially an East African term for 'person of foreign descent.' The term was first used by Africans to describe early European explorers. *See* OXFORD DICTIONARIES ONLINE, http://oxforddictionaries.com/definition/mzungu (last visited Nov. 17, 2011).
4. *See* Indego Africa, Transparency and Ethics, http://www.indegoafrica.org/transparency-and-ethics (last visited Nov. 17, 2011).
5. 'In-de-go' stands for 'independence,' 'development,' and 'governance.' IA submitted its 501(c)(3) application in February 2007 and received exempt status in July 2007. *See id.* at 501(c)(3) Tax Exemption Form 1023 Application.
6. *See* U.S. Dep't of State, Background Notes: Angola, http://www.state.gov/r/pa/ei/bgn/6619.htm (last visited Nov. 17, 2011) ('Angola is still recovering from 27 years of nearly continuous warfare, and is slowly beginning to tackle problems of corruption, lack of transparency[,] and economic mismanagement. Despite abundant natural resources and rising per capita GDP, it was ranked 146 out of 169 countries on the 2010 UN Development Program's (UNDP) Human Development Index.').
7. At 26,338 square kilometers with a population of approximately 11.4 million as of 2011, Rwanda's population density is currently the highest in continental Sub-Saharan Africa. *See* U.S. Dep't of State, Background Notes: Rwanda, http://www.state.gov/r/pa/ei/bgn/2861.htm (last visited Nov. 17, 2011).
8. For background information on the 1994 Rwandan genocide, see Chapter 4.
9. *See* THE REPUBLIC OF RWANDA, ECONOMIC DEVELOPMENT & POVERTY REDUCTION STRATEGY 2008–2012, at 2 (2007).
10. *See* Official Website of the Republic of Rwanda, Economic Development, http://www.gov.rw/Economic-development (last visited Nov. 17, 2011) [hereinafter Rwanda Economic Development] ('Rwanda was ranked one of the top ten global reformers in the World Bank Doing Business Survey 2010, and second global reformer out of 183 countries. Rwanda is also the 9th easiest place to start a business in the world and the 6th most competitive economy in Sub-Saharan Africa according to the 2010 World Economic Forum global Competitiveness Report.').
11. *See* Official Website of the Republic of Rwanda, Social Development, http://www.gov.rw/Social-Development (last visited Nov. 17, 2011) ('[E]ducation has become 18% of public expenditure for the continuous committed improvement of the quality and access to education.').
12. Currently, women head one-third of Rwandan households. Of those households, 62 percent lie below the poverty line compared to 54 percent of male-headed households. In 2003, Rwanda adopted one of the world's most progressive constitutions for women's representation with 56 percent female representation in Parliament. *See id.*; United Nations Development Programme, Rwanda: Poverty Reduction, http://www.undp.org.rw/Poverty_Reduction.html (last visited Nov. 17, 2011) [hereinafter UNDP Rwanda Poverty Reduction].
13. *See* Rwanda Economic Development, *supra* note 10 ('The real GDP growth increased from 2.2% in 2003 to 7.2% in 2010 with a peak growth of 11.5% in 2008. Overall, the average growth rate has been 7%.').
14. *See* UNDP Rwanda Poverty Reduction, *supra* note 12 ('Over 60% of individuals live in poverty and 42% in absolute poverty. Using the household as a unit, 57% live below the poverty line.').
15. *See* THE REPUBLIC OF RWANDA, CAPACITY DEVELOPMENT AND BUILDING A CAPABLE STATE: RWANDA COUNTRY REPORT, at 5 (2007).
16. For the official website of Gahaya Links, see http://www.gahayalinks.com/.
17. *See* Sarah DiLorenzo, *Macy's Partners With Rwandan Widows*, WASH. POST, Oct. 13, 2006,

*available   at   http://www.washingtonpost.com/wp-dyn/content/article/2006/10/13/
AR2006101300014.html ('Macy's imported 650 baskets last year [2005] in a successful test
run, and bought 31,000 more to sell this fall [2006] in stores in New York, Atlanta[,] and
Chicago[,] and online'). Plateau* baskets are flat, platter-like baskets that require up to seven
days to weave using needles and *imigwegwe* plant threads.

18. By June 2007, Rwanda was training 3,323 women in weaving, an initiative supported by the
     City of Kigali; Protection and Care of Families Against HIV/AIDS; the Ministry of
     Commerce, Industry, Investment Promotion, Tourism, and Cooperatives in Rwanda; the
     Rwanda Investment and Export Promotion Agency; the Rwandan Private Sector Federation;
     and the first lady of Rwanda, Jeannette Kagame. *See* Press Release, Imbuto Found., Mrs.
     Kagame Congratulates Agaseke Women on Completion of Training (June 1, 2007), *avail-
     able at* http://www.imbutofoundation.org/spip.php?article52.

19. Even with the Macy's order, the market was dominated by a single exporter, Gahaya Links,
     with 90 percent market control. *See* RWANDA MINISTRY OF TRADE AND INDUSTRY, RWANDA
     CRAFT INDUSTRY SECTOR STRATEGIC PLAN: FIVE YEARS 2009–2013, at 14 (2009).

20. 'Cooperative organizations are associations of natural or legal persons operating together in
     activities aiming at promoting their members in accordance with principles of mutual
     responsibility and self help, democracy, equity and equal rights to its assets.' *See* Codes and
     Law of Rwanda, Law No. 50/2007 Providing for the Establishment, Organisation[,] and
     Functioning of Cooperative Organizations in Rwanda, (O.G. n° 23 bis of 01.12.2007), *avail-
     able at* http://www.amategeko.net/display_rubrique.php?ActDo=ShowArt&Information
     _ID= 2062&Parent_ID=30698063&type=public&Langue_ID=An&ru bID=30698091.

21. Located about 35 kilometers south of Kigali, Nyamata is the site of a genocide memorial
     commemorating the massacre of approximately 10,000 people who sought sanctuary in a
     village church in April 1994. *See* JEAN HATZFELD, MACHETE SEASON: THE KILLERS IN
     RWANDA SPEAK xii (2005).

22. IA initially placed orders for 3,000 textile wine coasters from Ange and 120 *plateau* baskets
     from Covanya.

23. 'Fair wages are determined by a number of factors, including the amount of time, skill, and
     effort involved in production, minimum and living wages in the local context, the purchas-
     ing power in a community or area, and other costs of living in the local context. Wages are
     determined independently from North American wage structures and are designed to provide
     fair compensation based on the true cost of production.' Fair Trade Federation, Fair Trade
     Myths, http://www.fairtradefederation.org/ht/d/sp/i/198/pid/198 (last visited Nov. 17, 2011).
     IA became a member of the Fair Trade Federation on September 1, 2009. Letter from Mary
     R. Parrish, Membership Coordinator, Fair Trade Federation, to authors (Sept. 1, 2009) (on
     file with authors). For the official website of the Fair Trade Federation, see http://www.fair
     tradefederation.org/.

24. AGOA allows eligible countries in Sub-Saharan Africa to export certain products to the U.S.
     subject to zero import duty. *See* AGOA, H.R. 434, 106th Cong. § 506A(b)(i) (2d Sess.
     2000).

25. For the official website of Orrick, see http://www.orrick.com/.

26. For the official website of the Houston Holocaust Museum, see http://www.hmh.org/. For
     the official website of the U.S. Holocaust Memorial Museum, see http://www.ushmm.org/.

27. During the fiscal year that ended on December 31, 2007, IA recorded approximately
     US$4,800 in product sales revenue and US$23,000 in donations income.

28. For more information about GR, see Chapter 6.

29. In 2009, GR selected 27 scholars from among 2,700 applicants – a 1 percent acceptance rate.
     In 2010, GR selected 25 scholars from among 1,500 applicants – a 1.7 percent acceptance
     rate. *See* Generation Rwanda, Selection Process, http://www.generationrwanda.org/
     ?page_id=109 (last visited Nov. 17, 2011).

30. Born in February 1975 in the southern province of Rwanda, Nyiramana was a secondary
     school student when genocide erupted. Separated from her family, Nyiramana endured the
     next two months alone, eluding *génocidaires* in fields, jungles, and homes. The youngest of
     seven siblings, including three brothers and three sisters, Nyiramana emerged from hiding
     to discover that each of her brothers, her father, and two of her sisters' husbands had been

killed. In 1995, Nyiramana married, started a family, and relocated to Kigali. For the next decade, Nyiramana undertook a variety of odd jobs, including daily journeys of more than 25 kilometers to transport water. None of these jobs resulted in a daily wage exceeding US$0.25. Nyiramana joined Ange in 2006. Interview with Emelienne Nyiramana, Founder & Treasurer, Cocoki, in Kigali, Rwanda (Jan. 4, 2010) (on file with authors).

31. *Id.*
32. *See, e.g.*, Thomas Adcock, *Public Interest Projects*, N.Y.L.J., Sept. 19, 2008, http://www.newyorklawjournal.com/PubArticleNY.jsp?id=1202424629498; Amanda Royal, *Orrick Associate's One Client: Rwanda*, RECORDER 1 (Jan. 4, 2010).
33. During the fiscal year that ended on December 31, 2008, IA recorded approximately US$34,300 in product sales revenue and US$73,700 in donations income.
34. IA partnered with New York University School of Law's Law and Social Entrepreneurship Association and Columbia Law School's Law Students for Social Enterprise, both of which launched in February 2009. The partnership included the creation of a Fellowship Program at Columbia Law School for students (one per semester) to earn *pro-bono* credit, internships, and various speaking engagements through IA.
35. *See* Indego Africa, Speaking Engagements, http://www.indegoafrica.org/speaking-engagements (last visited Nov. 17, 2011).
36. *See* Social Enterprising: Indego Africa's Inside Look at Social Enterprise in Action, http://socialenterprising.indegoafrica.org/ (last visited Nov. 17, 2011) (posts include interviews and notes directly from the artisans).
37. *See* Harvard Business School & Kennedy School of Government, 2009 Social Enterprise Conference (Mar. 1, 2009).
38. *See* Kathleen L. McGinn, & Rachel Gordon, *The Indego Africa Project*, HARVARD BUSINESS SCHOOL, Case 911-011 (2010).
39. By 2011, IA had also launched regional boards in Chicago, Los Angeles, San Francisco, Boston, Houston, and Milwaukee.
40. *See* Interview with Valens Rutazihana, Management Team Leader, in Kigali, Rwanda (Apr. 16, 2010).
41. 'Functional literacy' is the general education needed to meet personal and social needs. *See* THE GREENWOOD DICTIONARY OF EDUCATION 148 (John W. Collins III & Nancy Patricia O'Brien eds., 2003). Studies have shown that even a minimum level of literacy education profoundly impacts women's filial income levels, reduces maternal and infant mortality rates, improves nutrition and general health, and fosters longer life expectancy. *See* UNESCO, THE HANDBOOK FOR LITERACY AND NON-FORMAL EDUCATION FACILITATORS IN AFRICA 55 (2006).
42. *See* Scott Baldauf, *French-Speaking Rwanda Turns to English*, CHRISTIAN SCI. MONITOR, Sept. 25, 2007, at 1.
43. *See* E-mail from Tom Mitro, Treasurer, Indego Africa, to authors (Sept. 11, 2009, 13:24:00 EST) (on file with authors).
44. Product sales decreased by 23 percent, or US$7,800, to approximately US$26,300 for the fiscal year that ended on December 31, 2009. Total revenue increased by 17 percent, or US$18,100, to approximately US$126,100 for the fiscal year that ended on December 31, 2009 due to an increase of 35 percent, or US$26,100, to approximately US$99,800 in donations income. 58 percent of such total annual revenue was earned during the fourth quarter.
45. Sixteen women from Cocoki and 28 women from Covanya participated in the social impact assessment. *See* INDEGO AFRICA, 2009 SOCIAL IMPACT REPORT, *available at* http://www.indegoafrica.org/socialimpact; INDEGO AFRICA, 2009–2010 SOCIAL IMPACT REPORT, *available at* http://www.indegoafrica.org/socialimpact.
46. IA's 2009 Social Impact Report showed a 336 percent increase in the number of women earning more than US$1 per day, 96 percent increase in the number of families eating at least twice per day, 17 percent increase in the number of women reporting some or all of their children attend school, 42 percent reduction in the number of women with no permanent residence, 153 percent increase in bank account ownership, and 585 percent increase in the number of women who are satisfied or very satisfied with their quality of life. INDEGO AFRICA, 2009 SOCIAL IMPACT REPORT, *supra* note 45.

47. *See* Press Release, Fair Trade Fed'n, Indego Africa Celebrated for Positive Change Created in Rwanda (Sept. 23, 2010), *available at* http://www.fairtradefederation.org/ht/a/ GetDocumentAction/i/14113.

48. For the official website of SURF, see http://www.survivors-fund.org.uk.

49. For the official website of Foundation Rwanda, see http://www.foundationrwanda.org.

50. SURF and Foundation Rwanda paid IA US$35,000 in several stages over a 22-month period (July 2010 to May 2012) to cover literacy, business, and sewing training, cooperative rent, member transportation, IA staff time, cooperative furniture, and registration fees. The women were also members of AVEGA-AGAHOZO, a non-profit run by and for genocide survivors. For the official website of AVEGA (*Association des Veuves du Génocide*)-AGAHOZO, see http://www.avega.org.rw/English.html.

51. *See* Interview by Alex Kennedy with Eugene Nteziyaremye, Literacy Program Intern, Indego Africa, in Kigali, Rwanda (Feb. 17, 2011).

52. At the request of Muteri and Umatesi, IA paid half of their monthly stipend of RWF 80,000 (approximately US$135) into Cocoki's account.

53. *See* E-mail from Sarah Dunigan, Rwanda Program Coordinator, Indego Africa, to authors (Oct. 10, 2010, 14:29:00 EST) (on file with authors).

54. *10,000 Women* is a US$100 million, five-year campaign launched by Goldman Sachs and the Goldman Sachs Foundation in 2008 to provide 10,000 underserved women around the world with business and management education. *10,000 Women* in Rwanda is organized by the William Davidson Institute at the University of Michigan in partnership with Rwanda's School of Finance and Banking. *See 10,000 Women* Initiative, http://www2. goldmansachs.com/citizenship/10000women/index.html (last visited Nov. 17, 2011).

55. Posting of Emelienne Nyiramana to Social Enterprising, *Stand Bold*, http://social enterprising.indegoafrica.org/2010/09/stand-bold-emelienne-blogs-goldman.html (Sept. 17, 2010).

56. Nyiramana wrote that the session on public speaking 'helped me to stand bold and present my business plan in front of many people.' *Id.*

57. Cocoki's annual gross revenues increased from RWF 700,000 (approximately US$1,300) in 2008 to RWF 4.2 million (approximately US$7,400) in 2009 to RWF 10.4 million (approximately US$17,600) in 2010. *See* Interview with Emelienne Nyiramana, *supra* note 30.

58. *Id.*

59. *See, e.g.,* Post of *Jacqueline Adams to Africa.com Blog, Powerful Businesswomen Collaborating in Rwanda and the United States*, http://www.africa.com/blog/blog,powerful_ businesswomen_collaborating_in_rwanda_and_the_united_states,119.html (Nov. 1, 2010).

60. *See* Noam Wasserman, *Founder-CEO Succession and the Paradox of Entrepreneurial Success*, 14 ORG. SCI. 149, 151 (2003) ('Founder-CEO succession may be the most critical succession event in the life of most firms.').

61. For the official website of Latham & Watkins LLP, see http://www.lw.com.

62. *See* Conor French, *Ashoka Helped Take Me From Lawyer to Social Entrepreneur*, Ashoka, Mar. 21, 2011, http://www.ashoka.org/story/ashoka-helped-take-me-lawyer-social-entre preneur. For more information about Ashoka, see the Foreword.

63. French worked for IA without pay until April 2011.

64. An American designer working in Rwanda assisted IA and Twiyubake in creating and proto-typing the banana leaf bracelet ordered by Polo Ralph Lauren.

65. *See, e.g.,* Rachel Jacoby, *What's Right Now: Ralph Lauren Sells Fair Trade Bracelets*, INSTYLE.COM, July 22, 2010, http://news.instyle.com/2010/07/22/ralph-lauren-sells-fair-trade-bracelets.

66. Nicole Miller is an American fashion designer with more than 1,200 independent specialty stores and namesake boutiques and generates US$650 million in annual sales. *See* Julia Chaplin, *Our Lady of Fiestas*, ELLE, Oct. 29, 2010, *available at* http://www.elle.com/Life-Love/Entertaining-Design/Our-Lady-of-Fiestas.

67. *See* Michelle Halpern, *Nicole Miller Designs Bangles for Africa*, STYLECASTER.COM, Oct. 29, 2010, http://www.stylecaster.com/fashion/9709/nicole-miller-designs-bangles-africa# 109334; Camden Janney, *Indego Africa's Color-Popping Bracelets*, ELLE.COM, Oct. 29, 2010, http://fashion.elle.com/culture/2010/10/29/indego-africas-color-popping-bracelets/.

68. Anthropologie (owned by Urban Outfitters) is a chain of retail stores with annual net sales of US$1,011,999,000. *See* Press Release, Urban Outfitters, Urban Outfitters Reports Record 4th Quarter Operating Profit (Mar. 7, 2011) *available at* http://news.urbn.com/phoenix.zhtml?c=115825&p=irol-newsArticle&ID=1536569&highlight.
69. *See, e.g.,* Chelsea Zalopany, *Feel Good Scarves at Anthropologie,* N.Y TIMES STYLE MAG., Sept. 30, 2010, *available at* http://tmagazine.blogs.nytimes.com/2010/09/30/feel-good-scarves-anthropologie/; Cheryl Krementz, *Anthropologie Class,* VOGUE KNITTING, Fall 2010, *available at* http://www.indegoafrica.org/media/docs/Multimedia/Indego.Africa-VOGUE.Knitting.pdf.
70. *See* DO WELL DO GOOD LLC, PUBLIC OPINION SURVEY ON CORPORATE SOCIAL RESPONSIBILITY SUMMARY REPORT (2010), *available at* http://dowelldogood.net/wp-content/uploads/2011/03/DWDG_CSR_Final.pdf.
71. Total revenue increased by 202 percent, or US$128,700, to approximately US$254,800 for the fiscal year that ended on December 31, 2010 due to an increase of 263 percent, or US$43,200, to approximately US$69,600 in product sales and an increase of 183 percent, or US$82,700, to approximately US$182,400 in donations income. 46 percent of such total annual revenue was earned during the fourth quarter.
72. Mitro joined Google's Africa team in London and continues as chairman of IA's board of directors. With Stone replacing Mitro as CEO, French transitioned into a joint Chief Operating Officer (COO) and CFO role.
73. In the first six months of 2011, IA issued its partner cooperatives purchase orders for approximately 6,440 products whereas, in the first six months of 2010, IA issued its partner cooperatives purchase orders for approximately 1,410 products. The 2011 six-month figure above does not include an additional 4,490 units ordered from Ingenzi Knit Union in July 2011.
74. *See* Emily Wax, *Trading Up,* WASH. POST, July 1, 2011, at C1 (quoting Nyiramana as saying: 'all the women of Cocoki have a dream: to become rich with their hands.'); *see also Nicole Miller's African Project,* WOMEN'S WEAR DAILY, July 27, 2011, *available at* http://www.wwd.com/fashion-news/fashion-scoops/manchester-uniteds-soccer-style-nicole-millers-african-project-5011897?page=2.
75. *See* Edmund Kagire & Linda Mbabazi, *Fashion Icon Wraps up Rwandan Tour,* NEW TIMES (Rwanda), Oct. 11, 2011, at 8, *available at* http://www.newtimes.co.rw/index.php?issue=14775&article=46097. Traditionally, IA (and companies like Gahaya Links) act as the intermediary between cooperatives and retailers by receiving a purchase order from the retailer and then issuing a separate purchase order to the cooperative.
76. For the official website of DANNIJO Jewelry, see http://dannijo.com. For the official website of Shopbop, see http://www.shopbop.com. For the official website of Steven Alan, see http://www.stevenalan.com.
77. In October 2011, J.Crew placed approximately US$70,000 in purchase orders with IA for approximately 9,000 textile wrap bracelets.
78. Interview by Alex Kennedy with Eugene Nteziyaremye, *supra* note 51.
79. *Id.*
80. Interview with Eugenie Ufitikirezi, President, Abasangiye, in Kayonza, Rwanda (Jan. 10, 2011).
81. *See Nicole Miller Partners with Rwandan Artisans,* WOMEN'S WEAR DAILY, Oct. 19, 2011, *available at* http://www.wwd.com/fashion-news/fashion-scoops/rwandan-artisans-meet-nicole-miller-5311243; Cocoki, Indego Africa & The NYT Visit DANNIJO for Breakfast, DANNIJO, http://dannijo.com/blog/?p=6482 (Oct. 26, 2011).
82. IA projected having to pay 78 percent of its aggregate fixed costs associated with the order, including purchasing raw materials, prepaying artisans at Ingenzi Knit Union, and paying customs costs, on or before June 1, 2011. IA could not expect payment from Anthropologie until November 2011. IA explored various debt financing options, including unsecured revolving loans, export credit facilities, purchase order factoring arrangements, and donor advances and guaranties. Two promising options included Grassroots Business Fund and Shared Interest. For the official website of Grassroots Business Fund, see http://www.gbfund.org. For the official website of Shared Interest, see http://www.sharedinterest.org. In the end, however, IA self-financed the order, with Anthropologie advancing

approximately 18 percent of the purchase order (US$19,375) and the Segal Family Foundation agreeing to advance certain committed future quarterly contributions if necessary.

83. IA and Ingenzi Knit Union successfully completed and delivered the order in October 2011. *See* Indego Africa, *Historic Scarf Order Hits Anthropologie Stores!*, Nov. 1, 2011, http://hosted.verticalresponse.com/289343/2a065244fb/1293000645/2058959f8b/.

84. In October 2011, IA verbally entered into a formal partnership agreement with the William Davidson Institute at the University of Michigan and the Goldman Sachs *10,000 Women* program in Rwanda.

85. Posting of Laila Qaimmaqami to Social Enterprising, *Indego Africa and VisionSpring Team Up to Provide Eyeglasses for Artisan Women in Rwanda*, http://socialenterprising. indegoafrica.org/2011/07/indego-africa-and-visionspring-team-up.html (July 29, 2011). For the official website of VisionSpring, see http://www.visionspring.org/.

86. Interview with Therese Iribagiza, Vice President, Cocoki, in Kicukiro, Rwanda (Sept. 9, 2011).

6. Transformation through education: Generation Rwanda and access to higher education for Rwanda's orphans and vulnerable youth

Dai Ellis, Jamie Hodari, and Oliver Rothschild

BACKGROUND

Two of us, Ellis and Rothschild, met in Kigali, the capital of Rwanda, in 2004. We were both working with U.S.-based NGOs, advising the Rwandan Ministry of Health as it launched Rwanda's first comprehensive national HIV/AIDS program. While we spent most of our time developing policy in Government of Rwanda (GoR) offices, we did our best to get into the field to meet people affected by HIV and AIDS. In a village called Kimisange, just outside Kigali, we came across an orphanage, Village de la Paix (Village of Peace), which was home to more than 70 children who had lost their parents to HIV/AIDS. The orphanage had enough funding to feed, clothe, and house all of the children, yet it operated without electricity and running water despite being located within a few hundred yards of the municipal access point to the electricity grid and water system. We decided to organize a modest fundraising drive among our friends and family in the U.S. to ameliorate this problem.

In 2004, our reaction to the orphanage's predicament set in motion a series of events that produced the organization that is now Generation Rwanda (GR) (known until 2010 as Orphans of Rwanda). We learned two key lessons from these early efforts to help solve specific problems that orphanages lacked the funds to address. First, donors in the U.S. were eager to make significant contributions that would benefit orphans and vulnerable children (OVCs) in Rwanda, provided that they knew that their money would be spent effectively.[1] Second, the orphanages we selected for assistance made clear to us that they were all struggling with a common problem: how to help older children – those graduating from secondary school and leaving the orphanages – to make the transition to independent adult life in the community. Based on these two realizations, we decided to establish a non-profit organization dedicated to aiding talented students in obtaining access to higher education and helping to prepare them to compete in the job market, to live independently, and ultimately to become leaders in their communities.

Since its founding in 2004, GR has grown from a small group of volunteers raising money from friends to a professional organization with six full-time staff in Rwanda and two in the U.S. One of us, Hodari, joined the organization in 2011 and serves as its second Executive Director.

GR works with partner organizations – orphanages, youth-focused community groups, and other local organizations – to identify motivated and talented young people who want to pursue a university education. Once selected for the program, these students receive comprehensive support from GR, which goes well beyond tuition to include healthcare, housing, language and life-skills training, and career development services. By 2011, GR supported 181 current university students while 45 young Rwandans had become university graduates through our program; the scholarships we provide are the most comprehensive university scholarships available in Rwanda today.

In building GR, we have sought to do things differently from other organizations working in education in the developing world. Many of our programs have been developed and executed following principles that challenge the conventional wisdom of many development organizations. As we will describe, GR has avoided spreading itself thinly across many countries due to our belief in the unique challenges presented – and unique responses required – by working in post-conflict Rwanda. GR has instead focused on developing a model of support that is best suited to the needs of the Rwandan people.

Sub-Saharan Africa is a notoriously difficult place to work. Non-profit organizations operating locally must contend with extreme poverty, a host of infectious diseases, and complex ethnic and cultural issues that can affect day-to-day program implementation. These problems form the backdrop for all development programs in sub-Saharan Africa, but working on education in Rwanda presents an additional set of obstacles.

The genocide of 1994 left Rwanda decimated: more than 10 percent of the Rwandan population was murdered in 100 days.[2] Widespread rape during the genocide helped spur the HIV epidemic in Rwanda. Since HIV is a sexually transmitted disease, it disproportionately affects people in the prime of their lives. Together, these two waves of destruction wiped out a large segment of Rwanda's intellectual capital and left hundreds of thousands of children without parents. In addition, many Rwandan orphans have no living grandparents, siblings, aunts, uncles, or cousins.

Not only was a generation of Rwandans orphaned, but the educational system was also left in ruins. Throughout sub-Saharan Africa, only 5 percent of students who finish secondary school end up pursuing tertiary education.[3]

In Rwanda, for the first decade after the genocide, this number is less than 2 percent.[4] In fact, in 2002, eight years after the genocide, less than one-half of 1 percent of Rwandans had received a tertiary diploma.[5]

The fact that Rwanda has extremely low rates of higher education, even in comparison to other sub-Saharan African countries, is particularly troubling in light of the importance of intellectual capital to Rwanda's development. A landlocked country with few natural resources, Rwanda currently lacks a diversified economy. According to a report published by USAID in 2010, nearly 80 percent of all Rwandans work in agriculture (which is responsible for approximately 34 percent of the nation's GDP).[6] Another challenge to Rwanda's growth is overpopulation; the most densely populated country in sub-Saharan Africa, Rwanda has more than 400 people per square kilometer.[7] Furthermore, the fertility rate per woman averages almost five children, which has contributed to Rwanda's quick population growth. [8]

With these challenges in mind, donors and analysts, as well as the GoR itself, recognize the need to expand the economy beyond farming. *Vision 2020*, Rwanda's strategic plan for promoting prosperity, provides the framework for the creation of a knowledge-based economy.[9] In order to implement this ambitious vision, Rwanda needs to harness its intellectual potential. While the information technology infrastructure in Rwanda is impressive for a developing nation, it still lacks the critical mass of talented professionals necessary for technology to become an effective growth engine.

Aspects of Rwandan culture and society pose challenges to the development of an entrepreneurial, knowledge-based economy. Deference to authority is pervasive, hindering entrepreneurship and risk-taking. In addition, the ethnic tensions that flared most brutally during the 1994 genocide continue to influence perceptions and decision-making in counter-productive ways. Finally, sexual violence and historic gender inequality have contributed to the creation of an intellectual elite in which women are underrepresented.

OUR MODEL

Our first step in 2004 when designing our interventions was to speak to both the orphanage directors and the youth for whom they cared. In the first of many conversations, we asked simply: how can we help? As we expected, we heard a litany of problems, but the most common was that older orphaned youths were having trouble transitioning out of orphanages and into Rwandan society. Even those who had obtained high school degrees had difficulty finding employment. As orphans, these young people were outside the social networks that permeate Rwandan society and provide access to employment opportunities. Out of the diverse challenges faced by these talented youth emerged GR's model and mission: to enable some of the young adults at orphanages to pursue university degrees, and thereby provide them with a foundation upon which to build a better future for themselves and for their families, communities, and country.

Conventional wisdom in donor circles holds that aid for education is most cost-efficient when it is targeted at young children, a trend encouraged by the belief that primary and secondary studies yield higher social returns than tertiary education.[10] In Rwanda, the government has deemed quality primary education one of its top priorities and is striving to reach its target primary school enrollment rate of 100 percent. The GoR now provides free and mandatory primary education for all children, and has set up campaigns encouraging parents to send their children to school.[11] This work is valuable and necessary: by 2009, primary school enrollment rates in Rwanda had risen to approximately 96 percent (up from 78 percent in 2004).[12] As Devesh Kapur and Megan Crowley of the Center for Global Development have noted, however, an unintended consequence of this approach has been that '[t]ertiary education has received short shrift in the international development community stemming from the belief that it yields lower social returns ... [than] primary and secondary education.'[13] In spite of this trend towards prioritizing primary and secondary education, listening to Rwandans inspired us at GR to develop programs that address education differently from other projects we encountered, filling the void created by the prevailing trend in development. We created an innovative model for supporting OVCs that allows us to leverage relatively limited resources to make a significant impact on Rwanda at a national level.

Support for Higher Education

Although the World Bank is one of the few development agencies that work on expanding access to higher education, in the past it has directed a comparatively small amount of aid toward tertiary education.[14] In our years of working in Rwanda, we have encountered only a handful of other international organizations dedicated to OVCs that work on the issue of higher education in sub-Saharan Africa, and none of these organizations operate in Rwanda. Guided by mistaken assumptions about the impact of aid at the university level, very few organizations take on higher education as a priority. Recently, however, these assumptions have been questioned by new academic research, by GR's experience, and perhaps most significantly, by those with whom we work in Rwanda.

In a 2006 report, *Higher Education and Economic Development in Africa*, David Bloom, David Canning, and Kevin Chan of Harvard University argue for increased investment in tertiary education. They emphasize the potential social returns, noting that higher university graduation rates may 'create greater tax revenue, increase savings and investment, and lead to a more entre-preneurial and civic society. [These higher rates] can also improve a nation's health, contribute to reduced population growth, improve technology, and strengthen governance.' The authors underscore the way in which university education has the potential to spur growth, citing India as an example: 'With regard to the benefits of higher education for a country's economy, many observers attribute India's leap onto the world economic stage as stemming from its decades-long successful efforts to provide high-quality, technically oriented tertiary education to a significant number of its citizens.'[15] Furthermore, the idea that higher education generally produces lower *private* returns than primary education has recently been challenged. In *The Returns to Education in Rwanda*, Gérard Lassibille of the University of Bourgogne and Jee-Peng Tan of the World Bank demonstrate that while the investment in an additional year of primary education in Rwanda yields a return of 19.4 percent (as reflected in increased earnings as an adult), investment in an additional year of university studies yields a return of 33 percent.[16] This discrepancy is largely explained by the fact that most well-compensated jobs in Rwanda's public sector and formal private sector require a university degree.

The importance of higher education is even more acute among OVCs because they lack strong social networks, financial resources, and back-up plans. Without enough money to support their studies, most OVCs discontinue schooling after completing their secondary studies. Children who grew up in orphanages or other institutional settings without parents or other adult contacts lack the social networks that are instrumental to finding employment. Finally, partly due to weak enforcement of property rights, most children lose their families' land when their parents die, further restricting their options and opportunities.

The admissions criteria for Rwandan universities are limited almost exclu-sively to the score a student achieves on the subject-specific national exam given at the end of secondary school. Students from relatively wealthy fami-lies who can afford to attend high-quality, expensive primary and secondary schools receive better training and preparation for the national exam. Equally important, such students are less likely to be hindered by the gaps in school attendance experienced by OVCs, who often must leave school for long peri-ods of time to earn income or care for family members. These significant differences lead to an unsurprising result: the vast majority of students pursu-ing tertiary education in Rwanda come from relatively wealthy families, which have a significant advantage in both the financial resources that can be dedi-cated to a child's education and the amount of time a student is able to dedi-cate to his or her studies.[17]

With few effective options for school loans, those who qualify for univer-sity but do not perform well enough to obtain a government scholarship can only proceed to university if they or their families can afford to pay tuition independently. Unfortunately, tuition and other costs related to attending university are well beyond the means of the vast majority of Rwandan families, let alone OVCs. Even within the wealthier strata of Rwandan society, the population of university students is skewed: men are more commonly encouraged to attend university than women and currently represent close to 60 percent of university students.[18]

The under-representation of vulnerable groups at the highest levels of education reflects deep inequality and threatens the country's development by limiting the potential of its people. Indeed, countries with entrenched inequality and low rates of social mobility appear to have lower growth rates than countries with lower degrees of inequality.[19] Moreover, OVCs have experienced great economic and social deprivation and are often motivated to address the country's problems. Delphine Mukamana, a GR graduate now working as an engineer in Kigali, voices her opinion of the current education system, and her desire to enact change: 'The problem with the schools in Rwanda is that the good schools are the schools that rich children attend. It's just an ambition, but I want to set up a big school, which could help orphans and children who don't have enough money to pay their school fees.'

GR takes an innovative approach to ensuring that students in our program do not merely get through university, but are empowered to thrive academically and professionally. In contrast to the traditional scholarship model, whereby students receive school fees and books only, we offer holistic scholarships that enable our supported students to focus on their studies. We also provide many students with their first true opportunity to live independently. The scholarship package includes healthcare, housing, and a monthly stipend. With this stipend, students have the financial resources that enable them to focus on their studies rather than their day-to-day survival. Furthermore, when a student joins GR, it is expected that the student will be dedicated 100 percent to their studies and cannot hold a full-time job. If the student had been contributing to the income of their family (if they have a family), the stipend gives the student an opportunity to provide some of that funding to their family to help mitigate the lost family income resulting from the student's departure from the workforce.

The healthcare component – both mental and physical – is crucial. Nearly all of the children we support have lived through extremely difficult events; some cared for their parents as they wasted away from disease, while others watched family members being murdered during the genocide, and still others have themselves been victims of horrific violence, including sexual assault. Suffering from trauma, one of our scholars lost her ability to speak for several days until she was able to obtain counseling. Many other GR-supported students missed weeks or months of school at the primary or secondary level due to post-traumatic stress, depression, malaria, and other recurring afflictions.

Our primary goal is to ensure that students in our program succeed, but we also hope to have an impact on a broader scale by increasing the number and proportion of OVCs who obtain higher education. Few Rwandans enter university at all, and even fewer graduate. Among these, most are wealthy, so the number of OVCs attending Rwandan universities on GR scholarships represents a significant increase in the number of OVCs graduating university nationally. Our goals are well aligned with those of the GoR, which has made expanding access to university education a national priority.

Empowering Students to Realize their Ambitions

Many of our students envision themselves as potential agents of change in Rwandan society. Whether our students hope to become dynamic business leaders, distinguished public servants, or successful entrepreneurs, we seek to empower them to pursue their highest aspirations. Yet, a significant number of GR-supported students have lived their entire lives in orphanages with only their basic needs met and little experience functioning on their own in society. We therefore balance initiatives intended to cultivate and sharpen long-term career goals with more immediate efforts to help students gain basic life skills and adapt to living independently.

GR's comprehensive scholarship package provides students with a number of transitional experiences. We set up an individual bank account for each student, depositing a modest stipend in it each month and coaching students on managing their own money for the first time. Students who have lived much of their lives in an orphanage get their first experience of living independently in houses rented by GR that serve as homes for seven to eight students each. These houses are an extremely important part of the GR scholarship: they create strong bonds among students and form an important social support system during this period of profound adjustment. The students who live together in houses frequently refer to their housemates as 'brothers' and 'sisters.'

Another major component of our work is our career development services. Our students are, by definition, the young people in Rwanda who lack the networks that can help them find employment. We therefore have a full-time staff member and a dedicated volunteer whose sole responsibility is to connect our students to part-time jobs and internships that will enable them to build their skill sets, develop their CVs, and figure out what their true interests are. In 2010, our students held 290 part-time jobs or internships (an increase of 51 percent over the prior year) and 91 percent of our students held part-time jobs or internships. In addition, 150 different employers hired our students, many for the first time – a development that reflects the strong reputation that GR students have earned over time. One of the main employers of GR's students is Indego Africa.[20]

Doing Things Differently: Building Generation Rwanda from the Ground Up

In addition to building a program that focuses on a neglected but crucial need, GR distinguishes itself from other international organizations in the way we implement our programs. Indeed, the original passion for creating GR was fueled partly by Ellis and Rothschild's frustrating observations gleaned during their day jobs. Rwanda's health sector witnessed a tremendous influx of donor support to combat HIV/AIDS, and the GoR was one of few sub-Saharan African governments that had developed sensible strategic plans on its own initiative and had demonstrated an ability to use funds responsibly.

Traditional development organizations share a number of common flaws in the way they operate, and we frequently observed behavior that bordered on the absurd. Large donors and NGOs tend to impose priorities in a top-down fashion, mandating certain pre-packaged aid programs regardless of recipients' specific needs or circumstances. One meeting we attended provides a perfect example. The GoR and a major donor met to discuss the donor's plans for supporting the fight against HIV/AIDS. When the GoR representative asked the donor's lead representative which part of the national HIV/AIDS plan her organization was most eager to support, she admitted that she had never consulted the national plan. Instead, the donor had created a parallel plan, paying foreign NGOs to implement it. When the GoR asked to review the donor's plans and budgets, the woman baldly refused, claiming that the money was their own and that the GoR had no right to second-guess their plans. In a separate meeting, we heard another donor representative wax eloquently about his close relationship with the GoR's Director of HIV/AIDS Testing – only to discover, rather embarrassingly, that the individual in question (whom the donor representative had never in fact met in person) was sitting directly across the table from him as he spoke.

The wasteful spending by donors and large NGOs is prodigious. In reviewing the HIV/AIDS program budgets of a number of major donors, it became apparent that in many cases one-third to one-half of these budgets was allocated to overhead expenditures – flying a small army of international consultants in from overseas on business class fares, buying hulking SUVs, and paying administrative fees to a series of organizations in a cascade of sub-contracts. Of the 'program' expenditures that remained, much of the funding was destined to be spent on trainings and conferences of vague purpose. One of our close Rwandan friends would often joke that, with luck, the money that would ultimately reach any given village in the countryside might just be enough to buy a card and envelope to thank the international donors for all their support.

Even the limited money that was spent on meaningful programs was often wasted due to poor coordination. Donors, including large NGOs, rarely aligned their plans with those of peer organizations to avoid gaps or redundancies. In the health sector, all the major international players scrambled to get a piece of the action in AIDS treatment, which left HIV prevention and a host of other health issues, such as malaria and maternal health, languishing with insufficient funding.

The creation of GR offered the chance to build a different kind of operation from the ground up. We highlight below just a few of the ways in which our model seeks to avoid the weaknesses we perceive in the traditional development model.

Promoting empowerment and listening
First and foremost, we are committed to empowering our students. We want to find capable, motivated students and help them to pursue their *own* priorities as aggressively and successfully as possible. GR intends its role to be a relatively modest one: supporting our students and holding them responsible for the achievement of measurable results. Our mission statement reflects the aspiration that our university graduates will become leaders in their communities and the economy. This can only happen if our students have the freedom to pursue their personal goals and passions, working with GR to develop the best possible system of support and using that support to maximal effect.

Implementing this vision has not always been easy and we have already learned a number of critical lessons about how to make this approach work. First, GR has had to become rigorously selective in identifying new scholarship recipients and local partners. Second, in post-conflict situations, and in a developing country such as Rwanda, the natural instinct is always to help as many people as possible in as many possible ways. Yet, a program model like ours, based on high levels of delegation and empowerment, only works if the beneficiaries are capable and motivated. These lessons have led to significant modifications of our selection process over the years. Our student selection process is now far more rigorous than it was initially, and is one of the most thorough searches for talent that occurs in East Africa: GR looks for a combination of academic potential, critical and analytical thinking, creativity, perseverance, and motivation through a multi-round admissions process that includes scrutinizing secondary school grades, class rank, and national exam scores, performance on a battery of GR-administered tests, multiple rounds of essays, and an extensive interview process. We believe these criteria are strong indicators not only of a student's ability to succeed in university, but also of his or her ability to handle the level of personal responsibility required of each GR scholar. After we create a final list of potential students to accept but before we officially invite those students to join the program, our staff verifies that the information they provided about their vulnerability status is indeed true; any student found to have falsified information on their application is disqualified from joining our program. The result is a highly competitive process: in 2010, for example, GR awarded scholarships to just over 1 percent of the 2,500 students that applied. In the final stage of the selection process, we conducted more than 100 interviews with candidates living in every region of Rwanda.

In order to ensure that our approach is sound, we have made a tremendous effort to become a 'listening' organization and to respond to the feedback of our students. We feel that we cannot truly understand and be responsive to our students' priorities if we operate as a group of foreigners constantly flying into and out of Rwanda. Instead, we try to make deeper connections in a number of ways. We believe it is critical to have a Rwandan in charge as Country Director. Our Country Director is responsible for developing strong relationships with NGOs, GoR officials, local partners, and students. Input from all of these stakeholders continuously informs the way GR plans for the future. GR also relies heavily on long-term volunteers who live in Rwanda, and actively discourages short-term volunteers from the U.S. or Europe who are only able to spend a few weeks or months in the country. Though this approach deprives us of a potentially limitless labor pool, we feel strongly that we need to build a dependable local presence and maximize organizational continuity and stability through our employees and volunteers.

Promoting organizational efficiency
Donors have long put a great deal of pressure on non-profit organizations – often too much pressure – to limit overhead costs and expenses while simultaneously demanding results. As the non-profit sector matures, however, many organizations find their programs hamstrung by systematic under-investment in core operational capacity. It is within this context that GR seeks to find a balance. Perhaps no endeavor undertaken by our organization illustrates this better than the development of our 'Measurement and Evaluation System.'

At the beginning of 2008, the organization lacked a centralized database that stored all student information. The fact that data were kept in various spreadsheets by different staff members made it difficult to retrieve data efficiently, to use quantitative information in order to assess student progress, and to monitor overall student trends. Throughout 2008, GR staff and volunteers with relevant expertise worked together to develop a customized online database that met our organization's needs. Staff members in both Rwanda and the U.S. can now easily access the database at any time to retrieve the academic, extracurricular, and demographic information that we track for all students. If, for example, the Executive Director in New York wants to learn whether a specific student attended the last all-student meeting, this information is readily available on the database; previously, retrieving this information was a time-consuming effort that required the participation of other staff members. Our student advising program supports the collection of data by providing the staff with regular opportunities to receive updates from students; after student advising sessions, staff members add new information to the database.

Centralizing and improving access to data were requisites for developing our Measurement and Evaluation System. Since 2009, we have been using the data to track our students' performance and to determine whether our program enhancements are having the intended impact. We now generate quarterly and annual reports that enable us to answer both basic and complex questions that we had previously been answering by combining analyses of incomplete data with anecdotal information. These questions include:

- Which students have improved academically over time and which students have declined or shown little improvement?
- Is there a direct correlation between success at university and having the highest secondary school grades and national exam scores?
- What is the connection between students' language skills and their academic performance?
- At which universities are students performing well and at which universities are they performing poorly?
- Do students with internships or part-time jobs perform better or worse academically?
- Is there a correlation between academic performance and attendance at student advising sessions and GR trainings?

These are just some of the issues that we can now investigate. The database enables us to perform analyses so that we can figure out why some students are excelling while others are not and which elements of our program are promoting our students' success. The crucial step in the development of this entire process was finding a volunteer – a highly experienced database developer – who created our customized system from scratch and who continues to this day to provide support to the staff on the system. In short, GR developed a tracking system unlike anything used by other NGOs working in Rwanda – and it cost us virtually nothing to build and maintain thanks to the dedication of a highly trained volunteer we recruited by posting an advertisement on Idealist.org.[21]

We should note that one question we often hear is what percentage of our budget is spent on overhead. We are firmly committed to ensuring that most of the money we receive goes to the students we support, and early in the development of our organization, we were nearly fanatical about this. Rather than hiring a full-time Country Director for Rwanda, we relied on one part-time staff member and a corps of volunteers. We could brag to our donors that we spent close to 0 percent of the funds we raised on salaries – and donors responded positively – but our programs began to suffer. The part-time Country Director and a few part-time volunteers could not keep up with the demands of a rapidly expanding organization. As our budget continued to grow, and as our programs became more involved and ambitious, we realized something had to change.

While we remain committed to keeping our overhead low, we have made significant investments in personnel. Our U.S.-based staff now consists of an Executive Director with a background in law and finance, and a Director of Operations and Marketing. In Rwanda, we have a Country Director, a Director of Programs, a Career Development Officer, a Health Officer, and two finance and administrative staff members. This team has enabled us to continue to grow quickly and to substantially increase our fundraising capacity while we continue to provide high-quality support to our students. While strengthening our human resources, we continue to benefit from the support of a dedicated team of long-term volunteers with professional expertise who assist our staff in numerous ways in both the U.S. and in Rwanda.

In addition to meeting our students' needs, we carefully respond to our donors' needs by providing regular updates about our work and the progress of our students. As we grow as an organization, donors seek more information about how our students perform and recent years have seen a marked increase in the reports and updates that our funders require. As an organization, GR is dedicated to ensuring that donors are fully aware of how their funds are spent and how those funds have an impact on the ground in Rwanda. Many NGOs see fundraising as a necessary evil and fail to realize that their donors have the potential to be active partners with the organization. GR seeks to establish long-term connections with our donors, but for us, the financial component is just one part of the relationship. Our students want to know who their generous supporters are and our donors want to know these talented students; over time, we are working to increase the link between the two through better information-sharing and more direct communication between donors and students.

Ultimately, we have learned through experience that, in order to be effective in the long term, we must answer first to the students we support and the local organizations with which we partner. While we are committed to keeping costs as low as possible, we believe that our investment in personnel and operational capacity is critical to running a truly exceptional organization. In the long run, GR's supporters will be more impressed by our students' successes than by our ability to cut costs.

REFLECTIONS

One of the most striking things one notices when traveling through rural Rwanda is Coca-Cola. Drive for hours down a washed-out road that requires four-wheel drive, then hike up a steep hill until you arrive at one of the country's many remote, rural health centers. Its shelves will likely be lacking a number of inexpensive, life-saving medications, but walk a few minutes farther into the community and you'll find a small convenience store where – no matter how far you have driven and walked – you can always find a Coke.

Why is it that government officials and expert consultants cannot design a system to ensure consistent availability of cheap antibiotic pills in health clinics to save lives, but thousands of storeowners who never attended a day of high school manage to fill their stores with Coke and never run out? What are the lessons that non-profit organizations such as GR can learn from considering these successful distribution systems?

The answers to these questions are the essence of social entrepreneurship. Large, traditional development agencies, advised by armies of consultants with PhDs and abstract theories, respond to economic and social problems with programs devised from afar and planned in advance. The storeowner, however, is much more agile. In order to stay in business, he must be able to adapt his plans to accommodate changing local demand.

Development agencies typically create and execute plans with little attention paid to whether the population wants their intervention. If an international organization wants to provide HIV/AIDS education, the organization often avoids any careful evaluation of whether the recipients need the education or are satisfied with the way in which it is being delivered. By offering a small incentive to anyone who shows up, the organization can run trainings in spite of a lack of true demand. Moreover, there is the problem of accountability: in the absence of rigorous performance measurement, the failure to achieve meaningful social impact rarely results in the termination of funding for ineffective development organizations. It takes little imagination to see what would happen to our storeowner if he ordered only Fanta but paid customers to take it so he could make sure to use up his stock.

Effective social entrepreneurship is development executed in the model of a storeowner on a remote hill in rural Rwanda. Instead of working to address poverty through top-down planning, effective social entrepreneurs identify their priorities based on demand from populations in the same way that storeowners decide which products to carry. We believe that addressing the problems we have confronted with this entrepreneurial approach has made – and will continue to make – an impact on GR's growth.

Adapting to our Customers' Needs

As a young organization under Ellis and Rothschild's exclusive direction, it took us a few months to find our focus. The idea was to support OVCs, but for the first few months, the interventions were scattershot. One day we would work to install water and sanitation systems and the next we would find ourselves developing an art therapy program. When we finally settled on the idea of supporting higher education, we felt that we had found the right solution for the following reasons: new research backed our approach; this was a concrete intervention that would have a broad impact; no one else was doing it; and, most important, higher education was what the individuals we sought to serve *wanted.*

We began by drawing up a five-year strategic plan and mobilizing our resources to put that plan into action. Because we had funded all educational expenses as well as health and auxiliary needs, we were sure that the students we were supporting could not fail. Until they did.

It started with language problems. When GR first began in 2004, university classes were held in either French or English (today, all university instruction takes place in English). At the time, the students we were supporting generally spoke one or the other. Without the benefit of well-educated, multi-lingual parents, GR's students were far behind their peers. These language problems were just the beginning. We soon began to see evidence that the basic package of healthcare support we were offering was insufficient. Students with chronic health problems were not getting the care they needed, and the basic package of support we were providing did not meet the needs of students with emergent problems.

Our original plan was based on the belief that identifying an innovative, empowering way to support these students was enough. But through this series of challenges, we learned that it is not sufficient to build programs based on long-term plans and then stick to them rigidly. Today, our language training program is – along with our career development services – the most important part of our program aside from the provision of the core scholarship (tuition, housing, living stipend, and healthcare).

While everyone does deserve an education, we soon realized that not everyone wants, or even needs, the same amount or kind of education. While the scholarship package we offered – comprehensive support for school, healthcare, and housing – was too good an opportunity for them to turn down, many of the first students who entered our program were not motivated or excited about their studies. We worked with them to get tutoring, to switch classes, and to resolve their healthcare problems, but after approaching students' issues from various angles, we realized that there was a limit to what GR could do. We had pushed our programs on some students who clearly were not interested. As we discussed this matter further with students, we heard several explanations. One student would have preferred vocational school. Another wanted to start his own business instead of continuing with academics. Finally, others simply expected that they could go through the motions: attend class most of the time but give none of the extra effort that GR expects of its students.

Because of these challenges, we overhauled our core university support program. We created a language training and tutoring program to help students catch up to their peers. We redesigned our program of healthcare support. Finally, we instituted a rigorous application process that resulted in a much lower rate of acceptance into GR's program but more qualified scholarship recipients. Although we had not planned these programmatic enhancements early on, we adopted them quickly when it became clear that our initial approach was not meeting our students' needs. As the World Bank economist William Easterly argues in his writing on social entrepreneurship: 'business success does not come from setting a prefixed goal and then furiously laboring to reach it. Rather, successful businessmen are searchers, looking for any opportunity to make a profit by satisfying the customers.'[22] GR's goal remained unchanged, but we quickly realized that if we were going to see the outcome we desired – a motivated, healthy, and high-achieving student body – an open, flexible approach would be the only way to achieve it.

Finding True Partners

In any development endeavor, the question of whom to help arises quickly. In Rwanda, the number of people who need help is virtually limitless. We needed partner organizations to refer students to us who would fit our program. We formed our first few partnerships with well-run organizations that we found through friends; these groups were working heroically for the youth they supported. Encouraged by early fundraising success, we planned to scale up our network of partners quickly so that we could recruit more students from throughout the country, not just from Kigali. It seemed obvious to us that other organizations would want to help us as we worked to achieve GR's mission.

As with our students, we confronted challenges with our partners. Some of the first partners we selected were slow to develop plans and did not respond to our requests. Initially, we took this as a sign that they were understaffed or overworked. While this was often true, it was rarely the whole story. Some of our partners simply did not share our goals or methodologies. Some were more concerned with a particular set of programs. Our first response was to push: we helped them build capacity and were patient with them as they conducted the process of selecting candidates for a GR scholarship. Despite months of work, we came to understand that certain individuals and partners did not always share our priorities. Today, there are 10 organizations throughout Rwanda that help us recruit students and we have refined our relationship with them so that everyone is on the same page about the goals that GR is working to achieve – and the roles that the partner organizations play in making the achievement of those goals possible.

Our experiences taught us to look for students and partners that share our values rather than pressuring people to work with us. We will not hand out our scholarships to just anyone who will accept them. Instead, our vision now is to find students and local organizations that both see the world as we do and can benefit from our help. After adopting this approach with partners, we have found great organizations that are excited to work with us in finding vulnerable students that would thrive in our program and in university. The chief executive of one of our key partners recently said that because of his passion for education, he considers it his 'duty' to work alongside us. Similarly, we are now selecting students who fully understand what it means to attend university and to be a GR scholar – and who are thrilled to accept these responsibilities (which are codified in a 'Student Contract' that all newly accepted scholars sign during the 10-week orientation program designed and administered by GR).

CONCLUSION

At GR, we believe we have found a way to leverage relatively modest resources to have a large impact not only on the students we support, but also on the country of Rwanda as a whole. We have done this not by planning in offices in the U.S., and not by consulting large organizations, but rather by talking and listening to the youth of Rwanda. If GR is an entrepreneurial venture, then students are our customers. They guide our programs, they let us know when we make mistakes, and, perhaps most importantly, they inspire us to work harder. And they – like the GoR and our partner organizations – are genuinely our colleagues in this endeavor. 'We are the young and we are many,' said one of our students, 'and we believe we can change Rwanda.'

NOTES

1. We use the term 'vulnerable children' broadly to refer to young people living in dire socioeconomic circumstances (even as compared with other poor individuals in Rwanda), whether their misfortune is purely economic or attributable to other challenging circumstances such as poor health, living situation, or social status.
2. For background information on the 1994 Rwandan genocide, see Chapter 4.
3. UNESCO INST. FOR STATISTICS, UIS STATISTICS IN BRIEF: EDUCATION (ALL LEVELS) PROFILE –

RWANDA (2009), *available at* http://stats.uis.unesco.org/unesco/TableViewer/document.aspx?ReportId=121&IF_Language=eng&BR_Country=6460&BR_Region=40540.

4. Gérard Lassibille & Jee-Peng Tan, *The Returns to Education in Rwanda*, 14 J. AFR. ECONOMIES 92, 94 (2005).

5. REPUBLIC OF RWANDA, MINISTRY OF FIN. & ECON. PLANNING: NAT'L POVERTY REDUCTION PROGRAMME, THE GOVERNMENT OF RWANDA POVERTY REDUCTION STRATEGY PAPER 23 (2002), *available at* http://www.imf.org/external/np/prsp/2002/rwa/01/ [hereinafter RWANDA NAT'L POVERTY REDUCTION PROGRAMME].

6. USAID, STRATEGIC REVIEW: FEED THE FUTURE (2010), *available at* http://www.feedthe future.gov/documents/RwandaFTFStrategicReview.pdf.

7. WORLD HEALTH ORG., COUNTRY PROFILE: RWANDA, http://www.who.int/countries/rwa/en/ (last visited Nov. 17, 2011).

8. CENT. INTELLIGENCE AGENCY, THE WORLD FACTBOOK: RWANDA, https://www.cia.gov/library/publications/the-world-factbook/geos/rw.html (last visited Nov. 17, 2011).

9. REPUBLIC OF RWANDA, MINISTRY OF FIN. & ECON. PLANNING: RWANDA VISION 2020 (2000), *available at* http://www.minecofin.gov.rw/ministry/key/vision2020.

10. DEVESH KAPUR & MEGAN CROWLEY, BEYOND THE ABCS: HIGHER EDUCATION AND DEVELOPING COUNTRIES 10 (2008), *available at* http://www.cgdev.org/content/publications/detail/15310/.

11. REPUBLIC OF RWANDA, NAT'L INST. OF STATISTICS OF RWANDA, MILLENNIUM DEVELOPMENT GOALS: TOWARDS SUSTAINABLE SOCIAL AND ECONOMIC GROWTH 22 (2007), *available at* http://statistics.gov.rw/images/PDF/MDGs%20final%20report%20Rwanda%20.pdf.

12. World Bank, Rwanda: Data and Statistics, http://go.worldbank.org/QLUDIRQB30 (last visited Nov. 17, 2011) [hereinafter World Bank Rwanda Data].

13. KAPUR & CROWLEY, *supra* note 10, at 10.

14. DAVID BLOOM, DAVID CANNING & KEVIN CHAN, HIGHER EDUCATION AND ECONOMIC DEVELOPMENT IN AFRICA 1 (2006), *available at* http://siteresources.worldbank.org/INTAFRREGTOPTEIA/Resources/Higher_Education_Econ_Dev.pdf.

15. *Id.*

16. Lassibille & Tan, *supra* note 4, at 106.

17. RWANDA NAT'L POVERTY REDUCTION PROGRAMME, *supra* note 5, at 48.

18. World Bank Rwanda Data, *supra* note 12.

19. Phillipe Aghion, Eve Caroli & Ceceilia Garcia-Penalosa, *Inequality and Economic Growth: The Perspective of the New Growth Theories*, 37 J. ECON. LITERATURE 1615, 1617–18 (1999).

20. For more information about IA, see Chapter 5.

21. Idealist.org is a website that features volunteer opportunities, non-profit jobs, internships, and organizations working to promote positive change in the world. For the official website of Idealist.org, see http://www.idealist.org/.

22. WILLIAM EASTERLY, THE WHITE MAN'S BURDEN 12 (2006).

7. Providing access to education for children orphaned or made vulnerable by HIV/AIDS: Orphans Against AIDS

Scott Grinsell and Andrew Klaber

INTRODUCTION

Background

HIV/AIDS[1] remains one of our generation's most widespread killers and most pressing public health concerns. The epidemic has tragically undermined individuals' familial and economic security throughout the world, especially in developing and post-conflict nations. Children are often most adversely affected by the disease, leaving them faced with a multitude of challenges. According to the UNAIDS/World Health Organization's 2010 Report on the Global AIDS Epidemic, by the end of 2009, HIV/AIDS victims had left behind as many as 18.8 million 'AIDS orphans.'[2] As many as 17 million children under 18 years of age have been orphaned by HIV/AIDS in sub-Saharan Africa alone[3] – a number larger than the entire population of Greece – and this figure is expected to rise in the coming years.[4] Children who live in households affected by the HIV/AIDS epidemic face challenges regardless of whether they are orphans. Young people whose parents are living with AIDS have increased vulnerability because a parent's illness often leads to a loss of family income, high medical expenses, and social stigma. Experiencing the death of a parent or guardian has significant consequences for a child, and this is all the more serious when such a person dies of AIDS due to the very nature of the disease. For example, a parent may transmit the virus to another parent unknowingly. The incapacitation or loss of one or both parents results in the family's loss of parental wages. Moreover, social ostracism and the 'wasting syndrome'[5] that accompany the epidemic have a particularly acute effect on children. A common result of these factors is reduced school attendance among orphans and vulnerable children (OVCs). Leaving school in order to care and earn money for ill parents and dependent siblings means sacrificing long-term potential for short-term needs. The child misses out on developing essential reading, writing, and math skills; she loses the opportunity for support from teachers and socialization among peers; and she often forfeits economic earning potential and self-esteem. Even if the child does remain in school, she may have trouble being accepted by peers and, as a result of the myriad distractions at home, harnessing the requisite concentration and study time to succeed academically. Moreover, those OVCs living with extended families or in foster care are prone to institutional and informal discrimination, including limited access to education, healthcare, and social services. Unfortunately, in too many communities, a misperception exists that OVCs are prone to spreading HIV/AIDS. In places where myths about the epidemic remain, many people falsely believe that the disease can be transmitted through casual contact at home, at school, or in the community.

While not a silver-bullet solution, education can help combat the epidemic's vicious cycle. As Donald Bundy, coordinator of the World Bank's Education and AIDS program, has observed: 'Education is the best vaccine that we have available at this time.'[6] We believe it is possible to leverage the important tool of education to promote OVC's improved self-esteem, employment opportunities, and health.[7]

Orphans Against AIDS

Orphans Against AIDS (OAA) was founded on the belief that providing educational funding to OVCs is one of the most sustainable and effective ways to combat HIV/AIDS. OAA partners with local organizations in the developing world to provide OVCs with educational funding and to cover these youths' healthcare and nutritional expenses. Additionally, OAA works with local partner organizations based in several countries throughout the world to develop their capacities for more effective and expansive operations, including advice on issues of governance or strategy, and helps with the implementation of new technologies such as improved websites. By working with its local partners, OAA helps them attract grants and donations from larger aid organizations, resulting in greater scale, impact, and a more diverse funding base.[8]

With OAA's support, each local partner organization selects the most vulnerable students to receive funding, oversees the program on the ground, and works with schools, physicians, community leaders, and families to monitor students' progress. The local partner organizations communicate regularly with OAA and provide its officers and directors with a current assessment of the participating children's psychosocial, physical, and educational well-being; an itemized budget of expenditures; and an analysis of available and needed finances. Last, OAA strives to be an incubator for young social entrepreneurs, affording its all-volunteer corps a first-hand development experience at an early age with the hope that these leaders will use their knowledge to empower underserved communities throughout their private, public, or non-profit careers.

OAA closely tracks its own progress and impact to ensure that funds are being used as effectively as possible. Of the 600 children whom OAA has sponsored over the last eight years, 98 percent have completed or are still in school.[9] In the past eight years OAA has raised over US$1 million from institutions like the Goldman Sachs Foundation, the Pfizer Foundation, the Medtronic Foundation, Google, Rotary International, the Magdalen College Trust and New College of the University of Oxford, as well as thousands of grassroots donors such as elementary schools, parent-teacher associations, and individuals.[10]

While we trust our in-country partners to develop informed selection criteria and operational procedures that best suit their specific communities, we do request that they follow certain guidelines. OAA requires that its local partners not select children who are simultaneously receiving support from the government or other NGOs when there are OVCs who are not receiving such assistance, and OAA mandates that its local partners not discriminate against female children in deciding who should receive funding. Following the best-practice of other NGOs that work with OVCs,[11] we ask our partners to assess the needs of all vulnerable children – not only those orphaned by AIDS – in determining those youths who should receive OAA support. We require our local partner organizations to maintain thorough records and provide us with receipts for expenditures. Furthermore, in assessing the academic progress and well-being of each sponsored youth, we rely on our local partners to determine when a student is in particular need of individualized attention or support.

Since OAA's founding in 2002, the majority of our efforts have been aimed at establishing new projects and developing our fundraising base. In the following part, we focus on the development of our organizational structure. A non-profit organization is an ever-evolving, organic entity. We will discuss how and why OAA decided to change its governance and work in several additional countries instead of focusing on one particular location. The story of OAA's growth from an organization with its sole operations in Chiang Mai, Thailand, to a venture with projects in multiple African countries is worth recounting; we hope that OAA's successes and failures can help guide other social entrepreneurs who are interested in founding an organization or extending the reach of an existing institution.

GROWING FROM ONE PROJECT TO SEVERAL

Founding a New Organization

Andrew Klaber had recently completed his sophomore year as an undergraduate at Yale University when he traveled to Chiang Mai during the summer of 2002. Like many who visit the developing world for the first time, he was deeply affected by the poverty he saw. In particular, he was struck by the impact of HIV/AIDS in the places he visited. While Klaber had read books about and seen pictures documenting the scope of the epidemic, he was less familiar with the effects of the disease on the victims' children. Many of these youths roamed the streets begging during school hours. Others stayed at home, afraid of the way their peers would treat them in class. Pre-teenage and teenage girls sold their bodies near the nighttime 'bazaar' to aid their families' financial predicament.

Klaber had learned about AIDS in Southeast Asia through his college coursework, but these studies mostly focused on those infected with HIV/AIDS, not the myriad ways in which the epidemic affects whole communities – especially children of HIV/AIDS victims – throughout the developing world. For Klaber, the full reach of the disease only became apparent once he traveled abroad. Statistics were merely numbers from the comforts of a university classroom. The scenes he saw in person were far more vivid and deeply affecting.

In Chiang Mai, large numbers of young children labor as sex workers on the streets in and around the nighttime bazaar. Klaber learned from many conversations with community members that these children were predominantly orphans who had become active in the sex trade after their parents had become sick or died as a result of HIV/AIDS. Since these children could earn up to 20 times more money from prostitution than they could by working in agriculture, the economic incentives could be almost coercive, especially given their ill parents' lost income, medication costs, and the needs of their siblings. These children were in some ways the forgotten victims of the epidemic – still largely absent at that time from popular Western media.[12] The story of these young girls and boys personifies the tragic cycle of HIV/AIDS – a phenomenon by which children whose parents died from the epidemic are more likely to contract the disease themselves.

Unable to forget the powerful Chiang Mai images involving these youths, Klaber used his recollections as motivation to consider what he, a young person, could do to make a difference in the places he visited. The idea that led Klaber to found a non-profit organization was in some ways very simple. Klaber concluded that by substantially lowering the personal expense of these children's education – subsidizing the cost of school fees, school uniforms, school supplies, transportation to and from school, school lunches, books, and basic health care – he could have a meaningful positive impact in the Chiang Mai community. Klaber recognized that the economic incentives in Chiang Mai had to be realigned, which would only be effective if OAA's educational support was comprehensive and focused on those youths who were most in need. Because Klaber would be returning to the United States at the end of the summer, he had to identify responsible local partners: physicians, business owners, school principals, and other local leaders who understood community norms and needs and had earned the trust of neighbors. While a larger organization with more resources might have elected to establish an on-the-ground presence in Chiang Mai immediately, Klaber thought, given his resources, it made the most sense to work to identify partners who had greater knowledge and contacts than he could amass in a single summer. In addition, the question of how Klaber would convince local community leaders to take him seriously – given that he had not yet raised any money nor spoke the Thai language – added another layer of difficulty.

A fortunate coincidence occurred when Klaber was walking the streets of Chiang Mai in late-June and saw a sign for a Fourth of July celebration at the United States Consulate.[13] The sign mentioned that a Yale *a cappella* group, the Whiffenpoofs, would be performing at the event. When he showed up at the Consulate on America's Independence Day, Klaber learned that the Consul General (the individual who is the head of the consulate) at the time was an alumnus of Klaber's home university, Yale, and was intrigued by the idea of creating a program to fund the academic, nutritional, and basic healthcare costs of local OVCs.[14] The Consul General graciously offered his contacts within the Chiang Mai government and non-profit, educational, medical, and business communities. He also arranged for meetings between Klaber and stakeholders from these communities to be held at the U.S. Consulate, affording Klaber much-needed credibility in his still nascent endeavor. The Consul General's generosity facilitated Klaber's access to community leaders and a wider set of contacts and lent more credibility than he would have had on his own.

The more local people with whom Klaber interacted and learned from, the clearer it became that providing educational support for children who had been orphaned or made vulnerable by HIV/AIDS would offer them a number of the tools necessary to avoid contracting the disease themselves. Everyone in the community in Chiang Mai seemed to agree that there was commonsense logic to the idea of providing these children with access to education, nutrition, and basic health care. Klaber became increasingly invested in the idea that a small non-profit organization could make a concrete difference in the lives of these children. Furthermore, Klaber learned that there was a stark supply-demand imbalance for such a scholarship scheme; little was being done to address the educational aspirations of OVCs considering the large number of these youths in the area.[15] By the end of the summer, Klaber had identified local partners and community leaders – primarily the Chiang Mai Sarapee Rotary Club – and estimated the cost to support each child.

The relatively small expense to send a child to school in Chiang Mai (US$100–US$150 a year in 2002) meant that Klaber and other college students could likely raise funds sufficient to have real impact. This was an exciting discovery for Klaber, because these figures put a significant social impact within reach of himself and other young people. He came to realize that relatively modest fundraising efforts and savings from summer jobs could make a crucial difference in these children's lives. Although Klaber was unsure how much money he could raise for these youths, he concluded that, even if the financial support was relatively limited and would therefore only impact a few children, the effect on each child's life would be truly significant, and so was worth the effort. Additionally, the sums of money to help each student were sufficiently small that there was likely a large pool of potential donors at home who could afford to contribute.

Upon returning to college for the start of his junior year, Klaber began the process of formally creating a new non-profit organization. First, he attended to the legal formalities. This involved filing incorporation papers with the government of the U.S. state in which an organization is to be located and 501(c)(3) forms with the Internal Revenue Service.[16] He learned from the umbrella community service and social justice organization at his university that the Yale Law School Nonprofit Organizations Clinic had incorporated and gained 501(c)(3) tax-exempt status for other non-profit organizations on a *pro bono* basis in the past.[17]

Next, Klaber began looking for potential partners at home who might be willing and able to help him with fundraising. He reached out to the headquarters of Rotary International in Evanston, Illinois, and requested contact information for individual Rotary clubs in the United States that might have a particular interest in issues related to HIV/AIDS or Thailand. Klaber, who had grown up near Evanston, in Buffalo Grove, knew of Rotary's generous matching grant program from high school community service activities. If Klaber could find a Rotary Club in the United States to partner with the Chiang Mai Sarapee Rotary Club, then a donation made by the U.S.-based club would be eligible for a matching grant by the District Rotary club (a confederation of Rotary clubs in the area); this doubled amount would in turn be eligible for a matching donation from Rotary International itself.[18] Klaber decided that pursuing this plan would be OAA's first strategic fundraising initiative since there was a strong possibility that any money raised at the individual Rotary club level would be quadrupled. Klaber spoke with a Rotary International official who covered projects located in southeast Asia, and learned of a Rotary club in Westport, Connecticut – another fortunate coincidence since Klaber's university was located in nearby New Haven, Connecticut – whose president had been a physician for many years in Thailand. Klaber arranged a meeting with the president of the Westport Rotary Club and subsequently made a presentation to the club. The Westport Rotary Club agreed to donate US$6,000, which quickly became US$24,000 after the Rotary District-level and Rotary International-level matching grant processes – enough funding to support 200 Chiang Mai OVCs for an entire year. Empowered by his experience with Rotary, Klaber leveraged a scholarship that he received during his sophomore year from Goldman Sachs to obtain a US$6,000 Social Entrepreneurship Fund grant from the company's Foundation.[19] Within its first year of existence, OAA had developed a growing fundraising base and was providing educational support for 250 OVCs in Chiang Mai.

From the outset, Klaber also sought to form collaborative partnerships between OAA and other international NGOs that either helped vulnerable children or worked to combat the HIV/AIDS epidemic. Through these partnerships, Klaber hoped to augment the scope of OAA's work in Chiang Mai while simultaneously building the organization's impact and reputation. The first partnership that OAA formed was with the Association of Hole in the Wall Gang Camps, founded by the actor and philanthropist Paul Newman.[20] By working with the Hole in the Wall Camps, OAA was able to coordinate week-long camp experiences for 50 children in Chiang Mai. OAA also partnered with Unite For Sight,[21] which had been founded by Jennifer Staple-Clark – Klaber's college friend – to provide vision screenings and eyeglasses for OVCs in Chiang Mai in July 2004.

These partnerships were an important resource in building the scope of services, impact, and reputation of OAA both within the Chiang Mai community and abroad as OAA grew during its first two years. Both Hole in the Wall and Unite For Sight have provided informal advice on new projects and, by working with OAA on projects, have lent OAA credibility with other international NGOs. Unite For Sight in particular became an important source of recommendations for potential local partners.

Adding New Officers and Establishing New Projects

During its first two years, OAA aimed to improve the lives of AIDS orphans and other vulnerable children in Chiang Mai and to strengthen the local community against the HIV/AIDS epidemic. Klaber ran the organization at this time with a number of friends from college but did most of the administrative work himself. The structure of the organization was essentially hierarchical: Klaber acted as president and a few other officers took on particular duties, such as grant writing.

Between 2004 and 2008, OAA's operations expanded to include five additional countries: Ghana, Kenya, Sierra Leone, South Africa, and Uganda. This period was the most significant in OAA's growth. We later reduced the number of programs that we fund to only three: Kenya, South Africa, and Uganda, in order to focus on the most successful projects that we believe we could scale over time.

OAA's governance structure changed considerably in this second phase of growth. The addition of projects was a result of the involvement of new officers who had interests and backgrounds in regions other than Asia. Some projects were discontinued because they proved for various reasons to be less viable than others. We also added three new officers and substantially changed the way that OAA raises and distributes money.

OAA evolved into a different organization. A key reason for OAA's rapid growth in this second phase of its development was the involvement of a different set of volunteers. When Klaber graduated from college, he went to Oxford University to pursue graduate studies in economics and finance. There he made four friends who came to comprise OAA's current leadership: Scott Grinsell, John Harabedian, and, until 2010 and 2011, respectively, Adam Grogg and Robert Schiff. They were impressed by the straightforwardness of the concept behind Klaber's organization and the work he had accomplished. Klaber's new friends asked how they could get involved, and Klaber saw a tremendous opportunity for the long-term prospects of OAA by having them participate. As they worked together, their friendships grew stronger, and the group began to reexamine the organization's structure and geographic focus.

Once Klaber and the new volunteer officers decided to expand the size of OAA, they needed to decide how to best utilize their resources. Klaber was particularly interested in maintaining the entrepreneurial model that had characterized OAA's first two years. His positive experience starting the organization motivated him to remain engaged in his work. He proposed the idea of a flat organizational structure in which each member of the organization would work on a project in a different country while he continued his work in Thailand. At first, it seemed strange to some of the new officers to decide to take this approach rather than to focus on building the project in Thailand because none of the new officers had firsthand experience running a non-profit organization in the developing world. OAA had stayed nimble in its first two years by operating in a single country. Additionally, few U.S.-based volunteers had been involved with the organization up to this point. Klaber wondered how increasing the scope of OAA's leadership might affect the institution's mission and outcomes.

Had OAA elected to grow vertically – by only remaining in Thailand and adding officers with subsidiary responsibility – a great deal of the agenda would have been set from the top and individual members of the organization would have needed to concentrate on one particular task, such as grant writing, fundraising, or advocacy within the context of this southeast Asian country. However, with such a structure, it can be difficult to create incentives for people to remain involved over time. The opportunity to work together with friends was one incentive, but it was not clear that this would be sufficient to motivate over the long term. The four new officers realized that part of Klaber's motivation was his ability to create something on his own, and they felt that independence would be an important source of motivation for the other officers as well.

The emerging group of officers elected to pursue a somewhat novel approach: while we would continue to operate our project in Thailand, OAA would invite these four new officers to join the organization as Project Directors with responsibility for a country or region of his or her choice. OAA's leadership relied on the small size of the group and its pre-existing friendship to ensure that each new officer would uphold his responsibility. This approach seemed best suited to ensuring that OAA would preserve the entrepreneurial spirit that had allowed Klaber to build OAA quickly into a fully functioning organization and would also give each new member of the organization the chance to pursue his or her own interests.

The decision to add projects proved to be a critical moment in OAA's growth. There were advantages to having several projects in different countries. First, multiple projects would help ensure that each officer could become a Project Director and would remain involved with his or her work by feeling genuinely, and directly, engaged in the political, economic, and social context of a given country. Importantly, not everyone shared Klaber's experience in Thailand, and some of the officers were more interested in working in different countries or regions. Since everyone was a volunteer, it made sense to give the officers freedom to follow their own interests. By working with partners in different countries, OAA as a whole would also be able to learn general lessons and best practices about the provision of funding to OVCs by drawing comparisons across contexts and gaining synergies from implementing successful programming initiatives in one location elsewhere. Moreover, OAA theorized that there would be some symbolic value to having projects in different countries. Insofar as OAA aims to contribute to the general public's understanding of the epidemic, OAA predicted that having projects in different countries would help to convey a stark statement about the global reach of HIV/AIDS. Another important benefit, which OAA subsequently made part of its stated mission, was that the expansion afforded new members of the organization the first-hand chance to learn about international development work by building a new project from the ground up.

OAA's new projects – in Ghana, Kenya, Sierra Leone, South Africa, and Uganda – took shape in a variety of different ways. Some were the result of connections Klaber had made with NGOs, while others were the product of new members' particular passions. The history behind the Uganda project is illustrative of OAA's expansion and the strengths of its model. Under the leadership of Grinsell and Schiff, the processes of securing a partnership with a Ugandan organization and developing OAA's relationship with it provide examples of the way in which we have grown as an organization. Close friends since high school, Grinsell and Schiff reconnected at Oxford, where both were studying for master's degrees. They met Klaber and appreciated what he had accomplished with OAA. They separately approached Klaber about becoming involved. While they were originally planning to work on their own projects, they ultimately agreed to team up and focus their efforts on Uganda, where Klaber had contacted a local NGO seeking assistance.

In December 2005, Schiff and Grinsell traveled to Uganda with the goal of establishing an OAA project there. Meanwhile, Grogg, Harabedian, and Klaber were traveling elsewhere in sub-Saharan Africa, visiting OAA's three other new South Africa projects and performing due diligence (i.e., researching governance structure and financial records) on potential local partners in Kenya. Grinsell and Schiff initially planned to concentrate their efforts on a local organization that worked primarily in the conflict areas of northern Uganda and that had focused on the rehabilitation of orphans who had become child soldiers. Staple-Clark had provided Klaber with a very positive recommendation of this organization. As Staple-Clark and Klaber started their nonprofit organizations around the same time, they often exchanged emails about pertinent issues and opportunities that they came across. In particular, when Staple-Clark and her volunteers would travel to a community to conduct free vision examinations and distribute complementary eyewear to those who needed it, they sometimes found OVCs who had the support of community leaders, educators, and physicians, but lacked the monetary resources to obtain a decent primary and secondary school education. Staple-Clark would contact Klaber to share these potential opportunities and Klaber would initiate a dialogue with these local stakeholders, assessing the number of OVCs and learning about the holistic needs and characteristics of the community. Klaber forwarded to Schiff and Grinsell one such dialogue that he was having with a Ugandan organization. Schiff had spent much of the summer communicating with this organization's officers and talking to other organizations, such as the Jewish World Service, which had previously worked with the Ugandan organization. Although Schiff and Grinsell were impressed by the northern Ugandan organization's work, the materials that its officers sent strongly emphasized its operations with children who had been orphaned by the horrific violence of the domestic war. A number of the directors of this Ugandan organization were former child soldiers who were interested in providing opportunities for and assisting in the rehabilitation of young people who had suffered a similar set of challenges.

While this organization was a potential partner (because it was involved in some HIV/AIDS work), Schiff and Grinsell eventually concluded that its primary focus was on the war and not on issues related to the epidemic. Given that OAA's explicit focus is on providing educational access, nutrition, and basic health care to youngsters who have been orphaned or made vulnerable by AIDS, OAA decided to forego a partnership with this northern Ugandan organization. Although the two issues of the war and HIV/AIDS are deeply intertwined in northern Uganda (rape, which is a frequent vehicle for transmitting HIV/AIDS, is among the atrocities frequently perpetrated on adults and children in the Internally Displaced Persons camps), given that OAA was a young organization and that its officers were still learning about international development, Schiff and Grinsell decided that it was more prudent for OAA to look for a partner whose mission was more narrowly focused on HIV/AIDS instead of the war more broadly.[22]

While in Uganda, Grinsell and Schiff also met with Friends in Need Integrated Development Project (FINIDP) on the recommendation of a graduate school classmate and friend, Michael Lamb, who had spent the previous summer working with the organization. Grinsell and Schiff met with Zziwa Ahmed, Bukenya Mohamed, and other members of FINIDP's leadership and spent a day examining several of their projects in the Mukono district, a rural area north of Kampala, Uganda's capital. FINIDP employs an integrated approach to development by running simultaneous projects that work in complementary ways, including on environmental sustainability, income generation, HIV/AIDS education, and the distribution of funding for the education of AIDS orphans and other vulnerable children. From meeting with leaders in the communities where Ahmed and Mohamed both work and from talking to them about the focus of their organization, it was clear that one of the more pressing problems in Mukono was the spread of HIV/AIDS. Second, both for FINIDP and for the community leaders, the provision of funds for orphan education was a very important goal. When Grinsell and Schiff asked open-ended questions about the area of greatest need in these communities, the need for funding for education (and for the education of AIDS orphans, in particular) was the most common answer. FINIDP had a genuine interest in establishing a project that would provide education to OVCs and this organization had the backing of the community's leaders since there was a desperate need for a program such as this in the area.

In addition to the good match of FINIDP's substantive work and local need with OAA's mission, the organization itself seemed well suited for a partnership with OAA. FINIDP was a small organization that operated on an annual budget of roughly US$5,000, but it seemed to have the capacity for significant growth. Both Ahmed and Mohamed were faculty members in the Department of Forestry at Makerere University in Kampala and both currently operate FINIDP on a voluntary basis in their spare time. Their written materials and financial records were detailed and sophisticated. It was clear that FINIDP had the capacity to effectively deploy significantly more funding than it had been able to obtain previously.

Grinsell and Schiff felt that OAA could help FINIDP reach its potential. They envisioned partnering with Ahmed and Mohamed over several years and working to build FINIDP's infrastructure, both by providing FINIDP with funding and by offering consultative support. Moreover, Grinsell and Schiff had a strong recommendation from a trusted friend that Ahmed and Mohamed would be reliable partners. After several long conversations about FINIDP's plans for the future and the needs of the communities where it operates, Grinsell and Schiff proposed that OAA form a partnership with FINIDP to establish a program for the education of OVCs in Uganda.

Upon returning to Oxford, OAA worked with FINIDP to develop a project agreement and, after both sides assented to its terms, OAA made its first transfer of funds to support 12 OVCs in Mukono. The program has been in place since 2006 and the number of OVCs supported has doubled. It is our hope that the FINIDP-OAA relationship will continue successfully for many years.

Adjusting to a New Structure and Managing Growth

As OAA's operations expanded from 2004 to 2007, we were surprised by how often our group discussions turned to questions about the governance structure of our organization. We began to realize that the partnership model we had chosen brought both benefits and unexpected challenges. The first and most pressing challenge involved the distribution of funds among the different projects. In the past, Klaber had raised all of the OAA donations and 100 percent of these resources went to the project in Chiang Mai. We now had several projects and were raising money both for these projects and for OAA as an umbrella organization, under which these projects functioned. In addition, it was not clear how much time each individual Project Director should spend raising funds for the general pool or even whether there should be a general pool at all. Should the common pool of funding be distributed to all projects equally, or according to need? If the latter, to what extent would we create problematic incentives? If we were to treat the common pool like an insurance fund to cover shortfalls in the event that a Project Director was unable to raise sufficient donations in a given year, would this affect the relationships among the partners in ways that might create resentment or otherwise harm the future of the organization?

Another challenge presented by the non-hierarchical partnership model was delegating OAA's increasing, collective organizational needs. In the past, Klaber had divided his time between, on the one hand, organizational and administrative tasks such as managing finances and the website, writing grants, and approaching large donors, and, on the other hand, operating the Thailand project. As OAA grew it became more difficult for one person to do all of this. Responsibility for OAA had to be delegated to a greater extent, and so a new organizational structure was necessary.

At the same time as we considered the division of duties, questions about how to distribute funds among the different projects still lingered. We suspected that applying only for individual projects on behalf of all of OAA would make it difficult to take advantage of each country project in our fundraising. Focusing on the organization as a whole would limit our ability to contact individuals or foundations with an interest in a particular country and tell the story of each project on its own. Indeed, our decision to work in many different countries proved to be an advantage with donors who were sometimes more interested in a particular country or region. At the same time, we would have to spend considerable effort coordinating our fundraising (so that individual projects would not apply to the same donor and compete for support); additionally, raising funds for each of the projects individually meant that we would not be able to devote as much time to developing programming or to the counseling side of our local partnerships – two initiatives that had become increasingly central to our mission. These questions led to many late-night conversations.

Establishing a Partnership Model

We discussed various ways of proceeding, including dividing OAA into multiple organizations or remaining with a hierarchical model. Neither of these positions seemed satisfactory. We eventually decided to continue OAA's operations as a loose federation of projects that would be governed by the existing group of officers. We opted for a 'partnership model' based roughly on the structure behind a law firm in which all of the partners contribute to a central pool of funds, work together to make important organizational decisions (and arrive at decisions on all important matters by consensus), and determine how central money should be divided. As in a law firm, some of the funds would be raised individually and some would be raised collectively. The funds would not be distributed simply on a performance basis, since we hoped that partners would continue to apply for some large grants on behalf of the whole organization when it was appropriate. At the same time, the consensus system would help to ensure that a partner's fundraising efforts for the whole organization would be reflected in the final share of the general pool that he or she received for his or her project. Partners, therefore, would raise some funds specifically for their projects, and others for the whole organization, but the distribution of the general funds would be the basis of the final deliberation of the partnership and in a way that responded to the needs, and potential, of individual projects.

At the core of this system is a consensus process in which all of the partners must agree on major decisions involving fundraising and the distribution of funds, organizational questions, and the establishment of new projects. Partners not involved in a particular project can also elect to abstain from making a decision about a project question. We decided that this structure would ensure that all of the partners were well informed about the operations of all projects and that this scheme would help to create an atmosphere of accountability for each Project Director. We also thought that this system would allow us flexibility to grow over time by adding new projects only when the whole partnership felt that it was financially prudent and in line with our mission. The partners could also eventually decide to abandon the partnership altogether or dramatically reduce its role, for example, by giving more authority to an executive director if appropriate. The partnership model gave us flexibility to evolve over time and to expand our operations in areas like fundraising. The partnership model has helped to spread responsibility and offer leadership opportunities to a larger number of people in the organization.

OAA has been operating with this new system since 2006, and the partners agree that it has largely been a success. Although the partnership model requires a relatively high volume of communication, it has not proven overly burdensome. Our governance structure has made us more aware of other projects so that we are able to collaborate effectively. That each officer has a say in how funds are spent seems to have heightened engagement and dedication to the organization as a whole. The energy that we gain by working together on these projects has proven to be an extremely valuable benefit of the new model.

REACTING TO GROWTH AND FINDING NEW FOCUS

From 2006 to 2009, we continued raising funds for the partner organizations and Klaber maintained his administrative role. The partnership, in that sense, constituted the core of our managerial structure. As we settled into this new pattern we made two key changes. First, we elected to decrease the amount of our in-country partners so that we could focus on those organizations with sustained impact and the greatest potential for future growth. Second, we decided to create a Board of Directors to provide a further level of strategic and governance oversight and to increase our fundraising capacity.[23] Specifically, OAA, with the advice of the Board of Directors, ultimately decided to reduce the number of countries in which it operates to three – Kenya, South Africa, and Uganda – since the lion's share of the children OAA now supports are located in these nations.

The partners were by now dispersed in different geographic locations in the U.S. Some went to law school or law and business school, and one took a job in management consulting. Over time, our personal and professional responsibilities grew, and we were no longer within a short bicycle ride or walk from one another. Occasional conference calls came to supplant the more sustained work we did during graduate school.

During this third period of OAA's development, it became clear that some of the projects we had established were not working as well as others. In some cases, we did not have adequate contact with a Project Director, and in other cases the in-country partner failed to maintain the level of email and phone contact with which we felt comfortable. The partners had numerous conversations about how to address these challenges. One possibility was traveling to each country to meet with the local partners. In these cases, we ultimately felt that it was best to discontinue projects that were not working and to focus on those that were. We also wanted to focus our efforts on those organizations for which we had made multi-year commitments and where children were counting on our year-to-year contributions for their school fees.

These were difficult decisions. In hindsight, they reflect both our eagerness to expand our programming and also the difficulties inherent in vetting partners that are very far away. These experiences led us to consolidate our work in ways that increased our impact. We learned what to look for in potential partners, which are the same things we came to value in our current partners: strong communication skills, attention to financial and organizational detail, and sound recordkeeping. Adding some of these projects was in some ways an overreach, and we would caution other non-profit organizations that adopt a model similar to ours to be even more careful in managing growth. Nonetheless, part of taking risk – even well-managed risk – is the possibility that some projects will do less well than others. In this vein, our project approach, which at one point involved eight projects in six countries, is similar to a social enterprise model. OAA works to support ambitious young social entrepreneurs who are passionate about the AIDS orphans crisis and, while not every project works out, those that do have been quite successful. Cutting the projects that were not working – while often emotionally difficult – proved to be an important step to allow us to focus on those partnerships that were the most reliable and that had the greatest impact.

Turning away potential in-country partners was especially hard in the context of the tremendous demand for academic scholarships, nutrition, and basic health care in communities ravaged by HIV/AIDS. There is an art to saying no. The importance of managed and cautious growth is something that we encourage other organizations to learn – and practice – early in their development.

The other major change to the structure of our organization was our decision to create a Board of Directors, in order to provide strategic and governance advice, oversight, and to increase our fundraising capacity. We could have decided to create a Board earlier in our growth, but we felt initially that the partnership structure alone was a sufficiently complex structure to manage. If a non-profit organization is not adequately prepared for volunteer or paid employee growth, adding more people to the organization can feel like more

of a managerial distraction than an asset. When OAA was a very small organization, and when each of us had more time, we could handle more of OAA's
work on our own. As we have grown, OAA tasks have been delegated to a far
greater extent between the volunteer partners, volunteer project managers, and
volunteer Board of Directors.

As we settled into our work as an organization, however, we began to see
the great value of having a Board. In addition, as each of us began careers, it
proved to be increasingly difficult to devote adequate time to fundraising and
strategic and governance counseling. Creating a Board allowed us to take
advantage of a much wider array of professional experiences than we had as a
small group and gave us access to an energetic group of young people who
could spread awareness of our work and assist in providing advice and
fundraising. We recruited the Board from our professional and personal
contacts, and we were fortunate that such an impressive group of individuals
decided to join us. The group is drawn from management consulting firms,
government, law firms, hedge funds and private equity firms, and graduate
programs and fellowships in law, public policy, and medicine.

The range of perspectives and experiences this group brings to our Board
meetings, held twice a year, has helped to redirect our strategic focus on the
programs that have been most successful. The Board has alerted us to new
fundraising opportunities and deepened our understanding of the issues
surrounding the AIDS orphan crisis.

Other volunteers, not directly involved in the Board, have been an immense
help as well. In one exceptional case, for instance, two friends of Grinsell's,
Mark and Meredith Wallace, spent nine days working with FINIDP in Uganda
and performing much needed due diligence on our operations there. The
Wallaces have since joined Grinsell as co-Project Directors for Uganda when
Schiff departed in 2011 as a result of increasing professional commitments.
Countless other volunteers have helped with our fundraisers and have
contacted individual donors on our behalf.

Thus, OAA today benefits from a deeply engaged Board, a wider community of volunteers and supporters, and a tightly knit group of partners who face
increasing demands on their professional and personal lives. The partnership
now must decide whether the current model is sustainable over time, especially as OAA continues to increase its fundraising capacity. For now, at least,
we believe that maintaining the partnership is the best course.

REFLECTIONS AND LESSONS

While our approach and structure are somewhat unusual, the issues we have
faced overlap to some extent with those many other non-profit organizations

encounter that begin as a small solution to a recognized problem and then grow over time into a more expansive form. Non-profit organizations are often the product of a personal experience, a chance meeting, a trip to a far off land, or a deep-rooted connection to a place. In our case, a new level of growth resulted from friendships that brought new people into the organization and an interest in one of the great public health issues of our day.

Many non-profit ventures depend upon the enthusiasm and dedication of their members to remain involved, and where their roles are necessarily limited, and their potential for innovation and impact is focused on a specific function, some members may lose motivation over time. An individual founder may provide the initial insight and follow through with early efforts of building a new venture, but in order for an organization to continue to have increasing and sustainable impact, the efforts of many people are necessary. For a group of people that is self-motivated and that is attracted to the idea of creating something new on their own, a decentralized model like the one OAA has used can provide helpful motivation by cultivating a sense of ownership. The partnership model we developed as an organization will not be an appropriate fit for every organization because not every program has the same geographic reach and not every officer has an interest in taking on the individual management of a particular program. Other young and especially all-volunteer organizations may find it more helpful to consider conventional, hierarchical methods for structuring their work. The corporate model of a CEO or executive director, and a staff who assists in various fundraising and managerial roles, may thus be more appropriate for some organizations.

In addition, OAA's story reveals one of the often-overlooked reasons that people join a non-profit organization: they enjoy spending time with each other and they enjoy fighting for a common cause together as a team. Social relationships are one of the strongest incentives that people have to volunteer large amounts of their time, even if the work itself is at first in an unfamiliar field. Indeed, our story reveals one very simple piece of advice for other aspiring social entrepreneurs: when a new organization needs volunteers and staff, one of the best places to look is around the social entrepreneur herself, whether that is in an educational community, a religious group, a neighborhood, or even to friends and family. The motivation provided by these social ties is a powerful incentive for volunteers to become – and remain – involved with important social causes.

In our experience, the fact that OAA is composed of a small group of people – all volunteers – who know each other well has yielded benefits and drawbacks. On the one hand, this close-knit staffing situation has created a climate of accountability that helps to ensure that everyone is similarly dedicated to the work and that everyone contributes as much time as he or she reasonably can. Because the organization is run by a group of people with a high level of familiarity and trust, we are able to confront a number of difficult organizational problems and to effectively negotiate solutions that have proven successful – although if often takes time to come to an agreement as a group on issues and to reach the consensus that we need to take action. In addition, the friendships that we have shared since graduate school can also make it more difficult to ensure that everyone is equally invested in the work when other personal and professional commitments inevitably arise. Compared to a more traditional hierarchical model with a clearer division of responsibilities, the partnership model that we have developed lends a feeling of openness to our decision-making that can make it tempting to side-step an issue – rather than confront it directly – to avoid offending someone in the group. We have learned, over time, to be more direct and open in our communication about outside work and family responsibilities. Because we know each other, we can appreciate how each other's lives are changing, and have found ways to reallocate tasks when members of our group are burdened by other obligations. We have also learned how to make it clear when work is not getting done. On balance, however, we believe that the trust and friendship on which OAA's organizational structure is founded has real value for our organization and the children we serve.

A comparison with Generation Rwanda (GR), also described in this book, helps to underscore the benefits and drawbacks of OAA's present management structure.[24] GR grew out of personal and professional relationships, and it also aims to address the AIDS orphan crisis. Its leadership, however, decided to structure the organization in a more traditional way, in which most of the members would have a role that focused on a particular set of tasks. In addition, GR decided to focus on one particular country, in part, perhaps, because two of the founders had spent significant time in Rwanda. Moreover, GR also hired a paid staff that remains on the ground in Rwanda, which is a sharp distinction from our decision to remain all-volunteer, and to work with small partner organizations to handle the day-to-day administration of our programs. The decisions that different organizations make about how to further even very similar missions are a reflection not only of the goals of the two organizations, but also of the particular personalities of the members of each organization, and the experiences that brought them together.

Since small organizations are often situated in particular communities, such as schools, towns, businesses, and other organizations, and are often the extension of pre-existing social networks, it does not always make sense to structure them in the same way as large non-profit organizations, which are more likely to comprise of people who do not know each other as well. This is especially true when they are run by a very small group of volunteers brought together by their friendships and their commitment to a particular cause. One of the most important lessons that OAA's experiences might offer other non-profit organizations is that it makes sense to take account of all the reasons that others might be motivated to join an organization – including social ties, an investment in a particular community, or passion for a particular issue – and to consider how these sources of energy and enthusiasm can best be put in service of the organization's mission. We have learned that we could become a more successful organization by drawing upon the ties among one another and using these relationships as added motivation for the work that we do.

Because we operate various projects under the umbrella of one organization, we have faced a set of questions that has led us to operate in a particular fashion. There are distinct advantages to the structure that we have chosen that we believe may be useful for other organizations that begin as a small project with a relatively modest mandate and would like to grow to have a broader impact. OAA was founded on the idea that our officers and project directors will be more effective if they are given the autonomy to create and manage their own projects. The fact that the officers and project directors have the ability to envision and then execute entrepreneurial projects means that all of us feel a personal investment in the work we do.

Additionally, OAA's partnership structure for raising and distributing funds is an attractive way of managing funds within an organization that has distinct projects that share similar goals. It is a structure that provides a balance of autonomy and collegiality and that allows individuals the opportunity to engage in some fundraising activities independent of the whole organization. Even if the goals of all of the projects within an organization are not as similar as the ones within OAA, it would still be possible to imagine a partnership structure as an effective way for running an organization composed of a number of different ventures, so long as the projects share enough of the same mandate that it is possible to raise common funds.

Placing several different projects under one organizational banner is a strategy that social entrepreneurs can use to quickly spread the reach of their work and motivate others to get or stay involved. For anyone interested in establishing a new social enterprise, the legal paperwork necessary to get an idea off the ground is enough to stop most people in their tracks. OAA has a very specific mandate focused on OVC education, nutrition, and basic health care and, as a result, all of our projects involve similar fundraising and consulting work. It has been possible to adapt what we have already accomplished to initiate even more social enterprises within our single organization. The advantages of this structure are also that individual social entrepreneurs are likely to be in close touch with one another and can therefore learn from each other's experiences.

Like entrepreneurial efforts in the business world, however, not all social enterprises will be successful, so there is some benefit to having several projects within one organization. That way, resources can be shared, repeat start-up costs can be avoided, and organizational risk can be spread. The knowledge and experience we have gained from working with our country partners is helpful for supporting the development of these organizations over the long term. We are able to draw comparisons across countries and contexts about best practices as a result of our successful – and less successful – in-country projects.

Consistent with this philosophy of sharing risks and experiences, we have learned a great deal from the success and failure of different projects over the course of our development. After our initial expansion, we ultimately decided that it was most beneficial for us to focus on those projects that had the greatest impact and upon which we had done the most complete due diligence. There is an argument that, given our limited resources, we perhaps expanded too quickly by adding several new countries in the early years of our organizational growth. On the other hand, by taking on these new projects we learned a great deal about what works and what does not in a partnership structure such as the one we embraced. We came to value the extent to which our partners communicated with us and the completeness of the records they sent. These lessons proved to be helpful as we focused our efforts on our current projects.

Another lesson that we would share with other social entrepreneurs is the significance of the partnerships we have had with others involved in similar work, and early on, especially with other young people. Over the course of our development, we have benefited tremendously from the advice we have received from other NGOs and, in particular, from the in-country contacts that have been recommended to us. Klaber's friendship with Staple-Clark has continued over several years, and we first learned about many of our in-country partner organizations from the organization she founded and leads, Unite For Sight. The fact that emerging organizations are in contact with and learn from one another and established organizations is also a significant lesson. OAA has been able to collaborate effectively with a number of groups, including Unite For Sight and Rotary International, over many years, and our growth is in many ways the product of these relationships.

We are determined to maintain OAA's project quality as we develop greater expertise and as our local partner organizations develop greater capacities to make use of our funding and other resources. Strengthening the NGO sector in the countries in which OAA operates is essential for these countries' economic development. While our primary focus has been upon serving the communities where we work, we have also learned to appreciate the power of collaboration with other social entrepreneurs. These relationships have greatly enhanced our work and enabled us to grow. Indeed, they have been our greatest asset.

By working with social entrepreneurs at home and abroad, we have been able to implement a relatively simple plan in a variety of countries, and we are hopeful that the impact, at least in small ways and in the places where we work, has been powerful. Rather than inventing a creative solution to a social problem in isolation, social entrepreneurs can work together in many different ways. We believe that this is a point often missed in the literature about the emerging field of social entrepreneurship. These human relationships, friendships, and collaborations across the world are what, for us at least, have enabled our organization to thrive.

NOTES

1. Throughout this chapter, we use 'HIV/AIDS' to refer to the epidemic as a whole.
2. *See* UNAIDS, UNAIDS REPORT ON THE GLOBAL AIDS EPIDEMIC 188 (2010), http://www.unaids.org/globalreport/Global_report.htm [hereinafter UNAIDS REPORT]. Throughout this chapter, we use 'AIDS orphans' to refer to children (0–17 years old) who have lost one or both parents to complications related to AIDS.
3. *Id.*
4. *See* UNAIDS, EXECUTIVE SUMMARY, REPORT ON THE GLOBAL AIDS EPIDEMIC 21, 24 (2008), http://data.unaids.org/pub/GlobalReport/2008/JC1511_GR08_ExecutiveSummary_en.pdf. Most of the AIDS orphans who live outside of sub-Saharan Africa reside in Asia, where the total number of orphans – orphaned for all reasons – exceeds 73 million. However, there is insufficient information available to provide figures for the number of AIDS orphans in individual Asian countries.
5. The 'wasting syndrome' that usually accompanies late-stage HIV/AIDS consists of involuntary loss of more than 10 percent of body weight, plus more than 30 days of either diarrhea or weakness and fever.
6. Donald Bundy, Lead Health Specialist, Afr., World Bank, Education and HIV/AIDS: A Window of Hope (May 7, 2002), http://web.worldbank.org/WBSITE/EXTERNAL/ TOPICS/EXTEDUCATION/0,,contentMDK:20042283~menuPK:282429~pagePK:640208 65~piPK:149114~theSitePK:282386,00.html. *See also* DONALD BUNDY, EDUCATION AND HIV/AIDS: A WINDOW OF HOPE xv (2002), *available at* http://www-wds.worldbank.org/ external/default/main?pagePK=64193027&piPK=64187937&theSitePK=523679&menuP K=64187510&searchMenuPK=64187283&siteName=WDS&entityID=000094946_02043 004023371.
7. It has been well documented that OVCs – largely due to increased stigma and poverty – are at a higher risk of contracting HIV/AIDS than other children. *See* UNAIDS REPORT, *supra* note 2.
8. Having a diversified funding base – as opposed to one large donor – is desirable because, should the one large donor be unable to contribute in a particular year under the latter scenario, significant strain is placed on the grantee organization; a diverse funding base helps mitigate this risk.
9. This figure does not include OVCs who can no longer attend school because of their being infected by HIV/AIDS. Most of the youths whom we support are not infected with HIV/AIDS.
10. OAA's more than US$1 million cumulative funds raised since 2002 includes our organization's expected 2011 donations.
11. *See, e.g.,* The Firelight Foundation, http://www.firelightfoundation.org.
12. *See* RANDY SHILTS, AND THE BAND PLAYED ON: POLITICS, PEOPLE, AND THE AIDS EPIDEMIC xxi (1988).

13. While the U.S. Embassy is located in Bangkok, the sole U.S. Consulate in Thailand is located in Chiang Mai.
14. It is said that luck is the intersection of preparation and opportunity, as is certainly evidenced here.
15. UNAIDS projections estimate that, as of 2010, Thailand has 1,054,000 orphans age 0–14 years old with one or both parents dead from any cause. This figure represented about 6.3 percent of the total population under 15. Of these orphans, 374,000, or about one-third, are estimated to be AIDS orphans. In 2006, UNAIDS estimated that there were 854,215 Thai orphans age 0–17 years old with one or both parents dead from any cause. This figure represented about 4.7 percent of the total population under 18. *See* UNGASS COUNTRY PROGRESS REPORT: THAILAND 130 (2010), http://data.unaids.org/pub/Report/2010/thailand_2010_country_progress_report_en.pdf.
16. 501(c)(3) status is the recognition the Internal Revenue Service grants to charitable organizations that permits donors to take deductions for financial contributions to them.
17. Dr. Zachary Kaufman, the editor of this book, would later serve as a member of this clinic while attending Yale Law School.
18. For example, a US$6,000 Rotary Club-level donation would be matched (US$6,000) by the District Rotary Club; moreover, Rotary International would match the Club-level and District-level donations (US$12,000) for an aggregate donation of US$24,000 (US$6,000+US$6,000+US$12,000).
19. For the official website of the Goldman Sachs Global Leaders Program, see http://www.iie.org/en/Programs/Goldman-Sachs-Global-Leaders-Program.
20. For the official website of the Association of Hole in the Wall Camps, see http://www.holeinthewallcamps.org/. Newman passed away on 26 September 2008.
21. For the official website for Unite For Sight, see http://www.uniteforsight.org/.
22. IRIN, *Uganda: IDP Camps, No Home Away From Home*, June 9, 2005, http://www.irinnews.org/report.aspx?reportid=54855.
23. For the biographies of the members of OAA's Board of Directors, see http://orphansagainstaids.org/meet-the-oaa-officers-a-board.html.
24. For more information about GR, see Chapter 6.

8. Inspiring generational change: Americans for Informed Democracy

Seth Green and Leah Maloney

INTRODUCTION

Americans for Informed Democracy (AID) empowers young people in the United States to address global challenges such as poverty, disease, climate change, and conflict through awareness and action. We began AID in 2002, hoping to empower young people who had studied abroad to bring the world home and showcase our common global values when they returned to the United States. The outpouring of sympathy from the international community for the United States in the aftermath of 9/11 inspired us to envision an organization that could help the United States better understand and work with other countries.

We recognized that students were not responding to traditional email and phone campaigns, and so we devised an innovative way of engaging the next generation of leaders in global education and advocacy. Our organization hosted fee-based weekend summits that educated young leaders about the interconnectedness of our world, connected these leaders with global campaigns, and offered them a comprehensive package of leadership and messaging guides to train them to be effective community organizers and advocates. Thanks to this fresh and scalable model, the organization quickly mushroomed from a shoe-string effort based out of a dorm room at the University of Oxford to a thriving non-profit organization with more than 20,000 members, foundation support exceeding US$500,000 annually, numerous revenue-generating streams of programming, and a high-profile, high-impact set of advisors and organizational partners. Community by community, we are educating Americans about global issues and building a robust constituency for international cooperation.

Ultimately, we seek to inspire and empower the developing generation to help the United States find a principled, collaborative role in an interconnected world. As part of this broader mission, we address many crucial issues, from genocide to humanitarian disasters, by raising public awareness and fostering positive, constructive dialogue about the U.S.'s role in global problems and solutions.

We believe that the public can and should play a role in every facet of our foreign policy, and that public values should help shape norms for international conduct. We also believe in the power of dialogue, not only to provide people with facts, but also to change the framework in which they receive and process information. Lastly, we view public involvement as critical for the maintenance of a genuine democracy. The true nature of a democratic society is not defined by its government but by its citizens.

The powerful role of the public in driving policy decisions is achieved by demanding certain norms of behavior and developing new standards of accountability for the government's foreign policy actions. In this development of norms, there is a vast political space that is left empty by both private individuals and the government. NGOs must encourage and facilitate an empowered public to fill this space. We do this at AID by providing information to a target audience of college-aged students. These students then organize events to spread that awareness in their communities. We also emphasize ways in which student leaders can use their knowledge to take constructive action. By increasing awareness and facilitating action, we seek to cultivate a robust and healthy U.S. democracy that responds to global problems with global solutions.

Americans are open to such global solutions. Indeed, one recent survey found that more than two-thirds of Americans prefer a collaborative approach, rather than a unilateral one, toward international affairs.[1] Surveys also indicate that the public overwhelmingly favors funding and support for international institutions, such as the International Criminal Court (ICC), that can respond to atrocities. Yet studies by the Program on International Policy Attitudes (PIPA) indicate that policy-makers consistently underestimate the actual public support for these institutions.[2]

We endeavor to change the standards that the U.S. government and citizens use when responding to problems affecting our world, and to ensure that the values held by most Americans are internalized in our policy responses. As a starting place, we seek to internalize an ethical code that ensures that the United States responds in a principled fashion to atrocities. In order for countries to obey norms of international engagement, they need to have integrated them into their individual code of appropriate behavior. Despite the fact that most Americans express support for a multilateral foreign policy, the American public perceives itself as unilateralist in nature.[3] We work to inspire young Americans to showcase and strengthen the multilateral framework and to advocate for this framework's adoption by the U.S. public and, eventually, the U.S. government. We seek to inspire a 'generational change,' wherein young people begin to subscribe collectively to a new way of thinking about America's role in the world. These young people then leverage this generational consensus to shape the perceptions of their parents and their children.

The result is ultimately a new vision for America's role in the world and a new foreign policy.

IMPETUS BEHIND AID

The motivating idea behind our work is that the United States is at a historic moment in its role in the world. In the post-Cold War era, the United States is unparalleled in both its economic and military might. We believe the United States should use this moment to set up an international architecture that will ensure the rule of law and protection of humanity. Currently, the U.S. government is largely disengaged in development and global governance issues that could provide solutions to the major atrocities of our time. The American government has not ratified either the Kyoto Protocol[4] or the ICC treaty. Even where the U.S. government has been engaged, such as on global health issues, the United States has at times made a conscious effort to offer its assistance unilaterally rather than through multilateral channels such as the Global Fund to Fight AIDS, Tuberculosis, and Malaria.[5] We thus identified a need for a group to galvanize the next generation of leaders to pressure today's leaders toward cooperative action.

Part of the problem is that Americans often have misconceptions about U.S. foreign policy.[6] This trend is apparent in their ideas about what proportion of America's federal budget is spent on foreign aid. While Americans believe that the government spends an average of 25 percent of the federal budget on foreign aid, in reality about 1 percent of the total federal budget is expended in this area. When asked what percentage would be appropriate for the government to spend, the mean answer was 10 percent.[7]

One of us (Seth Green) first identified this intense disconnect between the perception and reality of global issues during his time studying abroad. Green departed for London just weeks after the terrorist attacks of 9/11, wary of lacking the support he needed to digest the tragedy. To his surprise, he was met with intense sympathy from strangers who were living in the United Kingdom. He was often stopped on the street by strangers who noticed his American accent and wished to express their solidarity. The tragedy seemed to reveal the possibility for a global community of shared values and a truly global war against terror.

But foreign goodwill towards Americans quickly vanished and was replaced with anger and frustration over the actions of the U.S. government following 9/11. In the year that passed, the U.S. rejected the Kyoto Protocol, refused to ratify membership to the ICC, and pushed for a war with Iraq. Citizens around the world were baffled by the U.S. government's lack of concern for other countries' perspectives and its unwillingness to join crucial global efforts to address problems like global climate change. Green found that many non-Americans were now raising the question: 'Why should the international community support the U.S. if the U.S. is not willing to support the international community?'[8]

This unique opportunity of experiencing both the sympathy in the post-9/11 world and the intense disdain a year later allowed Green to realize the potential for the global community and the destructiveness of misunderstanding and unilateralism by and toward the United States. Green concluded that the initial sympathetic response must have been caused by an instinctual sense of a global community. But this inherent nature became buried as political leaders and media practiced a politics of division. Political leaders in the United States went so far as to rename food items to express disdain toward any Europeans that did not fully support the U.S. invasion in Iraq (e.g., 'Freedom Fries'). The media also focused on global differences rather than commonalities. Instead of looking at the opportunity for the United States to engage moderates in the Muslim world, the media focused on questions such as 'Who are the extremists and why do they hate us?' The world that most Americans therefore saw was one of disagreements and threats, not one of hope and opportunity.

Recognizing the failure of media to present a full picture of the rest of the world, a group of students at the University of Oxford created AID. The initial goal of this small group of Americans abroad was to inform fellow Americans about non-Americans' opinions, which were not being adequately communicated to the U.S. public. We wrote opinion pieces about the goodwill that embraced us and the rising anti-Americanism we witnessed since that fleeting post-September 11th moment. We organized email campaigns to government representatives and trained American students abroad to share their experiences after they returned home. Our overall purpose through these efforts was to provide other Americans a more complete picture of non-Americans and to help our countrymen realize how our government's actions were being received abroad. Originally, our focus was on informing policy-makers about these issues, but our focus eventually shifted to informing the public, with the conviction that policy changes would follow the demands of an informed and mobilized citizenry.

As our focus shifted, we realized that more needed to be done to foster increased understanding of the commonality of views between Americans and non-Americans and the failure of media on both sides to bring attention to these shared perspectives. We began to hold forums for Americans and non-Americans to discuss pressing issues and to see how our respective national media reported on each other. One event on comparing media was particularly successful. The goal was to show non-American peers at Oxford the diversity of viewpoints expressed by U.S. policy-makers in U.S. media in the lead up to the Iraq war. This media forum was held at Oxford in June 2002 and brought together American, European, Middle Eastern, and South Asian students.

Participants were shown news clips from a variety of American television networks: outlandish segments of cable news shows such as *Hannity & Colmes* and Pat Robertson's *700 Club*, along with segments from *Meet the Press* and NBC *Nightly News*. Non-American participants were shocked by the diversity of views expressed. Many of the European participants said that they did not know that a debate over Iraq was occurring at all in the United States because this debate went unreported in their local press.

Encouraged by these events throughout 2002, many students at Oxford became involved in AID, a large number of which were students from the United States studying abroad during their junior year of college. At the end of the academic year, these students returned to their home universities. In the following fall, many of these students organized town hall meetings across the United States on the future of relations between the United States and the Islamic world. These events have reached more than 1,500 people and have been highly successful in addressing the aftermath of the 9/11 attacks and misunderstandings between Muslims and non-Muslims in America.

One memorable town hall attendee that year was Sue Rosenblum, who lost her 28-year-old son, Joshua, in the 9/11 attacks. Rosenblum eloquently expressed the interconnectedness of today's world when she said:

> It is entirely possible that a member of the Islamic community sitting here today might have a distant relative who was directly or indirectly involved with the 9/11 attacks that killed my son. It is also possible that as an American and as a Jew I might have a distant relative who caused pain to a member of his family. But even if that were the case it will not stop me from reaching out my hand in friendship.[9]

Other attendees at the town halls uttered similar statements emphasizing the need to promote understanding of both the challenge of, and opportunity for, co-existence. The town hall meetings generally found consensus between Muslims and non-Muslims on key points. There was agreement that the United States should be more diplomatic toward the Islamic world and it should threaten the use of force only in situations where fundamental U.S. interests were at stake. At the same time, participants agreed overwhelmingly that the Islamic world needed more democratic institutions and emphasis on human rights. From this initial model of success, we began to develop a skeleton that could be put to work on a wide range of global issues, including those concerning atrocities.

DEFENDING HUMAN RIGHTS

Two of the areas in which AID has extensive programming are human rights and the prevention of atrocities. We define an atrocity as any event that infringes on basic human rights, whether it emanates from natural disaster, war, or genocide. Working with a network of student leaders, we educate students about atrocities and advocate for a productive U.S. role in setting up institutions to prevent and respond to atrocities. AID's focus is on raising awareness about global institutions, especially the ICC and the United Nations (U.N.), and educating about genocide. Atrocities such as the genocide in Darfur have been splashed across all forms of media, often making the public feel overwhelmed and impotent against the powerful forces that create such crises. We seek to present these issues in a way that makes understanding and activism possible.

In our work raising awareness about genocide, we have hosted talks by experts in the field, held film screenings, and supported the work of groups that focus on genocide. AID has facilitated speaking events with such leaders as Mark Hanis, then the president of the Save Darfur Coalition / Genocide Intervention Network;[10] Gregory Stanton, founder of Genocide Watch; and John Prendergast, then Special Advisor on Sudan for the International Crisis Group (ICG) and now co-Chair of the ENOUGH project.[11] AID brought these speakers to college campuses across the country, exposing students to both the reality of genocide and the possibility for action, such as starting a Students Taking Action Now: Darfur (STAND) Chapter at their university.[12] Throughout college campuses and community centers we held film screenings of 'Hotel Rwanda,'[13] a non-fictional depiction of the 1994 genocide in Rwanda, and 'Invisible Children,'[14] a documentary about the effects of the 20-year war in Northern Uganda. These powerful films help make these tragedies real to Americans and to motivate people to act. Many students watching these films participated in the rally in April 2006 to demand U.S. government inter-vention in Darfur. In our work raising awareness about genocide, we have seen increased activism on these issues. In the beginning of our work in this area, there was a real need for information to be spread about the reality of geno-cide; soon enough, a strong student movement for genocide awareness emerged. Organizations such as the Save Darfur Coalition / Genocide Intervention Network[15] and STAND responded to the need students expressed for information and activism on these issues. These groups – focused solely on genocide – were best equipped to tackle the issue and to give students concrete steps to help end genocide. Instead of continuing our own programming in these areas, we decided to support these existing networks, for example, by hosting workshops on how to most effectively communicate global issues to the non-expert public at STAND's 2005 conference at Harvard University.

While there is fortunately an impressive student movement committed to ending genocide, a similar student movement backing reform at long-term institutions such as the U.N. and the ICC has not yet emerged. These organi-zations could be vital partners in preventing genocide in the future. We have therefore concentrated our resources on building support for key reforms at these institutions. A large part of AID's programming on atrocities is dedicated to raising public awareness about the crucial work of the U.N. and the potential for it to be an even more effective organization. On March 21, 2005, U.N. Secretary General Kofi Annan presented a new report, *In Larger Freedom*, on sweeping reform in the U.N.[16] In his report, Annan calls for a collective security system to fight terrorism, an enlarged U.N. Security Council, a revamped U.N. human rights system, and new guidelines for military action. We continue to see these changes as essential to the U.N.'s effectiveness in preventing atrocities and alleviating suffering.

While the United States has backed some U.N. reforms, in particular greater transparency and administrative efficiency, the United States has opposed many substantive reforms such as the creation of the U.N. Human Rights Commission (UNHRC). U.S. leaders say they fear that such a commission will be monopolized and manipulated by countries with deplorable human rights records.[17] But the decision by the United States to disengage entirely from the process has only exacerbated this problem, as in the case of the confirmation of Sudan in 2004 to a third term on the UNHRC.[18] Sichan Siv, U.S. Ambassador to the U.N., walked out of the UNHRC meeting after the vote to confirm Sudan's membership was called.[19] As a result, no dialogue occurred between the U.S. and Sudanese ambassadors regarding the possible human rights violations in Sudan. In many ways, U.S. reluctance to support these necessary U.N. reforms reflects public inaction with regard to the U.N. reform process. We believe that it is critically important to encourage a set of international norms in favor of cooperation, mutual understanding, and peace. In response to this need, we developed the *Global Governance for a Changing World* initiative, which strives to transform the energy of globally conscious young Americans into an education and advocacy network for better U.S.-U.N. relations and ultimately U.S. support for critical U.N. reforms. In communities across the United States, we have worked with the United Nations Foundation and the Stanley Foundation to host town hall discussions on U.N. reform. These discussions allowed leaders from global NGOs and the U.N. system to talk directly with the next generation of leaders about their vision for the future of the U.N. system. Leaders speaking as part of this series have included ICG President Gareth Evans, former U.S. Ambassador Rich Williamson, former U.N. Assistant Secretary General Gillian Sorensen, and many others. These experts offered students practical information about how U.N. reforms would directly impact its effectiveness with regard to humanitarian aid and conflict prevention.

In order to promote understanding of the U.N.'s role in the world in a concrete way, we have also held screenings of 'The Peacekeepers.'[20] This powerful documentary about the U.N. peacekeeping mission in the

Democratic Republic of the Congo (DRC) has given viewers a look at the dramatic results of U.N. resolutions. The film documents the struggle to save 'a failed state,' taking the viewer back and forth between the U.N. headquarters in New York and events on the ground in the DRC from summer 2002 until spring 2004. Also in collaboration with the United Nations Foundation and the Stanley Foundation, our campus chapters have hosted more than 75 screenings of 'The Peacekeepers' across the United States. This campaign has provided thousands of citizens with an inside look at what the U.N. can accomplish and the local rivalries in war-torn countries against which it must battle.

In addition to supporting an effective U.N., we also seek to build U.S. support for the ICC. The twentieth century was the bloodiest in recorded history: 174 million people were killed in genocides and mass murders at the hands of dictators, warlords, and human rights violators.[21] After the devastation of World War II, the world was determined that never again should such blatant destruction of human life and dignity be permitted. Unfortunately, in the succeeding 50 years, the world sustained myriad atrocities without having recourse to any permanent, global mechanism for the prevention and punishment of such crimes. With the creation of the ICC, however, the world has begun to fulfill its post-World War II commitment.

Despite the merits of the ICC, the United States has refused to ratify its foundational treaty, the Rome Statute, for fear of politically-motivated trials against U.S. nationals.[22] In stark contrast to the widely admired commitment to the rule of law within its own borders and strong support for the ICC by most of the United States' closest allies, the United States was one of only seven nations (the others being China, Iraq, Libya, Yemen, Qatar, and Israel) to reject the Rome Statute in 1998.

In order to fill the void of understanding about the ICC, we offer public education through our campus chapters nationwide. With our network of globally conscious young leaders, we aim to engage diverse audiences such as student governments, fraternities and sororities, religious groups, and political organizations in the discussion of the purpose of and prospects for the ICC. Our *Darfur and Beyond: The Role and Future of the ICC* initiative strives to transform the energy of our globally conscious student network into an education network to engage their non-expert peers in learning about the international justice system. Specifically, we use leadership retreats to train and connect these young globally-minded students into a network. One such event was the *Young Global Leaders Summit on the Future of the International Criminal Court* that we hosted at Yale University on April 15, 2006. Over 350 students from more than 90 universities attended the conference to hear speakers such as Stephen Rickard, Director of the Open Society Institute's Washington, D.C. office, and Benjamin B. Ferencz, a prosecutor at the post-World War II

International Military Tribunal (popularly known as the Nuremberg Tribunal) and author of *New Legal Foundations for Global Survival*. Many of these student leaders went on to hold their own events on their campuses to raise awareness about the ICC and to connect them to advocacy campaigns in support of this international court.

DESIGN

Our organization addresses both the importance of global awareness and the need for activism to ensure this awareness results in informed policies. We interest students in our work by providing a model for student engagement that fits nicely with two major trends among the youth generation: increased global connectedness and a community-based, public-interest spirit. Today's university students are more connected to the rest of the world than ever before. They use online translators to access websites in foreign languages. They trade music with their counterparts abroad. And they chat about politics with their peers around the world through online message boards. Students' unprecedented global interaction is exemplified by the steady rise in the number of Americans choosing to study abroad. In 2008–09, more than 260,000 Americans studied abroad, an increase of four-fold over the last two decades.[23] Students are also increasingly eager to learn foreign languages; approximately 1.6 million American college students were enrolled in a foreign language class in 2009, an almost 50 percent increase from the approximately 1.1 million enrolled in 1995. Particularly interesting, the number of students studying Arabic from 2002 to 2006 leaped by 126.5 percent and from 2006 to 2009 surged by 46 percent.[24]

With so much international engagement, it is striking to hear today's students denounced for their apathy. To a generation who sees activism in terms of rallies and riots it may seem as if the age of student activism has passed. But a closer look at local involvement and issue-specific activist groups reveals that student activism is actually on the rise today. There is a difference between the generations in the way student activism is channeled, but passion among college students remains forceful. We have seized this new activism and internationalism with successful results.

Activism in the 1960s and 1970s consisted of campaigns of unified support for a single cause. Students across the country gained widespread media attention for their massive rallies, marches, and sit-ins around civil rights and the Vietnam War. These mechanisms were appropriate for mobilizing passionate, progressive, likeminded students on college campuses around issues of right and wrong, war and peace. But students today are less likely to see global issues in black-and-white terms, in part because their interaction with the rest of the world is so wide-ranging that they see many global issues from multiple perspectives.[25] The protest approach has limits among today's youth, which surveys indicate are politically more middle-of-the-road than past student generations.[26] These trends suggest that protest may not be a good way to tap the interest of many student leaders who are globally engaged.

Today's successful student efforts are more focused on smaller movements, which are more specifically tailored to students' interests and passions. Instead of symbolic rallies and marches, students use local involvement to rally behind national and international issues. Choosing concrete acts over symbolic statements, student activists have found great success. Students are putting emphasis on daily choices in a 'think globally, act locally' approach to global issues.[27] Students pressure their campuses to buy fair trade products, divest from Sudan, and become more environmentally friendly and self-sustaining.[28] Now more than ever, students are channeling their activism by acting within their communities to create change internationally.

It is no coincidence that these same students who value making a difference through local involvement are increasingly choosing public service work as part of their post-graduate experience. In 2009, the Peace Corps[29] received more than 15,000 applications, a 30 percent increase from just five years prior.[30] Other students are choosing domestic ways to channel their activism and volunteerism. More than 45,000 students applied to join Teach for America after graduation in 2010; this includes 12 percent of the senior classes at all Ivy League schools.[31] The same trend is consistent with applications for AmeriCorps*VISTA (Volunteers in Service to the United States).[32] Clearly students are eager to engage in international and domestic issues with the hands-on, local approach that defines this generation of activism.

Our approach to student activism moves alongside this generational trend. We offer initiatives on a wide range of issues to fit students' specific interests and we focus on how students can take positive action through education and activism in their own local community. We host ongoing leadership retreats on specific issues from climate change to global poverty. We select students for these summits through a competitive application process based on three criteria: demonstrated leadership skills, strong communication abilities, and a high-ranking academic record. At the summit, we provide students with toolkits that train them to be effective organizers and advocates on these issues in their community. We then help these empowered students to coordinate town hall meetings and international videoconferences; these forums connect communities to global issues and to people with whom they often feel disconnected. With a toolkit for each of our initiatives, students can pick an issue and simply follow the step-by-step instructions on how to run a successful town hall meeting or international videoconference. Our tools have provided many students with the skills to channel their activism further.

The reasoning behind this model of leadership summits followed by student-led education and advocacy comes from the original gathering of students at Oxford. We had the benefit of being able to recruit at its founding a large number of collegiate junior year abroad students. This enabled the group to start the following academic year with a nationwide support base of senior year university students, which proved to be a highly effective way of expanding our organization. The start of what would become AID developed largely out of this shared ownership environment. The participants were all students, eager to learn, and excited to play a leadership role in bringing awareness back to their community. These initial participants all had a clear vision for AID and put forth ideas for the best way to pursue this vision. We now replicate this experience through ongoing leadership summits.

One student in particular exemplifies the new activism on campuses through his work with AID. Yuri Beckelman, a graduate from California State University Monterey Bay, passionately cares about preserving our global environment. After attending one of our leadership retreats, where he learned of AID's Local Environmental Coalition Building toolkit, he returned to his community to host an educational forum and to build support in his local community for the Urban Environmental Accords. The Accords are a seven-year plan for local governments to improve the global environment by taking action locally. With AID's support network behind him, Beckelman built a broad coalition for the Accords and then successfully led this coalition to obtain the signature of Dennis Norton, the mayor of Capitola, California.

FUNDRAISING

AID works hard to gather the resources necessary to host its young global leaders summits and videoconferences, to offer small grants, and to sustain its central office and staff. This is a difficult task, especially as interest in our mission has grown and more people want to attend conferences and plan events. We have raised more than US$2.5 million from our founding in 2002 through 2011, mostly through foundation support. In the beginning, we applied to a wide range of foundations and were turned down. Over time, we were able to build a relationship with a number of grant-makers and show them the organization's work firsthand. As these funders became more familiar with our team and programming, they saw that their resources would be put to good use. Funders of AID include CarEth Foundation, Connect U.S. Fund, DarMac Foundation, Doris Duke Charitable Trusts, Ewing Marion Kauffman Foundation, Ford Foundation, Gates Foundation, Hewlett Foundation, JEHT Foundation, MacArthur Foundation, Open Society Institute, Planethood Foundation, Rockefeller Brothers Fund, Stanley Foundation, Summit

Foundation, United Nations Foundation, and the Wallace Global Fund. We are constantly applying for grants to fund specific initiatives and for general funding to expand the organization as a whole to meet current student demand.

STAFF

Despite the disparate nature of our work, our organization grew so rapidly and involved so many students that eventually it needed a full-time staff to keep up with the demand of students. Hiring staff is not easy for a small organization because one needs to find people with great talent who are willing to work 60 to 70 hours a week for low pay and to do mundane administrative jobs (e.g., filing, copying). The key in our experience has been finding people who have worked for our organization previously as volunteers, because they are sincere in their interest in AID and have already demonstrated a willingness to take on some of the more administrative tasks. Since our organization is based on engaging students, we target former student activists and prefer to hire people who have recently completed their undergraduate studies to ensure that AID's work continues to be relevant in its approach to young people.

As of July 2011, there are four paid staff members, three full-time and one part-time. The organization is additionally supported by a large network of volunteers on campuses, who organize town hall meetings and videoconferences, as well as an influx of summer interns. Some of these volunteers are designated as Regional Directors. These Directors coordinate activities between universities, help groups in their respective regions to solicit speakers, and organize regional conferences. The problem in hiring recent university graduates is a fairly high turnover of employees. Many recent graduates who come to work for us for a year have applications to graduate school pending. Our first two staff members, as an example, worked for one year and then moved on to graduate studies at Princeton and Harvard. Although this trend produces some strain requiring training new people, there are also some benefits to our overall mission of engaging students to have a fresh group of leaders who have just left their campuses joining our staff.

Our work is supported by an advisory board that provides us with expert advice and connections to important people in the field of international politics. AID's Advisory Board includes United Nations Foundation President Timothy Wirth, *Guardian* columnist Timothy Garton Ash, Yale Law School Professor Amy Chua, and former Starbucks Coffee Vice President Jonathan Greenblatt. AID also has a Board of Directors, which manages the group's work. At different points in our history, our board members have included leaders like Jacob Scherr, the Director of the Natural Resources Defense Council's International Program, and Anne Richard, the Vice President of

Government Relations and Advocacy for the International Rescue Committee. These members provide valuable oversight, as well as support to enhance our programming.

PROGRESS

Our goal as an organization is neither concrete nor static. Our work is not finished when a treaty is signed or a conflict is resolved. While the progress is difficult to measure, we do have indicators of success, which have been crucial in maintaining focus for our organization and judging the effectiveness of our methods. The quality of our public education is the most important indicator. This means working carefully to design town hall toolkits to ensure both substantive education and significant public participation. The quantity and diversity of students involved is another indicator – and we seek to reach the maximum number of people possible from different political viewpoints, religions, nationalities, and ethnicities.

We measure success in at least two other ways: media coverage and generational change. Most Americans get their information about global affairs from the local television news.[33] However, the local media typically only covers disasters – famines, earthquakes, wars. Consequently, Americans who depend on the local news for international information tend to perceive the world as a chaotic place in which their fellow citizens repeatedly try in vain to end crises.[34] However, when the same media shows footage of young Americans who are concerned about the rest of the world and who believe they are impacted by what happens on other continents, readers begin to see a different image of the world. For example, a 2005 *Chicago Tribune* headline about an AID event read 'Bringing Tsunami Home.'[35] The article emphasized the interconnectedness of American students and the tsunami victims. Likewise, the *San Francisco Chronicle* showed the same year interactions between students across the world in an article entitled 'Students Link with Aid Groups in Sri Lanka.'[36]

We view such positive media coverage as an indicator of a more significant, more sweeping goal: generational change. In an era of ignorance of international affairs among ordinary Americans who have an unparalleled amount of influence on the rest of the world, it is absolutely vital that the young generation leads the United States toward a more global perspective.[37] To that end, we are transforming latent global interest into action by opening up new opportunities for students to take action. Many students who have engaged with AID have never before been politically active. After their engagement, these individuals have led successful advocacy campaigns. In this way, AID is mobilizing a generation – one by one – to be champions for social change.

Another marker of progress is the exponential growth in the number of people actively involved in our organization. AID currently works on over 1,000 universities across the United States. During the academic year, an average of 17 AID events take place per week, each with an average audience of 75 students, which means that 1,250 students each week learn about global affairs at one of our forums. We also host as many as eight conferences a month, each with an average of 200 participants. We have received a significant amount of press coverage regarding these activities, exposing countless people to our mission beyond university campuses. Our events have been covered by over 750 news outlets, including *The New York Times*, *The Washington Post*, CNN, and C-SPAN. The public's interest in our work can also be seen in the fact that our website receives more than a quarter-million hits each year.

The diversity of viewpoints that we attract to our events is a final indicator of success. In an article for her school newspaper, Boston College student Katie Sellers lamented that '[t]ime and again I've found myself wanting, needing to have a conversation about any number of issues but unable to do so,' because of the lack of open, non-partisan forums.[38] Katie thanked AID for believing that 'moderates like me matter enough to be heard and to be further educated.'[39] We have been successful in providing passionate students with an opportunity to learn more about an issue without subscribing to a partisan ideology.

Including students from regions and religious institutions across the United States is another important facet of the organization. One 2008 conference attendee from Bob Jones University in South Carolina wrote in his campus newspaper, 'I was most impressed at how broad of a coalition it is – everything from free trade economic liberals to social liberals to feminists to evangelicals.'[40] This diversity of viewpoints enhances the dialogue and works for true change in the entire nation's consciousness.

SUSTAINABILITY

Sustaining an organization that is led by students and that is targeted toward grassroots education is never easy because ultimately the organization relies on the energy and passion of individuals. But we are fortunate that sustainability is in some sense at the heart of our mission. When students learn about global affairs, participate in our workshops, and apply our toolkits, they become an active part of our network and this helps to link their energy and passion into our network for the long term. Ultimately, the core of our mission is not in our headquarters or central staff, but the vision and activities carried out by our student volunteers. As long as we can maintain a strong and consistent vision, we believe that there will be an ample group of volunteers to help realize our mission.

Recognizing the costs of our programming, and the changing priorities of foundations, we have also begun to develop revenue-building and self-financing programs. For example, all of our 'Bringing the World Home' conferences abroad are tuition-based and now pay for themselves. We have also developed a tuition-based *Global Scholar* program, which is a two-week summer enrichment program that offers rising juniors and seniors in high school the chance to immerse themselves in college-level coursework on international relations. While these programs are intended to generate revenue for the organization, we continue to offer scholarships to students with financial need to ensure the programs are diverse and students from all backgrounds can attend.

Even with this planning, sustainability does not guarantee that one can maintain an organization at the same size over time. We were significantly smaller in 2010 than we were in 2007, with our budget at about half the size. The reason for this downsize is due to reduced foundation giving to organizations involved in foreign affairs, both as a result of the financial crisis, which adversely impacted endowments, and as a result of waning concern about U.S. foreign policy following the transition from the Bush administration's unilateralism to the Obama administration's multilateral approach. As soon as we recognized the changing funding environment, we began restructuring the organization to ensure our sustainability.

LESSONS LEARNED

The development of a non-profit organization requires a sixth sense about what the public responds to and what investors believe in. This sensitivity is necessary in order to see the opportunity for social entrepreneurship but it is also cultivated through working in the field. The mission of the organization needs to attract people on both intellectual and emotional levels. Appealing to people's core values is important for a volunteer organization because it is those values that compel people to act. While this grand vision must have vast emotional appeal, the organization must pursue realistic goals and a pragmatic, intellectually attractive approach to realizing them.

Maintaining focus on a single priority at the start of a project is also essential to success. Trying to tackle too many issues may result in paying inadequate attention to some of them. Our ultimate goal of raising consciousness nationwide began primarily with work in the northeast region of the United States. It was important to develop a model for an organization and to create infrastructure before introducing it nationally. Instead of trying to build a nationwide following immediately, we first developed the infrastructure with which to reach out to people beyond New England. To do so, we asked professors in relevant departments at universities in the New England region of the

United States to nominate student leaders for our program; we established partnerships with relevant organizations in that region; and we built a network of student leaders who were willing to help coordinate regional activities. Once we had accomplished these tasks, we were able to apply the model to other universities and regions throughout the country.

During the piloting and then growing of our model, AID has learned that it needs to evolve with the interests of its membership. When AID first began just after the September 11th attacks, students were learning about many international issues for the first time and were seeking unbiased information. At that time, AID sought to be largely an educational network, allowing young people to connect across borders. But as time has passed, and young people have increased their understanding of international issues, they have begun to ask 'What can I do to change unfair and unjust policies?' We have therefore become more focused on organizing and advocacy efforts to impact foreign policy. We have a history of educating the public and cultivating interest in international issues, and thus our challenge has been converting this engagement into action that creates substantive impact on foreign policy. We have responded by organizing advocacy trainings for our students as part of our broader campaigns. This shift follows the natural evolution of AID, which built its identity on the passions of its members. New research on youth political involvement reveals that the Millennial Generation prefers action over education alone and that this generation is more civically engaged than previous generations.[41] We have responded to this shift in the nature of our youth engagement. As one of our board members described the shift, 'Before we had an awareness movement ... but the big difference is that today's member really wants to take specific action to lobby the U.S. Government for change.'[42]

The most important lesson we have learned since our founding in 2002 is the importance of building a full leadership pipeline. We have always worked hard to develop the potential of our volunteer leaders and to create a pyramid of opportunities from being a participant to a campus organizer to a regional director to a staff member. But one part of the leadership pipeline that we only developed recently was our management team. Our historic staffing structure focused on an executive director and program staff divided by issue area (e.g., peace and security, global development, environment). As we grew to as large as seven full-time staff, we continued to have all program staff and one executive director. This meant that staff had limited upward mobility and tended to only stay for one to two years because they lacked real advancement opportunities. This also meant that when the time came for the founding executive director of the organization to transition out, there was no natural leader to take his place. This sent the organization looking to external candidates to fill the spot. While we were ultimately able to find a highly capable and resourceful candidate, she faced challenges upon entering the organization because she was not familiar with our work or history. In response, we have tried to establish additional promotion opportunities within our staffing structure both to improve our retention rates as well as to develop our leadership pipeline for the future.

CONCLUSION

Our organization seeks to 'bring the world home' by hosting town hall meetings, international videoconference dialogues, documentary screenings, discussions, and more – all to get Americans talking about the U.S. role in our increasingly interconnected world. We believe that the United States is at a historic moment in its role in the world. Climate change, global poverty, nuclear proliferation, and other global issues cross borders and require global solutions. We are a group of young advocates who want to ensure that the United States uses this historic moment in its role in the world to work collaboratively with other countries to address these compelling and urgent issues.

Students established AID to showcase the opportunities for the United States to play a more collaborative role in the world. We began hosting town hall forums to bring new questions to the U.S. public. We have also hosted international videoconferences that allow Americans to talk face-to-face with peers from around the world. Based on our own experiences abroad, we believed that if Americans developed new ways to connect with the rest of the world, new opportunities would arise for the United States to work with other countries in an effort to solve global problems. We do not seek to advocate a specific position or partisan ideology. Instead, we believe that if Americans simply had exposure to new issues and new perspectives, and had a chance to see the world in terms of both threats and opportunities, we would become more likely to support a collaborative U.S. foreign policy. In other words, we seek to inspire a more informed democracy.

We remain committed to this mission. Our organization comprises a large and growing network of over 20,000 students on more than 1,000 university campuses. Through our programming, we are empowering a passionate, young generation that can help America find a principled, collaborative foreign policy that is appropriate for our interconnected world.

Soon after the founding of AID, one of us explained our organization's mission this way:

> I never will forget my pain in the weeks following September 11, or my comfort when strangers on London streets shared my grief. Restoring that international cohesion will not be easy. America must be ready to embrace the world, and the

world must be prepared to accept American involvement. I hope that AID can play a part in bringing the world together, as it was in that fleeting moment after the attacks.[43]

We are succeeding in that effort to bring the world back together one student at a time. At a Darfur teach-in that we helped to organize at Bowdoin College in 2006, one sophomore expressed that the event showed her a number of ways to get involved and to make a difference. Another sophomore expressed the value she saw in learning not just about the issue but about activism more generally: 'It was inspiring to hear what students at other colleges have done.'[44] Audience members – at events discussing Darfur, war crimes, and relations between the west and the Islamic world – often express shock and anger at what is occurring and develop a new sense of motivation to impact the current political climate. A student at another Darfur event that we hosted at Binghamton College expressed the common frustration that 'People don't know what to do.'[45] After the event, this same student committed to joining AID to raise public awareness about the atrocities in Darfur, and to make a difference.

With just one experience of learning about Darfur, the student committed to taking action. This is the story of countless students who have been touched by AID's mission. More than 12,000 students have now signed agreements to hold events about global issues; thousands more have attended these events and been changed by the experience. We are proof that Americans are caring, intelligent, motivated citizens who, when given the information and tools, will fight to make this world a better place.

NOTES

1. ALEXANDER TODOROV & ANESU N. MANDISODZA, PUBLIC OPINION ON FOREIGN POLICY: THE MULTILATERAL PUBLIC THAT PERCEIVES ITSELF AS UNILATERAL 1–2 (2003), *available at* http://www.pipa.org/articles/todorov_opinion.pdf.
2. Steven Kull, U.N. Continues to Get Positive, Though Lower, Ratings With World Public, World Public Opinion.org, Jan. 24, 2006, http://www.worldpublicopinion.org/pipa/articles/btunitednationsra/163.php?nid=&id=&pnt=163.
3. *Id.*
4. The Kyoto Protocol is a protocol to the United Nations Framework Convention on Climate Change. This treaty's aim is to combat global climate change by reducing the emission of greenhouse gases. *See* Kyoto Protocol, http://unfccc.int/kyoto_protocol/items/2830.php (last visited Nov. 17, 2011).
5. For the official website of the Global Fund to Fight AIDS, Tuberculosis, and Malaria, see http://www.theglobalfund.org/en/.
6. STEVEN KULL & I.M. DESTLER, MISREADING THE PUBLIC: THE MYTH OF A NEW ISOLATIONISM (1999).
7. American Public Vastly Overestimates Amount of U.S. Foreign Aid, World Public Opinion.org, Nov. 29, 2010, http://www.worldpublicopinion.org/pipa/articles/brunited statescanadara/670.php?lb=btda&pnt=670&nid=&id=.

8. For more information on Green's experience, see Seth Green, *America, As Seen From Afar*, PRINCETON ALUMNI WKLY., Nov. 3, 2003, *available at* http://www.aidemocracy.org/students/america-as-seen-from-afar/.

9. *Id.*

10. The Save Darfur Coalition and the Genocide Intervention Network merged on November 1, 2010, into United to End Genocide. For the official website of United to End Genocide, see http://endgenocide.org/.

11. The ICG aims to prevent and resolve deadly conflict. For the official website of ICG, see http://www.crisisgroup.org. Co-founded by the Center for American Progress and the ICG, ENOUGH aims to end genocide and crimes against humanity. For the official website of ENOUGH, see http://www.enoughproject.org.

12. STAND is a student initiative that seeks to create awareness about, take political action on, and raise funds to relieve the genocide in Darfur, Sudan. For the official website of STAND, see http://www.standnow.org.

13. HOTEL RWANDA (MGM / United Artists 2004).

14. INVISIBLE CHILDREN (Invisible Children 2006).

15. The Save Darfur Coalition / Genocide Intervention Network envisions a world in which the global community is willing and able to protect civilians from genocide and mass atrocities. This merged organization (now known as United to End Genocide) works to empower individuals and communities with the tools to prevent and stop genocide. For the official website of the Save Darfur Coalition / Genocide Intervention Network, see http://www.genocideintervention.net.

16. UNITED NATIONS, IN LARGER FREEDOM: TOWARDS DEVELOPMENT, SECURITY AND HUMAN RIGHTS FOR ALL, para. 8 (2005), *available at* http://www.un.org/largerfreedom/.

17. Associated Press, *Sudan Retains U.N. Human Rights Post*, MSNBC.COM, May 4, 2004, http://www.msnbc.msn.com/id/4898975/#.TqmJHnF69bF.

18. *Id.*

19. *Id.*

20. THE PEACEKEEPERS (National Film Board of Canada 2005).

21. R. J. RUMMEL, DEATH BY GOVERNMENT 4 (1994).

22. Paul W. Kahn, *The International Criminal Court: Why the United States is so Opposed*, CRIMES OF WAR PROJECT MAGAZINE, Dec. 2003, http://www.crimesofwar.org/print/icc/icc-kahn-print.html.

23. INST. OF INT'L EDUC. OPEN DOORS 2010 FAST FACTS 2 (2010), *available at* http://www.iie.org/en/research-and-publications/open-doors.

24. NELLY FURMAN, DAVID GOLDBERG & NATALIA LUSIN, ENROLLMENTS IN LANGUAGES OTHER THAN ENGLISH IN UNITED STATES INSTITUTIONS OF HIGHER EDUCATION, FALL 2009 3, 14–15, 19–20 (2010), *available at* http://www.mla.org/2009_enrollmentsurvey.

25. HARVARD UNIV. INST. OF POLITICS, EXECUTIVE REPORT: HARVARD INSTITUTE OF POLITICS' SURVEY OF STUDENT ATTITUDES: THE GLOBAL GENERATION (2005), *available at* http://www.iop.harvard.edu/Research-Publications/Survey/Spring-2005-Youth-Survey/Executive-Summary.

26. Eric Hoover, *Student Groups Aim to Tap Interest in Politics*, CHRONICLE OF HIGHER EDUC., Jan. 30, 2004, *available at* http://chronicle.com/article/Students-Political-Awareness/29070.

27. *See, e.g., Student Activism Becoming More Personal, Yet More Global*, NAT'L ON-CAMPUS REPORT, 15 Oct. 15, 2005, at 1–4; Beth Walton, *Volunteer Rates Hit Record Numbers*, USA TODAY, July 6, 2006, http://www.usatoday.com/news/nation/2006-07-06-volunteers_x.htm.

28. Andrew Peters, *Students Urge Darfur Divestment*, DAILY CAMPUS, Feb. 20, 2007, http://www.dailycampus.com/2.7440/students-urge-darfur-divestment-1.1058481.

29. Peace Corps is a U.S. government agency devoted to world peace. Peace Corps volunteers work in 138 host countries on issues ranging from AIDS education to information technology and environmental preservation. For the official website of Peace Corps, see http://www.peacecorps.gov.

30. Karen Goldberg Goof, *Peace Corps' Popularity Jumps*, WASHINGTON TIMES, Nov. 11, 2009, http://www.washingtontimes.com/news/2009/nov/11/peace-corps-popularity-jumps/; Walton, *supra* note 27.

31. Press Release, Teach for America, Teach for America Fields Largest Teacher Corps in its 20-Year History (May 24, 2010), http://www.teachforamerica.org/newsroom/documents/20100524_Teach.For.America.Fields.Largest.Teacher.Corps.In.Its.20.Year.History.htm. Teach For America 'is the national corps of outstanding recent college graduates of all academic majors who commit two years to teach in urban and rural public schools and become leaders in the effort to expand educational opportunity.' For the official website of Teach for America, see http://www.teachforamerica.org. The Ivy League, also known as the Ancient Eight (in reference to an athletic league in the northeastern region of the United States), comprises Brown University, Columbia University, Cornell University, Dartmouth College, Harvard University, Princeton University, the University of Pennsylvania, and Yale University.

32. AmeriCorps is 'a network of local, state, and national service programs that connects more than 70,000 Americans each year in intensive service to meet our country's critical needs in education, public safety, health, and the environment.' AmeriCorps, Fact Sheets and Issue Briefs, http://www.americorps.gov/about/media_kit/factsheets.asp (last visited Nov. 17, 2011). For the official website of AmeriCorps, see http://www.americorps.gov. *See also* Walton, *supra* note 27.

33. ROCKEFELLER BROS. FUND & ASPEN INST., U.S. IN THE WORLD GUIDE 16 (2004), *available at* http://usintheworld.org/?page_id=744.

34. *Id.*

35. Sean D. Hamill, *Bringing Tsunami Home*, CHI. TRIB., Jan. 27, 2005, http://articles.chicagotribune.com/2005-01-27/news/0501270301_1_sri-lankan-tsunami-infrastructure.

36. Wyatt Buchanan, *Students Link with Aid Groups in Sri Lanka*, S.F. CHRON., Mar. 29, 2005, http://articles.sfgate.com/2005-03-29/bay-area/17363863_1_sri-lanka-tsunami-relief-coastal-areas/2.

37. Andy Zieminski, *Summit Calls For Moderation in U.S.-Muslim World Relations*, WORLDPRESS.ORG, Sept. 21, 2006, http://www.worldpress.org/Americas/2498.cfm.

38. Katie Sellers, *Finally, a Group for the Middle*, HEIGHTS (Boston College), Apr. 15, 2006, http://www.bcheights.com/2.6172/finally-a-group-for-the-middle-1.912613.

39. *Id.*

40. Michael Gembola, *Writer, History Major Attend Poverty Summit*, COLLEGIAN (Bob Jones University). Apr. 6, 2006, http://www.bju.edu/collegian/index.php?issue=43&article=369.

41. Catherine Beer, Nicole Gill, Rosale Richards, & Erin Weber-Johnson, The Future of Americans for Informed Democracy 23 (April 2010) (unpublished thesis, New York University Robert F. Wagner Graduate School of Public Service) (on file with author).

42. *Id.* at 24.

43. Green, *supra* note 8.

44. Miranda Yaver, *Students Called to Action at Darfur Panel Discussion*, BOWDOIN ORIENT, Feb. 10, 2006, http://orient.bowdoin.edu/orient/article.php?date=2006-02-10&section=1&id=5.

45. Matt Chayes, *Genocide or Civil War? Forum Seeks Answers*, BINGHAMTON PIPE DREAM, Apr. 29, 2005, http://www.aidemocracy.org/students/genocide-or-civil-war-forum-seeks-answers/.

9. Re-connecting cousins: Children of Abraham

Ari Alexander and Gul Rukh Rahman

INTRODUCTION

Many conflicts continue to rage between competing nationalisms, religious sects, and ethnic groups. Of all the regional conflicts since World War II, few, if any, have garnered as much media attention as the Arab-Israeli conflict. While the conflict between Arabs and Israelis in the Middle East has received enormous attention, the more widespread problem in global Muslim-Jewish relations is largely hidden from public view. The globalization of the Arab-Israeli conflict has created a worldwide phenomenon of mutual suspicion, separation, and even hatred between many Jews and Muslims from Jakarta to Johannesburg, from Sao Paulo to San Francisco. The majority of attention paid to this issue ignores the voices and projects that promote an alternative to the dominant narrative of conflict. However, both Hommes de Parole (based in France)[1] and the Muslim World League (based in Saudi Arabia)[2] have organized conferences in which Jewish and Muslim leaders from various parts of the world have participated in dialogue. We see this as part of a growing trend towards recognizing the importance of this issue on the global stage.

There are three primary arenas of the worldwide crisis in Muslim-Jewish relations. One version is a minority-minority dynamic, in which Jewish and Muslim communities live in Western (majority Christian) societies such as Canada, France, the Netherlands, the United Kingdom, and the United States. Most Jews in the world live in close proximity to Muslims. But the reverse is not true. Rather, most Muslims live in Muslim-majority countries, where there are few, if any, Jews. Many Muslims perceive the creation of the state of Israel and other developments in Muslim-Jewish relations as injustices that continuously traumatize Palestinians. These Muslims harbor hostility, suspicion, and condemnation towards Jews. Generations of Palestinian and many other Muslim children have been schooled in a language of hostility towards Israel. In Muslim-majority countries, most residents have never met a Jew, and their view of Judaism is often shaped by negative media coverage of Israel that only transmits Palestinian suffering. They memorize select verses of the Qur'an in a literal manner – without context, explanation, or modernization. The lines between anti-Israel and anti-Jewish sentiment have grown increasingly blurred, making legitimate criticisms of state policies hard to distinguish from wanton hatred. Most Muslims feel that it has become impossible to criticize Israeli policies due to the fear of being labeled as an anti-Semite. Some Jewish organizations that promote pro-Israel advocacy and fundraising as pillars of contemporary Jewish communal life have reacted to anti-Zionist claims as if they were anti-Semitic, which may be the case in some instances but not always.[3] These organizations' focus on Israel seems to reflect, rather than determine, the fact that many Jews in the contemporary world are much more identified with and connected to Israel than they are with religious aspects of their Jewish identities.[4]

The final arena of Muslim-Jewish tension is in Israel itself, where approximately 75 percent of Israelis are Jewish and over 90 percent of the non-Jews are Muslims. Though Israeli domestic inter-group relations are of primary concern to such groups as the Abraham Fund,[5] the New Israel Fund,[6] and the Inter-Agency Task Force on Israeli Arab Issues,[7] they are of limited relevance to relations between Muslims and Jews elsewhere.

This Jewish-Muslim dynamic also continues to evolve in the context of a broader conflict between the Muslim world and the West. While neither the Muslim world nor the West is monolithic, observers view each to be fundamentally in conflict with the other. For more than half a century, it is the Jew who has frequently been singled out and blamed for most of the political, economic, and social problems the Muslim world faces. Mainstream newspapers from Morocco to Indonesia often cite Jewish conspirators, pressure groups, or devious plans. Zionism captivates much of the contemporary Muslim world. Widespread Jewish support for Zionism leads most Muslims to single out Jews in Muslim expressions of shock, humiliation, and hatred. The radicalization of Islam is widely perceived to be a serious threat to the world at large, and not just to Jews or Zionists, as evidenced by terrorist attacks over the past several years in, among other places, Amman, Dar es Salaam, Istanbul, London, Madrid, Mumbai, Nairobi, New York, and Washington, D.C. Incidents such as the Israelis' 2010 raid[8] on a flotilla headed towards the blockaded Gaza Strip and the deaths of protesters fuel ongoing feelings of Muslim disempowerment, which in turn furthers recruitment of radical groups within the larger Muslim world.

IMPETUS

Children of Abraham (CoA) was born in New York City in 2004. One of us – Alexander, a Jew who had previously been a graduate student – was the co-founder and co-Executive Director until 2008. The other of us – Rahman, a Muslim who had previously been a software engineer – joined in 2006 and served as co-Executive Director until 2009.

We designed CoA to improve Muslim-Jewish relations. The bilateral relationship between these two religious groups is of great importance to the geopolitical environment but has only modest institutional support outside of the Israeli-Palestinian context. Our programs targeted young people between the ages of 15 and 20. With their capacity to inflict harm and to inspire hope, young people should be seen as central actors on the global stage. This particular age group is old enough to discuss critical issues at a sophisticated level, yet young enough to be receptive to powerful teachings and vulnerable to ideological forces. The message of CoA was that Muslims and Jews share fundamental similarities that deeply connect them to one another. We were competing with extremists for the hearts and minds of young people. If we had decided to work with students at the post-secondary level, we would likely have been too late for meaningful intervention. If we had focused our efforts on children younger than 15, then the participants would have been much less comfortable with Internet technology and much less likely to have basic English language skills that would enable them to communicate with their peers around the world.

By working with this 15- to 20-year-old age group, we witnessed two seemingly opposing trends in their lives. On the one hand, these young people were incredibly hopeful, open to challenging assumptions, curious to explore the world. On the other hand, they or their peers were often fighting wars or joining youth groups with militant wings. Young people have the power to inspire their elders by reminding them of the potential in humanity to do more and be better, rather than to accept as inevitable some of the injustices and patterns to which they have grown accustomed. Equally true, however, is that young people are often the greatest forces of destruction in our world. They comprise the majority of terrorists and soldiers.[9] While terrorists and soldiers in most cases are not morally equivalent, both are actors who inflict harm through the use of physical force. Whether committed in the name of suicidal fundamentalism or the perceived defense of democratic ideals, violence puts teenagers on the frontlines.

Many observers of youth-centered organizations, whether they be press, potential donors, or even peer leaders in the field, mistakenly treat young people as if their relevance is entirely relegated to the future. Adults cannot afford to dismiss youth as irrelevant in practical terms. These young people are not the future. They are not a cute investment for an undisclosed time. They are the now. They matter right now.

DESIGN

CoA sought to build an international community of Muslim and Jewish youth who celebrated their religious identities. Through an engaging project involving a photographic exploration of Jewish and Muslim communities around the world, and unflinchingly honest online dialogue, participants had formed a network of advocates and 'ambassadors'[10] for groundbreaking Muslim-Jewish relations. We sought to improve the culture of Muslim-Jewish relations by creating a peer youth network that works together to foster mutual understanding and respect in local communities. Voices publicly advocating Muslim-Jewish dialogue are non-existent in nearly all of the places in which our participants live. We had hoped CoA would be the springboard from which some of these courageous voices would emerge.

CoA's mission was to host the first online community for the world's Jewish and Muslim students to spend time together using the most effective technologies available. We harnessed the power of the Internet to enable students in societies that have no or few members of one group to interact with members of the other group, as well as to have the broadest impact at the lowest possible cost. We aimed to restore a healthy relationship between these two ancient peoples and to honor our common heritage, reaffirming the essential principles that lie at the heart of our faiths. We used photography to open up lines of communication between Muslims and Jews by illustrating shared rituals, habits, and customs. We partnered with local educators, businesspeople, and organizations to create programs in countries with limited prior history of educational opportunities specifically for Muslims and Jews to learn about each other.

CoA created the Global Discovery Program (GDP) in the summer of 2004 to facilitate a dialogue exclusively on the Internet using discussion boards that drew 61 students from 23 different countries, with just over half of the students being Muslim and just under half being Jewish. The program was evaluated and improved through three other iterations. The last GDP ran in the early part of 2008, and, in total, we had 210 graduates (representing 45 countries) of our online programs.

All four iterations of the program had shared two primary components: e-dialogue and photograph exchanges. By e-dialogue, we mean the modern equivalent of traditionally face-to-face small group facilitated conversations that aim to achieve greater mutual understanding through the medium of Web-based discussion boards. Research assessing the impact of contact programs in transforming attitudes concluded that inter-group contact reduces inter-group prejudice.[11] While none of the studies analyzed focuses on e-dialogue, we saw that students' views of their peers of the other religion were transformed by their participation in CoA.[12] Through our work, we hoped to contribute to research on the impact of Web-based inter-group contact programs.

In the photography component of our online program, we asked participants to take original photographs of their families, neighborhoods, places of worship, food, clothing, rituals, and other windows into their local culture. Between 2004 and 2008, the 210 graduates of our programs submitted over 2,000 digital photographs. The traveling photo exhibition used to raise awareness about CoA drew entirely from this collection. Photography had been an essential tool in the success of our work. Though books about Islam, Judaism, and Muslim-Jewish relations have been written by serious scholars,[13] hundreds of pages of textual analysis and comparison often do not move the average Muslim or Jew to view the other with curiosity and appreciation. However, by asking each of the participants in CoA programs to share photographs of their families, their communities, and their customs, participants became mutually humanized. Photography inspired questions and enabled sensitive conversations to occur.[14]

The combination of the high cost of international travel and strict visa requirements makes it nearly impossible for the majority of people in Muslim countries to meet Jews. (Although the cost of international travel and visa requirements may also make travel for Jews to Muslim-majority countries prohibitive, it is easier for Jews to meet Muslims since, as discussed above, Jews often live near them.) The Internet was the chosen medium of CoA because 'meeting virtually' is the only way for most Muslims and Jews to meet each other. Fortunately, the Internet is not a marginal medium, but one to which access is expanding rapidly across the developing world.[15]

Many people conflate Palestinians and Israelis with Muslims and Jews, respectively. Despite the fact that only one in five Muslims is Arab, many people in the United States use the terms 'Muslims' and 'Arabs' interchangeably, just as many in the Muslim world use 'Jews' and 'Israelis' interchangeably although only three out of four Israelis is Jewish, and four out of 10 Jews are Israeli.[16] As a result of this confusion, we found ourselves in the unexpected side business of providing background education for most of our potential supporters to dispel widespread ignorance about Judaism and Islam and their relationship to each other as religions and as diverse global communities. Similarly, Seeds of Peace has worked since 1993 to bring Israelis, Palestinians, and others together in Maine, a northeastern state in the United States, to learn to co-exist in a safe context far from the day-to-day conflict and danger at home.[17] Hundreds of small initiatives bring Israelis and Palestinians together.[18] The Abraham Fund gives grants to projects that foster equality and co-existence between Jewish and Arab citizens of Israel.

It is vital that governmental and non-governmental institutions in Muslim and Jewish communities create more opportunities for Muslims and Jews (and Christians) to work and live together in peace and harmony. We had found in launching this enterprise that there was an urgent need for the work we had begun in CoA to invest in education around the world due to the fallout from the Arab-Israeli conflict on global Muslim-Jewish relations. Arab-Israeli dialogue is only one part of Muslim-Jewish dialogue.

We saw ourselves as being on the frontlines of creating a model for Internet-based conflict resolution. The best programs in the world that depend upon face-to-face encounters are intrinsically limited in their impact to a very small number of individuals and have a high cost per participant. Only creative, strategic uses of global communication technologies have the capacity to scale messages of respect to reach millions, rather than thousands, in seeking to enable young people from different and mutually misunderstood backgrounds to educate each other directly. In founding and launching CoA, we had begun a process the aim of which was to enable a message of Muslim-Jewish mutual respect to 'go viral' through a network of Internet-connected teenagers.

Taking into account the evaluation of the 2006 online program cycle, we made a strategic shift in our thinking. We had measured success largely in terms of the geographic reach and diversity of our online participants. Upon review of our programs, we decided that we could not realistically support alumni of our programs as isolated individuals scattered throughout the world. This led us to focus our attention on a select number of countries where we could make the greatest impact. In 2007, we divided planned programming into two areas: the GDP and Domestic Discovery Programs (DDPs).

We implemented the more geographically-limited GDP in 2007. The program directors selected Muslim students from countries with some of the most significant concentration of Muslims: Syria, Iran, Indonesia, Saudi Arabia, and the United Arab Emirates. The program directors likewise selected Jewish students from countries with some of the most significant concentrations of Jews: the United States, the United Kingdom, Canada, and France. During the first part of the GDP, students discussed their stereotypes and assumptions about, and hatred for, the other. Of particular interest to the educational process was whether animosity in each case tended to be rooted in religious, political, or economic factors. The students discussed the role of the media and political/religious leaders in creating their perceptions, and critically examined the level of accuracy of local representations of the 'other.'

In the second stage of the program, students engaged in guided weekly conversations about prayer, ritual, holidays, community, women's rights, religious scriptures, history, and politics. Simultaneously, they photographed the weekly themes as they applied to their own lives, where appropriate. The students then used Wiki[19] technology to log on to password-protected virtual classroom spaces in order to collaboratively create multi-media educational materials out of their own dialogue and photography that could be used for presentations and educational materials. Selected alumni from past online programs were brought into the process as mentors to the new group of students. The continuity helped to build a support network that was crucial to some of the new students who were anxious about the process of getting to know the 'other.'

DDPs were the second type of program CoA administered. Muslim-Jewish dialogue exists mainly as a concept and on the ground in only a handful of countries. In other countries, however, where Jews and Muslims co-exist, no organization invests resources in targeted educational programs to enable members of the two communities to learn more about each other. CoA considered the Muslim-Jewish dynamics and political contexts in Morocco, Turkey, Germany, the Netherlands, Russia, Iran, and France – countries with some of the most potential for active engagement between Muslims and Jews – to determine where we as an organization could add the most value on the ground. We initially chose Morocco and subsequently selected France as the place to devote our most significant resources.

Morocco seemed like the ideal place to pilot a DDP. CoA undertook a fact-finding mission to Morocco in July 2006 that included meetings with two of the King's senior advisors, ministers in the government, journalists, and community and religious leaders. A follow-up trip three months later focused on solidifying relationships and expanding the network of partners. CoA staff determined that there was great interest on the part of the Government of Morocco in supporting CoA's work, and that the program most likely to add value in the Moroccan context was the creation of oral histories to enable young people to learn about the radically different state of Moroccan Muslim-Jewish relations 50 years ago. Despite the efforts of our tireless representative in Morocco, bureaucratic red tape and political officials' fear to get involved during national elections ultimately stalled our progress on initiating a program there.

Our board then turned to France as our next area of operations. CoA favored France over some other candidate countries because of what we anticipated to be open access to decision-makers needed to scale programs, significant Jewish and Muslim communities, and a safe political context in which to enable discussion of Jewish-Muslim issues. Our board then asked us to spend significant time in Paris in order to focus on establishing a network of supporters and creating a CoA sister organization, Generation Dialogue, in and for the people of France. A better chance of success than what we had encountered in Morocco, in other words, would be dependent upon an ongoing on-the-ground commitment preceded by a long-term analysis of the situation. The two of us spent two months in late 2007 living in Paris and meeting with over 150 individuals to learn about the French context and where we could most add value. We presented our findings to our board, which asked us to relocate indefinitely to Paris in February 2008.

We led the organization through a very exciting transition. In Paris, we were focused on bringing our experience facilitating online Muslim-Jewish dialogue to the very tense situation between French people of different backgrounds in Paris and its suburbs. We had successfully established the French NGO, Generation Dialogue, which was set to launch two significant projects in France: a web-based classroom-to-classroom educational exchange tool that would have paired French students who live and go to school in socially segregated neighborhoods, as well as an experiential educational center dedicated to educating French youth about different cultures and religions. Our organization's president in France was His Excellency, Ambassador Jacques Huntzinger, a former French Ambassador to Israel and Macedonia.

STAFF

CoA was founded on a commitment to Muslim-Jewish balance at all levels of our organizational staff. We, a Muslim and a Jew, served as Co-Executive Directors of the organization, and as the organization had the capacity to absorb additional full-time staff, this structure of a balanced executive would have likely remained. When, in September 2005, the first Muslim co-director left the organization, there was uncertainty about whether the organization could survive such a transition before its first anniversary. CoA recruited to fill the post via craigslist.org[20] and idealist.org,[21] and then invited 10 candidates to interview for the job of Muslim co-director. Three of the candidates were then hired to begin working on October 10, 2005. One was hired to be the Co-Executive Director, one to be the Director of Education, and one to be the Director of Development (even though all were interviewed for the job of co-director). A moment of crisis and near collapse was turned into an opportunity for dramatic and healthy growth.

In hindsight, this choice to hire three Muslims simultaneously was a hasty decision made out of the misguided assumption that it would be exceedingly difficult to recruit Muslim staff members. While candidates were interviewing for one available position, two new positions were created in the process to allow the organization to bring on three talented new staff at the same time. Suddenly, Muslim staff members outnumbered Jewish staff members, three to one. The Jewish chairman and the Jewish co-director of the organization felt no shame in boasting about this fact to everyone who assumed such work would be dominated by Jews.

The Director of Development was not a good fit for the organization. He did not last through the six-month trial period he was offered during which he was to secure US$100,000 in pledges from Muslim donors. He left the organization in mid-January 2006 because of personal differences with the other three full-time members of the CoA staff. The Director of Education, who seemed to be quite enthusiastic for the first few months, grew increasingly uncomfortable as the 'third wheel' in what was then a three-person organization. Much of this discomfort was the responsibility of the two of us, as we had not clearly established where our responsibilities ended and hers began. What was an entirely professional problem became personal as another round of staff tension temporarily derailed the process of developing the organization. The individual serving as Director of Education left CoA in May 2006 at the conclusion of the GDP, which she directed.

Three clear lessons can be learned from these staff hirings and departures. First, it is worth conducting extensive inquiries into the previous employment of new staff, particularly for such a sensitive organization as CoA. Only by speaking with past employers can recruiters gain a sense of the candidate's interpersonal skills and professional history. Second, precise and clear staff roles need to be articulated before interviewing a new staff member. It is wise to spend the necessary time planning for staff expansion and to recruit appropriate people that meet those needs. Shortcuts cannot be taken by having new people come into an organization with an expectation that they will fix old problems that predated them. Third, those in management positions should have experience, or at least training, in organizational change and development. The seeds of both eventual staff departures in 2006 were planted by a transition that was handled unwisely. We would be foolish not to recognize the rudimentary nature of these missteps, but we also observe from peer organizations that they are frequent rookie errors, and thus deserving of mention in spite of the obvious nature of the advice to check references and be prepared for new employees. It is no excuse that we were busy thinking about the macro state of Muslim-Jewish relations. Attention to day-to-day logistical detail is crucial.

Partially in response to earlier experiences, we had learned that we must rely heavily on volunteer office interns to manage some of the administrative responsibilities of the organization. Ranging in age from 15 to 35, interns have often directed day-to-day CoA business while we were out of the office attending to potential donors, conferences, or research. We have learned that it is worth spending time on the front end of each new relationship explaining as much as possible and being as specific as possible with what is wanted or needed from an intern. Achievable goals and regular check-ins help tremendously. As is the case with new staff, advanced thinking and planning prior to the arrival of interns dramatically increases their efficiency and helpfulness upon arrival.

WEBSITE

Although an Internet-based organization, CoA spent remarkably little money on web design and technical support. In total, we spent less than 5 percent of our budget on website development over our first two years. As a result, we had an inefficient back-end structure that required significant time and money to update in 2007. We had relied on hundreds of donated hours of technical support by a close friend.

Eventually, we had the English-language website translated into five languages (Arabic, French, German, Indonesian, and Spanish) by volunteer translators. We anticipated needing to pay translators in the future to maintain an updated multi-lingual site.

Our intent was to build our website into the primary site on the Internet for Muslim-Jewish relations. As CoA grew, we planned to add certain features, such as an interactive map with demographic information about the communities in which we had participants, a virtual pen pal program to connect Jews and Muslims to the 'other' for anonymous chatting, an online resource library with relevant texts from both traditions, and an interactive museum-like exhibition featuring photos of visually compelling similarities with explanations.

As most small non-profits tend to be creative when it comes to using available financial and in-kind resources, we also made the best of in-kind support from initial web design to technical support. In the short term, this approach saved CoA thousands of dollars. However, in the long run, more investment earlier into our web-based organization would have been beneficial to CoA, as paid designers would likely have produced better results. CoA's website would thus have been more attractive to funders, the general public, potential participants, and all those interested in the issue. We should have better recognized the short-term and long-term trade-offs when making budget decisions in our non-profit organization.

In 2007, as CoA's website was being redesigned and re-launched by a team based in Cairo, the Internet was exploding with social networking websites like Facebook and MySpace, attracting millions of users. Muslim-Jewish chat groups were created online using these available resources. While we were thrilled to see other online groups attempting to bring these two communities together, we secretly worried about possibly being pushed into competing to attract participants. Our programs were educational and structured and we worried that these characteristics could make them less appealing than unstructured online conversations.

Should CoA have tried to partner with Facebook or any other social networking site to expand its reach? Would such a partnership have allowed more time for the staff to focus on research and programming? Could that have allowed us to fulfill our dream of a state-of-the-art web-presence, a reference point in Muslim-Jewish relations? In hindsight, these are some of the questions that we should have explored when we had the chance. CoA's website should have been its strongest pillar as our mission was to create the first online Muslim-Jewish community.

PROGRESS

Because young non-profit organizations usually have more failures than successes, it is natural for staff to become pessimistic. Our organization remained focused on our successes as we sought to create a new field of international Muslim-Jewish dialogue. This part summarizes the most important accomplishments during CoA's five years of operations, from 2004 to 2009.

Between 2004 and 2007, we facilitated online educational programs for Muslim students and Jewish students from 45 countries. During that time, we also created a board of 25 advisors who are religious scholars in 14 different countries. Their involvement brought credibility and expertise to our mission as many Jews and Muslims believe it is contrary to their religion to engage in dialogue for the sake of understanding and respect of the 'other.' Working with our board, we created a strategic plan that focused us and functioned as a roadmap for our work. Between August 2007 and January 2009, we did not run any programs. This was the period of time during which we relocated to, and worked on establishing our presence in, France. During this time, we also were invited to speak and present at various international forums. In 2008 alone, we made a feature presentation at the Emir of Qatar's conference on Interfaith Dialogue; participated in the G8 Religious Leaders Summit in Osaka and Kyoto, Japan; and contributed to the World Conference on Dialogue in Madrid, under the patronage of King Abdullah Ibn Abdul Aziz Al Saud of the kingdom of Saudi Arabia.

Our traveling photo exhibition had been on display at international conferences (including the Congress of Imams and Rabbis for Peace and the World Association of NGOs) and in government buildings (including the Israeli Knesset) in Jerusalem, Brussels, Seoul, New York, and Washington, D.C., as well as at several U.S. universities and Islamic and Yeshiva high schools.

In 2007, we built a second version of our website that was easier to navigate and featured a simpler, more streamlined design. The website had mirror sites in French and Indonesian. As part of this effort, we launched an experimental public forum that had 3,000 unique contributors, before our board decided that it should be de-activated because of a number of posts spewing hatred. Our programming and operations as an organization ceased in 2009.

The international press had been responsive to our work. CoA's efforts were featured in local, national, and international media in Arabic, English, Farsi, French, and Indonesian, including in Canada, Cyprus, France, Indonesia, Iran, Israel, Morocco, the Netherlands, Saudi Arabia, Syria, Tunisia, the United Kingdom, and the United States.

In addition to these successes, quite a number of mistakes taught us an enormous amount about the effective management and growth of an organization. It was an invaluable experience to learn not to be afraid of failure. In addition to the staffing problems discussed earlier, we made other missteps.

Due to a staff turnover issue, we failed to collect post-program surveys from our second group of participants and therefore lost the ability to seriously evaluate between the second and third iterations. This misstep taught us to always collect data from our participants for use in invaluable evaluation research.

We established our strongest base in New York City, despite the fact that the American context and what many Muslims consider to be an overwhelming Jewish presence made our work to achieve international credibility and balance that much more challenging.[22] Additionally, the most active members of our board were disproportionately located in the United States and Europe, and we had difficulty building strong relationships with individuals in Muslim countries. There were several challenges that prevented us from cultivating meaningful and strong relationships with a wider group of individuals in Muslim countries. The first one was the distance factor; we learned that despite technological strides made in communications, Muslims valued face-to-face time, especially at the onset of a relationship. In eastern cultures, there is perhaps more emphasis on developing a personal relationship and email, phone calls, and faxes have limited success in our line of work. Limited time and resources prevented us and other staff from undertaking such trips.

We waited too long to create high-end, professional-looking promotional materials, thereby squandering many potential opportunities early on to raise the profile of the organization and attract new donors. Later, we had exceptional brochures in Arabic, English, Farsi, and French, which provided potential donors with a wonderful first impression of CoA.

FUNDRAISING

We in CoA committed ourselves from the outset to obtaining balanced fundraising between Muslim and Jewish sources. Our operating expenses for our first fiscal year (2004–05) came to under US$150,000, which was contributed evenly by His Excellency Mohammad Ali Alabbar and Mr. Eli Epstein.[23]

During our second fiscal year (2005–06), our budget nearly doubled. The support of our two leading patrons was joined by financial assistance from the Rosenzweig-Coopersmith Foundation, the Nathan Cummings Foundation, and individuals in Brussels, Los Angeles, and New York. We had explored funding for future expansion with the Saudi Arabian government, the Richard and Rhoda Goldman Fund, the Coexist Foundation, and additional individuals in Doha, London, Los Angeles, and Manama, but our organization ceased to operate before we could conclude such discussions.

The generosity of our two lead donors enabled us to postpone creating and implementing a comprehensive development strategy, as well as a governing board of trustees. This unusual good luck, in fact, stunted our growth, in the sense that we did not adequately plan for our expansion that would require a wider donor base. The cultivation of relationships with a variety of potential donors would have ensured a broad and sustainable base of support as we moved forward.

SUSTAINABILITY

The sustainability of CoA remained an underlying question. Our growth until January 2009 had been the result of a 'two steps forward, one step backward' path. In addition to the mismanagement issues already discussed, we had also found this pattern of progress and regress to apply in developing, evaluating, and reforming online programs that promoted respect between Muslim and Jewish teenagers. Each setback brought with it a new round of uncertainty about CoA's viability. Still, no one involved doubted the cause or intended to abandon the vision.

For our first two years (2004–06), we worked out of the International Center for Tolerance Education (ICTE) in the trendy Down Under Manhattan Bridge Overpass (DUMBO) section of Brooklyn, New York. This absolutely magnificent site was sponsored by the Third Millennium Foundation. The ICTE was a pioneering initiative to incubate start-up non-profit organizations. Following the expiration of our two-year lease at the ICTE, we began to pay office rent for the first time, and selected a shared office arrangement in midtown Manhattan.

In making the transition to France (in 2007), we began working from our respective apartments in a start-up phase that felt quite similar to the initial months of CoA in New York. In order to sustain ourselves as an organization, we needed to secure the public support of the Government of France, as well as significant funds from both Muslim and Jewish sources, which would have enabled us to administer programs that make a measurable impact on inter-group relations in France. The belief of our board, in asking us to work in Paris, was that we could have a real chance to make a name for our organization through our work in France. Our hope was that our work would be able to be replicated in other European countries, and so would gain us notoriety and a seat at the table in related conversations in other regions.

However, things did not turn out as we had hoped and worked for. Our board mandated us to gain formal support of the Government of France and to identify and develop new programs. Our target was to get financial and political support from the French State, which would have been matched by our supporters in the United States and the Arab world.

In hindsight, the decision to relocate to France was not in CoA's best interest financially or programmatically. France's foundations have been built on 'laïcité' or 'secularism.' Laïcité is a core concept in the French constitution, Article 1 of which formally states that France is a secular republic.[24] The French environment was not and is not open to projects that address religious and cultural identities. Pressing issues like socio-economic disparity, racism, and debates on French identity continue to remain the focal point.

Just as it often felt in past years that we were trying to grow an organization that single-handedly tackled a major global problem affecting more than 1 billion people, so, too, in France did it often feel like we two outsiders were trying to lead reluctant policy-makers to work on one of France's most difficult social issues. We continued to struggle with attracting resources to support innovative ideas that do not neatly fit into boxes that people are familiar with when talking about related issues. In the French context, the very words we used to analyze the problems and describe possible solutions were often very different from the words French people are accustomed to using.[25] We sought to strike a balance between challenging French partners to think outside the box, while respecting French history, culture, and discourse on issues that play out differently than they do in the American context.

In other words, we not only faced challenges common to all non-profit organizations, struggling to raise funds and establish a brand, but we also found ourselves contributing to the creation of a discourse that often does not exist even in the circles of our most likely potential donors. We were not 'Islam v. the West.' We were not 'Arab-Israeli.' We were not an open tent for all faiths to talk about the underlying similarities all human beings share. These are the categories people who have some experience talking about related issues are comfortable using. We promoted Muslim-Jewish dialogue globally. We promoted intercultural dialogue in France. We promoted respect for difference. We focused on young people and enabling them to communicate with each other directly. Even though it felt like there should be more natural partners, it was more difficult than we had imagined to find organizations with these same purposes.

We were naïve to think that the French Muslim and Jewish communities as well as the authorities would jump on such an initiative and adopt it wholeheartedly. There are fierce debates going on inside the Muslim and Jewish communities about survival, empowerment, or disempowerment, and representation or lack thereof. Thus, interest from these communities was nominal. At the same time, the French administration that had banned the *hijab* (Muslim headscarf) along with other religious symbols in public schools proved to be an unlikely partner in CoA's projects.

In 2005, a police chase led to the death of two teenagers and left others with serious injuries, which started the worst riots in the *banlieue* (suburbs) of Paris.

These riots were a symbol of deep-rooted social issues that to date have not been addressed. It is worth noting that most people of immigrant origins, particularly Muslims, live in these *banlieue*. The following two years saw further unrest in France amongst the marginalized community. There was political and social stigmatization of the French Muslims. In such a backdrop, CoA offered to build bridges between not only French Muslims and Jews but also between secular and non-secular citizens of the French republic. In hindsight, this was a no-win position. It led to frustrations and at times doubts about the wisdom of our mission.

The best strategy for us to pre-empt the danger of internal organizational pessimism was to set exciting but achievable goals six to 12 months into the future. We engaged with high-level diplomatic contacts in France about the possibility of initiating programming in Paris. Potential growth in France provided the type of motivation that made it impossible for people as passionate as we were to abandon this organization. Similarly, the reactions we frequently received to our speeches elicited an enthusiastic response amongst our supporters. Additionally, we were regularly asked to share information about the GDP and are reminded by our alumni via email how transformative the experience was for them.

CoA, like most other non-profit organizations, fundraised from individuals and institutions. However, a generous but small group of patrons had always supported CoA. The scale of our vision of improving Muslim-Jewish relations led us to overlook key strategic decisions, including about how to achieve financial sustainability. We at CoA did not clearly devise a plan that would have supported a financially viable organization. Mistakenly, financial independence was not one of our core principles.

In the end, despite all our efforts, enthusiasm, motivation, and commitment from our supporters, the decision to move to France changed the course of CoA. Sadly, CoA evolved from a vibrant, small yet effective New York-based organization into a defunct organization. As one of us (Alexander) left the organization in 2008, the other of us (Rahman) was left to wrap things up.

LESSONS LEARNED

We have learned important lessons about the nature of social entrepreneurship and the tradeoffs involved in this professional endeavor. These lessons can be divided into day-to-day effectiveness, strategic thinking, and lifestyle choices.

Day-to-day Effectiveness

One of the biggest challenges in social entrepreneurship is the effective building of a helpful and efficient network of financial supporters and consultants.

CoA staffers formed hundreds of relationships while we were operating. There were many more potential partners and interested individuals spread throughout the world. We always needed to determine exactly what we needed from each individual or organization with which we met. There is a fine line between gradual relationship development and 'cutting to the chase.' There may be no more important feature of a successful enterprise than efficiency. However, it is inappropriate and thus ineffective in many situations to be too practical and business-minded when so many of the stakeholders have never previously interacted with someone from the other religion and were hearing about an organization with our mission for the first time. Minimizing disappointment by determining which contacts are most valuable, figuring out what the goals of each meeting are, and setting deliverable dates all aid in efficiency. But we were in the business of building trust and challenging assumptions, and it often takes patience and genuine empathy to be able to engage effectively in any work-related relationship. This is doubtless true in many other fields, but we believe it is particularly true in social entrepreneurship.

We confronted the fact that it is typical for contacts to make promises that they are ultimately unable or unwilling to keep. Apathy and personal failures are common. This should not be surprising to anyone who is fighting for a social cause against the dominant trend. However, the idealism that brings us social entrepreneurs to our respective causes means that regular rejections can have a devastating impact on energy levels. Days went by during which we wondered whether we had any chance of making a real difference.

We cannot overstate the importance of celebrating and publicizing good news and achievements. It is essential that people working against the odds to accomplish social change pause and rejoice when mini-victories are won. Being too serious, too intense, and too focused on doing more work at a time when celebration is called for may be a sign of an organization headed for a crash. Few people can be sustained indefinitely without sufficient joy in their professional lives.

This brings us to our next lesson: persistence. Our commitment to fundraising propelled us from our first major gift to our second major gift. Our perseverance in recruitment, including during a period of time in which we perceived disinterest, enabled us to hire two new board members. Persistence is also the key to many of the little things that need to happen that could otherwise get lost in endless multi-tasking.

Strategic Thinking

We have also learned important strategic lessons in launching this enterprise. We cannot overemphasize the importance of clarity in laying out goals and methodology. Most problems have several possible solutions. We would argue that a multi-faceted approach is needed to significantly alter the crisis in Muslim-Jewish relations. While there are government officials, think tanks, and other NGOs dedicated to issues and concerns related to CoA, there is only a small number of other people in the world who have committed themselves full-time to the improvement of global Muslim-Jewish relations. As a result, with good intention but lack of foresight, we spread ourselves too thin.

We needed greater focus, and it took us over a year to gain the discipline, maturity, and understanding to realize that what we needed to do was exclude particular populations in order to better serve others. We could not possibly be successful until we knew exactly what we were aiming to achieve. Our goal was to launch an educational project that for the first time would be globally inclusive of Muslim and Jewish teenagers. By reaching students in over 40 nations on six continents, we felt quite positive about what we had achieved in a short time. But we had come to realize that this manner of measuring success prevented us from making a sustained impact on specific communities. While in Paris, we believed that the problem could best be addressed by seeing significant change in Paris, and moving forward by determining the next place for us to invest our skills and resources. The opportunity to work on these issues in many different locations was exciting, but we needed to determine how best to focus and sustain our efforts. In order to do so, we needed to establish criteria for selecting regions where we could have the greatest impact. We also anticipated developing greater clarity about optimal methods to achieve our goals as the organization evolved.

This leads to another very important lesson: American models of dialogue and bridge building are not necessarily adaptable to other cultures. One of the biggest criticisms we hear in the fields of social entrepreneurship, development, and peace and conflict resolution concerns the 'one-size-fits-all' approach. It has been proven time and again that this approach is short-sighted and yet organizations continue to repeat the same mistake. As outsiders, our understanding of French sensitivities, cultural and social references, political and historical narratives, and issues pertaining to Muslim and Jewish communities, were at best nominal. We spoke to hundreds of people, but in hindsight, living through and in a society as part of it and being an observer from the outside are two different things. We were two individuals, neither of whom was French nor had any French language ability at the outset, representing an American organization, touching upon one of the most volatile issues in France.

Cultural relativity and sensitivity are the cornerstones of social entrepreneurship; overlooking them even unconsciously can have disastrous results. We overlooked them in several ways. With the best of intentions, we at CoA believed that we should be in France working on French issues forgetting that simply our name, Children of Abraham, would cause discomfort with its religious undertones. It was for this reason that we eventually created a sister organization, Generation Dialogue, which sounded more secular and neutral, to operate in France. We wondered, though, whether we shouldn't have just done away with the name 'Children of Abraham' altogether.

Before organizations venture into other countries and cultures, they must conduct an in-depth study of how the intervention would be effective and how changes made because of the new context might affect the existing organization. We did research in the last two to three months of 2007 and made the move in February 2008. We now wonder, though, whether an internal research document produced by our staff without French language ability was adequate. Perhaps a better alternative would have been to have a local organization conduct a feasibility survey.

Another key consideration is the strategic lesson learned about the careful building of a relationship between us board members and the president of our organization. We were incredibly fortunate to work with a stellar human being as our president and greatest champion, Eli Epstein. He surrounded himself with many wonderful people whom we had the opportunity to meet and who gave us important counsel and moral support. Most of the strength in our relationship with Mr. Epstein derived from his exceptional character and ability to trust us and view us as emerging experts in the field of Muslim-Jewish relations. In return, we were attentive to his needs, sentiments, and enthusiasm. We prioritized him and were honored to change our schedules at short notice to accommodate his frequent desire to help CoA.

Another lesson learned is to put in place accountability and governance procedures. Although any of our board members could ask for a report at any time, we had not put in place procedures that would have lasted long after certain staff had moved on. Regular reporting procedures, like those in the private sector, keep organizations running smoothly and efficiently. In times of crisis, a functional board can make decisions to help avoid staff discontent or provide staff with necessary guidance, or to prevent the staff from derailing the organization's mission.

One of our managerial shortcomings was that we did not mentor others to take over from us. In France, we were two pillars of the organization trying to keep it together – to recreate a new mission and vision in a country we hardly knew. We were still grappling with our new mission and lacked time and resources to hire and groom new staff members. This recognized error leads us to a related lesson: the need to clearly articulate the organization's mission statement. An organization may possess a global, lofty vision, but must retain at its core a pragmatic, step-by-step, focused approach to building organizational capacity. An organization must avoid mission-creep, as it can dilute the original mission and may cause unintended and undesired (not to mention undesirable) outcomes.

When we moved to France, we created two ambitious multi-million dollar projects. Each of us hoped that we could garner support for one project and on its success the other would be easily accepted. What started with such motivation, soon turned into a competition. The board wanted to know which one to shelve and which one to work on; both of us wanted to continue working on our own projects. We learned a great deal from this experience. Organizations should not create an internal environment in which staff members compete for project implementation; this only leads to discontent and fragmentation within the team. Sadly, at a later stage, we went down this road; a healthy, honest, and respectful working relationship turned painful and sour.

The final strategic lesson learned relates to branding.[26] We came to understand that most observers would associate CoA with a similar organization with which they were familiar. In our case, these organizations included Seeds of Peace, Abraham's Vision,[27] the Abraham Fund, and two local projects based in the U.S. (Brooklyn and Detroit) also with the name Children of Abraham. The key to establishing a unique brand name is simplicity. Strangely, this has required a near 180-degree shift in orientation from our academic and journalistic training. In the past, it seemed that nuance, subtlety, and complexity were the marks of seriousness and respectability. In our work as social entrepreneurs, we found that simplicity sells and that we needed to learn more from leading companies than from leading scholars. To get things done as a social entrepreneur, one needs to be able to simplify, to exclude, to push forward, and to take advantage of opportunities. Because we gained the confidence that we were guided by a vision and moved to help more Muslim and Jewish young people learn about and from each other, we found that *acting* quickly often served us better than *thinking* deliberately. We recognize that it is unwise for many people in such situations to act before they think. But we discovered for ourselves as educated social entrepreneurs that our concerns usually laid on the other side of the spectrum, by not acting efficiently and quickly enough.

Lifestyle Choices

A third area of lessons learned can generally be thought of as lifestyle trade-offs. When we compare ourselves with many of our peers, we recognize that we have had unusual professional lives as social entrepreneurs. We came to work when we wanted. We left when we wanted. Sometimes we spent days in coffee shops, and others in the office. We took trips where we wanted, when we wanted, and other times we chose to stay in New York or Paris, our primary bases. Moving our headquarters to Paris at the direction of our board was one of the few examples of decisions made for us, instead of by us, that significantly impacted our lives. This development reflected a key milestone in the maturity of our organization, as we had become less free-spirited and more responsible to others. This proved to be a challenging but exciting transition. We could have earned significantly higher salaries elsewhere than we did while working for CoA. Working with CoA, however, we embraced our jobs with passion. In doing so, we undertook significant international travel and experienced personal and professional growth through challenging our assumptions about, expanding our knowledge of, and gaining exposure to a variety of foreign cultures. There is little structure in the job of social entrepreneur except the structure the social entrepreneur creates. At times, this job characteristic excited us, and at times it hampered productivity. We found that setting work goals for specific days helped to focus us and keep our priorities straight.

This brings us to the related point about email maintenance. Some weeks were consumed entirely with email correspondence. On a typical week, we used to receive close to 1,000 email messages. Since we did not have secretaries or administrative assistants, maintenance of our correspondence proved a major work challenge. We often accomplished this correspondence at night and on the weekends in order to clear out the workweek for meetings, writing, delivering proposals, fundraising, and program development.

It is unfortunate that although we were both passionately committed to working with people to talk through differences and to discover each other, we sat in front of computer screens all day. We would prefer to be talking to people. We would have preferred to be 'in the field' more. But to launch an enterprise that had the power to involve many thousands of people in cutting-edge Muslim-Jewish dialogue activities, both virtual and face-to-face, required us to spend most of our time building the infrastructure of an institution. And the reality today is that the majority of that institution building happens on computers. We both could have taken jobs that would have enabled us to spend more of our time away from computers doing small-scale dialogue work. But because we chose to build an enterprise, there was no way around the fact that most of the hours get logged in front of the computer.

To engage in a social enterprise, one needs to understand that evenings can often be filled with meetings. Work anxieties or stress can interrupt nights of sleep. Weekends can sometimes feel like weekdays. Once launched, balance and boundaries are essential in order to sustain the enterprise. We are both people who value our friends, families, and hobbies. Once we began to spend too much time at work and not enough time attending to the other dimensions of our lives, we started to resent work. This formula was a recipe for failure. Personal sustainability as a social entrepreneur is largely dependent on careful planning, efficiency, and a commitment to setting boundaries that ensure ample private time where work is not on one's mind. And for most initiatives, personal sustainability as a social entrepreneur is more than likely indistinguishable from the sustainability of the enterprise itself.

We found the experience of launching a social enterprise to be deeply meaningful. We are people who like to be challenged, who are driven by optimism and determined to stay grounded in reality. We are certain that we worked on an issue and at an organization about which we remain highly passionate. We realize that we were giving up more lucrative and potentially less stressful opportunities in our professional lives. Though we had never thought of ourselves as social entrepreneurs, we can only hope our story plays a part in convincing some readers to get involved in such work, perhaps that of another organization featured in this collection, or to start a new social enterprise.

NOTES

1. Hommes de Parole is a French humanitarian organization with projects ranging from interfaith dialogue to environmental action. For the official website of Hommes de Parole, see http://www.hommesdeparole.org/. For the organization's official website about high-level conferences assembling religious leaders, see http://www.imamsrabbis.org/.
2. The Muslim World League, according to its English-language website, 'is a broad based international Islamic non-governmental organization.' *See* Muslim World League, http://www.muslimworldleague.org/mwlwbsite_eng/index.htm (last visited Nov. 17, 2011). For the website of the referenced conference, see http://www.world-dialogue.org/english/english.htm.
3. 'Zionism,' coined in 1890 by Nathan Birnbaum, refers to the movement supporting a sovereign Jewish homeland. *See, e.g.*, A Definition of Zionism, Jewish Virtual Library, http://www.jewishvirtuallibrary.org/jsource/Zionism/zionism.html (last visited Nov. 17, 2011).
4. According to one leading study, 81 percent of American Jews feel that being Jewish involves caring about Israel 'a lot or some.' UNITED JEWISH COMMUNITIES, ISRAEL CONNECTIONS AND AMERICAN JEWS 4 (2003), *available at* http://www.jewishfederations.org/page.aspx?id=108513. The executive summary of a study of the American Jewish community states:

    > [S]maller proportions [of Jews] – generally between a quarter and a third – report involvement in other religious and communal activities. Among these are always or usually lighting Shabbat candles, keeping kosher at home, attending religious services monthly or more, belonging to a [Jewish Community Center] or other Jewish organization, making a personal or household contribution to Jewish federal campaigns, volunteering under Jewish auspices, participating in adult Jewish education programs, and having visited Israel.

    JEWISH FED'NS OF N. AM., NATIONAL JEWISH POPULATION SURVEY 2000-01, 7 (2003), *available at* http://www.jewishfederations.org/getfile.asp?id=3905.
5. For the official website of the Abraham Fund, see http://www.abrahamfund.org/.
6. For the official website of the New Israel Fund, see http://www.nif.org/.
7. For the official website of the Inter-Agency Task Force on Israeli Arab Issues, see http://www.iataskforce.org/.
8. Edmund Sanders, *Israel Draws Global Outcry for Fatal Raid*, L.A. TIMES, June 1, 2010, at A1.
9. For example, the median age of foreign-born individuals who travelled to Iraq to fight between August 2006 and August 2007 was 22 to 23 years old. *See* CNN, *Report: More Libyans Joining Militants in Iraq*, Dec. 20, 2007, http://edition.cnn.com/2007/WORLD/meast/12/20/iraq.main/index.html. The average age of Palestinian suicide

bombers is from 18 to 24 years old. *See* Tracy Wilkinson, *In Growing Numbers, Palestinian Boys are Choosing the Brief Life of a 'Martyr,'* L.A. TIMES, June 10, 2002; § Main News, at 1; *Karachi: Into the Mind of A Suicide Bomber*, July 21, 2007, DAWN (Pakistan), http://www.dawn. com/2007/07/21/local17.htm.

10. We use the term 'ambassador' to describe alumni of our programs. Having gone through a process of mutual discovery, our alumni were in the best position to market our organization, to recruit students for subsequent programs, and to push the agenda of improved Muslim-Jewish relations in their local media and communities.

11. *See* Thomas F. Pettigrew & Linda R. Tropp, *A Meta-Analytic Test of Intergroup Contact Theory*, 90 J. PERSONALITY & SOC. PSYCHOL. 751–83 (2006).

12. Two examples of quotations from participants that illustrate CoA's impact are as follows:

- From a participant in Vancouver, British Columbia: 'These past few weeks of communication on the CoA message boards have completely blown me away. I've found myself learning far more than I ever expected, strengthening my own faith and opening my eyes to viewpoints I have never before been exposed to.'
- From a participant in Malmö, Sweden. 'I guess that all of us are really challenging what we have been brought up with. It is also for that reason that we should be even more patient and to the extent that we should avoid getting upset if somebody expresses a discriminating or prejudiced opinion. Just the mere fact that a person is daring to step out of their shell and question things that they have felt for no specific reason more than they have been told so by family and friends is superb. I have actually noticed how people have been daring to ask themselves "why" and I think that seeing a thing like this has made the CoA worthwhile. Well done everybody!'

13. These scholars include F.E. Peters, William A. Graham, Harry Austryn Wolfson, Raquel Ukeles, and Reuven Firestone.

14. A selection of the photographs that highlight visually compelling similarities between Islam and Judaism have also been made available to the general public via a photo gallery on our website (which is still operational) and a traveling photo exhibition that has been shown to over ten thousand people on four different continents. *See* Photo Gallery, Children of Abraham, http://www.childrenofabraham.org/render/Public/Photo_Gallery_Categories/ (last visited Nov. 17, 2011). The emphasis on similarities stems from the great number of parallels between the two faiths that is unknown to the majority of adherents of both (and other) religions and serves as an effective way to frame the process of developing mutual respect on which CoA was based.

15. To be sure, the digital divide is still quite significant. According to one 2011 study, 11.4 percent of Africans, 23.8 percent of Asians, 58.3 percent of Europeans, 31.7 percent of Middle Easterners, 78.3 percent of North Americans, 36.2 percent of Latin Americans/people from the Caribbean, and 60.1 percent of Australians/people from Oceania are Internet users. *See* Internet World Stats, World Internet Users and Population Stats, http://www.internetworldstats.com/stats.htm (last visited Nov. 17, 2011).

16. For Muslim figures, see JOHN ESPOSITO, ISLAM: THE STRAIGHT PATH 2, 43 (3rd rev. upd. ed. 2004); JOHN ESPOSITO, WHAT EVERYONE NEEDS TO KNOW ABOUT ISLAM 21 (2002). Approximately 5.7 million Jews live in Israel out of a global Jewish population of approximately 13.3 million. Central Bureau of Statistics, Israel in Figures 2010, 10 (2010), *available at* http://www1.cbs.gov.il/reader/cw_usr_view_Folder?ID=141; Jewish Agency for Israel, http://www.jewishagency.org/JewishAgency/English/Jewish+Education/Compelling +Content/Eye+on+Israel/Demography/Suggested+Educational+Exercises.htm (last visited Nov. 17, 2011).

17. According to its official website, as of 2011, Seeds of Peace had trained more than 4,300 young people, most through its three-week summer camp program in Maine. Many of the organization's alumni are Israelis and Palestinians. For the official website of Seeds of Peace, see http://www.seedsofpeace.org/.

18. Just Vision manages a leading database of joint Israeli-Palestinian grassroots initiatives and the Alliance for Middle East Peace has encouraged many of the leaders in the field to pool their resources to mobilize the U.S. Congress to increase funding towards these efforts. For the official website of Just Vision, see http://www.justvision.org/. For the official website of Alliance for Middle East Peace, see http://www.allmep.org/.

19. According to Wikipedia, a wiki is 'a website that allows the creation and editing of any number of interlinked web pages via a web browser using a simplified markup language or a WYSIWYG text editor. Wikis are typically powered by wiki software and are often used collaboratively by multiple users. Examples include community websites, corporate intranets, knowledge management systems, and note services.' *See* Wikipedia, Wiki, http://en.wikipedia.org/wiki/Wiki (last visited Nov. 17, 2011).

20. Craigslist describes itself as the following: 'Local classifieds and forums – community moderated, and largely free.' It reports more than 20 billion page views per month, with more than 50 million users in the United States alone. *See* Craigslist, Fact Sheet, http://www.craigslist.org/about/factsheet (last visited Nov. 17, 2011).

21. According to its website, 'Idealist.org is an interactive site, social network, and community for people and organizations dedicated to building a better world, where all people can lead free and dignified lives.' *See* Idealist.org, About Idealist: Terms and Conditions, http://www.idealist.org/info/About/Terms (last visited Nov. 17, 2011).

22. After Tel Aviv, New York City is home to the second largest community of Jews in the world. World Jewish Population, http://www.simpletoremember.com/vitals/world-jewish-population. htm (last visited Nov. 17, 2011). With approximately 2 million Jews, over one-third of all Jews in the United States live in New York City. Lance J. Sussman, *Jewish History Resources: New York Jewish History*, New York State Archives, http://www.archives.nysed.gov/ a/research/res_topics_pgc_jewish_essay.shtml (last visited Nov. 17, 2011).

23. Eli Epstein is a businessman based in New York and is involved in investments and commodity trading. He currently is a Managing Director of Aminco Resources LLC, which manufactures industrial carbon products. From 1990 to 2001, he served as CEO and majority owner of Calco, a joint venture with Conoco Phillips Oil Company. He traveled widely in the Middle East and developed close business and personal relationships with business leaders in the Arab world. As an Orthodox Jew, he was drawn to the similarities of the Jewish and Muslim worlds and had committed himself to creating constructive dialogue and better understanding for both communities.

    H.E. Mohammed Alabbar is a senior aide to Dubai's ruler and the Vice-President / Prime Minister of the United Arab Emirates, Sheikh Mohammed bin Rashid Al Maktoum. He currently serves as the Director-General of Dubai's Department of Economic Development, and Chairman of Emaar Properties, one of the world's largest real estate companies. Emaar is the largest construction and development company in the UAE and has built over 1,000 residential units and office complexes during the real estate boom in Dubai. Emaar is also responsible for the development of Burj Dubai, which is the tallest tower in the world. Alabbar has spoken in a number of international forums, representing the UAE several times at the World Economic Forum in Davos, Switzerland.

24. In French, the relevant portion of the constitution reads: 'La France est une République indivisible, laïque, démocratique et sociale.'

25. We had numerous conversations with public authorities, politicians, and other stakeholders. A consistent theme emerged in the use of language. As an example, terms like 'Muslim-American' and 'Jewish-American' were a part of our conversations while 'French-Muslim' (or 'Muslim-French'), 'Algerian-French' or 'French-Moroccan' are not considered politically correct terms as they go against the French notion of 'equality' for all. Many of them saw being discreet with regards to their religious identity as a part of being French. Thus, at times our focus on looking at religious identities made these conversation challenging.

26. For the importance of branding and effective strategies, see RITA CLIFTON & JOHN SIMMONS, BRANDS AND BRANDING (2003); IAIN ELLWOOD, THE ESSENTIAL BRAND BOOK (2000).

27. For the official website of Abraham's Vision, see http://www.abrahamsvision.org/.

10. Social entrepreneurship in the age of atrocities: Lessons learned and conclusion

Zachary D. Kaufman

INTRODUCTION

Having presented the first-hand narratives of social entrepreneurs who have focused on atrocity issues, this book now turns to reflecting on those separate experiences as a whole. This concluding chapter thus compares each of the preceding case studies of social entrepreneurship – highlighting Americans for Informed Democracy (AID), Asylum Access (AA), Children of Abraham (CoA), Generation Rwanda (GR), Indego Africa (IA), the Kigali Public Library (KPL), the National Vision for Sierra Leone (NVSL), and Orphans Against AIDS (OAA) – with lessons learned interspersed throughout.[1] The topics below draw upon only as many case studies from this book as necessary to illustrate a particular point.

SIMILARITIES

Certain traits are shared by some of the social enterprises while others are shared by all. As noted in the Introduction, this book profiles social enterprises led by young Westerners who focus on atrocity issues, whether ongoing or post-conflict. This part explores some of those shared characteristics in greater depth, concentrating on youth leadership and focus, motivation, luck, failure, institution-building, management, friends and family, technology, intersections with academia, and potential personal risks, costs, and benefits.

Youth: Leadership and Focus

Social enterprises, including all of those profiled in this book, are often founded, led, and staffed by young people, ranging in age from 18 to 30 years old. While people of all ages and experience levels are engaged in social entrepreneurship, youth often provides the requisite time, idealism, energy, enthusiasm, and boldness to launch a social enterprise – traits that perhaps an older group of individuals would not possess in part or in toto. Bill Drayton and Dr. Cheryl Dorsey emphasize these dynamics in the Foreword and Afterword, respectively. Archbishop Desmond Tutu has similarly noted: 'Youth are uniquely equipped to change the world because they dream. They choose not to accept what is, but to imagine what might be.'[2]

Yet these efforts by youth are not always viewed positively. Guidance counselors often criticize students – and parents are often frustrated by their children – for having vague notions of their future careers, such as that they 'want to help people.' Far from many of their peers with meticulously-planned careers, youthful social entrepreneurs do not necessarily strive for linear professional paths. These instincts should be cultivated and encouraged; as these young people learn about the world's needs and develop skills, they will be ready to apply their knowledge and expertise when they confront problems and opportunities that inspire them to act in concrete ways.[3]

While social entrepreneurship has certainly become professionalized, such activities may also be performed and treated as a 'hobby,' especially among such youthful, socially-conscious individuals. Young people often start off as part-time social entrepreneurs, as a kind of extra-curricular activity, and may or may not eventually pursue the field full-time. Social entrepreneurship concerns often emotionally and economically taxing problems involving human struggles. Social entrepreneurs should pay careful attention to the toll those problems take on their personal lives so those problems do not become overwhelming. Young people – with their ever-changing interests and priorities – often exercise little patience and long-term commitment. Since the broader goals of social enterprises may take longer than even a lifetime to accomplish, they must have leaders who are dedicated to prolonged participation or who develop and implement realistic succession plans, as discussed further below.

Furthermore, relatively young leaders are sometimes naïve, immature, undisciplined, inexperienced, and ignorant in ways that may be harmful or even catastrophic to an organization. Therefore, social enterprises requiring a relatively large amount of knowledge, diplomacy, or sensitivity may also require a greater amount of 'adult supervision,' which can mean incorporating into the organization an experienced, engaged Executive Director and/or Board of Directors/Trustees/Advisers (and IA, for example, features both a Board of Directors and a Board of Advisers). While we should not doubt the vigor of youth, we should remember to learn from the wisdom of elders.

In addition to the fact that the profiled social enterprises are run, at least in part, by young people, these ventures also primarily focus on aiding young people. CoA targeted youth between the ages of 15 and 20. GR and OAA both concentrate on orphans and others who have not yet completed their education. AID aims its awareness-raising and training efforts at American youth. The KPL strives to serve, in part, children's educational needs. The NVSL used its exhibit, in part, as a forum for educational activities benefitting children in school and youth groups. AA has provided legal assistance to young people, including those in danger of being forced to become child soldiers. IA's efforts have enabled more of its partner cooperative members' children (some of whom were born of rape from the genocide) to attend school.

Why are these youthful social enterprises so focused on youth? Because the social entrepreneurs profiled in this book are young, they naturally gravitate towards their peer age group. Furthermore, young people play a critical role, whether for good or ill, in the international arena. CoA emphasizes this point, which may be especially acute in the minds of young social entrepreneurs: 'With their capacity to inflict harm and inspire hope, young people should be seen as central actors on the global stage.' Moreover, young people, even if they are not central actors now, will grow up to be. AID focuses on university-level students and the KPL in part aims to serve children, both noting that young people are future leaders and so must be a focal point for change in the present.

Motivation

Social entrepreneurs initiated each venture to fill a gap they perceived in attempts to address problems. GR was inspired by its founders' dual beliefs, based on their first-hand observations, that donors, NGOs, and the GoR have not focused sufficiently on tertiary education and that existing aid initiatives were too often wasteful and incompetent. The latter view echoes the critique some commentators, such as Philip Gourevitch – a staff writer at *The New Yorker* who also wrote one of the best and earliest books on the 1994 Rwandan genocide[4] – hold about the often self-defeating and poorly-executed foreign aid/development industry.[5]

Like GR, OAA originated in response to its founder's personal experience of witnessing the plight of children in particularly dire circumstances. Andrew Klaber established OAA after seeing the tragedy of Thai children whose parents were infected with HIV/AIDS. And like GR and OAA, the KPL community was inspired to undertake its campaign to build Rwanda's first public library by what it observed – or, crucially, the public library it did *not* observe – in the country.

Given the experiences of GR, the KPL, and OAA, it is clear that some social enterprises grow out of the time social entrepreneurs spend in a particular community working on other matters, rather than some venture conceived, designed, and executed from a distance. Travel – particularly to developing countries, where the potential impact of social entrepreneurship is often the greatest – can thus directly lead individuals to identify gaps in development needs and, consequently, the inspiration to supply social entrepreneurship work there. (A notable exception to this phenomenon is IA, the founder of which decided to base the venture's operations in Rwanda, which he had never visited, after determining that his initial instinct favoring Angola was problematic.)

The other enterprises are similarly gap-filling initiatives. IA facilitates – and grows – a market by aligning the supply of handicrafts from Rwandan women's collectives with the demand for such goods from foreign consumers. AA seeks to narrow the difference between refugees' need for and access to legal resources. OAA strives to bridge the gulf between the basic requirements of and ability to afford those requirements by particular communities of orphans. The NVSL sought to merge the desire and opportunity for survivors of atrocities in West Africa to express themselves. CoA aspired to fill the space between the perceived benefit and existing avenues of communication between Muslims and Jews. AID seeks to connect the divide between essential and actual knowledge and training on global affairs. It is this gap-filling that is the lifeblood and purpose of an entrepreneur, whether social or another type.

Luck

Luck plays a role in social entrepreneurship, just as it does in life more generally. The experience of OAA typifies this fact. Klaber was fortunate to hear about a college alumni event at a U.S. consulate in Thailand, to attend that event, and, finally, to meet by chance the Consul General, who facilitated Klaber's work in developing OAA. Klaber's discovery of a Rotary Club near his undergraduate university that was willing to partner with a Rotary Club he identified overseas was, likewise, serendipitous.

Then again, perhaps the extent of luck is overstated in such cases. As Bear Bryant, the legendary University of Alabama football coach, proclaimed: 'Luck is when preparation meets opportunity.'[6] Klaber, like other social entrepreneurs profiled in this book, was prepared, and therefore able, to seize opportunities.

Failure

Like luck, failure is a common part of everyday life and work and can possibly be productive. Arnold-Fernández did not obtain an Echoing Green Fellowship on her first try, but the application process itself yielded rewards in challenging – and refining – AA's business model. All of the profiled enterprises have faced various setbacks along the way. As discussed in the Introduction, perseverance and carefully identifying, analyzing, and applying lessons learned are key qualities of social entrepreneurs.

Institution-building

Social entrepreneurs face similar questions and problems when considering how to build their institutions effectively and efficiently. These issues include the adaptation of existing models; credibility; local learning, engagement, and buy-in; fundraising; partnerships; organizational evolution; organizational creation and alternatives; profitability; and the interplay among these issues.

Adaptation of existing models
One of the striking features of social entrepreneurship is that many of the ideas involved are not, in a strict sense, new. AA notes that it sought to build on existing, successful models of refugee legal aid. Though a public library had not existed in Rwanda, the KPL campaign enjoyed precedent in other public libraries throughout the world. GR and OAA, in pursuing holistic support for orphans, were path-breaking in their regions, but not unique in their efforts either. The non-profit IA had a model, in the for-profit Gahaya Links, of a Rwandan handicraft business that exported goods on a large scale to the United States. Social entrepreneurship may thus be best understood in some cases as adapting or applying existing models in new ways or at least to new places rather than creating an entirely new type of venture.

Credibility
Because local community members and potential funders are sometimes skeptical of the motives and abilities of social entrepreneurs and their ventures, a social enterprise's credibility is critical, particularly in the early phases of work and especially when led by young, inexperienced individuals with unformed reputations. Building such trust and confidence – in both the social entrepreneur and the social enterprise – played a critical role in different aspects of at least three of the case studies profiled in this book.

Meeting space provided by the U.S. Consulate in Chiang Mai, introductions the U.S. Consul General made to community leaders, and partnerships with more established organizations endowed OAA with credibility early in its development.

Similarly, the KPL secured its credibility through a number of initiatives and relationships. The imprimatur of Rotary International, of which the RCKV is a part, bestowed legitimacy on the RCKV's flagship project. The designation of 501(c)(3) tax-exempt status in the United States provided the AFKPL with the validity of being a bona fide American non-profit organization. In addition, the first series of donations to and fundraisers for the KPL, one of which was hosted by the then-United States Ambassador to Rwanda and another of which was hosted by the then-Rwandan Ambassador to the United States, attributed even more reliability and trustworthiness to the KPL's leaders and the campaign itself.

IA has determined the credibility of artisans before partnering with them, by placing test orders to judge for itself the quality and timeliness of the goods. IA has then often provided U.S. retailers with prototypes of its artisan partners' handicrafts so that those retailers can ascertain for themselves the quality of the goods before placing large orders. Recognition from independent organizations like Harvard Business School, the Fair Trade Federation, and Goldman Sachs *10,000 Women*, and early, high-profile clients such as Polo Ralph Lauren, Anthropologie, and Nicole Miller have solidified IA's credibility as a serious, high-quality social enterprise.

Local learning, engagement, and buy-in

Former British Prime Minister Winston Churchill once declared: 'Courage is what it takes to stand up and speak; courage is also what it takes to sit down and listen.'[7] The successful social enterprises profiled in this book have been thoughtful and deliberate about their interventions, attempting, through listening and learning, to be sensitive to the true requirements and desires of local populations.

Since a local community knows its particular needs best and is the primary beneficiary of a social enterprise's work, it is both necessary and useful to engage the local community when designing a project. Consequently, successful social enterprises stress the importance of listening to and learning from local stakeholders before and during the execution of a project. GR and OAA staffers have solicited input from locals about how they could more successfully combat HIV/AIDS. IA managers have relied upon their local staff to advise them on the sensitive social and economic contexts in which their artisan partners operate. The design of the KPL reflects Rwandan art and culture and was generated through a competition in the local community. Moreover, the KPL stocks materials on subjects of particular interest to the local community, such as African history. The NVSL emphasizes the significance of having involved locals in the project's work.

If possible, then, as early as the design phase of a social enterprise, social entrepreneurs should raise local interest and involvement in the project. For example, some sort of public competition could be held to design an aspect of the project, such as an advocacy campaign. Competitions, conferences, consultations, or some other means of involving the public could promote participation within the local community, raise public awareness about the project, and spur media interest.

One enterprise acknowledges not having done sufficient research before launching, or while conducting, its intervention. CoA notes that the French culture was not receptive to its religiously-oriented mission, in part because secularism is enshrined in the French constitution and in part because the country has other priorities. CoA's experience is a reminder that thorough research on the beneficiary community must be conducted before initiating a social enterprise to ensure that, however well-intentioned, the venture itself – or at least the way in which it is conceived and executed – is also welcome.

Closely related to the concepts of credibility and local learning is the concept of local buy-in, whereby the local community subscribes to the social enterprise's mission and activities. Indeed, local buy-in is an expression of the credibility conferred by the target community. Learning from the indigenous population helps ensure local buy-in, because the local community is – and feels – involved in the process. Each profiled social enterprise has required some minimum local buy-in, recognizing that indigenous stakeholders should, and often do, play a critical role in the design, operation, and success of a social enterprise. Only if Rwandans are comfortable with certain patron procedures will the KPL be able to function successfully. IA believes that Rwandan artisans will continue their partnership with IA only if they consider IA to be reliable. Consequently, IA has promoted transparency in its pricing calculations and internal cost structure as well as responsiveness to artisans' feedback on improving training programs. GR believes that its mission of facilitating university education for Rwandans will be realized only if these students are fully committed to their studies and engaged in their career planning. Some students rejected certain aspects of GR's assistance; GR took note and refined its approach.

If the local community is not involved, no matter how positive the project and no matter how genuine 'the kindness of strangers,'[8] the venture may be rejected because it is perceived as yet another good or service that a third party, often from the West, offers a needy community, either as some sort of neo-imperialist or neo-colonialist endeavor or perhaps as simply unnecessary. The local community, without buy-in, may even forcibly attempt to sabotage or to resist a social enterprise.[9]

When engaging the local populace, it is important to consider which community members will likely be helpful and which may be harmful, perhaps even unintentionally. The involvement of particular community members may not elicit the increased credibility, legitimacy, and acceptance for the project that the social entrepreneur seeks. Yale Law School Professor Amy Chua, who authored the Preface to this book, has drawn attention to the phenomenon of what she terms 'market-dominant minorities,' or 'ethnic minorities who, for widely varying reasons, tend under market conditions to dominate economically, often to a startling extent, the "indigenous" majorities around them.'[10] These minority groups, such as Rwandan Tutsi, Indians in Kenya, or ethnic Chinese Burmese, are often the elites of developing countries, and thus attractive in-country candidates for social entrepreneurship partnership. However, the disproportionate amount of economic power they hold and exert has often elicited, as Professor Chua documents, ethnic hatred, which has led to bloodshed, including genocide.[11] On the one hand, the majority's possible resentment towards minority individuals or groups may be further directed at any social enterprise in which those minorities are involved as much as if only outsiders led the venture. This could occur precisely because the majority may consider many of these minorities, even if long-time residents and citizens, to be outsiders themselves.[12] On the other hand, minorities' involvement in social enterprises that benefit the local community could help them dispel some of the suspicion and antipathy they suffer, which may be part of the reason they seek to participate in the first place. Social entrepreneurs must thus carefully weigh the potential benefits and drawbacks of involving certain members of the local community in their work.

Fundraising

Funding makes much of social entrepreneurship possible, and a significant amount of a social enterprise's time and resources will therefore be dedicated to fundraising. However, each social enterprise is different and so must have its own fundraising strategies to meet unique challenges.[13] For example, CoA had two generous donors that made additional fundraising mostly unnecessary for the organization's short-term purposes. However, as CoA notes, the fact that the organization did not undertake wider and more diverse fundraising even when the organization was financially secure later hindered its ability to develop broader support for sustainability and future expansion. A narrow pool of donors may also unintentionally convey the notion that an organization has limited support or is a vanity project. A diverse and large pool of funders, as most of the other social enterprises have had, can enhance the credibility of an organization and its underlying mission.

Fundraising success will likely naturally fluctuate, sometimes greatly, over time. As the KPL experience shows, the first stage of fundraising, when a project and its participants are still new and relatively unknown, is often the slowest and most difficult. Even after the threshold is met where potential donors are no longer skeptical of the commitment of staff and their likelihood of success, fundraising may still vary over time. One such reason is donor fatigue. Repeat donors may finally decide not to give any more if they are frustrated by the project's slow progress. Other reasons relate to competition for the already scarce resources for such social enterprises. As the KPL illustrates, there are three basic types of competition: competing interests in a different issue area in the same country, competing interests in the same issue area in a different country, and competing interests in different issue areas in different countries. Social entrepreneurs must remain aware of these competing interests and try not to be discouraged while donors are pulled in multiple directions.

Successful fundraising for a social enterprise may include pursuing mutually beneficial endeavors for donors. As the KPL recommends, social entrepreneurs should brainstorm incentives that can help persuade potential donors that contributing is a 'profitable' activity. A realistic fundraiser recognizes that some will donate only if it is in their self-interest to do so. Some of those self-interested reasons to donate include gaining positive publicity and furthering the donor's own cause. Many donor benefits thus involve various ways of formally publicizing the donor's generosity, such as by including the donor's name or logo on the social enterprise's website, letterhead, brochure, and other promotional materials. (Of course, such donor benefits must be designed such that they do not sacrifice the independence or sully the public image of the social enterprise.) Even then, some donors may decide to give anonymously, which still could allow for a contributor to promote her cause by conditioning the donation on some sort of adjustment in the social enterprise or enabling the venture to expand in a way that furthers the contributor's agenda.

In the process of fundraising, it pays to be creative, patient, diligent, and reflective. Successful fundraisers are those who employ a multitude of tactics and who are willing to take risks and abandon ineffective methods.

Partnerships
Unlike the 'solopreneurs,'[14] or entrepreneurs who work alone, in other types of innovative ventures, social entrepreneurs rarely operate in a vacuum. To echo the English poet John Donne, no social enterprise is an island.[15] In fact, social entrepreneurs usually collaborate with and rely heavily upon partners to develop and execute their plans. OAA depends on local partners to select students who receive funding and to oversee programs that OAA supports. In order to register itself officially with the Thai government, AA-Thailand identified itself as a project of a separate, umbrella organization in the country. The NVSL partnered with the RSLAF to provide Sierra Leonean soldiers with training on the SL TRC, to share the NVSL exhibition, and to solicit 'Visions' from the military. Instead of pursuing its own programming and in order to promote its advocacy in the area of atrocities, AID has featured representatives from, supported the networks of, and hosted workshops with the Save Darfur Coalition/Genocide Intervention Network (subsequently merged and called United to End Genocide) and STAND. The KPL campaign comprises multiple partners, particularly the RCKV, the AFKPL, and donor organizations, such as the Government of Rwanda, Project BIG, and LWB, which have provided not only funding and in-kind contributions of goods and

services, but also valuable ideas. IA and GR are two social enterprises profiled in this book that have partnered with each other (among others). IA has provided valuable (to both the individual and IA) internships (as skills trainers for IA's artisan partners) to candidates GR has rigorously vetted. In addition, IA has partnered with multiple cooperatives and retailers in varying types of relationships.

Journalist and author Malcolm Gladwell provides helpful nomenclature and descriptions of different types of personalities that are critical to facilitating what Gladwell calls 'social epidemics,' or ideas, behavior, and messages that spread quickly.[16] Gladwell suggests that one such group of people is 'Connectors,' individuals with unusually broad and varied social networks. As Gladwell puts it, Connectors 'link us up with the world ... [they are] people with a special gift for bringing the world together.'[17] Connectors, whom Gladwell also calls 'people specialists,'[18] possess this ability because they 'know lots of people. They are the kinds of people who know everyone.'[19] Given the number and diversity of partnerships involved in social entrepreneurship, the most effective social entrepreneurs are usually Connectors. Social entrepreneurs often thrive when connected to like-minded individuals and organizations. Where such strategic alliances exist, trust is a necessary component of social entrepreneurship – and it must be built, solidified, and re-affirmed over time. To use the words of former U.S. President Ronald Reagan, social entrepreneurs should 'trust, but verify.'[20] For example, OAA issues guidance to, reviews expenditures of, and receives regular reports from its local partners: trusting – but verifying – their work.

Organizational evolution

Each venture has evolved – a phenomenon indicating that changemakers themselves, while seeking to change particular communities and perhaps the entire world around them, may change even their own work and thinking over time. These organizations changed in different ways and to different extents.

Some ventures altered their operations. GR made its student selection system more rigorous over time. Other enterprises transformed their structure. OAA morphed from a hierarchy to a partnership.

Still other ventures revised their mission and scope. AA initially raised funds to support AMERA-Egypt but soon broadened its mission to serve as a new human rights organization that would help catalyze the refugee legal assistance movement itself. OAA opened in one country (Thailand) but then expanded to five others (Ghana, Kenya, Sierra Leone, South Africa, and Uganda) and later contracted to three (Kenya, South Africa, and Uganda). Because of the time-consuming efforts of fundraising for multiple country projects, OAA began spending less time on its other missions of programming and counseling. In addition to its student selection process, GR grew from an initiative focused on helping a particular orphanage to a country-wide program, and GR also evolved from performing varied development assistance to focusing exclusively on supporting higher education. The NVSL began as a two-month campaign focused on soliciting input from the Sierra Leonean public for the Recommendations section of the SL TRC's final report. The NVSL then became a more robust campaign to engage the Sierra Leonean public in a cultural and artistic dialogue on the objectives of the SL TRC, including truth and reconciliation. Moreover, the NVSL produced a Handbook to the SL TRC final report and co-sponsored a related conference, which were complementary ventures aimed at making the TRC's findings accessible to the Sierra Leonean public. Other social enterprises may also want to consider broadening their original objectives but they should balance that impulse against the phenomenon of 'mission creep,' whereby a venture continues to expand its goals until it reaches failure.

Most of the enterprises began informally but became more professional in their structure, staff, and operations over time. IA and GR both evolved from small groups of volunteers with modest budgets to organizations of several full-time staff members with significant financing. OAA began as one person's quest to assist individuals he personally met, but eventually became an organization with several staff members in multiple countries. That each enterprise became more professional as it grew in size is no coincidence: larger organizations generally need more skilled administrators and greater bureaucracy.

Some of these organizational changes have been driven by larger political, economic, or cultural developments. GR, IA, and the KPL responded to the fact that, in recent years, the Rwandan educational system switched from Francophone to Anglophone. For GR and IA, this development necessitated more training and tutoring in English. For the KPL, this transformation prompted the acquisition of a greater proportion of English-language library materials.

In some cases, internal developments rather than outside forces brought about organizational changes. OAA's leadership modified its structure, mission, and scope to satisfy the desire of each of the organization's multiple officers to recognize ownership and leadership stakes in his own project, and to work on and in a particular country that interested him.

Those ventures that became more professional reflect the reality that many social entrepreneurs come to their work young and inexperienced. Over time, however, these innovators learn lessons and develop increasingly ambitious goals that provide the ability and necessity to restructure their work. These changes also reflect that, as a social enterprise grows, expands, and becomes more ambitious, budget apportionments for overhead may increase. Expending additional resources on internal operations and staff may be a positive development, as it may signify that more – especially experienced and professional – staff are being recruited, hired, and retained, and that ever more ambitious fundraising and programmatic activities are being undertaken.

The two ventures that dissolved did so for different reasons, and their leaders' responses to those dissolutions also differ. On the one hand, the directors of the NVSL reflect on its obsolescence as a natural course of events, in that the project fulfilled its mission of collecting and showcasing artistic and literary 'Visions' while Sierra Leone confronted the immediate aftermath of its recent conflict. On the other hand, the leaders of CoA reflect on its cessation in reluctant and regretful terms, as the result of internal mismanagement, mistakes, miscalculations, and missed opportunities.

The experiences of the ventures profiled in this book demonstrate that it is desirable, and perhaps necessary, for social enterprises to be flexible and adaptive to both internal as well as external circumstances. As a result, social entrepreneurs must accept that their ventures can and do evolve, often in unexpected, increasingly ambitious ways that may be either positive or negative.

Organizational creation and alternatives

All of the enterprises profiled in this book were newly created organizations, not components of another project. This phenomenon is unsurprising given that it is often the instinct of social entrepreneurs, precisely because of their innovative streaks and concepts, to form their own organizations and pursue their own initiatives.

At the same time, many social enterprises are interconnected with existing organizations, usually in the same region or issue area. For example, IA and OAA have collaborated with VisionSpring and Unite For Sight, respectively, to provide eye care. Other social enterprises have overlapping agendas, and some have already shared information and efforts on the issue areas of refugees, orphans, economic development, education, and ethnic tensions.

The experiences with partnerships and organizational evolution profiled in this book suggest a model for promoting efficiency and effectiveness. Individuals wanting to affect social change should seriously consider addressing a problem by broadening or combining existing ventures' operations, structures, missions, or scopes rather than creating a new organization with a similar agenda. While competition and varied approaches can improve quality (as the theory of free-market commerce holds), the continual proliferation of social enterprises may not necessarily be a productive development. Organizations working within the same issue area, particularly within the same geographic communities, may become detrimentally competitive or inefficient as they pursue limited funds from donors, similar labor pools, and attention from local, national, and international communities. Uniting resources, talent, and experience may be the more effective path to success than constantly establishing new organizations. The 2010 merger of the Genocide Intervention Network and Save Darfur Coalition (into what is now known as United to End Genocide) was thus a refreshing and welcome union of two groups, with increasingly overlapping missions and resources, to comprise the world's largest anti-genocide organization.[21]

Profitability

All of the ventures profiled in this book are not-for-profit. A prominent example of a for-profit social enterprise is Ethos Water. Founded in 2002 by Peter Thum and Jonathan Greenblatt, then acquired in 2005 by the Starbucks Coffee Company, Ethos Water is a bottled water company that raises awareness about what it calls 'the World Water Crisis' and donates a portion of its profits to provide clean water in developing countries, especially for children.[22] Another example of such a venture is GoodSearch. Founded in 2005 by Ken and JJ Ramberg, GoodSearch is a Yahoo!-powered search engine that donates 50 percent of its revenues to charities and schools.[23] Yet another example is Stonyfield Farm Yogurt, the world's largest manufacturer of organic yogurt, which consciously employs innovative, cost-effective, environmentally sustainable business principles and operations.[24] Jacqueline Novogratz, a former investment banker who founded and leads Acumen Fund, which combines principles of capitalism and aid, signifies and champions such for-profit social entrepreneurship.[25]

Turning social problems into business opportunities is a mixed bag. Through for-profit ventures, experienced professionals can bring proven management and efficiency principles to bear on issues requiring more than simple charity and good intentions. Conversely, for-profit ventures may, or may be perceived to, shamelessly and opportunistically capitalize on and exploit suffering and desperation.

Whether a social enterprise is – or even should be – not-for-profit or for-profit depends on the range of solutions that can address a given problem. Not-for-profits and for-profits may work simultaneously, even cooperatively, to complement each other's efforts to address the same problem.

Cultures of not-for-profits and for-profits often differ, attracting distinct kinds of staff and espousing dissimilar priorities. Either type of venture can be successful and deliberately benefit a social cause, but the process and people involved may vary greatly.

Management

There are numerous common experiences and lessons learned by social entrepreneurs regarding management; such topics include morale, decision-making, and sustainability.

Morale

Much of social entrepreneurship is driven by personal motivation and monetary, in-kind, and time contributions by staff members who often forgo more
lucrative and perhaps less personally taxing career options. Because of its
difficulties and sacrifices, social entrepreneurship requires high levels of
morale. It is part of human nature to respond favorably to positive feedback.
Both CoA and the NVSL note the importance of achieving and publicizing
small victories along the way, so staff members can celebrate progress at regular intervals between more significant accomplishments.

Decision-making

Decision-making structures and procedures are a recurring topic throughout this
book – one fraught with difficult choices that significantly impact social enterprises. OAA considers it such an important topic that a large portion of its chapter is dedicated to describing the evolution from a hierarchy to a partnership and
related challenges. AA notes that RLAP's staff devolved into factions over
whether decisions should be made by consensus. That case study also notes that
AA's approach at first was, naïvely, not to concern itself much with management, particularly as it related to fundraising. The NVSL notes that its non-hierarchical structure and consensus-based decision-making, which were originally
attractive in their collegiality and informality, proved to be paralyzing on occasion. The NVSL thus proposed that decision-making rules, roles, and responsibilities be clearly delineated and defined. CoA similarly stresses that the
departure of two of its four leaders was due to mismanagement, including insufficient background checks on candidates, as well as unclear job descriptions for
new staff. CoA also notes the importance of building and clarifying relationships
between a social enterprise's advisory board and its day-to-day leaders.

These experiences highlight that, while social enterprises may begin informally by one person or a small group of people with pre-existing relationships
(e.g., friends, relatives), additional staff and more ambitious goals necessitate
more structured decision-making, more rigorous bureaucracy and management, and greater expertise. A venture's increasing formality can indeed be
desirable, even necessary. Such developments demand that time and thought
be invested in intra-group dynamics to ensure the group's work is not
impaired, as befell the CoA experiment. Moreover, as AA, IA, and the KPL
suggest, it is insufficient, if an organization is to grow and operate effectively,
for staff members to possess only subject-matter expertise. Organizational
competence, fundraising acumen, and public relations knowledge, among
other skills, will also be required. This may require the hiring of a COO, a
CFO, or a CEO, perhaps one that is full-time, paid, and empowered to make
executive decisions. Some social enterprises, such as IA, feature all of these
positions and staff who serve in more than one of them.

Sustainability

Each venture must consider long-term maintenance and sustainability. Social entrepreneurs should estimate the project's lifespan and adjust their commitment accordingly. AID, for example, describes how the students it trains perpetuate the organization's mission. The KPL, as a living institution, will need constant upkeep, preservation, and support, and so has envisioned a management structure to oversee ongoing fundraising, decision-making, and stewardship. IA's ultimate goal is to provide training to its artisan partners that will enable them to manage their own quality control and production processes and to become independent in dealing with foreign buyers. Until then, however, IA sustains itself with a combination of philanthropic investment in women's education and aggressive, creative involvement in the consumer goods market.

Without an effective strategy to maintain the social enterprise, even the most promising venture may fail. Not only is it important to anticipate such sustainability needs, but it is also critical to communicate at the outset the plan to address those needs. Potential donors want assurance that their support will be used wisely and will contribute to a long-term solution, and affected community members want assurance that interest in their needs is not a passing fad.

Maintenance and sustainability include both sufficient resources and staff to manage the venture over a long period of time, even perhaps after the social entrepreneur and other staff who initiated and set up the project have left the organization. The budget should therefore clearly anticipate and include adequate funds, and the social enterprise's plan should include additional fundraising, staff recruitment, training, and necessary stewardship of any physical infrastructure.

The human resource aspect of sustainability is often the most delicate and potentially conflicted. Because many social entrepreneurs are – and, as Bill Drayton argues in his Foreword and Dr. Cheryl Dorsey argues in her Afterword, should be – young, a large number of them will eventually leave the organization once they develop other interests, if competing personal or professional commitments take priority, or because the organization ultimately requires more experienced leadership and staff. Some social entrepreneurs may even move on to other ventures, as 'serial social entrepreneurs.' Given the inevitable attrition among youthful social entrepreneurs, long-term planning within any social enterprise should include 'personal exit strategies' – provisions for the organization's durability after key individuals sever ties, or what is often referred to in the private sector as 'succession planning.' Others, however – especially young social entrepreneurs who have founded an organization and helped it grow over an extended amount of time – may be reluctant to relinquish their leadership positions. Their sense of ownership over an organization is both emotional and psychological. But that hesitation may inhibit the organization's, and the individual's, growth, development, and potential.

Social entrepreneurial staff must thus learn how and when to let others take over a project, even if they gave birth to and nurtured the venture. Sustainability plans need to include succession processes and must incorporate efforts to recruit and train the organization's next generation of leaders and other workers. One risk the plan should consider is that the succeeding staff may pursue an agenda that the founders of the organization would not have supported, as is alleged in the case of the Ford Foundation, which is accused of betraying its conservative founders' intentions by supporting liberal causes.[26] Implementing clear objectives, drafting an organizational mission statement, and recruiting staff members who subscribe to that vision can help maintain an organization's integrity as it passes from older leadership to new. In addition, as social entrepreneurs depart from their previous leadership positions in a venture, they may continue on in a capacity that enables them to remain involved and influential. For example, the founder and first CEO of IA is now the chairman of its Board of Directors.

Friends and Family

Of the close relationships she developed with her fellow Balkan war correspondents in the 1990s, Pulitzer Prize-winning author Samantha Power says, 'when it comes to fighting the good fight, there is no fuel like friendship.'[27] The same can be said of family.

Friendship is a central theme of the OAA case study. Friends become partners in the OAA organization and friends of OAA staffers suggest, facilitate communication with, and perform due diligence on potential partner organizations.

Close personal relationships are also mentioned in two other chapters, on the KPL and IA. Friends and relatives of existing RCKV and AFKPL volunteers have become volunteers themselves and some of the most generous donors to the KPL. The first CFO of IA was the founder and first CEO's father and the second CEO was the first CEO's close friend from college. IA raised its seed funding from friends and family and focused on Rwanda after the idea was suggested by a friend of the founder's family.

Young people, whether social entrepreneurs or not, often become or remain involved in activities because of their friends and relatives. These social bonds, beneficial in attracting people and maintaining their loyalty, dedication, and generosity, also may be detrimental, or at least present challenges, in other ways. As Klaber and Grinsell indicate, because of the particular social relationship among the officers, OAA expends more time than it otherwise might on fostering social ties within the organization if the officers had a purely professional relationship. (Conversely, however, as much or more time might be required to build the relationships necessary for a productive working environment if the officers were not already well acquainted.) Friends and relatives may try to exploit their close relationship with a staff member to shirk their responsibilities, such as by securing extensions on deadlines or by submitting work of poor quality. It is emotionally difficult for a staff member to discipline or fire a friend or relative.

A further detriment – possibly catastrophic to any organization – may occur if the personal relationships among staff members sour. As in the case of CoA, an organization may suffer a breakdown in communication, perhaps to the fatal detriment of the organization and its work. Because their commitments may be more to persons than to projects, estranged friends and relatives may leave an organization. The organization may even dissolve entirely if too many of the relationships upon which it is built irreparably break. Social entrepreneurs, as much as any professionals, must thus consider the benefits and drawbacks of working with friends and family, and put into place contingency plans that anticipate the possible deterioration of such sensitive relationships.

Technology

Each venture has employed modern technology to achieve its objectives. Leveraging cutting-edge technology maximizes internal communication as well as external networking, public awareness-raising, fundraising, and staff recruitment while minimizing overhead costs in terms of both money and staff time. In many cases, through savvy and effective use of the Internet, these social enterprises can reach more potential donors and staff and larger numbers of media outlets and interested stakeholders than they might otherwise.

All of the profiled social enterprises use, or used, various websites, such as Change.org, Doostang, Facebook, Friendster, Global Giving, Google+, Idealist.org, LinkedIn, MySpace, Network for Good, Plaxo Pulse, Skype, Twitter, and YouNoodle to boost their recruiting, fundraising, social networking, and internal conversations and deliberations. The SRLAN mentioned in the case study on AA uses websites and listservs to facilitate information-sharing and discussion among its member organizations. The NVSL also harnessed modern technology to communicate with staff members, who were located on three continents. AID has used film screenings (of 'Hotel Rwanda,' 'Invisible Children,' and 'The Peacekeepers,' among others) to educate and inspire young Americans to become more effective advocates for U.S. engagement in the world, and has also used videoconferencing to promote dialogue among students across the world. CoA solicited and published online thousands of images of Jews and Muslims as a means of humanizing each group to the other and highlighting similarities between them. Indeed, because of financial and visa restrictions on travel, but also because of the ability to reach more people than would be possible in person, the Internet (often through wikis) was the primary, if not exclusive, means for Muslims and Jews to meet and communicate through CoA's programs. If anything, given the fact that it was mostly an Internet-based enterprise, CoA regrets not investing more, and earlier, into online resources.

Whereas most of the profiled social enterprises note their use of social media, CoA, unique among the ventures in its fostering of online dialogue, admitted a sense of competition with these less structured and more casual sites. In addition, three ventures – CoA, IA, and the KPL – noted that online relationships are not a full substitute for face-to-face communication, especially at the beginning of a connection. Consequently, social entrepreneurs would do well to remember that online communication can facilitate a relationship, but sometimes only after it is established in person.

Intersections with Academia

All of the case studies cite academic sources in their narratives to support their methodologies and claims. Furthermore, some of the case studies also note how participants have produced their own academic literature related to their work or otherwise have contributed to scholarly discourse. Michael Kagan, in the AA case study, has written scholarly works on refugee legal aid. AID has hosted many of its conferences and workshops on university campuses. KPL volunteers have published and spoken widely about the venture's efforts. IA staff have lectured at various academic institutions, and a business school developed a case study on their work. Indeed, this book itself aims to contribute to the scholarly and practical study of social entrepreneurship.

The intersection of academia and social entrepreneurships is logical. First, social entrepreneurship is a complicated, increasingly popular, and self-consciously novel field that employs – as well as enables contribution to – such disciplines as business, law, political science, public policy, economics, sociology, anthropology, and social psychology. Indeed, as noted in the Appendix to this book, there are a significant and growing number of social entrepreneurship fellowships, centers, courses, conferences, and competitions at universities throughout the United States and Europe, and around the world.

Second, young people – the focus of the social entrepreneurs in this book – primarily use academic networks to draw insights and contacts. Universities are hubs for young people who possess the time and motivation to explore new ideas and to get involved in new initiatives. University students and campuses serve as communities of potential starters, staff, and supporters of social enterprises.

However, CoA notes the limits of academia in aiding social entrepreneurship. At least in the realm of branding, CoA drew the lesson that it will be more successful to pursue simplicity than the complexity usually promoted in scholarly works.

Potential Personal Risks, Costs, and Benefits

Social entrepreneurs face a number of potential risks, costs, and benefits resulting from their work. These matters implicate both individual social entrepreneurs and social enterprises as a whole. Such issues involve opportunity costs, office administration, fundraising and office space, safety, autonomy, and intersections among these aspects of social entrepreneurs' personal and professional lives. Because of the nature of social entrepreneurship work, which is often initiated informally and at the expense of its founders, the professional is often the personal, and vice versa. As is discussed below, CoA, in particular, reflects on the benefits and drawbacks of this phenomenon.

Opportunity costs

In order to pursue a social enterprise, social entrepreneurs may forgo attractive professional opportunities, even those that are potentially more lucrative and less stressful, and personal relationships. Because their work may be focused on a particular geographic region, social entrepreneurs may also forgo the ability to have more control over where they work and thus end up living in less desirable places. As a result, social entrepreneurs may need to reside far from friends, family, and other loved ones. CoA's Board, for example, decided that CoA's co-founders would relocate, at great personal cost, to France, which was far from their homes.

Office administration

Because of the usual resource-poor aspects of social entrepreneurship, and in order to keep administrative overhead costs low, social enterprises may not fund such office amenities as administrative assistants. Consequently, as CoA notes, relatively more time may need to be allocated to such mundane activities as scheduling, correspondence, and filing, thereby reducing the amount of time that social entrepreneurs can spend focused on the venture's overall mission. This administrative burden can limit both time spent on other work (and thus limit possibilities to scale the venture) and personal time, further blurring the line between the office and home, and eating into rest and relaxation, which can lower morale. In order to keep morale and efficiency high, social entrepreneurs should, as GR and IA illustrate, consider expending necessary funds to hire administrative staff, treating their work like other types of enterprises.

Fundraising and office space

As AA, IA, and the KPL describe, social entrepreneurs often fundraise for start-up or seed money through personal networks of friends, relatives, schoolmates, and colleagues, and by investing their own money in the venture. Also, as AA, CoA, and the KPL explain, early on in the life of a social enterprise office space may be located in one or more staff members' homes, and may make use of their personal computers and other equipment. Social entrepreneurs may also need to personally finance transportation, phone calls, housing, food, supplies, materials, and website design/hosting unless or until the venture has raised sufficient funds to provide work-related living and travel expenses. As several of the case studies illustrate, some expenses social entrepreneurs personally assume can be pricey.

Some have raised the concern that social enterprises, frequently self-funded by social entrepreneurs themselves, are limited to the exclusive realm of the financial elite. This observation may be accurate in some cases. (All of IA's senior managers, for example, are former attorneys at global corporate law firms who saved enough money to work for IA full-time for extended periods either for free or at significantly reduced salaries.) However, this critique overlooks several burgeoning aspects of social enterprise support. First, social entrepreneurs may borrow money or incur debt to finance their work. Second, several universities and foundations provide fellowships and grants, in addition to training, office space, and networking opportunities, for emerging social entrepreneurs.[28] Third, as AA, IA, and OAA note, legal assistance (on incorporation, for example) can be provided *pro bono* by a law school clinic or law firm. Fourth, social entrepreneur incubators, which provide office space at a reduced rate and offer networking and other opportunities, are proliferating. Such institutions may include either dedicated incubators (for example, Ashoka and Echoing Green) or makeshift ones (such as, in the case of IA, a law firm, Orrick, that was willing and able to provide office space, staff assistance, and funding). Financial and logistical support for social entrepreneurship is available and expanding; changemakers can and should be as entrepreneurial about investment in their own work as they are about how that work can help address a pressing problem.

Safety

The most significant personal cost to a social entrepreneur is illustrated by the NVSL. Artemis Christodulou, a founding member of the NVSL and the individual to whom this book is dedicated, was seriously injured while involved in her social entrepreneurship work, leaving both her own and the NVSL's future in jeopardy. Christodulou's accident cautions us to remember two things. First, social entrepreneurs may knowingly or unwittingly engage in activities that pose physical risks (illness, injury), particularly if those activities occur in developing, conflict, or immediately post-conflict regions. Social entrepreneurs must thus take necessary precautions, and supervisors must implement safety procedures for their subordinates. When operating in risky regions or on dangerous activities, social entrepreneurs should strongly consider obtaining insurance for themselves and their subordinates if they are not otherwise covered. Second, in order to plan for the unexpected, social enterprises, like other organizations, must create procedures for the continuation of their work in the event that a key team member becomes unwilling or unable to remain involved. As noted by AID, CoA, and IA, and also discussed above, succession procedures are critical and can include training and grooming existing staff members for promotions.

Autonomy
In addition to the potential personal risks and costs discussed above, there are, or can be, significant personal benefits to social entrepreneurship work. As CoA describes, changemakers and their staff, much like in any entrepreneurial organization, have a significant amount of control over their day-to-day work/life balance: they often can decide the amount, timing, and nature of their work. Such liberties, while exciting to some, may be overwhelming, isolating, and paralyzing to others. Remedies include setting personal daily goals and hosting regularly scheduled team meetings to discuss progress. Social entrepreneurs must also accept that, as with serious commitments to other challenging endeavors, they may work long hours under stressful conditions not of their choosing.

DIFFERENCES

Social entrepreneurship is a diverse industry. The ventures profiled in this book are different in several ways, including design and operations, scalability and obsolescence, staff, local leadership, and social entrepreneur multipliers.

Design and Operations

The profiled social enterprises vary in terms of their design and operations, particularly concerning their issue areas, geopolitical and geographic considerations, output, and political involvement.

Issue areas
The enterprises discussed in this book focus on different, sometimes multiple issue areas within the larger theme of addressing atrocities. Some ventures

(CoA, GR, IA, the KPL, OAA) have concentrated on education. Some (GR and OAA) are primarily concerned with helping orphans. Others (CoA, the NVSL) have specialized in reconciliation. Still others (AA, AID, GR, IA) have dedicated themselves to empowering concerned or affected individuals. This range in sub-specialties indicates just how diverse the field of atrocities is and how great its needs are.

One enterprise (CoA) focused on religion, whereas all others are secular. Two ventures (AID, CoA) have based their efforts in developed countries (for AID, the U.K. and the U.S.; for CoA, France and the U.S.), whereas the rest (AA, GR, IA, the KPL, OAA, the NVSL) have been based mostly in developing countries. Some enterprises employ a more holistic approach than others to solving a problem. In addressing educational needs, GR and OAA both also provide health care, recognizing that illness can hinder a student's concentration and achievement by causing school absence and incomplete homework. AID seeks to empower young people in the United States to address global challenges as diverse as poverty, disease, climate change, conflict, human rights, and support for and reform of international institutions, such as the UN and the ICC. In contrast to AID, GR, and OAA, other ventures have been more narrowly focused on a particular project. The NVSL used various communication strategies to educate Sierra Leoneans about the legacy of the SL TRC and related issues of human rights and reconciliation. The KPL has focused on building, outfitting, and operationalizing a single library. IA concentrates on handicrafts. These differences indicate that operational approaches and bases of social entrepreneurship can vary widely even within a single issue area (here, responding to atrocities).

Geopolitical and geographic considerations
Some of the profiled enterprises (AA, CoA) focus on ongoing conflicts, whereas others (GR, IA, the KPL, the NVSL, OAA) are primarily concerned with post-conflict issues. AID focuses on both conflict and post-conflict issues. The context of each type of venture is different, as a region with ongoing conflict is usually less stable, which may make travel to the area and networking with certain contacts more difficult and dangerous.

Most of the profiled enterprises (AA, AID, CoA, GR, IA, the KPL, the NVSL) have had permanent offices at the site of their work, whereas one (OAA) has not. Some ventures (AA, CoA, GR, IA, the KPL, the NVSL) have had at least some of their leaders based in the target communities, whereas the leaders of the other ventures (AID, OAA) have been based primarily in their home or resident countries.

Some enterprises (GR, IA, the KPL, the NVSL) have focused on a single country whereas the others (AA, AID, CoA, OAA) have concentrated on multiple countries or an entire region. In some cases, the geographic focus of an organization is natural and self-evident. As the KPL has been exclusively focused on building and now sustaining Rwanda's first public library and GR concentrates on supporting young Rwandans, these two organizations are limited to working on and in Rwanda. Similarly, the NVSL's work was dedicated to Sierra Leone. Conversely, the broader missions of AA and CoA have compelled them to work across borders in the countries where the communities they serve are found. For other social enterprises, though, the territorial boundaries are not self-evident. AID started in the UK because its leadership happened to live there at the time, although any number of countries could have been suitable locations for initiating a project to educate Americans living abroad about global issues. IA chose to work in Rwanda only, although nothing in the venture's mission of providing market access and skills training to needy artisans requires IA to work in – or only in – that particular country. GR and OAA both focus on supporting OVCs. GR consciously decided to limit its work to a single country, believing that Rwanda's recent background required specialized and exclusive attention, precluding the multi-country approach OAA has taken. OAA deliberately decided to work across borders and continents to appeal to its leadership. As a result, OAA is able to learn lessons across contexts and apply best practices to each individual country project.

This range in geographic focus reflects the fact that some social enterprises take place locally, whereas others may be far away, even overseas.[29] Because of the distance among an organization's offices and the site of the project it seeks to accomplish, the dynamics of such long-distance enterprises require special consideration.

Project staff working in different regions may seldom, if ever, meet in person. A social entrepreneur must be particularly mindful in such cases to build a sense of camaraderie through email, mail, phone, video conference, and online social networking. Staff may also find it beneficial, as IA and the KPL have, to form local or regional sub-groups or committees based on overlapping geographic location.

In addition, staff at an organization's primary office may seldom, if ever, witness the project's progress first-hand. A social entrepreneur must be particularly mindful in such cases to keep all staff informed of developments. Sharing images and video of and testimony from locals about the project are two methods of addressing this challenge and boosting morale.

Output
Some enterprises provide services. AA, AID, CoA, GR, and OAA have concentrated on raising awareness, education, and technical and support services. Other ventures supply both goods and services. IA facilitates the production of handicrafts while offering training programs to its artisan partners. Still other

ventures focus on a combination of 'bricks-and-mortar' initiatives and activities. The NVSL collected and showcased tangible artistic and literary
'Visions.' The KPL has built Rwanda's first public library, which will also
eventually develop and implement programs, such as story-hours for children,
now that the prerequisite institutional infrastructure of the library itself is
completed.

With tangible projects, the project design, deadlines, and communication of
development and growth are usually straightforward. These milestones
provide objective metrics of progress, which can be monitored, measured, and
shared with staff, the media, and existing or potential donors. Where intangible projects are concerned, it may be more complicated, for example, to
encourage or discourage a particular viewpoint, and to determine whether
progress is being made to that end.

Funders are sometimes more willing to support programmatic activities
over 'bricks-and-mortar' projects. Because campaigns to raise capital or to
influence opinion often take long periods of time to complete, both tangible
and intangible projects may find it difficult to hold the interest of staff and to
receive multiple rounds of funding from the same source.

Political involvement

While all social enterprises are inherently political to some extent, some are
more overtly politically engaged than others. On the one hand, GR, IA, the
KPL, and OAA may all be considered politically neutral efforts, since they do
not support or oppose partisan positions on particular issues. AA and AID, on
the other hand, are directly engaged in political matters.

A social entrepreneur must determine whether to politicize an otherwise
politically neutral enterprise. If so, the venture may alienate potential supporters. If a social entrepreneur decides to politicize the problem or project herself,
then she must be ready to address criticism, such as the charge of undertaking
the project for personal, even selfish political gain. Typically, such politiciza-
tion is unnecessary, as observers will draw obvious connections between a
social enterprise and the larger political context.

Scalability and Obsolescence

AA notes that one of the criteria of the business plan portion of the Echoing
Green Fellowship competition is a strategy to 'scale impact.' Some of the
enterprises consciously focus on scaling the impact of their work. AA queried
how legal aid can reach a sufficient number of refugees to make a difference,
AID describes itself as developing a 'scalable model,' and IA deliberately
constructs its business infrastructure with an eye towards scale. Other ventures
are content to focus on a particular challenge and not necessarily expand their

work. The NVSL was a mechanism for the public to participate in the work of the SL TRC. After building Rwanda's first public library, the KPL is now focused on sustaining the institution, and does not currently have plans to build other libraries in Rwanda or elsewhere. (Since construction of the KPL is now complete, however, some staff members might decide to continue library-building efforts elsewhere.)

Scalability is thus not necessarily a component of all social entrepreneurship, even those ventures that are successful and have a significant impact. Although some social enterprises are not intentionally scalable, others might embrace their work as models, hence indirectly scaling their work.

Closely related to the issue of scalability is the matter of obsolescence: a social enterprise that is obsolete is by definition not scaling itself. Some of the profiled ventures (CoA, the NVSL) have ended whereas others (AA, AID, GR, IA, the KPL) continue. Still others (OAA) have ceased portions of their activities (i.e., projects in particular countries) while continuing others. OAA decided to discontinue certain projects in order to consolidate its work and continue pursuing its most promising and fruitful initiatives. The NVSL ceased its operations and transferred its 'Visions' to other institutions for their preservation and memorialization because the project had run its natural course. CoA stopped its operations for another set of reasons. First, its projects were not embraced in France. Second, its staff became competitive, which poisoned what had been a productive and positive working environment. Third, CoA staff members were not able to limit (or accept) the encroachment of their work on their personal lives, which further decreased their morale.

Non-scaling or discontinued social enterprises need not be seen as failures. These developments may simply reflect that the venture has reached a natural conclusion by achieving its goals or that the social entrepreneurs calculated that their efforts were better spent on other endeavors. It also may be the case that some issues – such as, in the case of CoA, Muslim-Jewish relations – are ill-suited to social entrepreneurship, at least at a particular time, in a certain region, or through a specific mechanism.

Staff

Social entrepreneurs must be conscious of what they do not know. Although they often begin their venture driven by a passion stemming from a recognized need, social entrepreneurs do not necessarily have at their disposal all or even most of the skills necessary for the enterprise. Social entrepreneurs thus often recruit others to fill those gaps. In doing so, social enterprises employ different kinds of staff. These staff members may be volunteer or paid, short- or long-term, novices or experts, part- or full-time, or some combination. The type of staff a social enterprise employs may change over time and will help dictate how efficiently the venture uses it resources and how successfully the venture achieves its objectives.

Some of these enterprises (the NVSL, OAA) have used an all-volunteer staff, whereas others (AA, AID, CoA, GR, IA, the KPL) have employed at least some paid staff. Some ventures (AA, AID, CoA, GR, IA, the KPL, the NVSL) have relied on full-time staff (although not necessarily, as in the cases of GR and the KPL, of their founders, and not necessarily, as in the cases of AID and the KPL, since their inception), whereas one venture (OAA) has retained only part-time staff. GR deliberately and proactively discourages short-term volunteers from the West, believing that such a transient workforce would be, over-all, unproductive. Instead, GR prefers longer-term volunteers from within Rwanda. Similarly, IA has evolved from relying on volunteers and low-paid staff (who often exhibited poor performance) to a more professional staff paid at market rates (who possess greater skills and demonstrate better integration). Conversely, many of the KPL's staff are located outside Rwanda and may seldom, if ever, visit the country. Those individuals, who focus more on fundraising, raising public awareness, and book-collecting aspects of the KPL than design and management, are able to pursue their work despite – or perhaps because – they are not located in Rwanda. In 2011, however, the KPL hired its first Executive Director, whose leadership of the KPL is a paid, full-time job, a component of which is to hire and supervise additional full-time staff.

Volunteers are often young people, serving in their positions for a relatively short term and on a part-time basis. Through their efforts, volunteers can gain valuable contacts, skills, knowledge, experience, and exposure to paid work opportunities.[30] Volunteers may also be more motivated to work for a social enterprise for experiential value – to see a particular region and to learn about its poverty and other challenges – than to contribute fully to the venture, a phenomenon that has pejoratively come to be known as 'Voluntourism.'[31]

In order to work as a volunteer, the staff member must have the financial means to do so. Economic downturns may affect whether, which, how many, and for how long individuals pursue volunteer positions. On the one hand, some people may seek paid work instead of volunteer opportunities and thus accept perhaps less substantive and meaningful positions because they need the financial support. On the other hand, some individuals may not be able to obtain paid positions and instead choose volunteer opportunities that are inter-esting and enable them to develop certain skills and knowledge that may be unobtainable in more traditional, salaried jobs. As discussed above regarding social entrepreneurs themselves, the fact that volunteers are self-funded may lead some to criticize them – or their enterprise – as located in the realm of the financial elite, even if the reality is otherwise.

AID, CoA, IA, the KPL, and the NVSL reveal benefits and drawbacks to youthful staff. Such an age group, while bringing significant enthusiasm, passion, and fresh ideas, may not possess much relevant experience and, again, as discussed above with social entrepreneurs themselves, may only be willing or able to commit a limited amount of time before venturing off to other opportunities, whether educational, professional, or personal.

As IA and the NVSL demonstrate, there are also benefits and drawbacks to a majority- or all-volunteer staff. The time commitment these individuals are able to make initially or sustain cannot be taken for granted. Therefore, planning for the long term may be difficult, as it can be naïve to assume that a particular volunteer will increase or even maintain her initial level of engagement.

The experience of the NVSL also suggests that, if social entrepreneurs or their staff are not members of a particular social class, there may be barriers to entry or execution of their work. Local officials may have discriminated against indigenous NVSL staff members based on superficial traits (e.g., appearance, speech) when those staff members attempted to register the NVSL as an NGO. There may unfortunately be some level of bias within the field of social entrepreneurship that social entrepreneurs may need to recognize and struggle to overcome.

Acquiring staff thus entails a cost-benefit analysis of various considerations including supervision, training, turnover, and safety, including a built-in recognition of the fluidity and attrition especially of staff that are young, short-term, part-time, and/or volunteer. As a result, despite knowing that this policy limits their 'labor pool,' some ventures (GR, IA) opt to hire more experienced, long-term staff than to use short-term volunteers. Other ventures are grateful for any help they are offered. The particular characteristics of a social enterprise significantly determine the type of staffing that is most helpful and appropriate. And, as social enterprises evolve over time, staffing needs may similarly change.

Moreover, when developing the social entrepreneurial organization, designers should create institutional protections against problematic staff. One such mechanism is to mandate and incorporate into the official constitution or by-laws (or the less formal documents and guiding principles that govern the social enterprise) term limits and/or periodic elections for all officials or senior staff of the organization. Where these institutional features are not instituted, alternative, *ad hoc* impeachment and removal proceedings can be time-consuming and morale-draining. Through term limits or periodic elections, the organization can implement a less or non-confrontational method of eliminating undesirable staff members or preventing someone ineffective or counterproductive from assuming – or retaining – a senior position.

Local Leadership

Some of the ventures have benefited from the participation of local leaders. GR employs Rwandans as Country Director and in other staff positions. Many members of IA, the RCKV, and the AFKPL are also Rwandans. Most team leaders of AMERA-Egypt are Egyptian. AA draws advocates from within the refugee community itself. OAA mandates its local partner organizations to oversee programs on the ground.

Such local leadership can facilitate, among other things, the credibility and local learning, engagement, and buy-in mentioned above that are often crucial to successful social entrepreneurship. Other social enterprises do not have local community members serving in leadership positions. As with staffing, decisions on leadership placement require a cost-benefit analysis of various factors, including availability, experience, and chemistry with other leaders.

Social Entrepreneur Multipliers

The development of indigenous social entrepreneurs is yet another positive benefit of engaging the local population in a social enterprise. By involving members of the local community, those individuals will be exposed to and learn lessons from the social enterprise. In turn, these community members may apply that knowledge to other problems and activities. In short, by engaging the local population, a social enterprise may generate a multiplier effect on native social entrepreneurship.

In addition, by watching social entrepreneurs work, other individuals interested in replicating their success may obtain knowledge of practices that have proven successful. In this sense, social entrepreneurs can cause ripple effects that can impact other social enterprises.

Most of the profiled ventures have produced, whether intentionally or not, additional social entrepreneurs. Other library entrepreneurs in Rwanda have learned from, and adopted, the KPL's practices in establishing or restructuring their own library ventures. IA has implemented a 'training of the trainers' program to teach Rwandans business skills that they can then share with other Rwandans. GR's students view themselves as potential changemakers in Rwandan society. OAA assists its partner organizations in developing their capacities and implementing new technologies and OAA incubates young social entrepreneurs by training and educating its volunteers and providing them with valuable experience. The NVSL, particularly concerned about the lack of employment opportunities in Sierra Leone, was committed to fostering participation and leadership among its domestic volunteers and paid staff. CoA alumni facilitated communication among participants. AID works to inspire young people to pursue multilateral solutions to global problems, and provides them with tools to channel their activism.

CONCLUSION

In the course of founding and managing a social enterprise, social entrepreneurs learn many general lessons they can share to help make other social enterprises – and themselves – more successful. Indeed, the way in which a social enterprise is formed, structured, and operated significantly affects the likelihood of achieving its objectives.

One important lesson is to keep administrative costs low. This effort will ensure that as many precious resources go directly to the project as possible, which is best for the venture and reassuring to potential donors, further encouraging them to contribute initially or repeatedly. A second lesson is that almost all social enterprises require a team of dedicated, intelligent, bold staff, many of whom can and should be *ad hoc*, to maintain a constant infusion of fresh ideas and vigor.

Once a project is initiated, it must be sustained. Plans for maintenance must be built into the design and execution of the social enterprise from the very beginning. A social enterprise's overall potential is limited only by the organization's vision, creativity, communication, patience, and diligence.

It is critical to involve the local community in as many phases of the social enterprise as is practicable. No social enterprise can be a completely 'outside-in' initiative, as those types of activities, no matter how beneficial, are often resented and rejected as paternalistic, neo-colonialist, or neo-imperialist. Local involvement and ownership is also crucial to the success of a social enterprise because the local population is most aware of its needs and the effectiveness of potential solutions. That said, some minority members of the community, if already resented for other reasons, may provoke ire against the social enterprise if these minorities become involved. In addition, where social enterprises operate in foreign countries, staff must be thoughtful and respectful to the local population for the intervention to be successful. Project staff thus must take time to learn about the country, its language(s), customs, culture, economy, history, and politics, to be able to engage sensitively and effectively with the local population. Working in a small country can be simpler, as smaller communities are often easier to get to know.

The diversity among the profiled social enterprises demonstrates that there is no single, correct way to effect social change. As Grinsell and Klaber note in comparing OAA to GR, the manner in which social enterprises with even similar missions structure themselves and carry out their work is a reflection of the differing objectives, personalities, experiences, and philosophies of their leaders and staffs.

The social enterprises profiled in this book identify and seek to address problems within larger constellations of demanding needs. Rather than tackling an unmanageable, amorphous challenge, these social enterprises have focused on specific, practical projects. Some social entrepreneurship concentrates not on the most critical needs within an issue area or geographic region, but rather on a problem that the social entrepreneur determines to be ignored. In such cases, social entrepreneurs may be motivated because others are already focusing on those other needs or because the chosen problem seems likely to yield a successful outcome.

By acknowledging that their own resources are finite while the pool of beneficiaries is potentially huge, the profiled organizations implicitly indicate that there is need for even more social enterprise. Whether this need can better be addressed in a particular context by expanding or merging existing social enterprises, or by establishing new ones, is an open question. As the field of social entrepreneurship grows, participating individuals and organizations should establish better coordination to minimize redundancy and to maximize efficiency and effectiveness. To this end, the field – and the communities it seeks to help – would greatly benefit from the creation of more robust networks of social entrepreneurs (beyond the elite network Ashoka has developed and the few others that currently exist[32]) that can facilitate the sharing of experiences and engagement in collaborative endeavors. As various chapters in this book discuss, networking is a critical component of social entrepreneurship, both because it raises public awareness about and funds for social enterprises, and also because it helps the projects' managers coordinate their work and recruit staff. Social entrepreneurs often operate at the cutting edge of technology, making use of new online social networking outlets. However, networking space entirely dedicated to social entrepreneurship is still lacking.

Social entrepreneurship already is – and holds even greater potential to be – a significant actor in many political, economic, and cultural arenas. Social entrepreneurs may work alone, with each other, or in partnership with governmental, religious, or private sector institutions. Such synergistic efforts hold enormous potential to effect positive change in the world. For example, U.S. President Barack Obama's creation of the White House Office of Social Innovation and Civic Participation, a component of his administration that focuses on social entrepreneurship,[33] signifies the greater attention and priority on public-private partnerships this field has received in recent years from the highest levels of government. The public has increasingly grown to respect social entrepreneurs. Indeed, self-identified social entrepreneurs, such as Tom Perriello,[34] have recently campaigned for and won elected office. These developments suggest that political relationships among citizens and leaders on social causes are strengthening and that this trend will likely continue.

Businessperson, philanthropist, and writer William Clement Stone once said: 'Aim for the moon. If you miss you may hit a star.'[35] Even if a project takes longer than initially planned or if it eventually fails to achieve its principal objectives, the venture still may have accomplished a great deal. First, the social entrepreneur will have raised public awareness about a problem. Second, the social entrepreneur will have learned lessons and developed skill sets for herself and others that can be applied to other projects, including how to launch and run an organization, fundraise, manage public relations, and work with people of various backgrounds, languages, customs, and cultures. Finally, the social entrepreneur will have expanded her network and perhaps even developed strong and lasting relationships with individuals she may have never otherwise met and who also care deeply about the same cause. As illustrated by CoA, not all social enterprises will succeed in realizing their primary goals, but even these ventures may achieve some useful results.

If you are a social entrepreneur, or are considering becoming one, I hope that this book has provided insight into the field and inspires and assists you along the way. Good luck!

NOTES

1. For shorthand, this concluding chapter refers to an organization's name when meaning the case study chapter about that organization.
2. Desmond Tutu, *Foreword* to KINKADE & MACY, *supra* Chapter 1 note 63, at 9, 9.
3. *See also* James Dao, *For Injured Veterans, Healing in Service to Others*, N.Y. TIMES, Nov. 2, 2011, at F9 (noting that 'there is a natural progression from military service to community or humanitarian work in the civilian world' because '[m]any troops enlist for idealistic reasons, wanting "to serve and protect"').
4. GOUREVITCH, *supra* Chapter 4 note 4.
5. Philip Gourevitch, *Alms Dealers*, NEW YORKER, Oct. 11, 2010, at 102. *See also* Chapter 1, note 52.
6. HARRY E. CHAMBERS, THE BAD ATTITUDE SURVIVAL GUIDE: ESSENTIAL TOOLS FOR MANAGERS 30 (1998) (quoting Bryant).
7. CHURCHILL BY HIMSELF 572 (Richard Langworth ed., 2008).
8. TENNESSEE WILLIAMS, A STREETCAR NAMED DESIRE 178 (1947).
9. Some possibilities include threatening, kidnapping, or killing staff, or damaging or destroying offices, supplies, or other infrastructure. *See, e.g.*, Carlotta Gall, *In Afghanistan, Helping Can Be Deadly*, N.Y. TIMES, Apr. 5, 2003, at B13; Kirk Semple, *Iraq is Struck by New Wave of Abductions*, N.Y. TIMES, Nov. 30, 2005, at A1; Shimali Senanayake & Somini Sengupta, *Aid Workers Face Obstacles and Threats in Sri Lanka*, N.Y. TIMES, Aug. 18, 2006, at A9.
10. CHUA, WORLD ON FIRE, *supra* Preface note 2, at 6.
11. *Id.* at 163–75.
12. For example, 'the belief in inherent differences between Hutu and Tutsi' that has violently manifested, most recently in the 1994 Rwandan genocide, has been due in part to the view that 'Hutu in Rwanda represented the majority and rightful inhabitants of Rwanda, while the Tutsi were alien invaders from Abyssinia (Ethiopia) who had colonised and subjugated the Hutu for 400 years.' Jean Baptiste Kayigamba, *Without Justice, No Reconciliation: A Survivor's Experience of Genocide, in* AFTER GENOCIDE, *supra* Chapter 1 note 58, at 33, 34.
13. While this book has focused on philanthropy from the perspective of the fundraiser, it is equally important for social entrepreneurs and other potential grantees to understand philanthropy from the perspective of the donor. For an incisive look at donors' philanthropic strategies, see PETER FRUMKIN, STRATEGIC GIVING: THE ART AND SCIENCE OF PHILANTHROPY (2006).
14. *See, e.g.*, Eilene Zimmerman, *A Small Business Made to Seem Bigger*, N.Y. TIMES, Mar. 2, 2011, at B11.

15. JOHN DONNE, DEVOTIONS UPON EMERGENT OCCASIONS 108–09 (1624) ('No man is an island, entire of itself; every man is a piece of the continent, a part of the main. If a clod be washed away by the sea, Europe is the less, as well as if a promontory were, as well as if a manor of thy friend's or of thine own were; any man's death diminishes me, because I am involved in mankind, and therefore never send to know for whom the bell tolls; it tolls for thee.').

16. MALCOLM GLADWELL, THE TIPPING POINT: HOW LITTLE THINGS MAKE A BIG DIFFERENCE 21 (2000).

17. *Id.* at 38.

18. *Id.* at 59.

19. *Id.* at 38.

20. Ronald Reagan, U.S. President, Remarks on Signing the Intermediate-Range Nuclear Forces Treaty (Dec. 8, 1987), *available at* http://www.reagan.utexas.edu/archives/speeches/1987/120887c.htm.

21. Ashoka, Merging Missions, Nov. 2010, http://usa.ashoka.org/merging-missions; Advocacy Groups Save Darfur Coalition and Genocide Intervention Network Announce Merger to Create Powerful Constituency Focused on Preventing Genocide and Mass Atrocities, Save Darfur, Nov. 1, 2010, http://ww20.savedarfur.org/index.php/pages/press/advocacy-groups-save-darfur-coalition-and-genocide-intervention-networ.

22. For the official website of Ethos Water, see http://www.ethoswater.com/.

23. For the official website of GoodSearch, see http://www.goodsearch.com/.

24. *See* GARY HIRSHBERG, STIRRING IT UP: HOW TO MAKE MONEY AND SAVE THE WORLD (2008).

25. Acumen Fund states that its mission is 'to create a world beyond poverty by investing in social enterprises, emerging leaders, and breakthrough ideas … . We believe that pioneering entrepreneurs will ultimately find the solutions to poverty. The entrepreneurs Acumen Fund supports are focusing on offering critical services – water, health, housing, and energy – at affordable prices to people earning less than four dollars a day.' Acumen Fund, About Us, http://www.acumenfund.org/about-us/about-us.html (last visited Nov. 17, 2011). For the official website of Acumen Fund, see http://www.acumenfund.org/. For Jacqueline Novogratz's self-described background and philosophy, see NOVOGRATZ, *supra* Chapter 1 note 67.

26. *See, e.g.,* John J. Miller, Op-Ed., *Charity Begins at Home, but Must It Stay There?*, N.Y. TIMES, May 15, 2006, at A21.

27. Power, *Why Can't We*, *supra* Chapter 1 note 41.

28. For a list of such universities and foundations, see the Appendix.

29. For a discussion of local v. oversees social work, see, e.g., Zachary D. Kaufman, Ltr to the Ed., *Young Americans, Doing Good*, N.Y. TIMES, Mar. 24, 2006, at A18; Nicholas D. Kristof, Op-Ed., *On the Road, You and Me*, N.Y. TIMES, Mar. 21, 2006, at A17.

30. *See, e.g.,* John Leland, *Volunteering Rises on the Résumé*, N.Y. TIMES, Nov. 2, 2011, at F12.

31. Social Edge, The Voluntourism Debate, Jan. 2011, http://www.socialedge.org/discussions/responsibility/the-voluntourism-debate.

32. For a list of existing networks in the field of social entrepreneurship, see the Appendix.

33. On May 5, 2009, the White House announced that President Obama would 'ask Congress to request US$50 million in seed capital for the Social Innovation Fund to identify the most promising, results-oriented non-profit programs and expand their reach throughout the country.' The White House Office of Social Innovation and Civic Participation was designated to coordinate these efforts. *See* Press Release, Office of the Press Sec'y, White House, President Obama to Request $50 Million to Identify and Expand Effective, Innovative Non-Profits (May 5, 2009), http://www.whitehouse.gov/the_press_office/President-Obama-to-Request-50-Million-to-Identify-and-Expand-Effective-Innovative-Non-Profits/. For more information about the White House's Social Innovation Fund, see White House Blog, What Is the Social Innovation Fund? (May 6, 2009), http://www.whitehouse.gov/blog/What-Is-the-Social-Innovation-Fund/. For a discussion of the White House Office of Social Innovation and Civic Participation, see Clayton M. Christensen, *The White House Office of Social Innovation: A New Paradigm for Solving Social Problems*, HUFFINGTON POST, July 1, 2009, http://www.huffingtonpost.com/clayton-m-christensen/the-white-house-office-on_b_223759.html. On June 30, 2009, President Obama met with Fellows of Echoing

Green, the organization Dr. Cheryl Dorsey, who authored the Afterword to this book, leads, to discuss public-private partnerships in solving social problems. *See* Echoing Green, President Obama Meets with Echoing Green Fellows, June 30, 2009, http://www.echoing-green.org/blog/obama-talks-social-innovation-today.

34. In January 2009, Tom Perriello, a Democrat, unseated a six-term Republican incumbent to become a member of the U.S. Congress representing Virginia's 5th district. Perriello describes himself as a 'social entrepreneur' and his peer group as 'the Service Generation.' *See* Gail Russell, *Social Activists Hunt for Congressional Seats ... in G.O.P. Districts*, CHRISTIAN SCI. MONITOR, July 10, 2008, at 1; Ian Shapira, *A New Breed of Congressman: Va.'s Perriello Envisions a 'Service Generation,'* WASH. POST, Jan. 7, 2009, at B1.

35. *See* JOYCE GUCCIONE, THE POWER OF CHOICE: THE GREATER ADVENTURES OF HUMPTY DUMPTY 199 (2007) (quoting Stone).

Afterword

Cheryl L. Dorsey

As I finished reading the last chapter of *Social Entrepreneurship in the Age of Atrocities: Changing Our World*, I was incredibly buoyed and heartened by what this book means for the state of conversation and activity within the field of social entrepreneurship. As the new kid on the social change block, social entrepreneurship is still finding its footing: grappling with definitions, jockeying to raise public awareness, and positioning itself alongside and occasionally in opposition to other change theories and methodologies. Much of the recent scholarship and research has focused on providing insight into some of the fundamental questions about the field as well as rigorous academic analyses of social entrepreneurship theory and a framework for future research. Dr. Zachary Kaufman's work on this book is so important and needed not only because it provides additional data for researchers and scholars through case study methodology but also because it gives voice to the critical perspectives and insights of practitioners – those on the ground actually doing the work – and recognizes the contributions of one of the important players in the field: young, emerging social entrepreneurs.

As the President of Echoing Green, a global social venture capital fund providing start-up financing and support to some of the world's most promising social entrepreneurs, I understand and have watched in awe the power of young people to change the world. I strongly believe that young people brimming with optimism, uninhibited by authority and limitations, and outraged by inequity and injustice, remain our greatest flame for igniting social change. Since 1987, Echoing Green has seeded over 500 emerging social entrepreneurs working in over 40 countries around the world. With initial investments totaling over $30 million, Echoing Green Fellows have gone on to establish vibrant social change organizations serving millions of people across the globe focusing on areas as disparate as health care, education, community and economic development, and civil and human rights. These young, mission-driven, and results-oriented women and men are energizing social movements by introducing new models of impact, injecting relentless energy and passion into the hard, long-term work of social change, and inspiring other people – both young and old – to join their cause.

Historian Doris Kearns Goodwin once noted that it is the magic of leadership that allows a leader's example to reach down to people's self-definition and change it.[1] This observation is, in fact, what may be social entrepreneurs' greatest contribution to society: their ability to embody and personify the power of individuals to get involved and make a difference. I encourage readers not to underestimate the power of narrative and the importance of public example as a way to test one's own assumptions and catalyze personal change. As I mentioned earlier, I am so pleased by Zachary's contribution to the field because he has highlighted the achievements of *young* social entrepreneurs through narrative. I often hear from young people interested in social entrepreneurship that they find the typical examples and models of outstanding social entrepreneurs inaccessible and distant. They have difficulty seeing themselves as the feted and award-winning veteran social entrepreneur running a global multi-million dollar social enterprise. However, they can and *do* see themselves in all of the young people profiled in this book. Their stories provide an on ramp and permission, if you will, to engage in meaningful, effective ways in the work of social change.

The chapter on Asylum Access (AA) and legal aid for refugees in the Global South is co-authored by 2007 Echoing Green Fellow Emily E. Arnold-Fernández.[2] While the work of Emily and her colleagues to develop and promote new models of legal aid services in a global context is important, so too is Emily's personal story as a model for identity and values formation and commitment. In 2002, Emily arrived in Cairo as a second-year law student to work for the summer as a legal advocate. Emily's first client was a Liberian boy who had been denied refugee status after fleeing to Egypt to avoid being abducted to fight as a child soldier. Her work and personal investment to ensure his safety and well-being were transformative, forever changing the course of both of their lives. It is what Echoing Green calls her 'moment of obligation.' Upon deep personal reflection on her values and purpose, Emily envisioned her potential impact on the lives of thousands of other refugees who needed legal advocates to defend their fundamental human rights.

A moment of obligation is quite simply a discovery of exactly what inspires you. While anyone can experience a moment of obligation, *responding* to these moments requires comfort with the unfamiliar and an abundance of optimism typical of young minds. More specifically, it requires recognition of one's ability to make a unique contribution as well as garnering the courage to take the first small steps of action. Emily fully embraced her moment of obligation and ushered in her idea for a new model of legal aid from concept to reality. In 2005, she founded AA to provide refugees with access to legal advocates on the ground in the Global South.

It is often said that 'demography is destiny.'[3] I subscribe to this theory in as much as I believe that generational shifts are important precursors to social change. I remain impressed by the power of younger generations, especially the 'millennial generation,' to usher in seismic changes in how we both take ownership of the world's toughest problems – such as the atrocities that are the focus of this book – and ultimately go about solving them. I look at the good works of the social entrepreneurs profiled in *Social Entrepreneurship in the Age of Atrocities* and the thousands of social entrepreneurs working across the world and think that our toughest societal problems are simply no match for the 'audacity of hope'[4] and the gall to think big.

NOTES

1. On January 21, 2009, Doris Kearns Goodwin appeared on *The Oprah Winfrey Show* to discuss the inauguration of Barack Obama as President of the United States. Goodwin alludes to Obama's leadership in this paraphrased statement.
2. For more information about AA and Arnold-Fernández, see Chapter 3.
3. This phrase is usually attributed to Auguste Comte, a nineteenth-century French philosopher.
4. The phrase 'audacity of hope' was popularized by the title of Barack Obama's second book: BARACK OBAMA, THE AUDACITY OF HOPE: THOUGHTS ON RECLAIMING THE AMERICAN DREAM (2006).

Appendix: Social entrepreneurship resources and institutions[1]

SOCIAL ENTERPRISES PROFILED IN THIS BOOK

Africa & Middle East Refugee Assistance (http://www.amera-uk.org/)
Americans for Informed Democracy (http://www.aidemocracy.org/)
Asylum Access (http://www.asylumaccess.org/)
Children of Abraham[2]
Fahamu Refugee Programme (http://www.srlan.org/)
Generation Rwanda (http://www.generationrwanda.org/)
Indego Africa (http://www.indegoafrica.org/)
Kigali Public Library (http://www.kigalilibrary.org/)
National Vision for Sierra Leone[3]
Orphans Against AIDS (http://www.orphansagainstaids.org/)
Southern Refugee Legal Aid Network (http://www.srlan.org/)
Stichting 3R (http://www.stichting3r.nl/)

EXAMPLES OF OTHER WESTERN SOCIAL ENTERPRISES FOCUSING ON ATROCITIES

Before Project (http://www.beforeproject.org/)
Campaign for Innocent Victims in Conflict (http://www.civicworldwide.org/)
CeaseFire (http://www.ceasefirechicago.org/)
Coalition for the International Criminal Court (http://www.iccnow.org/)
Darfurian Voices (http://www.darfurianvoices.org/)
Enough (http://www.enoughproject.org/)
Facilitating Opportunities for Refugee Growth & Empowerment (http://www.forgenow.org/)
Falling Whistles (http://www.fallingwhistles.com/)
Global Youth Connect (http://www.globalyouthconnect.org/)
Humanity in Action (http://www.humanityinaction.org/)
International Center for Transitional Justice (http://www.ictj.org/)
International Peace & Security Institute (http://www.ipsinstitute.org/)

Invisible Children (http://www.invisiblechildren.com/)
Khmer Legacies (http://www.khmerlegacies.org/)
Mercy Corps (http://www.mercycorps.org/)
Not on Our Watch (http://www.notonourwatchproject.org/)
Peace Direct (http://www.peacedirect.org/)
Peace Dividend Trust (http://www.peacedividendtrust.org/)
PeacePlayers International (http://www.peaceplayersintl.org/)
Play31 (http://www.play31.org/)
Polaris Project (http://www.polarisproject.org/)
Res Publica (http://www.therespublica.org/)
Right to Play (http://www.righttoplay.com/)
SMS: Legal (http://legal.frontlinesms.com)
Stand (http://www.standnow.org/)
Stop Genocide Now (http://www.stopgenocidenow.org/)
A Thousand Sisters (http://www.athousandsisters.org/)
Unite For Sight (http://www.uniteforsight.org/)
United to End Genocide (http://www.endgenocide.org/)
Witness (http://www.witness.org/)

BOOKS

Aaker, Jennifer and Andy Smith (2010), *The Dragonfly Effect: Quick, Effective, and Powerful Ways to Use Social Media to Drive Social Change*, San Francisco, CA: Jossey-Bass.

Acs, Zoltan J. and David B. Audretsch (eds.) (2nd ed. 2010), *Handbook of Entrepreneurship Research: An Interdisciplinary Survey and Introduction*, New York, NY: Springer.

Alcacer, Juan and Ozgur Demirtas (2011), *Understanding Social Entrepreneurship: The Relentless Pursuit of Mission in an Ever Changing World*, New York, NY: Routledge.

Alter, Sutia Kim (2000), *Managing the Double Bottom Line: A Business Planning Reference Guide for Social Enterprises*, Washington, DC: Pact.

Ashoka (2004), *Leading Social Entrepreneurs: Elections in 2002 and 2003*, Arlington, VA: Ashoka Innovators for the Public.

Ashoka (2006), *Leading Social Entrepreneurs: Elections in 2004 and 2005*, Arlington, VA: Ashoka Innovators for the Public.

Ashoka (2008), *Leading Social Entrepreneurs: Elections in 2006 and 2007*, Arlington, VA: Ashoka Innovators for the Public.

Ashoka U and Debbi D. Brock (3rd ed. 2011), *Social Entrepreneurship Education Resource Handbook*, Arlington, VA: Ashoka Innovators for the Public.

Ashton, Robert (2010), *How to Be a Social Entrepreneur: Make Money and Change the World*, Mankato, MN: Capstone.

Bessant, John and Joe Tidd (2nd ed. 2011), *Innovation and Entrepreneurship*, Chichester, West Sussex, United Kingdom: Wiley.

Binder, Linda (2009), *Ten Ways to Change the World in Your Twenties*, Naperville, IL: Sourcebooks.

Bishop, Matthew and Michael Green (2008), *Philanthrocapitalism: How the Rich Can Save the World*, New York, NY: Bloomsbury Press.

Bloom, Paul and Edward Skloot (2010), *Scaling Social Impact: New Thinking*, New York, NY: Palgrave Macmillan.

Blossom, Eve (2011), *Material Change: Design Thinking and the Social Entrepreneurship Movement*, New York, NY: Metropolis Books.

Bornstein, David (2004), *How to Change the World: Social Entrepreneurs and the Power of New Ideas*, New York, NY: Oxford University Press.

Bornstein, David (2005), *The Price of a Dream: The Story of the Grameen Bank and the Idea that is Helping the Poor to Change Their Lives*, New York, NY: Oxford University Press.

Bornstein, David and Susan Davis (2010), *Social Entrepreneurship: What Everyone Needs to Know*, New York, NY: Oxford University Press.

Borzaga, Carol and Jacques Defourny (eds.) (2001), *The Emergence of Social Enterprise*, New York, NY: Routledge.

Branson, Richard (2011), *Screw Business as Usual*, New York, NY: Portfolio.

Brinckerhoff, Peter C. (2000), *Social Entrepreneurship: The Art of Mission-Based Venture Development*, New York, NY: Wiley.

Brinckerhoff, Peter C. (2012), *Smart Stewardship for Nonprofits: Making the Right Decision in Good Times and Bad*, Hoboken, NJ: John Wiley & Sons, Inc.

Bronfman, Charles and Jeffrey Solomon (2009), *The Art of Giving: Where the Soul Meets a Business Plan*, San Francisco, CA: Jossey-Bass.

Brooks, Arthur C. (2008), *Social Entrepreneurship: A Modern Approach to Social Value Creation,* Upper Saddle River, NJ: Prentice Hall.

Bugg-Levine, Antony and Jed Emerson (2011), *Impact Investing: Transforming How We Make Money While Making a Difference*, San Francisco, CA: Jossey-Bass.

Choi, David Y. and Edmund R. Gray (2011), *Values-Centered Entrepreneurs and their Companies*, New York, NY: Routledge.

Church, Linda and Jeff Church (2011), *A Thirst for Change: How Social Entrepreneurship Can Make the World a Better Place*, La Jolla, CA: Church Family Productions.

Cleveland, Odell and Robert Wineburg (2011), *Pracademics and Community Change: A True Story of Nonprofit Development and Social Entrepreneurship During Welfare Reform*, Chicago, IL: Lyceum Books.

Clinton, Bill (2007), *Giving: How Each of Us Can Change the World*, New York, NY: Alfred A. Knopf.

Collier, Paul (2007), *The Bottom Billion: Why the Poorest Countries Are Failing and What Can Be Done About It*, New York, NY: Oxford University Press.

Collins, Daryl, Jonathan Morduch, Stuart Rutherford, and Orlanda Ruthven (2009), *Portfolios of the Poor: How the World's Poor Live on $2 a Day*, Cape Town, South Africa: University of Cape Town Press.

Counts, Alex (2008), *Small Loans, Big Dreams: How Nobel Prize Winner Muhammad Yunus and Microfinance Are Changing the World*, New York, NY: John Wiley & Sons, Inc.

Crutchfield, Leslie, John V. Kania, and Mark R. Kramer (2011), *Do More than Give: The Six Practices of Donors Who Change the World*, San Francisco, CA: Jossey-Bass.

Crutchfield, Leslie R. and Heather McLeod Grant (2008), *Forces for Good: The Six Practices of High-Impact Nonprofits*, San Francisco, CA: Jossey-Bass.

Dees, J. Gregory, Peter Economy, and Jed Emerson (eds.) (2001), *Enterprising Nonprofits: A Toolkit for Social Entrepreneurs*, New York, NY: John Wiley & Sons, Inc.

Dees, J. Gregory, Peter Economy, and Jed Emerson (eds.) (2002), *Strategic Tools for Social Entrepreneurs: Enhancing the Performance of Your Enterprising Nonprofit*, New York, NY: John Wiley & Sons, Inc.

Dorsey, Cheryl and Lara Galinsky (2006), *Be Bold: Create a Career with Impact*, New York, NY: Echoing Green.

Drucker, Peter F. (1985), *Innovation and Entrepreneurship*, New York, NY: Harper & Row.

Drucker, Peter F. (1999), *Management Challenges for the 21st Century*, New York, NY: Harper Business.

Duhl, Leonard J. (1990), *The Social Entrepreneurship of Change*, New York, NY: Pace University Press.

Durieux, Mark B. and Robert A. Stebbins (2010), *Social Entrepreneurship for Dummies*, Hoboken, NJ: Wiley Publishing, Inc.

Easterly, William (2006), *The White Man's Burden: Why the West's Efforts to Aid the Rest Have Done So Much Ill and So Little Good*, New York, NY: Penguin Books.

Elkington, John and Pamela Hartigan (2008), *The Power of Unreasonable People: How Social Entrepreneurs Create Markets that Change the World*, Boston, MA: Harvard Business Press.

Ellis, Tania (2010), *The New Pioneers: Sustainable Business Success through Social Innovation and Social Entrepreneurship*, New York, NY: Wiley.

Emerson, Jed and Fay Twersky (eds.) (1996), *New Social Entrepreneurs: The*

Success, Challenge and Lessons of Non-Profit Enterprise Creation, San Francisco, CA: Roberts Foundation.

Fayolle, Alain and Harry Matlay (eds.) (2011), *Handbook of Research on Social Entrepreneurship*, Northampton, MA: Edward Elgar.

Frances, Nic and Maryrose Cuskelly (2008), *The End of Charity: Time for Social Enterprise*, Crows News, New South Wales: Allen & Unwin.

Frumkin, Peter (2006), *Strategic Giving: The Art and Science of Philanthropy*, Chicago, IL: The University of Chicago Press.

Galinsky, Lara (2011), *Work on Purpose*, New York, NY: Echoing Green.

Gardner, Howard, Mihaly Csikszentmihalyi, and William Damon (2001), *Good Work: When Excellence and Ethics Meet*, New York, NY: Basic Books.

Gaudani, Claire and David Graham Burnett (2011), *Daughters of the Declaration: How Women Social Entrepreneurs Built the American Dream*, New York, NY: Public Affairs.

Gergen, Christopher and Gregg Vanourek (2008), *Life Entrepreneurs: Ordinary People Creating Extraordinary Lives,* San Francisco, CA: Jossey-Bass.

Gladwell, Malcolm (2002), *The Tipping Point: How Little Things Can Make a Big Difference,* Boston, MA: Back Bay Books.

Goldsmith, Stephen (2010), *The Power of Social Innovation: How Civic Entrepreneurs Ignite Community Networks for Good*, San Francisco, CA: Jossey-Bass.

Goldstein, Jeffrey A., James K. Hazy, and Joyce Silberstang (2009), *Complexity Science and Social Entrepreneurship*, Litchfield Park, AZ: ISCE Publishing.

Greenfield, Sidney M. and Arnold Strickon (1986), *Entrepreneurship and Social Change*, Lanham, MD: University Press of America.

Gunn, Robert and Chris Durkin (eds.) (2010), *Social Entrepreneurship: A Skills Approach*, Portland, OR: Policy Press.

Hammond, Darrell (2011), *Kaboom!: How One Man Built a Movement to Save Play*, New York, NY: Rodale Books.

Hansmann, Henry (1996), *The Ownership of Enterprise*, Cambridge, MA: Belknap Press of Harvard University Press.

Hart, Stuart (2005), *Capitalism at the Crossroads: The Unlimited Business Opportunities in Solving the World's Problems*, New York, NY: Wharton School Publishing.

Heegaard, Peter A. (2008), *Heroes Among Us: Social Entrepreneurs Strengthening Families and Building Communities*, Minneapolis, MN: Nodin Press.

Hersey, Paul, Kenneth H. Blanchard, and Dewey E. Johnson (eds.) (9th ed. 2008), *Management of Organizational Behavior: Leading Human Resources*, Upper Saddle River, NJ: Pearson Prentice Hall.

Hirshberg, Gary (2008), *Stirring It Up: How to Make Money and Save the World*, New York, NY: Hyperion.

Hockerts, Kai, Johanna Mair, and Jeffrey Robinson (eds.) (2010), *Values and Opportunities in Social Entrepreneurship*, New York, NY: Palgrave Macmillan.

Hollender, Jeffrey and Stephen Fenichell (2004), *What Matters Most: How a Small Group of Pioneers is Teaching Social Responsibility to Big Business, and Why Big Business is Listening*, New York, NY: Basic Books.

Hopkins, Bruce (2001), *Starting and Managing a Nonprofit Organization: A Legal Guide*, New York, NY: John Wiley & Sons, Inc.

Hubbard, R. Glenn and William Duggan (2009), *The Aid Trap: Hard Truths About Ending Poverty*, New York, NY: Columbia Business School Press.

Jarvis, Jeff (2009), *What Would Google Do?*, New York, NY: Collins Business.

Johnson, Steven (2010), *Where Good Ideas Come From: The Natural History of Innovation*, New York, NY: Riverhead Books.

Kanter, Beth and Allison H. Fine (2010), *The Networked Nonprofit: Connecting with Social Media to Drive Change*, San Francisco, CA: Jossey-Bass.

Kanter, Rosabeth Moss (2009), *SuperCorp: How Vanguard Companies Create Innovation, Profits, Growth, and Social Good*, New York, NY: Crown Business.

Karlan, Dean S. and Jacob Appel (2011), *More than Good Intentions: How a New Economics is Helping to Solve Global Poverty*, New York, NY: Dutton Adult.

Karnani, Aneel (2011), *Fighting Poverty Together: Rethinking Strategies for Business, Government, and Civil Society to Reduce Poverty*, New York, NY: Palgrave Macmillan.

Kerlin, Janelle A. (ed.) (2009), *Social Enterprise: A Global Comparison*, Medford, MA: Tufts University Press.

Kickul, Jill, Sophie Bacq, Davis Gras, and Mark Griffiths (eds.) (2012), *Social Entrepreneurship*, 2 vols, Northampton, MA: Edward Elgar.

Kidder, Tracy (2004), *Mountains Beyond Mountains: The Quest of Dr. Paul Farmer, a Man Who Would Cure the World*, New York, NY: Random House.

Kinkade, Sheila and Christina Macy (2005), *Our Time is Now: Young People Change the World*, New York, NY: Pearson Foundation.

Kopp, Wendy (2003), *One Day, All Children … : The Unlikely Triumph of Teach for America and What I Learned Along the Way*, New York, NY: Public Affairs.

Kourilsky, Marilyn L. and William B. Walstad (2007), *The Entrepreneur in Youth: An Untapped Resource for Economic Growth, Social Entrepreneurship, and Education*, Northampton, MA: Edward Elgar.

Kouzes, James M. and Barry Z. Posner (4th ed. 2007), *The Leadership Challenge*, San Francisco, CA: Jossey-Bass.

Krakauer, Jon (2011), *Three Cups of Deceit: How Greg Mortenson, Humanitarian Hero, Lost His Way*, New York, NY: Anchor Books.

Kristof, Nicholas D. and Sheryl WuDunn (2009), *Half the Sky: Turning Oppression into Opportunity for Women Worldwide*, New York, NY: Alfred A. Knopf.

Light, Paul C. and Catharine B. Reynolds (2010), *Driving Social Change: How to Solve the World's Toughest Problems*, Hoboken, NJ: Wiley.

Light, Paul C. (2008), *The Search for Social Entrepreneurship*, Washington, D.C.: Brookings Institution Press.

London, Manuel and Richard G. Morfopoulos (2009), *Social Entrepreneurship: How to Start Successful Corporate Social Responsibility and Community-Based Initiatives for Advocacy and Change*, New York, NY: Routledge.

Lynch, Kevin and Julius Walls, Jr. (2009), *Mission, Inc.: The Practitioner's Guide to Social Enterprise*, San Francisco, CA: Berrett-Koehler Publishers, Inc.

Mair, Johanna, Jeffrey Robinson, and Kai Hockerts (eds.) (2006), *Social Entrepreneurship*, New York, NY: Palgrave Macmillan.

Mortenson, Greg (2009), *Stones into Schools: Promoting Peace with Books, Not Bombs, in Afghanistan and Pakistan*, New York, NY: Penguin.

Mortenson, Greg and David Oliver Relin (2006), *Three Cups of Tea: One Man's Mission to Fight Terrorism and Build Nations – One School at a Time*, New York, NY: Viking.

Moss, Todd J. (2007), *African Development: Making Sense of the Issues and Actors*, Boulder, CO: Lynne Rienner Publishers.

Moyo, Dambisa (2009), *Dead Aid: Why Aid is Not Working and How There Is A Better Way for Africa*, New York, NY: Farrar, Straus, and Giroux.

Mulvany, Clare (2009), *One Wild Life: A Journey to Discover People Who Change Our World*, Cork, Ireland: Collins.

Munoz, Joseph Mark (2010), *International Social Entrepreneurship: Pathways to Personal and Corporate Impact*, New York, NY: Business Expert Press.

Nicholls, Alex (ed.) (2006), *Social Entrepreneurship: New Models of Sustainable Social Change*, Oxford, United Kingdom: Oxford University Press.

Northouse, Peter G. (5th ed. 2010), *Leadership: Theory and Practice*, Thousand Oaks, CA: Sage Publications.

Novogratz, Jacqueline (2009), *The Blue Sweater: Bridging the Gap Between Rich and Poor in an Interconnected World*, New York, NY: Rodale Books.

Noya, Antonella (ed.) (2009), *The Changing Boundaries of Social Enterprises*, Paris: Organisation for Economic Co-operation and Development.

Nunn, Michele (ed.) (2006), *Be the Change: Change the World, Change Yourself*, Atlanta, GA: Hundreds of Heads Books.

Nyssens, Marthe (ed.) (2006), *Social Enterprise: At the Crossroads of Market, Public Policies, and Civil Society*, New York, NY: Routledge.

Oster, Sharon M., Cynthia W. Massarsky, and Samantha L. Beinhacker (2004), *Generating and Sustaining Nonprofit Earned Income: A Guide to Successful Enterprise Strategies*, San Francisco, CA: Jossey-Bass.

Perrini, Francesco (ed.) (2005), *The New Social Entrepreneurship: What Awaits Social Entrepreneurial Ventures?*, Northampton, MA: Edward Elgar.

Petit, Patrick U. (2011), *Creating a New Civilization Through Social Entrepreneurship*, New Brunswick, NJ: Transaction Publishers.

Pitcoff, Winton (2004), *Investing in People: Building the Capacity of Community Development, Training, and Social Enterprise Practitioners*, New York, NY: Rockefeller Foundation.

Polak, Paul (2008), *Out of Poverty: What Works when Traditional Approaches Fail*, San Francisco, CA: Berrett-Koehler.

Prahalad, C.K. (2010), *The Fortune at the Bottom of the Pyramid: Eradicating Poverty Through Profits*, Upper Saddle River, NJ: Wharton School Publishing.

Praszkier, Ryszard and Andrzej Nowak (2011), *Social Entrepreneurship: Theory and Practice*, New York, NY: Cambridge University Press.

Quinn, Robert E. (2000), *Change the World: How Ordinary People Can Accomplish Extraordinary Results*, San Francisco, CA: Jossey-Bass.

Ridley-Duff, Rory and Mike Bull (2011), *Understanding Social Enterprise: Theory and Practice*, Thousand Oaks, CA: Sage Publications.

Roberts, Sam (2009), *A Kind of Genius: Herb Sturz and Society's Toughest Problems*, New York, NY: Public Affairs.

Robinson, Jeffrey A., Johanna Mair, and Kai Hockerts (eds.) (2006), *Social Entrepreneurship*, New York, NY: Palgrave Macmillan.

Robinson, Jeffrey A., Johanna Mair, and Kai Hockerts (eds) (2009), *International Perspectives on Social Entrepreneurship*, New York, NY: Palgrave Macmillan.

Rodriguez Heyman, Darian (ed.) (2011), *Nonprofit Management 101: A Complete and Practical Guide for Leaders and Professionals*, San Francisco, CA: Jossey-Bass.

Rosenberg, Tina (2011), *Join the Club: How Peer Pressure Can Transform the World*, New York, NY: W. W. Norton & Co.

Sagawa, Shirley (2010), *The American Way to Change: How National Service and Volunteers Are Transforming America*, San Francisco, CA: Jossey-Bass.

Sampson, Danielle N. (ed.) (2011), *Social Entrepreneurship*, New York, NY: Nova Science Publishers.

Sandler, Michael R. (2009), *Social Entrepreneurship in Education: Private Ventures for the Public Good*, Lanham, MD: Rowman & Littlefield Education.

Saul, Jason (2011), *The End of Fundraising: Raise More Money by Selling Your Impact*, San Francisco, CA: Jossey-Bass.

Saul, Jason (2011), *Social Innovation, Inc.: 5 Strategies for Driving Business Growth Through Social Change*, San Francisco, CA: Jossey-Bass.

Schutz, Aaron and Marie G. Sandy (2011), *Collective Action for Social Change: An Introduction to Community Organizing*, New York, NY: Palgrave Macmillan.

Schwartz, Beverly (2012), *Rippling: How Social Entrepreneurs Spread Innovation Throughout the World*, San Francisco, CA: Jossey-Bass.

Scofield, Michael R. (2011), *The Social Entrepreneur's Handbook: How to Start, Build, and Run a Business that Improves the World*, New York, NY: McGraw-Hill.

Sexton, Donald L. and Raymond W. Smilor (eds.) (1986), *The Art and Science of Entrepreneurship*, Cambridge, MA: Ballinger Publishing Company.

Seymour, Richard (ed.) (2012), *Handbook of Research Methods on Social Entrepreneurship*, Northampton, MA: Edward Elgar.

Shannon, Lisa (2010), *A Thousand Sisters: My Journey of Hope into the Worst Place on Earth to be a Woman*, Berkeley, CA: Seal Press.

Social Enterprise Alliance (2010), *Succeeding at Social Enterprise: Hard-Won Lessons for Nonprofits and Social Entrepreneurs*, San Francisco, CA: Jossey-Bass.

Social Enterprise Knowledge Network (2006), *Effective Management of Social Enterprises: Lessons from Businesses and Civil Society Organizations in Iberoameria*, Cambridge, MA: Harvard University Press.

Shore, Bill (2001), *The Cathedral Within: Transforming Your Life by Giving Something Back*, New York, NY: Random House.

Sommerrock, Katharina (2010), *Social Entrepreneurship Business Models: Incentive Strategies to Catalyze Public Goods Provision*, New York, NY: Palgrave Macmillan.

Southern, Alan (ed.) (2011), *Enterprise, Deprivation, and Social Exclusion: The Role of Small Business in Addressing Social and Economic Inequalities*, New York, NY: Routledge.

Steyaert, Chris and Daniel Hjorth (2006), *Entrepreneurship as Social Change*, Northampton, MA: Edward Elgar.

Stout, Chris E. (2009), *The New Humanitarians: Inspiration, Innovations, and Blueprints*, 3 vols, Westport, CT: Praeger.

Strong, Michael (2009), *Be the Solution: How Entrepreneurs and Conscious Capitalists Can Solve All the World's Problems*, Hoboken, NJ: Wiley.

Sztompka, Piotr (1994), *The Sociology of Social Change*, Oxford, United Kingdom: Blackwell.

Theobald, Robert (1987), *The Rapids of Change: Social Entrepreneurship in Turbulent Times*, Indianapolis, IN: Knowledge Systems.

Tierney, Thomas J. and Joel L. Fleishman (2011), *Give Smart: Philanthropy that Gets Results*, New York, NY: Public Affairs.

Tough, Paul (2008), *Whatever it Takes: Geoffrey Canada's Quest to Change Harlem and America*, New York, NY: Houghton Mifflin Harcourt.

Vago, Steven (5th ed. 2003), *Social Change*, Upper Saddle River, NJ: Pearson Prentice Hall.

Wankel, Charles (ed.) (2008), *Alleviating Poverty through Business Strategy*, New York, NY: Palgrave Macmillan.

Wei-Sillern, Jane, James E. Austin, Herman Leonard, and Howard Stevenson (2007), *Entrepreneurship in the Social Sector*, Thousand Oaks, CA: Sage Publications, Inc.

Welch, Wilford (2008), *The Tactics of Hope: How Social Entrepreneurs are Changing our World*, San Rafael, CA: Earth Aware Editions.

White, Jerry (2008), *I Will not be Broken: 5 Steps to Overcoming a Life Crisis*, New York, NY: St. Martin's Press.

Wolk, Andrew M. and Kelley Kreitz (2008), *Business Planning for Enduring Social Impact: A Social-Entrepreneurial Approach to Solving Social Problems*, Cambridge, MA: Root Cause.

Wood, James (2006), *Leaving Microsoft to Change the World: An Entrepreneur's Odyssey to Educate the World's Children*, New York, NY: Collins.

Wooster, Martin Morse (2002), *By Their Bootstraps: The Lives of Twelve Gilded Age Social Entrepreneurs*, New York, NY: Manhattan Institute.

Yunus, Muhammad (1999), *Banker to the Poor: Micro-Lending and the Battle Against World Poverty*, New York, NY: Public Affairs.

Yunus, Muhammad (2007), *Creating a World Without Poverty: Social Business and the Future of Capitalism*, New York, NY: Public Affairs.

Yunus, Muhammad (2010), *Building Social Business: The New Kind of Capitalism that Serves Humanity's Most Pressing Needs*, New York, NY: Public Affairs.

Ziegler, Rafael (ed.) (2009), *An Introduction to Social Entrepreneurship*, Northampton, MA: Edward Elgar.

FOUNDATIONS AND FELLOWSHIPS

Acumen Fund (http://www.acumenfund.org/)

Ashoka (http://www.ashoka.org)

– Ashoka's Youth Venture (http://www.genv.net/)

Aspen Institute's Nonprofit Sector & Philanthropy Program (http://www.aspeninstitute.org/site/c.huLWJeMRKpH/b.612023/k.22C4/The_Nonprofit_Sector_and_Philanthropy_Program.htm)

Bill & Melinda Gates Foundation (http://www.gatesfoundation.org/)

Blue Ridge Foundation New York (http://www.brfny.org/)

Bridgeway Foundation (http://www.bridgewayfoundation.org/)

Canadian Social Entrepreneurship Foundation (http://www.csef.ca/)

Case Foundation (http://www.casefoundation.org)

Clinton Global Initiative (http://www.clintonglobalinitiative.org/)

Compass Partners (http://www.compasspartners.org/)

Draper Richards Foundation (http://www.draperrichards.org/)

Echoing Green (http://www.echoinggreen.org/)

Ewing Marion Kauffman Foundation (http://www.kauffman.org/)

Ford Foundation (http://www.fordfoundation.org/)

Forest Foundation (http://www.theforestfoundation.net/)

Global Giving (http://www.globalgiving.org/)

Google.org (http://www.google.org/)

Humanity in Action Foundation (http://www.humanityinaction.org/)

Humanity United (http://www.humanityunited.org/)

International Youth Foundation (http://www.iyfnet.org/)

John D. & Catherine T. MacArthur Foundation (http://www.macfound.org/)

Joshua Venture Group (http://www.joshuaventuregroup.org/)

Lemelson Foundation (http://www.lemelson.org/)

Manhattan Institute for Policy Research's Social Entrepreneurship Awards (http://www.manhattan-institute.org/html/social_entrepreneurship.htm)

Mulago Foundation (http://www.mulagofoundation.org/)

New Profit (http://www.newprofit.com/)

NextBillion (http://www.nextbillion.net/)

Open Society Institute & Soros Foundations network (http://www.soros.org)

Peter F. Drucker Foundation for Nonprofit Management (also known as the Leader to Leader Institute) (http://www.pfdf.org/)

Rainer Arnhold Fellows (http://www.rainerfellows.org/)

Root Cause (http://www.rootcause.org/)

Samuel Rubin Foundation (http://www.samuelrubinfoundation.org/)

Schwab Foundation for Social Entrepreneurship (http://www.schwabfound.org/)

Skadden Fellowship Foundation (http://www.skaddenfellowships.org)

Skoll Foundation (http://www.skollfoundation.org/)
Sparkseed (http://www.sparkseed.org/)
StartingBloc Institute for Social Innovation (http://www.startingbloc.org/)
Synergos (http://www.synergos.org/)
UnLtd (http://www.unltd.org.uk/)
Unreasonable Institute (http://unreasonableinstitute.org/)
Venture Philanthropy Partners (http://www.vppartners.org/)

ACADEMIC INSTITUTIONS

American University, School of International Service: Social Enterprise
    Initiative (http://www.american.edu/sis/socialenterprise/index.cfm)
Ashoka U (http://ashokau.org/)
Babson College
– Arthur M. Blank Center for Entrepreneurship (http://www.babson.edu/
    Academics/centers/blank-center/Pages/home.aspx)
– Lewis Institute for Social Innovation (http://www.babson.edu/
    Academics/centers/the-lewis-institute/Pages/home.aspx)
Belmont University: Center for Social Entrepreneurship and Service-Learning
    (http://www.belmont.edu/csesl/index.html)
Berea College: Entrepreneurship for the Public Good (http://www.berea.edu/
    epg/)
Bocconi University: Social Entrepreneurship & Philanthropy Management
    (http://www.unibocconi.it/wps/wcm/connect/SitoPubblico_EN/Navigation
    +Tree/Home/Departments/Department+of+Management+and+Technology
    /Research/CSR+Unit/Research+Units/Social+Entrepreneurship+%26+Phil
    anthropy+Management/)
Brown University, Swearer Center for Public Service: Social Innovation
    Initiative (http://swearercenter.brown.edu/sii/)
Carnegie Mellon University, H. John Heinz III College: Institute for Social
    Innovation (http://heinz.cmu.edu/institute-for-social-innovation/index. aspx)
Case Western Reserve University, Weatherhead School of Management: Fowler
    Center for Sustainable Value (http://weatherhead.case.edu/centers/ fowler/)
Claremont Graduate University: Drucker Institute (http://www.drucker
    institute. com/)
Clark University: Innovation & Entrepreneurship (http://www.clarku.edu/
    departments/ie/)
College of the Atlantic: Sustainable Business (http://www.coa.edu/
    sustainable-business.htm)
Colorado State University, College of Business: Global Social & Sustainable
    Enterprise (http://biz.colostate.edu/gsse/pages/default.aspx)

Columbia University, Columbia Business School
- Research Initiative on Social Entrepreneurship (RISE) (http://www.rise project.org/)
- Social Enterprise Program (http://www4.gsb.columbia.edu/social enterprise/)

Cornell University
- Samuel Curtis Johnson Graduate School of Management, Center for Sustainable Global Enterprise (http://www2.johnson.cornell.edu/sge/index. cfm)
- Social Entrepreneurship (http://entrepreneurship.cornell.edu/about-us/ social-entrepreneurship)

Duke University
- Fuqua School of Business: Center for the Advancement of Social Entrepreneurship (CASE) (http://www.caseatduke.org/)
- Law School: Law & Entrepreneurship LLM Program (http://www. law.duke.edu/llmle/)

Elon University: Social Entrepreneurship Scholars Program (http://org.elon. edu/ses/ep.html)

Harvard University
- Harvard Business School: Social Enterprise Initiative (http://www.hbs.edu/ socialenterprise/)
- Harvard Business School: Social Entrepreneurship Fellowship (http://www. hbs.edu/socialenterprise/careers/socialentrepreneurship/)
- John F. Kennedy School of Government: Catherine B. Reynolds Foundation Fellowship in Social Entrepreneurship (http://www.ksg.harvard.edu/ leadership/reynolds/)

Hult International Business School: Master of Social Entrepreneurship (http://www.hult.edu/masters-program/programs/social-entrepreneurship)

INSEAD, Social Entrepreneurship Programme (http://executive.education. insead.edu/social-entrepreneurship)

Johns Hopkins University: Hopkins Social Innovation Partnerships (HOP-SIP) (http://www.jhu.edu/csc/specialinitiatives.shtml)

Keio University: Social Innovation (http://ic.sfc.keio.ac.jp/about-sfc/study-opportunities-at-sfc/social-innovation/)

Marquette University: Social Innovation Initiative (http://www.marquette.edu/ social-innovation/)

Massachusetts Institute of Technology: Abdul Latif Jameel Poverty Action Lab (http://www.povertyactionlab.org/)

Miami University, Farmer School of Business: Center for Social Entre-preneurship (http://www.fsb.muohio.edu/centers/social-entrepreneurship)
- Legatum Center for Development & Entrepreneurship (http://legatum. mit.edu/)

National University of Singapore, Business School: Asia Centre for Social Entrepreneurship & Philanthropy (http://bschool.nus.edu/Research Publications/ResearchCentres/ACSEPHome/AboutUs.aspx)

New York University

– Catherine B. Reynolds Program in Social Entrepreneurship (http://www.nyu.edu/reynolds)

– Leonard N. Stern School of Business: Berkley Center for Entrepreneurial Studies: Stewart Satter Program in Social Entrepreneurship (http://w4.stern.nyu.edu/berkley/social.cfm?doc_id=1868)

Northeastern University, College of Business Administration: Social Enterprise Institute (http://www.northeastern.edu/sei/)

Northwestern University, Kellogg School of Management: Social Enterprise at Kellogg (SEEK) (http://www.kellogg.northwestern.edu/academic/seek/)

Pace University: Wilson Center for Social Entrepreneurship (http://appserv.pace.edu/execute/page.cfm?doc_id=15819)

Pennsylvania State University, School of Engineering, Design, Technology, and Professional Programs: Humanitarian Engineering and Social Entrepreneurship (http://www.sedtapp.psu.edu/humanitarian/index.php)

Portland State University, School of Business Administration: Social Innovation Incubator (http://www.sba.pdx.edu/sii/)

Roskilde University: Centre for Social Entrepreneurship (http://magenta.ruc.dk/paes_en/cse/)

Santa Clara University: Social Entrepreneurship (http://www.scu.edu/scunews/ourstories/Social-Entrepreneurship-at-SCU.cfm)

School for Social Entrepreneurs (SSE) (http://www.sse.org.uk)

Social Enterprise Academy (http://www.theacademy-ssea.org/)

Stanford University, Graduate School of Business

– Center for Social Innovation (CSI) (http://www.gsb.stanford.edu/csi/)

– Executive Program in Social Entrepreneurship (http://www.gsb.stanford.edu/exed/epse/)

– Social Innovation and Entrepreneurship (SIE) Program (http://sie.stanford.edu/)

Tata Institute of Social Sciences: M.A. in Social Entrepreneurship (http://www.tiss.edu/TopMenuBar/admissions/masters-programmes)

Tulane University: Social Entrepreneurship Program (http://tulane.edu/socialentrepreneurship/)

University of Alberta, School of Business: Canadian Centre for Social Entrepreneurship (CCSE) (http://www.bus.ualberta.ca/ccse/)

University of California at Berkeley, Haas School of Business: Lester Center for Entrepreneurship and Innovation (http://entrepreneurship.berkeley.edu/)

University of Cambridge: Transforming Business (http://www.transforming-business.net/)

University of Cape Town, Graduate School of Business: Bertha Centre for Social Innovation and Entrepreneurship (http://www.gsb.uct.ac.za/s.asp?p=389)

University of Colorado at Boulder: Social Entrepreneurship for Equitable Development & Sustainability (SEEDS) (http://housing.colorado.edu/residences/residential-academic-communities/residential-academic-programs/social-entrepreneurship-eq)

University of Liège, Centre for Social Economy: Master in Management of Social Enterprises (http://www.ces.ulg.ac.be/en_GB/education/master-in-management-of-social-enterprises)

University of Maryland, Robert H. Smith School of Business: Center for Social Value Creation (http://www.rhsmith.umd.edu/svc/)

University of Michigan: William Davidson Institute (http://wdi.umich.edu/)

University of North Carolina, Kenan-Flagler Business School: Center for Sustainable Enterprise (http://www.kenan-flagler.unc.edu/sustainable-enterprise)

University of Oxford, Saïd Business School
- Centre for Entrepreneurship and Innovation (http://www.sbs.ox.ac.uk/centres/entrepreneurship/Pages/default.aspx)
- Skoll Centre for Social Entrepreneurship (http://www.sbs.ox.ac.uk/skoll/)

University of the Pacific: Global Center for Social Entrepreneurship (http://globalctr.org/)

University of San Diego: Center for Peace and Commerce (http://www.sandiego.edu/cpc/)

University of Stirling: Social Enterprise (http://www.socialenterprise.stir.ac.uk/)

University of Texas at Austin, Lyndon B. Johnson School of Public Affairs: RGK Center Institute on Social Entrepreneurship (http://www.rgkcenter.org/programs/ISE)

University of Wisconsin-Madison: Center for Nonprofits (http://centerfornonprofits.wisc.edu/programs/entrepreneurship.html)

Yale University, School of Management: Program on Social Enterprise (PSE) (http://pse.som.yale.edu/)

JOURNALS AND BLOGS

Acumen Fund Blog (http://blog.acumenfund.org/)
Ashoka (http://www.ashoka.org/news/clippings)
Ashoka's Youth Venture blog (http://blog.youthventure.org/)
Audeamus (http://www.audeamus.com/)
Beyond Profit (http://www.beyondprofitmag.com)

Bottom Billion Blog (http://bottombillion.com/blog/)

Change.org Blog (http://www.change.org/?page=3)

Changemakers (http://www.changemakers.net)

Chris Blattman's blog (http://chrisblattman.com/)

Companies for Good Blog (http://www.thenetworkforgood.org/t5/Companies-For-Good/bg-p/CompaniesforGood)

Dani Rodrik's weblog (http://rodrik.typepad.com/dani_rodriks_weblog/)

David Bornstein's blog (http://davidbornstein.wordpress.com/)

Do Good Well (http://dogoodwell.wordpress.com/)

Dowser (http://dowser.org/)

E-180 (http://e-180.com/)

Eastside Social Enterprise Blog (http://www.socialenterpriseconsulting.co.uk/)

Eco Africa Social Ventures Blog (http://www.ecoafricasocialventures.org/ blog/)

Enterprise Africa (http://mercatus.org/enterpriseafrica)

Entrepreneur (http://www.entrepreneur.com/magazine/index.html)

Envision Good (http://envisiongood.com/)

Fixes (http://opinionator.blogs.nytimes.com/category/fixes/)

Foley Hoag's Corporate Social Responsibility and the Law Blog (http://www.csrandthelaw.com/)

Generation Rwanda's Isoko Blog (http://www.generationrwanda.org/?cat=21)

GiveWell Blog (http://blog.givewell.org/)

Global Development: Views from the Center for Global Development (http://blogs.cgdev.org/globaldevelopment/)

Good (http://www.goodmagazine.com/)

Good Intentions Are Not Enough (http://goodintents.org/)

Harvard Business Review (http://hbr.org/)

Indego Africa's Social Enterprising blog (http://socialenterprising.indegoafrica.org/)

Innovations (http://www.mitpressjournals.org/loi/itgg)

Innovations for Poverty Action (http://www.poverty-action.org/blog)

It Takes a Village (http://tashanda-africa.blogspot.com/)

Joseph Scarantino's blog (http://josefscarantino.com/)

Journal of Business Ethics (http://www.springer.com/social+sciences/applied+ethics/journal/10551)

Journal of Social Entrepreneurship (http://www.tandf.co.uk/journals/rjse)

Katya's Non-Profit Marketing Blog (http://www.nonprofitmarketingblog.com/)

Knowledge@Wharton (http://knowledge.wharton.upenn.edu/)

LawForChange (http://www.lawforchange.org/)

MIT Sloan Management Review (http://sloanreview.mit.edu/)

Network for Good Blog (http://networkforgood.blogspot.com/)

Next Billion (http://www.nextbillion.net/)

No Limits Magazine (http://www.unltd.org.uk/template.php?ID=29& PageName=downloads)

Nonprofit Management and Leadership (http://www.josseybass.com/ WileyCDA/WileyTitle/productCd-NML.html)

Nonprofit Management 101 (http://nonprofits101.org/nonprofits101-blog/)

NonProfit Times (http://www.nptimes.com/)

Nubian Cheetah (http://nubiancheetah.blogspot.com/)

Ode (http://www.odemagazine.com/)

Philanthropy 2173 (http://philanthropy.blogspot.com/)

Philanthropy Action (http://philanthropyaction.com/)

Philanthropy Journal (http://www.philanthropyjournal.org/)

Philanthropy Media (http://www.philanthromedia.org/)

Pulling for the Underdog (http://www.denniswhittle.com/)

RazEsquire (http://razesquire.wordpress.com/)

Sasha Dichter's blog (http://sashadichter.wordpress.com/)

The Skoll Foundation's Social Edge (http://www.socialedge.org/)

Small Enterprise Development (http://www.ingentaconnect.com/content/ itpub/sedv)

Social Business (http://www.thesocialbusiness.co.uk/blog/)

Social Earth (http://www.socialearth.org/)

Social Enterprise Journal (http://www.emeraldinsight.com/products/journals/ journals.htm?id=sej)

Social Enterprise Law (http://socentlaw.com/)

Social Enterprise Reporter (http://www.sereporter.com/)

Social Entrepreneurship in the Age of Atrocities (http://www.socialentre preneurship-book.com/)

Social Entrepreneurship@Work (http://socialentrepreneurshipwork.blogspot. com/)

Social ROI: A Social Entrepreneurship Blog (http://socialroi.com/)

Solutions Magazine (http://www.solutionsmag.net/)

Stanford Social Innovation Review (http://www.ssireview.org/)

Strategic Entrepreneurship Journal (http://sej.strategicmanagement.net/)

Tactical Philanthropy (http://www.tacticalphilanthropy.com/)

Trailblazers for Good (http://www.care2.com/causes/trailblazers/)

Venture Capital for Africa (http://www.vc4africa.com/)

Weekly Way (http://www.weeklyway.blogspot.com/)

What's a BOPreneuer (http://bopreneur.blogspot.com/)

Wonderment Woman (http://wondermentwoman.com/)

The World Bank's Private Sector Development blog (http://blogs.worldbank. org/psd/)

CONFERENCES AND COMPETITIONS

Ashoka Changemakers: Staples Youth Social Entrepreneur Competition (http://www.changemakers.com/competition/staplesyv)

Ashoka U Exchange (http://ashokau.org/exchange/)

Columbia University, Columbia Business School: Social Enterprise Conference (http://columbiasocialenterprise.org/)

Dell Social Innovation Competition (http://www.dellsocialinnovation competition.com/)

Duke University, Fuqua School of Business: Sustainable Business and Social Impact Conference (http://dukembanetimpact.org/)

Global Social Venture Competition (http://www.gsvc.org/)

Harvard University, Harvard Business School
– Social Enterprise Business Plan Contest (http://www.hbs.edu/social enterprise/businessplan/)
– Social Enterprise Conference (http://socialenterpriseconference.org/)

Massachusetts Institute of Technology:
– IDEAS Global Challenge (http://globalchallenge.mit.edu/)
– Lemels-MIT Award for Global Innovation (http://web.mit.edu/invent/a-award.html)

Net Impact Conference (http://netimpact.org/)

New York University
– Leonard N. Stern School of Business, Robert F. Wagner Graduate School of Business & New York University Law School: NYU Annual Social Innovation Symposium (http://nyustern.campusgroups.com/sea/social-innovation-symposium/)
– Leonard N. Stern School of Business, Berkley Center for Entrepreneurship & Innovation:
  • $200K Entrepreneurs Challenge (http://www.stern.nyu.edu/experience-stern/about/departments-centers-initiatives/centers-of-research/berkley-center/programs/venture-competitions/how-to-enter/index.htm)
  • Conference on Social Entrepreneurs (http://www.stern.nyu.edu/experience-stern/about/departments-centers-initiatives/centers-of-research/berkley-center/programs/social-entrepreneurship/annual-conference-of-social-entrepreneurs/index.htm)
  • Social Venture Competition (http://www.stern.nyu.edu/experience-stern/about/departments-centers-initiatives/centers-of-research/berkley-center/programs/venture-competitions/about/index.htm)

Northwestern University, Kellogg School of Management: Innovating Social Change Conference (http://kellogg.campusgroups.com/isc/h/)

Social Capital Markets (SOCAP) Conference (http://www.socialcapital markets.net/)

Social Edge: Social Entrepreneurship Competition (http://www.socialedge. org/features/opportunities/social-entrepreneurship-competition/? searchterm=None)

Social Enterprise Alliance: Social Enterprise Summit (https://www.se-alliance.org/summit.cfm)

Social Enterprise Bootcamp (http://www.socialenterprisebootcamp.org/)

Social Enterprise Trust: Beyond Business as Usual (http://www.beyond businessasusual.org/)

Social Venture Partners International: Social Venture Partners Conference (http://www.svpi.org/annual-conference)

Stanford University: BASES Social Entrepreneurship Challenge (http://bases.stanford.edu/150k/sociale)

Sustainatopia: Impact Conference (http://www.sustainatopia.com/)

Tufts University, School of Engineering, Gordon Institute: Business Plan Competition (http://gordon.tufts.edu/entLeader/competition/index.asp)

Unite For Sight: Global Health & Innovation Conference (http://www.unite forsight.org/conference/)

University of California at Berkeley, Haas School of Business, Center for Responsible Business & Lester Center for Entrepreneurship: Ideas to Impact (http://ideastoimpact.squarespace.com/)

University of Johannesburg: Social Enterprise World Forum (http:// www.sewf2011.com)

University of Maryland, Robert H. Smith School of Business: Global Challenge (http://www.rhsmith.umd.edu/globalchallenge/)

University of Oregon, Lundquist Center for Entrepreneurship: New Venture Championship (http://www.nvc.uoregon.edu/)

University of Oxford, Saïd Business School
- Centre for Entrepreneurship and Innovation: 21st Century Challenge Competition (http://www.sbs.ox.ac.uk/CENTRES/ENTREPRENEUR SHIP/PROGRAMMES/Pages/21stCenturyChallenge.aspx)
- Skoll Centre for Social Entrepreneurship:
  • Emerge Conference (http://www.theemergeconference.org/)
  • Skoll World Forum on Social Entrepreneurship (http://www.skoll worldforum.org/)

University of Virginia, Darden School of Business, Olson Center for Applied Ethics: Building an Ethical World Video Contest (http://conference. darden.virginia.edu/olssonevent/index.asp)

University of Washington, Foster School of Business: Global Social Entrepreneurship Competition (http://www.foster.washington.edu/centers/ gbc/globalsocialentrepreneurshipcompetition/Pages/GSEC.aspx)

Villanova University: Social Entrepreneurship Competition (http://vsec.
weebly.com/)
Wake Forest University, School of Business: Social Competition (http://
business.wfu.edu/default.aspx?id=938)
William James Foundation: Sustainable Business Plan Competition
(http://www.williamjamesfoundation.org/)
World Economic Forum (http://www.weforum.org/)

NETWORKS

Acumen Fund's Community (http://community.acumenfund.org/)
Africa Gathering (http://www.africagathering.org/)
AIESEC (http://www.aiesec.org/)
Ashoka (http://www.ashoka.org/)
Change.org (http://www.change.org)
Do Something (http://www.dosomething.org/)
Endeavor (http://www.endeavor.org/)
European Research Network (http://www.emes.net/)
Institute for Social Entrepreneurship in Asia (http://isea-group.net/index.html)
International Network of Social-Eco Entrepreneurs (http://inse.groupsite.com)
Jumo (http://www.jumo.com/)
Microlinks (http://www.microlinks.org/)
MojaLink (http://www.mojalink.com/)
National Center for Social Entrepreneurs (http://www.nationalcenterforsocial
entrepreneurs.org/)
Net Impact (http://www.netimpact.org/)
Peace & Collaborative Development Network (http://www.international
peaceandconflict.org/)
Purpose (http://www.purpose.com)
SEEP Network (http://www.seepnetwork.org/)
Shift (http://www.shift.org)
Social Enterprise Europe (http://wwww.socialenterpriseeurope.co.uk/)
Social Enterprise Knowledge Network (http://www.sekn.org)
Social Venture Network (http://www.svn.org/)
TakePart (http://www.takepart.com/)
University Network for Social Entrepreneurship (http://www.university
network.org/)

OTHER ONLINE RESOURCES

4Nonprofits (http://4nonprofits.org/)
10 Ways to Change the World in Your 20s (http://www.tenways.org/)
CherryCard (http://cherrycard.org/)
Entrepreneurship (http://www.entrepreneurship.org/)
GiveWell (http://www.givewell.org/)
GlobalGiving (http://www.globalgiving.com/)
GuideStar (http://www.guidestar.org/)
Institute for Social Entrepreneurs (http://www.socialent.org/)
Kiva (http://www.kiva.org/)
The New Heroes (http://www.thenewheroes.org/)
Next Billion (http://www.nextbillion.net/)
Omidyar Network (http://www.omidyar.net/)
RSF Social Finance (http://rsfsocialfinance.org/)
Social Enterprise Alliance (http://www.se-alliance.org/)
SocialVest (https://www.socialvest.us/)
Tactics of Hope (http://www.tacticsofhope.org/)
TED (http://www.ted.com/)
Wikipedia's entry on 'Social Entrepreneurship' (http://en.wikipedia.org/wiki/
    Social_entrepreneur)

NOTES

1. This appendix focuses on social entrepreneurship, but also includes selections from the closely related fields of leadership, activism, non-profit management, philanthropy, development, foreign aid, and private sector investment in developing countries. Some other books on social entrepreneurship also include an appendix on social entrepreneurship resources and institutions. *See, e.g.*, ASHOKA U & DEBBI D. BROCK, SOCIAL ENTREPRENEURSHIP EDUCATION RESOURCE HANDBOOK (3rd ed. 2011); BORNSTEIN, HOW TO CHANGE THE WORLD, *supra* Chapter 1 note 7, at 303–12; DAVID BORNSTEIN & SUSAN DAVIS, SOCIAL ENTREPRENEURSHIP: WHAT EVERYONE NEEDS TO KNOW 133–39 (2010); JEFFREY HOLLENDER & STEPHEN FENICHELL, WHAT MATTERS MOST: HOW A SMALL GROUP OF PIONEERS IS TEACHING SOCIAL RESPONSIBILITY TO BIG BUSINESS, AND WHY BIG BUSINESS IS LISTENING 271–98 (2004); WILFORD WELCH, THE TACTICS OF HOPE: HOW SOCIAL ENTREPRENEURS ARE CHANGING OUR WORLD 199–217 (2008). This appendix builds on some of those appendices, updating and expanding the ever-growing list of relevant sources of information on this field. Because of space constraints, this appendix does not list articles concerning social entrepreneurship.
2. As CoA no longer operates, it does not have a functional website.
3. As NVSL no longer operates, it does not have a functional website.

Index